PRENTICE HALL
FOUNDATIONS OF MODERN SOCIOLOGY SERIES

Alex Inkeles, Editor

THE SOCIOLOGY OF MEDICINE

a participant observer's view

RENÉE C. FOX

University of Pennsylvania

Prentice Hall, Englewood Cliffs, New Jersey 07632

Library of Congress Cataloging-in-Publication Data

Fox, Renée C. (Renée Claire)
   The sociology of medicine.

   (Prentice-Hall foundations of modern sociology series)
   Includes bibliographies and index.
   1. Social medicine. I. Title. II. Series
RA418.F662 1989   362.1   88-17957
ISBN 0-13-820507-8

Editorial/production supervision
  and interior design: Serena Hoffman
Manufacturing buyer : Peter Havens

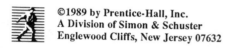

©1989 by Prentice-Hall, Inc.
A Division of Simon & Schuster
Englewood Cliffs, New Jersey 07632

Printed in the United States of America

10 9 8 7 6 5 4 3 2 1

ISBN   0-13-820507-8

PRENTICE-HALL INTERNATIONAL (UK) LIMITED, *London*
PRENTICE-HALL OF AUSTRALIA PTY. LIMITED, *Sydney*
PRENTICE-HALL CANADA INC., *Toronto*
PRENTICE-HALL HISPANOAMERICANA, S.A., *Mexico*
PRENTICE-HALL OF INDIA PRIVATE LIMITED, *New Delhi*
PRENTICE-HALL OF JAPAN, INC., *Tokyo*
SIMON & SCHUSTER ASIA PTE. LTD., *Singapore*
EDITORA PRENTICE-HALL DO BRASIL, LTDA., *Rio de Janeiro*

To Willy De Craemer,
with gratitude for all that he has taught me
over the years about the deepest meaning
of health, illness, and medicine.

CONTENTS

CHAPTER **4**

THE EDUCATION, TRAINING, AND SOCIALIZATION OF PHYSICIANS: RESIDENCY AND PRACTICE   108

CHAPTER **5**

THE HOSPITAL: A SOCIAL AND CULTURAL MICROCOSM   142

CHAPTER **6**

MEDICAL SCIENCE AND MEDICAL RESEARCH   181

PREFACE

It has taken a long time to write this book. I began to plan its contents in the summer of 1973, after I accepted Alex Inkeles's invitation to contribute to the Prentice Hall *Foundations of Modern Sociology* series (of which he is editor), by authoring a monograph on medical sociology. The gracious letter that I received from him describing what was expected stated soothingly, "We do not want anyone 'to make a big production' . . . out of this assignment. I am writing to experts who are presumably on top of the material," he explained, "and I am asking them to set down what they are already presenting in their daily professional activity."

By virtue of sheer longevity, I was qualified to be considered such an expert. I have been a continuous participant in medical sociology as a researcher, teacher, and writer since 1951—even before the field was officially recognized as a subspecialty by the American Sociological Association.[1] Because of this history, and in spite of the editor's reassurances, "setting down" the medical sociology on which my "daily professional activity" is based was destined to become a very "big production" indeed. Somehow, all those years of first-hand medical sociological work that made me eligible to write this book had to be distilled and compressed into it. The prospect and the task were overwhelming.

I was intimidated by what the writing of this book entailed, and I was also too immersed in the field to clearly see its contours. At the same time, my relationship to medical sociological materials was part of my daily professional round. They were so familiar that it was hard to feel a sense of discovery or a rush of creative élan in attempting to write about them. Partly because of my intense involvement in medical sociology, I was acutely aware of its deficiencies as well as its strengths. I was especially troubled by the persistent gaps and sharp discontinuities that I saw in the medical sociological literature, and by the missed intellectual opportunities, capriciousness, and bias that I felt they represented.

When I turned my attention to medicine, health, and illness, I was impressed with the enormity of their scope, their increasing symbolic as well as empirical importance in American and other modern Western societies, and by the magnitude of scientific, technological, social, and cultural change that revolved around them. It seemed to me that only a small, highly selective part of these developments had as yet been addressed by sociologists.

My sentiments grew out of a very "*un*detached concern" about a field to which I have a lifetime commitment. They made it difficult for me to write about the state of medical sociology, and even harder to mold that writing into a reasonably concise book that would interest readers in the field. After much pondering and hesitation, starting and stopping, prolonged episodes of muteness, and then, at last, an exhilarating breakthrough of sustained writing, here is the book that has finally emerged.

In addition to being uncommonly long for the *Foundations of Modern Sociology* series, this book has several other distinctive characteristics. Although it is built upon a systematic, comprehensive review of the sociology of medicine literature, it draws upon materials and authors that extend beyond what professional sociologists have written. Certain articles and books by anthropologists, psychologists, historians, biomedical scientists, physicians, nurses, and science writers, among others, are cited and extensively discussed. There are several reasons why I have chosen to do this.

Without being disrespectful of the special competence of sociologists, I consider medical sociology to be inherently interdisciplinary. Linking medicine, biology, and the social sciences, it deals with some of the deepest, most basic, human concerns. I have been especially inclined to rely on the work of nonsociologists to fill in empty spaces in the field that result from inattention to particular topics and phenomena that I think merit more consideration. I also believe it important for medical sociologists to have a strong historical sense (all the more so, in light of the revolutionary changes that biology and medicine have undergone since World War II), to have a cultural and cross-cultural perspective, and to be sufficiently interested in and knowledgeable about biomedical science to be able to recognize and interpret the social and cultural materials that lie deeply within it. The outlook and data of colleagues in other fields are essential to the development and enrichment of these capacities.

In many instances, I have not only described an author's work in detail, but I have quoted abundantly from it. More than scholarly fastidiousness was involved. Some thirty-five years of ethnographic medical sociological research have powerfully reinforced my fieldworker's penchant for respecting and savoring the exact way that people say things, and my appreciation of the nuances of thought and perception that verbatim speech and texts convey. I also hope that the fullness of these excerpts will stimulate readers to consult the works from which they were taken.

The passages that I have reproduced include both published and unpublished field materials. Usually the unpublished data are my own. In a few cases, I have had privileged access to observations, interviews, and primary documents collected by younger researchers for their doctoral dissertations. The field materials presented are not just decorative or atmospheric. They contain an extra dimension of information that other forms of available data lack.

The book is written from the vantage point of a highly participant observer in the field. I have incorporated into it a wide and varied cross-section of works of medical sociological relevance with which I am familiar, including my own. I have also made my observations on the state of the field a part of the text, and one of the determinants of its contents and emphases.

It could be said that my medical and sociological overview is more cultural than social organizational. This book reflects the fact that in my medical sociological endeavors and in my career as a sociologist, I have been consistently interested in the clusters of values and beliefs, symbols and rituals, meanings and motivations that are components of social life—of its ambiance, ethos, and world view. I have related these sociocultural aspects of health, illness, and medicine to their social structural attributes and processes in a framework that interweaves micro and macro levels of analysis and interpretation.

I have taken account of the increasing degree to which health, illness, and medicine have become "primary symbolic media through which American society [is grappling] with fundamental questions of value and belief,"[2] in a period marked by explosive developments in medical science and technology, far-reaching structural transformations in the delivery of medical care, and major social and cultural change that extends beyond the domain of health and medicine. Many of the editorial revisions that I made en route to completing this book were in response to the challenging problem of dealing adequately with such dynamism.

This book consists of seven chapters. It begins with a chapter on the meaning and significance of health and illness that explores the ways in which social and cultural factors influence what is defined as illness in a given society (or a particular group within a society)—how it is interpreted and experienced, and how it is dealt with physically, psychically, interpersonally, and existentially. The second chapter examines the attributes of professions in general, and those of the medical and nursing professions in particular. Chapters 3 and 4 are concerned with the socialization of medical professionals at different stages in their careers, especially with the intertwined learning of knowledge and skills, and of attitudes, values, and behavior patterns that takes place during the prolonged and intensive years of professional education and training. These chapters also outline some of the most significant changes that have been occurring in American medical education and medical care over the past few decades, and suggest ways in which this has affected the socialization of physicians. The fifth chapter contains a sociological portrait of the hospital—the social and cultural microcosm that stands at the center of the institutions that are integral to modern medicine. Chapter 6 focuses on modern biomedical science and technology and the processes of research through which they are developed. It describes and analyzes both the ideal and the actual patterns of medical science and research and how they are socioculturally as well as biomedically shaped. The seventh and final chapter is about the emergence of bioethics—a relatively new area of inquiry and action on the American scene—the societal and cultural questions surrounding modern medicine from which it emanates, and its simultaneously aloof and strained relationship to medical sociology.

Because the subject matter of this book is so closely connected with the pain and mystery and meaning of illness, with birth and life and death, and with all the patients, caretakers, and researchers I have known as a medical sociologist, I hope that the picture of the field that I have presented—of what it is and of what it could and ought to be—will help it to grow in humane understanding as well as in intellectual quality.

ACKNOWLEDGMENTS

Many generous people have accompanied me and helped in my work as a sociologist of medicine. To these teachers, students and colleagues, nurses, physicians and allied health professionals, patients, and biomedical researchers, I want to express my enduring gratitude.

There are several persons essential to the writing and production of this book I particularly want to acknowledge:

(The late) Talcott Parsons: At a time when medical sociology was not yet an established field, he opened this area of reflection and inquiry to me and taught me to recognize its larger cultural significance.

Henrietta and P. Fred Fox: I shall never take for granted the education and loving encouragement I received from my parents.

Alex Inkeles: He taught me when I was a graduate student, invited me to author this book, and with patient understanding awaited its completion.

Martha Rosso: She typed the manuscript with the impeccability and intelligence that she always confers on my work.

Judith C. Watkins: She checked every reference this book contains and constructed the index, with fastidious and devoted scholarship.

Troy P. Gately, copy editor of *The Wilson Quarterly*: She applied her expertise to eliminating errors in the page proofs.

Above all, there are two intimate colleagues and friends to whom I am indebted for the realization of this book, and for whatever value it may have:

Judith P. Swazey: During the summer of 1981, when she and I were in the field in Tianjin, China, the nurses and physicians dubbed us the "Team of Two." And so we have been, since 1968. I have been continually enriched by her intellect, uplifted by her moral standards, and warmed by her friendship. She read every word of this book and pruned it with the caring skill of an editorial "gardener."

Willy De Craemer: For more than twenty-five years, in Europe, Africa, and the United States, he has been at the vital center of my work and its wellsprings. It is to him that this book is dedicated.

Renée C. Fox

NOTES

1. My earliest work in the sociology of medicine was done in 1951, while I was still a graduate student. The American Sociological Association's Section on Medical Sociology was established in 1960, as an outgrowth of the Committee on Medical Sociology organized by August B. Hollingshead of Yale University in 1955. Medical Sociology is currently the largest ASA section. In 1986 it had a membership of 1,049 out of a total ASA membership of 11,500.
2. Renée C. Fox, "The Medicalization and Demedicalization of American Society," in *Doing Better and Feeling Worse: Health in the United States*, ed. John H. Knowles (New York: W.W. Norton and Company, 1977), p. 21.

CHAPTER 1

THE SOCIAL AND CULTURAL SIGNIFICANCE OF HEALTH AND ILLNESS

NEGATIVE AND POSITIVE MEANINGS OF ILLNESS

In all societies, the state of freedom from disease, and the well being or capacity to function optimally that is culturally defined as health, are considered to be desirable. What is regarded as sickness of body or mind is viewed as undesirable. Everywhere, illness is apprehensively associated with misfortune, suffering, pain, disability, the ebbing of the life force, and the approach of death.

It is only under special circumstances that illness takes on positive significance. The power of religious beliefs to infuse the experience of illness with transcendent meaning usually effects this transformation. In traditional Christian thought, for example, illness is seen as an evil related to original sin, and in some cases to personal sin. But it is also an ordeal permitted by God, from which some greater good can come. If sick people respond to their illnesses with patience, fortitude, trust in God, and penitence, then it can make them more profoundly human, ennoble them, redeem them, and bring them Salvation.[1]

In the mid-1970s, at the height of a wave of social criticism in the United States concerning the excessive "medicalization" of American society and the "professional domination" of physicians over health and illness, Ivan Illich published a book entitled *Medical Nemesis* that attracted a great deal of attention. It was widely regarded as a provocatively radical, humanistic statement. However, certain aspects of Illich's perspective on health and illness, suffering, life and death are as orthodoxly Christian and Catholic as they are revolutionary.[2] Illich deliberately played down and, to a degree, camouflaged these wellsprings of his thesis through the skillful use of sophistry, embedding key parts of his argument in language that blends Rousseau, Marx, and Catholic "Liberation Theology."

Wherever in the world a culture is medicalized, the traditional framework for habits that can become conscious in the personal practice of the virtue of hygiene is progressively trammeled by a mechanical system, a medical code by which individuals submit to the instructions emanating from hygienic custodians. Medicalization constitutes a prolific bureaucratic program based on the denial of each man's need to deal with pain, sickness, and death. . . . Medical civilization is planned and organized to kill pain, to eliminate sickness, and to abolish the need for an art of suffering and of dying. This progressive flattening out of personal, virtuous performance constitutes a new goal which has never before been a guideline for social life. Suffering, healing, and dying . . . are now claimed by technocracy as new areas of policy-making and are treated as malfunctions from which populations ought to be institutionally relieved. . . .

Traditional cultures confront pain, impairment, and death by interpreting them as challenges soliciting a response from the individual under stress; medical civilization turns them into demands made by individuals on the economy, into problems that can be managed or *produced* out of existence. . . .

Patience, forbearance, courage, resignation, self-control, perseverance, and meekness each express a different coloring of the responses with which pain sensations were accepted, transformed into the experience of suffering, and endured. Duty, love, fascination, routines, prayer, and compassion were some of the means that enabled pain to be borne with dignity. . . .

Pain has ceased to be conceived as a "natural" or "metaphysical" evil. It is a social curse, and to stop the "masses" from cursing society when they are pain-stricken, the industrial system delivers them medical pain-killers. Pain thus turns into a demand for more drugs, hospitals, medical services, and other outputs of corporate, impersonal care and into political support for further corporate growth no matter what its human, social, or economic cost. . . .

Man's consciously lived fragility, individuality, and relatedness make the experience of pain, of sickness, and of death an integral part of his life. The ability to cope with this trio autonomously is fundamental to his health.[3]

Illich goes on to affirm that "[w]hen dependence on the professional management of pain, sickness and death grows beyond a certain point, the healing power in sickness, patience in suffering and fortitude in the face of death must decline."[4] For Illich, this state is not only psychologically and socially destructive; it is also morally and spiritually dangerous. Because it entails "hubris" in the form of what he deems arrogant and excessive human intervention in a medical form, it invites "Nemesis," the retribution of the gods.

A more secularized variant of a Christian outlook on the positive significance of illness, its attendant suffering, and its relationship to death is the romantic image of tuberculosis that pervaded English, French, and American literature and art in the early mid-nineteenth century, and also influenced conceptions of beauty, fashion, and life style during that period. In *The White Plague*, René and Jean Dubos present an intriguing, pastel-colored word portrait of the way that "consumption" (tuberculosis) was "sentimentalized" in that "romantic age."[5] According to the authors, exquisitely sensitive persons and those of extraordinary intellectual or artistic giftedness were believed to be especially susceptible to tuberculosis. When stricken by this consumptive disease (which involved "lofty and noble parts of the human body"), they supposedly became more beautiful in a way that physically reflected their "refinement," endowment, and state of election. The pallor, languor, slenderness, even emaciation associated with tuberculosis were admired and cultivated by others.

In this idealized nineteenth-century picture of the disease, "the fire" that wasted the bodies of those stricken with consumption was supposed to kindle their minds and their spirits. They became more brilliant, creative, loving, and celestial. And in a feverish state of sublimity, at the height of their youth, they eventually succumbed to what was baroquely described as a "painless, poetic death."

In certain non-Western, nonmodern societies, it is not only the signs and symptoms of a disorder that ultimately determine whether it is viewed as a religious event, but also what consequences for the community these manifestations bring in their wake. For example, the visionary leaders who initiate the kinds of religious movements that characteristically occur in Central African societies often behave in ways that are at first perceived as physically abnormal. Whether or not these "aberrations" come to be defined as illness, as possession, or as a sign of supernatural inspiration depends on what ensues. If the person in question goes into retreat and subsequently emerges to deliver to the community a new religious message that is compatible with their cultural tradition, that person is accepted as a visionary leader. Under these circumstances, "the *ex post facto* explanation that the community gives for [the leader's] prior derangement is that it was the precondition for the realignment of rituals, symbols, beliefs and myths to which he has introduced them."[6] Here, a tentative collective diagnosis of psychic illness or spirit possession is revoked and replaced by a religious interpretation, which elevates the leader and uplifts the community.

The degree and kind of importance that are attached to health, illness, and medicine differ from one society to another and can also vary from one historical period to another. For example, the significance of phenomena associated with health-illness-medicine in American society has progressively increased since the end of the 1950s in a variety of symbolic as well as empirical ways that will be discussed as this book unfolds.

Despite these differences and fluctuations, there is no society in which health, illness, and medicine are assigned a minor or a peripheral status. For health and illness and a society's way of dealing with them are associated with the capacity of individuals to perform and fulfill their social roles, and with their ability to relate to one another in and through these roles. Health, illness, and medicine are also closely linked to some of the most fundamental values and beliefs of any society, and to the problems of meaning that the primal experiences of birth, life, pain, suffering, anxiety, accident, aging, mortality, and death seem to evoke, individually and collectively, in all persons and human societies.

THE NATURE, RANGE, AND INCIDENCE OF ILLNESS

Illness is a panhuman occurrence. There is no known illness-free society or group, and the "I have never been sick a day in my life" individual is a rarity in any part of the world. The range of disorders with which men, women, and children may be stricken is impressively large. The emergence of new illnesses or the "back to the future" rediscovery of old ones continuously takes place, along with the progressive control and, in some cases, elimination of "old" ones.[7]

AIDS is a particularly dramatic contemporary instance of the development and discovery of a new disease. From its appearance and identification at the beginning of the 1980s, with its "puzzling occurrence of unusual malignancies, opportunistic infections, and immune system abnormalities that mysteriously develop in previously healthy individuals,"[8] AIDS rapidly escalated in "little more than five years from a clinical oddity to a virtual epidemic."[9] The surprised and fearful reactions that AIDS has elicited are a complex sociocultural phenomenon, to which its lethal nature and its association with high-risk sexual activity and intravenous drug abuse have contributed powerfully. On another level, at this point in Western biomedical history, when it has become commonplace to suppose that infectious and epidemic diseases have been eradicated in advanced modern societies like our own, the American medical profession and public alike were experientially and attitudinally unprepared for the surfacing of a disease like AIDS:

> In an era when many young physicians have never seen a case of measles or polio and when once life-threatening bacterial infections disappear in two or three days with antibiotic therapy, the AIDS epidemic seems almost unreal. The temptation to believe that a vaccine or a miracle drug is just over the horizon may be overwhelming for both health care providers and the general public. But [a]s the infection spreads, it is crucial that messages about risk reduction reach as wide an audience as possible. . . . The characteristics of the virus place it just out of reach of the most advanced therapeutic drugs.[10]

New mental disorders also have crystallized in American society during the 1980s. Three such disorders were proposed for inclusion in the third edition of *The Diagnostic and Statistical Manual of Mental Disorders*, the American Psychiatric Association manual generally regarded as representing the consensus of the psychiatric profession on officially recognized diagnoses. The new diagnostic categories are:

> "Premenstrual dysphoric disorder," a version of premenstrual syndrome that emphasizes the accompanying mood and behavioral changes; "paraphillic coercive disorder," designed to identify a subset of sexual offenders who are sexually aroused by the coercive nature of the act; and "self-defeating personality," a broad category of personality disorders characterized by masochistic and self-destructive behavior.

In contradistinction to the undisputed acceptance of AIDS as a syndrome, these new psychiatric categories have aroused opposition among mental health professionals. "Feminist psychiatrists and psychologists, and groups concerned with the victims of sexual abuse, contend that the proposals could contribute to sexual inequality and legitimize attempts to 'blame the victim' in some cases of assault."[11]

The question of whether disease and illness are inherent to life and the human condition cannot be definitively answered at our present stage of knowledge. It is still unclear whether there will ever be a scientifically based answer to such a question, or whether this is the sort of query to which primarily philosophical and religious responses must be made. But at this juncture in our understanding, the same biomedical, environmental, and behavioral data call forth quite different opinions from scientists. For example, physician-researcher Lewis Thomas believes that there is a finite number of major diseases that will be conquered by medical science:

> But what about that short list . . . of diseases whose mechanisms we did not understand 50 years ago? As it has turned out, fifty years after the beginning of what everyone acknowledges to be a revolution in medical science, we still have such a list, and it is still a roster of important, disabling and sometimes fatal illnesses that we are unable to deal with as effectively as we, and our patients, hope. . . . But the difference today—and it is a very great difference indeed—is that all the items on the list have changed from blank mysteries to approachable scientific problems. And ultimately, given the right kind of research and a certain amount of luck, all of them can be solved.[12]

Microbiologist René Dubos, on the other hand, insisted that "complete freedom from disease and from struggle is almost incompatible with the process of living":

> The very process of living is a continual interplay between the individual and his environment, often taking the form of a struggle resulting in injury or disease. The more creative the individual, the less he can hope to avoid danger, for the stuff of creation is made up of responses to the forces that impinge on his body and soul. Complete and lasting freedom from disease is but a dream remembered from imaginings of a Garden of Eden designed for the welfare of man.[13]

Dubos considered belief in the attainment of a diseaseless state to be utopian, and the conception of "conquering disease" through the vigorous application of medical science and technology to be a distinctively Western and particularly American expression of this outlook. He also recognized that "the illusion that perfect health and happiness are within man's possibilities has flourished in many different forms throughout history."[14] Such a vision is implicit in the *summum bonum* view of health that is a part of the cultural tradition of many different societies: "a state of complete physical, mental and social well-being and not merely the absence of disease or infirmity."[15]

In numerous cultures, this perspective also implies that health is "natural," whereas a great deal of illness is "unnatural." If people or communities are in harmony with their physical, social, and metaphysical environments, then illness and other forms of adversity are not likely to befall them. But if this equilibrium is upset through their own behavior, their conscious or unconscious thoughts and feelings, or those of significant others, then the situation is conducive to the illness-engendering play of malignant supernatural forces. Human agents often are considered to be the media through which these supernatural presences are triggered into action. In this view, illness is a nonnatural occurrence in several senses. Ideally it ought not to exist, and would not so frequently develop, except for the predominantly psychic and social disharmonies that set noxious physical and metaphysical influences into motion. This kind of health-illness paradigm, or a variant of it, is characteristic of a large number of societies: ancient Greece, classical China, India, a variety of East, West, and Central African societies, as well as a series of North American Indian societies, to cite just a few.[16] It appears that this framework is likely to predominate in nonmodern societies or subsocieties whose beliefs and practices relating to health and illness have been called "primitive," "folk," or "ethno" medicine by social scientists. In fact, from a cross-cultural perspective, the tendency of modern Western societies to emphasize so-called natural, biological, and physical aspects of health and illness, separate them from psychological and social factors, and rarely consider the relevance of religious and magical influences, is an uncommon, even peculiar orientation.

Cultural differences notwithstanding, it seems that a certain array of acute, infectious, and chronic diseases have occurred in most societies: for example, plague, cholera, influenza, pneumonia, tuberculosis, smallpox, typhoid fever, diphtheria, venereal diseases, dysentery, measles, and poliomyelitis; cardiovascular and renal disorders, malignant neoplasms; diabetes mellitus, ulcer of the stomach and of the duodenum; various psychoses, particularly schizophrenia or its equivalent, and various psychoneuroses.

A society's geographical zone and its stage of development also affect the profile of diseases to which its population is subject. For example, malaria is likely to be endemic and even epidemic in a tropical society that either does not have the scientific, public health, and technological knowledge to control the breeding of anophales mosquitoes, and to use chloroquine to help prevent and reduce the severity of malaria attacks, or the culturally adapted medical, political, and economic means to effectively implement this knowledge. In contrast, a society with a north temperate climate, like the United States, that is highly industrialized and urbanized, and that through medical scientific means, public health measures, and life style changes has brought most infectious diseases under control, characteristically is confronted with cardiovascular disorders, cancer, mental illnesses, automobile and work-incurred accidents, and suicide and homicide as major sources of disability and causes of death. Epidemiologists and demographers are now predicting that the United States is moving into what they define as "the age of delayed degenerative diseases":

According to the theory of epidemiologic transition there are three stages that have been characterized generally by a substitution of degenerative diseases for infectious diseases, and life expectancy at birth reaching approximately 70 years in the third stage. Based upon the analysis of mortality, life expectancy, and survival data for the United States from the turn of the century to 1980, and projections to the year 2020, the United States appears to have recently entered a fourth stage . . . characterized distinctly by rapid mortality declines in advanced ages that are caused by a postponement of the ages at which degenerative diseases tend to kill. This redistribution of degenerative diseases has been referred to as "The Age of Delayed Degenerative Diseases"—a stage that will propel life expectancy into and perhaps beyond eight decades. . . . [This] represents an unexpected and perhaps welcome era in our epidemiologic history, an era that requires new ways of thinking about aging, disease, morbidity, mortality, and certainly how life will be lived in advanced ages in the very near future.[17]

SOCIOMEDICAL IMPLICATIONS OF CULTURALLY SPECIFIC ILLNESSES AND SYNDROMES

Many aspects of illness are profoundly influenced by social and cultural factors as well as those of personality and biology. Sociocultural factors influence what is defined as an illness in a given society, what it is called, how it is interpreted and experienced, and how and whether it is detected and diagnosed. Social and cultural factors also affect decisions about to whom an illness is confided; what kinds of help, if any, are sought for dealing with it and from what sorts of persons in which statuses and roles; what therapies are administered, with what effects; what the prognosis is; and whether and how it is thought to be preventable. Nowhere are these influences more apparent than with respect to what have been alternatively called "folk illnesses" or "culture-bound syndromes," which are distinctive to particular societies or groups within them. These illnesses seem to be integrally related to particular beliefs, values, and social organization, and especially to the stresses and conflicts generated by the group's cultural outlook and social structure. As with other recognized forms of illness, the culture they are embedded in provides etiological and diagnostic explanations of their causes, nature, and modes of prevention, treatment, and cure.

Here, for example, is the way that Scott Preston, a Navajo medicine man, explained such a syndrome to a group of "white doctors" working on the reservation:

> There are some things which we medicine men know the white doctor is better able to cure. One of these is appendicitis; another is tuberculosis. Then there are such things as snake bite which both the medicine man and the white doctor can cure, each using his own medicine. And there is still a third kind of illness which only the Navajo medicine man can cure. For example, a person may be too near a tree struck by lightning. Right now there are probably some patients in this hospital who are sick from that illness. You white doctors wouldn't know that person is sick. You have no way of even finding out what is wrong with them. But we medicine men can, and we are able to cure such cases. In the Navajo way, we think that is just as important as treating the person in pain with appendicitis.[18]

"In the Navajo way," this kind of incident with lightning means that evil-producing forces of witchcraft are actively present, and that they have been directed at the person near the tree. Because of its cultural significance, irrespective of whether or not the people are physically hit by lightning, they may develop the somatic and psychic symptoms that Navajos define and experience as being "sick" with this "standing near a tree when it is struck by lightning" illness.

SUSTO: A LATIN AMERICAN FOLK ILLNESS

Since the beginning of the 1980s, there has been "a great revival of interest in culture-bound psychiatric syndromes."[19] One of the most important first-hand studies to appear is an analysis of "susto" (the word itself means fright), a particularly well-known and well-documented folk illness.[20] Although susto is socially and culturally shaped, it is not narrowly culture-bound. Rather than being restricted to a population speaking a distinctive language or to a singular cultural background, it is widespread throughout Latin America. It has been studied by anthropologists Arthur Rubel and Carl O'Nell, separately and together, for over twenty years. Their recent book, written in collaboration with physician Rolando Collado-Ardón, is a carefully designed, interdisciplinary study of the biological, emotional, social, and cultural characteristics of persons who are *asustado*—"suffering susto"—in comparison with those who are not. The study was done in three village communities in the state of Oaxaca, Mexico (two Indian and one Latino), chosen because they were comparable in demography, income, gender-role expectations, form of governance, and the influence of outside change agents such as Catholic priests, schoolteachers, or physicians, while differing in maternal language, cultural heritage, and social history.

Rubel, O'Nell, and Collado-Ardón's findings break through some of the commonplace assumptions about folk and culturally imprinted illnesses in ways that have conceptual as well as empirical implications for how "to comprehend people of other cultures when they complain of being sick and attribute their condition to causes that do not 'fit' our medical concepts."[21] All susto sufferers manifest the same symptoms: "The victim is (1) restless during sleep and (2) otherwise listless, debilitated, depressed, and indifferent to dress and personal hygiene."[22] But these symptoms are considered to be susto only if the patients, their families, and/or healers attribute them to "an essential part of the person being separated from the body,"[23] as the result of a frightening event. Thus, the villagers' casual explanation of the susto problem is as important to its phenomenological reality as its "cohering set of characteristics";[24] and their interpretation of susto is associated with certain metaphysical concepts and beliefs that have no counterpart in modern Western medicine and psychiatry:

> Suffering susto, being *asustado*, is based on people's understanding that an individual is composed of a body and an immaterial substance, an essence, that may become detached from the body and either wander freely or become a captive of supernatural forces. This essence may leave the body during sleep, particularly when the individual is dreaming, but may also become detached as a consequence of an unsettling or frightening experience. Among Indians, this essence is believed held captive because the patient, wittingly or not, has disturbed the spirit guardians of the earth, river, ponds, forests, or collectivities of animals, birds, or fish. Its release depends upon expiation of the affront.[25]

Susto, then, is not just a familiar syndrome of the West that is called by a different name and shaped by a different culture. Nor is it "simply a way of explaining mental illness for people who lack the education to understand its true significance,"[26] as some researchers have maintained. Rather, Rubel, O'Nell, and Collado-Ardón contend that their investigation of susto "demonstrates how cultural and disease processes interact to form an entity unfamiliar to cosmopolitan medicine.[27]

Although the investigators used what they called an "open-system model" to probe the biological, social, psychological, and cultural dimensions of susto, they themselves were surprised to discover that asustados had more signs and symptoms of organic disease than their matched controls, "and these were more impairing and life-threatening."[28] The major hypothesis around which their study had turned was a social one. They had predicted that susto would be most closely and significantly "associated with a person's perception of his or her inadequacy in the performance of critical social roles":[29]

> Although the hypothesized relationship between a susto complaint and a victim's inadequate level of role performance was demonstrated, it proved insufficient to explain susto. Finding that asustados also suffered an uncommonly heavy burden of biological disease obliged us to reappraise the premises with which we began. Now it is inadequate and inappropriate to conceive of susto as a form of unique social behavior on the one hand, or as a purely biomedical phenomenon on the other. Before collection of these data, we had argued that a susto complaint simply legitimized "time off" from the exigencies of everyday roles. . . . However, our new findings demonstrate that the life burdens of ordinary Oaxacans overburden the asustados. Doubly taxed by a perceived inability to perform critical role assignments and an excessive load of disease, the asustado finds it impossible to carry out his normal responsibilities. Rather than electing the sick role to legitimize a respite from their obligations, asustados are *forced to the sidelines* by excessive demands on their adaptive resources.[30]

Touching on the larger implications of their study, the authors go on to say that it "remains a theoretical possibility that other folk illnesses could be credibly explained as either uniquely social or uniquely biological processes." However, in their opinion, such a conclusion "must . . . remain in doubt until empirical research has taken the other, rival possibility into account and seriously probed its explanatory value."[31]

CULTURAL PATTERNING OF ILLNESS IN CONTEMPORARY JAPAN

The most abundant literature on culturally specific syndromes pertains to developing societies and communities within them. But the interplay between biological, social, and psychological factors in the etiology, definition, diagnosis, and treatment of illness in modern societies is no less intricate or culturally distinctive. In her "anthropological view" of *Illness and Culture in Contemporary Japan*, Emiko Ohnuki-Tierney vividly and sensitively documents this fact. Her book "illustrates that, despite industrialization and significant advances in modern science, including biomedicine, in contemporary Japan, Japanese concepts and behavior regarding health and illness are to a large extent culturally patterned, even when they are couched in biomedical terms."[32] For example, "the greatest attention by far is given to the abdomen, . . . called *hara* or *ichō* in Japanese":

> Numerous illnesses in this part of the body are recognized. . . . The Japanese give extra attention to the stomach and use various means to protect it. The use of the *haramaki*, a piece of material wrapped around the abdomen, has a long history and illustrates the importance of this part of the body. . . . The *hara* used to be considered the seat of the soul. . . . In contemporary Japan, the term *hara* may be used to mean either the entire area between the thorax and the pelvis, including the flesh and the internal organs (stomach, intestines, liver), or the lower abdomen, excluding the stomach. . . . [T]he *hara* is not simply an equivalent of the heart in Western

thought, but instead represents a combination of the heart and the brain. It is the seat of both thought and feeling, or intellect and affect. . . . No contemporary Japanese thinks of the *hara* as the seat of the soul, just as no American believes the anatomical heart to be the locus of love. Nevertheless, the content of the metaphor remains germane, just as the notion of love claims a central place in the contemporary American value system, and is expressed in the icon of the St. Valentine's heart.[33]

Ohnuki-Tierney observes that although Japanese "emphasize psychobehavioral symptoms," they "pay little attention to emotions in illness causation, and consequently have little interest in 'psychotherapy.'"[34] Rather, they attribute most ordinary illnesses to the body, and to "other material and physiological agents in the universe."[35] For example, *shinkei*, or "nerves" in the physiological sense, is "a frequent etiology of illnesses with a wide range of self-perceived symptoms":

[I]n many cases the Japanese explanation of *shinkei* as the etiology of a certain ailment or illness is further elaborated by whether it is a disorder of the autonomic nervous system or of the peripheral nervous system. The imbalance of the sympathetic and parasympathetic nervous systems is also a frequently cited disorder. . . . Although in the United States some of these disorders or their symptoms would be viewed as purely physiological, affecting the nervous systems, many would be interpreted as psychosomatic symptoms. In the case of Japanese diagnosis, they are usually perceived as disorders of *shinkei* . . . nerves in their physiological sense. As a corollary, prescribed treatments all aim at the restoration of the normal balance in the nervous system through physiological and physical treatments such as bathing, massage, acupuncture, and medicine.[36]

Among the intriguingly Japanese health-illness patterns that Ohnuki-Tierney reports are those connected with what she refers to as "the aborted fetus as etiological agent." A sudden increase in the popularity of "the age-old practice of *mizuko no kuyō*, the memorial service for an aborted fetus," has been occurring in Japan. "These services are held primarily by women who have undergone recent abortions and often are suffering from what we call psychosomatic illnesses":[37]

The service can take several forms. For example, one can purchase a tomb for the fetus. . . . The tomb consists of a stone carved in the figure of a jizo, a buddha in charge of children, wearing a red bib, and with flowers and a pinwheel on each side. On the tomb is written a *kaimyō*, a posthumous name given to a deceased person in Buddhism. Many cannot afford to buy a tomb; instead, they acquire a *kaimyō* from a priest, who will write it on a tablet. The tablet is placed in the ancestral alcove of the family, and people observe the regular memorial services as they do for other ancestors. Another form of holding a memorial service is the use of *ema*, which the Japanese have used for a long time for various purposes. *Ema* are wooden boards with roof-shaped tops. People write prayers on them, asking, for example, for the cure of particular illnesses, or for a successful passage of the entrance examination to a university. They are then hung at a specified place in temples and shrines. Although *ema* have long been very popular among the Japanese, it is only in the past few years that innumerable *ema* have appeared with prayers for and apologies to aborted fetuses. They are hung most often at temples that are known for the protection of children.[38]

The fact that Japanese women seem to be experiencing an increased amount of psychosomatic illnesses which they associate with their aborted fetuses, and that they are trying to cope with these illnesses through the observance of traditional magico-religious rituals, is unexpected. For Japan is a society that has long been known for its very high incidence of abortion and for what has appeared to be the remarkable ease with which it is practiced.

SOCIAL VARIABILITY IN WHAT IS NOT REGARDED AS ILLNESS

As we have seen, illnesses configurations exist that are particular to a culture, society, or group. Conversely, there are conditions distinctively *not* defined as illness in a given cultural or social milieu that would be defined, experienced, and treated as such in others. This is the case, for example, with Navajo attitudes toward what non-Indian Americans define as a serious disorder, congenital dislocation of the hip. The prevalence of this condition among Navajos has been found to be quite high, and it has been "strongly suspected that cultural factors, notably the use of cradle-boards, contribute substantially either to the condition itself or to the degree of permanent disability resulting from it. For, on the cradleboard, the infant is securely laced with the outstretched legs bound together in a position that does not favor continued insertion of the head of the femur in the pelvic joint."[39] Even when hip dislocation is bilateral, it "is not viewed as a disease or . . . as a particularly important disability" in Navajo culture:

> Boys with this condition are not generally mocked, and girls who have it have no difficulty in obtaining husbands and raising families. Indeed, the fact that one child in a family has congenital hip disease appears to be regarded, not quite as a positive blessing, but as a sort of continuously visible relative blessing. By this is meant a blessing in the sense that when evil struck the family, this was the worst it could do, and evil is not apt to strike one family on too many occasions.[40]

As the Navajo example suggests, even within the same society, what one group regards as an illness or a disability is not necessarily regarded as such by other groups. In a society as heterogeneous and differentiated as American society, a person's ethnic and religious background, level and type of education, region of the country and type of community, as well as sex, age, marital status, occupation, income, and social class status may influence what the individual defines as illness, and how he or she responds to it when it occurs.

In this connection, Earl L. Koos's *The Health of Regionville*, published in 1954, was a pioneering study of how the social stratificational system of an upper New York State town affected "what the people thought and did" about health and illness.[41] Over a period of four years, Koos regularly interviewed 500 families about their health- and illness-relevant attitudes and behaviors. He found that they varied significantly according to the socioeconomic classes to which a person belonged:

Class I (business and professional people); Class II (skilled and semiskilled workers); Class III (unskilled workers). For example, whereas approximately half the members of Classes I and II were inclined to define a persistent backache as a medical symptom and seek a physician's advice about it, less than 20 percent of those in Class III were likely to do so. Their attitudes are reflected in the following statements made by Class III respondents:

> I'd look silly, wouldn't I, going to see a doctor for a backache. My mother *always* had a backache, as long as I can remember, and didn't do anything about it. It didn't kill her, either. . . . If I went to the doctor for that, my friends would hoot me out of town. That's just something you have, I guess. Why let it get you down? [42]

Money and time constraints, of course, helped to make such working class people more reluctant to seek medical aid than those of higher socioeconomic status. But as the foregoing quotation suggests, subcultural factors were also involved in the stoical outlook on what unskilled workers defined as the inevitable aches and pains of life.

EXPRESSIVE AND SYMBOLIC ASPECTS OF ILLNESS: THE INFLUENCE OF ETHNICITY

The emotions that illness evokes and the form in which people express these feelings are also significantly influenced by social and cultural factors. Some of the best observations made on the powerful role that social background and cultural tradition can play in the expressive and symbolic aspects of an illness experience have come from social scientists interested in the relationship between ethnicity, health, and the sick role. Sociologist/social psychiatrist Marvin K. Opler, for example, has reported consistent cultural differences both in the affective behavior of Italian-American and Irish-American hospitalized schizophrenic patients, and in the emotional conflicts that seem to have contributed to their illness.[43] He described the Italian patients whom he studied as physically active, verbally noisy, emotionally volatile, dramatic, overtly flouting of authority and authority figures, and engaging in various other concrete and symbolic forms of aggressive behavior. In comparison, Irish schizophrenic patients appeared to be quiescent, taciturn, compliant, withdrawn, and disinclined to show defiance in any outward form other than through passive resistance. Whereas the majority of the Irish patients observed by Opler suffered from feelings of guilt and sinfulness about their sexuality and were prone to delusions, Italian patients were relatively symptom-free in these regards. However, the Italian patients were more anxiously preoccupied with what might be wrong with their bodies, and were inclined to be vociferous about what the medical staff deemed hypochondriacal complaints. Opler alleged that these consistent differences in the emotional structure, ambiance, and content of the psychotic illnesses of Italian and Irish patients were consistent with differences in their cultural traditions, the conflicts institutionalized in their respective milieux, and the socioculturally preferred ways that each ethnic group has developed for dealing with those conflicts.

Anthropologist Anne Parsons's work with schizophrenic patients of southern Italian origins in the United States (Boston) and in Italy (Naples) reinforced and enriched a number of Opler's findings. In contrast to Opler, however, she found that many Italian patients were subject to delusional perceptions and thinking, and she noted that the content of these delusions was different for Italian patients in a Boston mental hospital from what it was for comparable patients in a quite similar Neapolitan hospital. The Boston patients not only defined certain individuals as "enemies," but also attributed the same kinds of threatening, dangerous qualities to such abstract institutional and ideological entities as the hospital, an advertising agency, a business firm, or the Communists.[44] The Naples patients' delusions, however, were almost exclusively particularistic and concrete, focusing on people and events within their families and neighborhoods.

Parsons demonstrated how profoundly social and cultural influences can penetrate unconscious layers of the personality, so that they shape and color the imagery and symbolism as well as the meaning of a psychotic illness. She also illustrated the role that social and cultural factors can play in ritualizing patients' emotional responses to their mental illness and hospitalization. Focusing on the "repetitive pleading" for discharge from the hospital in which "crowds" of patients in southern Italian psychiatric institutions continuously engaged, Parsons interpreted the clamorous, chorale-like way in which they repeated, "I wanna go home," over and over again, as a "collectively supported ritual for the maintenance of contact with the outside world [that] at the time [has] the function of supporting denial of the problems which confront patients in it."[45] Here, then, the ritualization of affect that *simulates* what an ethnic group considers to be normal expressiveness serves as a culturally conditioned defense mechanism.

The impact of social and cultural factors on some of the physiological phenomena that accompany illness or injury is as impressive as their relationship to psychological symptoms. In his classic study of *People in Pain*, Mark Zborowski has documented this association through his detailed analysis of the ways in which patients from several "ethno-cultural groups" respond to "the pain experience."[46] The patients he observed and interviewed were male veterans of World Wars I and II and the Korean War at the Kingsbridge Veterans Hospital in the Bronx, New York. They were of Jewish, Italian, and "Old American" (white, native-born, and Protestant) origins. All had neurological conditions, primarily herniated discs and spinal lesions. The Jewish and Italian patients were inclined to express their reactions to pain openly and emotionally through "words, sounds and gestures. . . . [They felt] free to talk about their pain, complain about it and manifest their sufferings by groaning, moaning, crying, etc." According to Zborowski, they were "not ashamed of this expression." Rather, they recognized that when in pain, they complained a great deal, called for help, and expected the responsive presence of members of the medical staff, friends, and especially relatives, from whom they required continual sympathy and active help.

In contrast, the "Old American" patients did not publicly cry out in pain. Instead, when examined by physicians or attended by nurses they tended to give a clinical report on their pain with something approaching the detached professional manner of medically trained persons. When their pain became overwhelming, their inclination was to withdraw, and express their anguish only when alone. The ideology of these patients regarding appropriate, effective ways of coping with pain differed as much from that of Jewish and Italian patients as their behavior. "Old

American" patients believed that keening over their pain "won't help anybody," whether it be themselves, members of the medical team whose efficacy ideally ought not be impeded by patients' emotional outbursts, or concerned kin. On the other hand, they viewed pain as a serious symptom, indicative of something significantly wrong with their health, and they welcomed the most energetic, scientific, and technological interventions that the medical team and hospital could provide in the way of diagnosis and treatment.

One of the subtlest aspects of Zborowski's study is that after identifying the manifestly similar ways that Jewish and Italian patients reacted to pain, and contrasting their responses to those of "Old Americans," he went on to show that the meaning of their pain-related behaviors could not necessarily be deduced from their actions. Although both Jewish and Italian patients were exclamatory about their pain, the Jewish patients were primarily anxious about its "symptomatic meaning"—its significance for their own and their family's health and welfare—whereas the chief concern of Italian patients was the pain experience *per se* and its hoped-for relief. Thus, for example, although Italian patients welcomed being treated with analgesic drugs and benefitted from them pharmacologically and psychologically, Jewish patients, in contrast, worried about the potential side-effects of the drugs, received less physical comfort from them, and even when temporarily relieved of their pain were anxiously preoccupied with the "uncured" medical condition from which it originated. In this respect the attitude of Jewish patients resembled that of the "Old Americans" more than the Italians', although their outward behavior differed greatly. Both the Jewish and "Old American" patients' anxiety about pain was more generalized and "future-oriented" than that of Italian patients. Where they diverged attitudinally was that the Jewish patients were characteristically skeptical, and frequently pessimistic, about the ability of medical science and its practitioners eventually to solve their illness problems, while the "Old Americans" were more confident and optimistic in their belief that the medical profession could and would do so.

THE SOCIAL SHAPING OF MEDICAL CARE DECISIONS

Characteristically, an individual who experiences certain forms of physical, psychological, or interpersonal malaise considers the possibility that these may be indicative of an illness or disorder. (As already shown, the society, culture, and group to which one belongs influence what are regarded as signs and symptoms of illness.) He may or he may not choose to mention his difficulties to others: for example, to a family member, a colleague at work, a friend, or even a stranger with whom he enters into ostensibly casual conversation. How prone he is to acknowledge his symptoms and to talk about them is not only a function of his personality characteristics but also of his social and cultural background.

In some instances, the initial signals that some health problem is manifesting itself may come from onlookers rather than from the incipiently ill person. For example, relatives, friends, or associates may suggest to an individual that he does not seem to be looking or acting well and should take better care of himself, temporarily diminish or suspend part of his usual activities, and seek expert health advice. Once again, social and cultural factors, along with psychological and biological ones, play a major part in determining whether significant others in an ailing person's milieu will intervene, which individuals in what statuses and roles will do so, what measures they will advocate, and how the person about whom they are concerned will respond to their suggestions.

The arrival of a person with a health problem at the door of a medical practitioner is rarely an unhesitating, straight-line process in any society or group. There is likely to be much inner and outer dialogue, considerable vacillation, and numerous intermediaries en route. Nor can it be assumed that those who do not confer with a practitioner are free of illness. In most cases, what sort of medical practitioner people eventually consult, if they do so, is profoundly influenced by their status and role set, the groups with which they identify, and by their values, beliefs, and attitudes, as well as by their physical and psychological signs and symptoms and economic situation.

There are very few studies of the process by which people wend their way to a particular practitioner or set of practitioners, what they expect to receive from those whose advice and care they seek, how these expectations affect their response to the recommendations and treatment, and their willingness to continue the relationship that they have established with the practitioner. *Grosso modo*, we know that most people consider both technical competence and humanity to be the earmarks of a good practitioner; they tend to attach equal weight to the two criteria. In most instances, the outcome of the practitioner's ministrations—how well it is explained to the patient what is wrong and what is being done to allay it, the degree of physical and psychological comfort provided, and how much progress is made in managing or curing the patient's underlying problems—constitute the ultimate bases for the patient's judgment of the practitioner's technical, interpersonal, and moral excellence. And in societies where a supernatural as well as a natural explanation is sought for the occurrence of an illness or injury, the success of the practitioner in these regards is also considered to be indicative of the degree of metaphysical power that he or she wields.

Social Class and Mental Illness, by sociologist August B. Hollingshead and psychiatrist Fredrick C. Redlich, is a landmark study of the manifest and latent ways in which individuals' social and cultural characteristics influence their "paths" to medical practitioners and patienthood, the types of treatment processes they undergo, and what the outcomes of those treatments are likely to be.[47] As the title of their book indicates, Hollingshead and Redlich were primarily concerned with the interrelationships between social class and mental illness in these regards, but their analytic paradigm and methodology are also applicable to the interplay between other social and cultural factors and other forms of illnesses. Basing their research in the community of New Haven, Connecticut, in the 1950s, and using a combined battery of census, interview, and case study techniques, Hollingshead and Redlich studied extensive and intensive samples of psychiatric patients and nonpatients, psychiatric facilities, and psychiatrists of different therapeutic orientations.

They discovered, for example, that persons of higher social class status were most likely to come to psychiatrists through self-referral or the referral of family or friends, whereas individuals of lower class status were more likely to be referred to psychiatrists by clinic physicians, social agencies, and (in the case of those diagnosed as psychotically ill) by the police and the courts. An inverse relationship was found to exist between social class and the prevalence of psychiatric patients in the community; the largest proportion of patients came from the lowest social classes, and the lower the class, the higher the rate of psychotic disorders.

Hollingshead and Redlich also demonstrated that, in a number of different respects, the treatment of psychiatric patients was affected both by their own social class background and by the background of the psychiatrists. Thus, higher status patients were more likely to receive psychotherapy, while lower status patients were more frequently the recipients of organic therapies.[48] Furthermore, lower-class patients who did enter psychotherapy generally did less well than higher status patients. Partly because they were less likely to have undertaken treatment voluntarily, lower status patients were often more antagonistic, or at least resistant. In addition, they expected physical rather than "talking" methods of treatment; they were more comfortable with authoritarian, "order-giving" behavior from physicians than with a collegial, nondirective approach; and they were less accustomed to engaging in the psychotherapy-relevant modes of self-analysis, verbalization, and symbolization than higher status patients.

The problems that lower class patients experienced in psychotherapy, then, stemmed in part from the fact that the psychotherapeutic method itself proved to be more compatible with certain attitudes, values, and behavior patterns with which middle- and upper-class patients were more familiar than lower-class patients were. In turn, this contributed to the difficulties that many psychiatrists experienced in communicating with lower-class patients, understanding them, liking them, and feeling heartened by their responses to treatment.

However, as Hollingshead and Redlich documented, the most fundamental sources of difficulty in the psychiatrist-lower class-patient relationship stemmed from the fact that the physician's own social class origins and culture were so different from those of the patient that he had difficulty empathizing with him as well as reaching him. Thus, the middle-to-upper-class-oriented psychiatrist "did better" with higher status patients. Finally, Hollingshead and Redlich observed that the social backgrounds of the psychiatrists were not distributed at random and were significantly correlated with their treatment orientation. Those who had an "analytic and psychological orientation," for example, were archetypically very upwardly mobile, first- or second-generation American men of Jewish origin; those who had a "directive and organic orientation" were usually men from Old American, Protestant origins who had not experienced the same degree of social class mobility.

Why People Go To Psychiatrists, by Charles Kadushin, built on the Hollingshead and Redlich analysis but attached special importance to the role that a "social circle of influencers" can play in leading persons to the decision that they are in need of psychological help, and in directing them towards a particular kind of practitioner.[49] In 1959–1960, using questionnaires, interviews, and clinic records, Kadushin collected data on 1,452 applicants to ten New York City psychiatric clinics, out of a universe of 61 such clinics open to the general public at that time. Since New York is the "world capital of psychotherapy, every imaginable type of clinic [was] represented" among the city's clinics.[50] Kadushin's sample included psychoanalytic, psychotherapeutic, religio-psychiatric, and hospital clinics.

He found that, partly as a consequence of the great heterogeneity of psychiatric facilities in New York, applicants to the different types of clinic were already self-selected. The applicants to psychoanalytic clinics, like patients in private therapy, tended to be young, single, well-educated, white, American-born, Jewish, nonreligious, and sophisticated "insiders" about psychotherapy. Those who applied to psychotherapeutic clinics had similar characteristics, though their social class standing was not quite as high. Religio-psychiatric clinics, on the other hand, attracted middle-aged, married, white, Protestant businessmen, and, to an even greater degree, their wives. In contrast, the hospital clinics drew people who belonged to the urban working classes or who were on relief, and who were less exclusively white than applicants to the other types of clinic, were older, and were more likely to be women.

Most of the persons in Kadushin's study had seen a psychiatrist or another psychotherapist at least once before presenting themselves to a particular clinic. The first professional seen turned out to be the key to the patient's subsequent choices. And the selection of this first professional proved to have less to do with the specific problems that a patient eventually presented to a clinic than with his or her social circle, social class, and ability and motivation to pay for private psychotherapy.

The informal social circle to which Kadushin devoted the most attention is one that he called "Friends and Supporters of Psychotherapy." "This mythical but nonetheless very real social organization," he wrote, "consists of a loose social circle of people knowledgeable about and interested in psychotherapy."[51] It influenced every step in the progressive process by which those affiliated with it decided to go to a psychotherapist or psychiatric clinic: "the realization of a problem, consultation with laymen, choice of type of healer, and choice of an individual practitioner."[52] The Friends and Supporters of Psychotherapy not only had certain social background traits in common (intellectuals, artists, and professionals, often of a literary bent, who were frequently Jewish), but they tended to define their problems in ways that were compatible with the psychoanalytic ethos. In their self-conception and self-presentation, they emphasized the self-worth, sexual, and interpersonal difficulties they were experiencing. Characteristically, they were more inclined than nonmembers of this circle to discuss their problems with friends and relatives, and voluntarily to select psychiatrists or analytic clinics for help with their problems. By and large, they knew what to expect from this type of therapy, and partly as a consequence responded well to treatment.

THE SICK ROLE

In any society, whatever the path a person may have travelled to get there, seeing a medical practitioner usually implies at least a tentative definition of that individual as ill. (This continues to be true despite the efforts that have been made in numerous societies to emphasize preventive rather than curative or palliative medical care.)

As Talcott Parsons emphasized, illness is not just a biological or psychological condition or an unstructured social state. It is also a social role, characterized by certain exemptions, rights, and obligations, and shaped by the society, groups, and cultural tradition to which the sick person belongs.

Parsons's formulation of what he termed "the sick role" is perhaps the most important and frequently discussed conceptual contribution that has been made to the sociology of medicine. He first articulated the notion of the sick role in 1948 in an essay on "Illness and the Role of the Physician."[53] He developed it more fully in a pathmaking chapter in *The Social System* that played a crucial historical part in making the "situations" of physicians and patients and the "institutional pattern of medical practice" amenable to sociological analysis.[54] Over the years Parsons published a number of other essays that further elaborated his conception of the sick role and its larger sociocultural implications. These included the sick role's relationship to family and kinship, occupations and professions, science, religion and magic, social motivation, deviance and social control, and to the value system of an advanced modern, Western society like the United States.[55] His last publication on the sick role, in 1975, was "a restatement of certain aspects of the . . . sick role, and its relation to the performances and functions of physicians, or more generally therapeutically oriented health service agencies."[56] It was written as a consequence of Parsons's own more extensive theoretical and substantive thinking, and in response to the voluminous printed and oral responses by social scientists to his ideas about the sick role that had continued unabatedly since his first publication on the subject.

To this day, commentary on the sick role goes on. Yet, despite the thousands of pages that have been written about the sick role and its attributes, about its application to empirically relevant contexts, and about the merits and demerits of the way that it was delineated by Parsons, it is rarely presented by those who write and speak about it with the nuances that its originator intended and built into it.

Parsons's conception of the sick role is based on the assumption that what is regarded as illness by different societies and groups encompasses a wide range of conditions: physical or organic disorders; psychosomatic illnesses; what might be called socio- or culturo-somatic syndromes such as so-called folk illnesses and culture-bound syndromes; psychological or mental illnesses; and existential conditions—states of "spiritual malaise" or "possession" that are viewed as metaphysical illnesses.

Running parallel to the spectrum of illness that is inherent to Parsons's paradigm is his notion of a sliding scale of "the 'motivatedness' of illness." In his view, conscious and unconscious psychological and sociocultural factors range from being of negligible to very great importance in the etiology, prognosis, and outcome of different sorts of disorders. Parsons cautioned, however, that "the interweaving of motivated and nonmotivated factors at both conscious and unconscious levels is complex indeed and any simple formula about these matters is likely to prove misleading."

> It seems to me quite clear that modern knowledge of unconscious motivation makes a much more extended scope of the concept of motivatedness entirely acceptable than older common sense, including that of the medical profession, has allowed for. I would not, however, at all claim that this covers the whole ground. Certainly human beings, like other categories of organism, are subject to pathogenic influences of many sorts which are altogether independent of the processes we call motivational. Thus, doubtless, most cases of bacterial or viral infection or of degenerative processes may be so regarded, as can some of the traumatic consequences of accidents. . . .
>
> [But] we can . . . speak of accident-prone people even though the physical consequences of an accident, once it has occurred, are not clearly analyzable in motivational terms. Such people . . . may unnecessarily expose themselves to the risk of such accidents. Probably somewhat similar considerations apply to such fields as infections, and indeed, to the degenerative diseases like cancer.[57]

How motivated an illness is considered to be is significantly influenced by the cognitive, belief, and value systems of the society or group within which it occurs.

For instance, within the thought and belief systems of what Parsons analytically classified as post-primitive or archaic societies, a high proportion of the sicknesses, injuries, accidents, and other forms of misfortune that occur are considered to be caused by the conscious or unconscious negative thoughts and feelings of others, who have called into play the action of malevolent supernatural forces.

> In the archaic view, illness is "unnatural." Ideally, it ought not to occur, and empirically, it would not, without the intervention of transhuman forces, mediated by human agents who are either intentional or unintentional evildoers. Illness is presumed to be caused by the evil thoughts, feelings, or motives of a significant other person. It may result from feelings of envy, jealousy, resentment, hatred, aggression, destructiveness, or the like on the part of an individual who is not necessarily aware of the fact that he harbors these emotions or that he is deliberately intent on harming the person who is his "victim." . . . But it is also possible that illness is due to the conscious and overt malevolent thoughts, feelings, and motives of an individual who has used symbolic, ritualistic means to cause the harm that has occurred. . . . In either case, the thoughts and feelings of the malefactor have the capacity to harm, because they are believed to harness the power of one of the numerous kinds of spirits that move back and forth between the spheres of the dead and the living, filling the cosmic space between the Supreme Being or Creator and Man.[58]

To take an example from a modern societal context, Kadushin has shown that particular sets of signs and symptoms are much more likely to be defined as psychological in nature by persons who belong to the subculture he called the "Friends and Supporters of Psychotherapy," than by those who do not. Independent of the stage of development of a society, or the attributes of a group, there is a self-fulfilling prophecy relationship between shared social and cultural beliefs that an illness is motivated and the objective probability that motivational factors will play a significant role in its etiology and outcome.

SICK ROLE EXEMPTIONS

The major parameters of the sick role, according to Parsons, consist of two dynamically interrelated sets of exemptions and obligations. First, the sick person is exonerated from certain kinds of responsibility during the illness. The person is not held morally accountable for being sick—it is not considered his "fault"—and he or she is not expected to get better by sheer determination or without the help of others. Second, the sick individual is viewed as someone whose capacity to function "normally" is impaired, and who ought to be relieved of some usual role-related activities and responsibilities (in the family, at work, in connection with school, and so on). The nature and extent of these exemptions is determined by the limitations that the illness is assumed to impose, by the restrictions that are considered to be conducive to recovery, and by the curtailments that are believed necessary to protect others from contracting the illness or from harm caused by the sick person's malperformance of usual role responsibilities.

Exempting a person defined as sick from responsibility for having fallen ill does not necessarily exclude recognition that motivational elements may be involved in the origin of the disorder or in the person's response to it. Rather, it means that the person is not judged to be morally blameworthy for the state or condemned for having succumbed to it. "If being sick is to be regarded as 'deviant,' as certainly in important respects it must," Parsons has written, "it is as we have noted distinguished from other deviant roles precisely by the fact that the sick person is not regarded as 'responsible' for his condition, 'he can't help it.'"[59]

The ways in which the exemptions of the sick role are institutionalized—their scope and duration, expressive style, and cultural meaning—vary considerably from one society to another. A particularly vivid example of this variation is provided by contemporary Japan, a modern society characterized by what Ohnuki-Tierney describes as a highly indulgent, "'pampering' attitude toward the sick":

> The average length of hospitalization in Japan is by far the longest in the world. . . . One of the major factors . . . is a basic "pampering" attitude toward the sick. . . . The Japanese think of many more conditions as "illnesses" than biomedicine recognizes as "diseases." . . .
>
> Part and parcel of the Japanese attitude toward illness is the emphasis on *ansei* (peace and quiet, or bed rest) as the major treatment for virtually any illness, from a minor cold to a major disease. . . . Lengthy hospitalization, then, may be seen as the official sanctioning of *ansei*, the most cherished treatment method of popular Japanese medicine. Long hospitalization periods thus affirm the legitimacy of, and provide the institutional support for, sickness. . . .
>
> For both men and women, there is an implicit and sometimes explicit expectation on the part of the patient, approved by family members and doctors, that hospitalization is a form of "vacation," a reward for hard work. This attitude may be linked to the limited use of paid vacation time by Japanese employees. Illness legitimizes the "vacation" Japanese workers otherwise feel pressured not to utilize. Needless to say, the connection between these two phenomena is not always consciously recognized.[60]

In some societies, the exemption from responsibility dimensions of the sick role may complicate the "problems of meaning" that are likely to arise when a person falls seriously ill. This is true of many modern societies, for example, in which the predominant framework for defining and explaining illness is a scientific one:

> Illness is believed to be a "natural" rather than a supernatural happening: a state of disease and dysfunction impersonally caused by microorganisms, inborn metabolic disturbances, or physical or psychic distress. No mythical beings, spirits or gods are assumed to be at work bringing sickness to bear on particular individuals; nor are persons considered to be motivated or able to use arcane, magical powers to do so. Furthermore, as Parsons indicated, one of the attributes of the sick role in a modern society is that the person who falls ill is not supposed to have caused his condition by displeasing the gods, the ancestors, or "significant others" in his social milieu who, as a consequence, magicoreligiously afflict him.[61]

Yet in a modern society, no less than in others, an encounter with serious illness evokes questions about *why* it has happened, in the minds of the sick person, the family and friends, and sometimes even among the members of the medical team who care for her or him:

Why do some people get sick and others stay perfectly healthy? . . . Why are the people in here [the hospital] sick, and those outside well? . . . Why am *I* sick? . . . You lie there and think, "Why? Why Leo? Why me?" I've tried to be a good man. I've gone to Temple, given money, never cheated, tried to help my fellow man. . . . I don't understand. . . . I don't know. . . .[62]

"But who of us really believes that his own bodily infirmities and the approaching death is a purely natural occurrence, just an insignificant event in the infinite chain of causes?" anthropologist Bronislaw Malinowski has written. "To the most rational of civilized men health, disease, the threat of death, float in a hazy emotional mist, which seems to become denser and more impenetrable as the fateful forms approach."[63] Modern medicine provides no legitimation for the occurrence of such problems of meaning and no institutionalized means for dealing with them. Its "scientificness" addresses and provides some explanations for the "hows" of illness, but does not recognize, dispel, or answer the questions of "why" that inevitably arise. Exempted from responsibility for having fallen ill, confronted with some of the most fundamental enigmas of what Parsons termed "human condition" matters of "ultimate concern," the sick person in a modern society is often faced with a greater explanatory void than those who fall ill in a traditional premodern society, and have culturally given recourse to interpersonal, moral, and metaphysical interpretations of their predicament.

The fact that a sick person is exempted from some of the role responsibilities normally expected of healthy individuals is another potential source of strain. For one thing, the person who is defined as ill is not permitted to decide independently which social activities will be continued, and which ones will be relinquished. The attributes of the illness, the opinions of family, friends, and colleagues, and the prescriptions and proscriptions of the medical practitioners all contribute to the exemptions that the ill person is granted. From one point of view, these exemptions are special privileges; but from another, they are an imposed set of obligatory restrictions. Although they may constitute what has been called "secondary gains" for some, they are experienced as painful deprivations by others. The role exemptions associated with sickness are likely to be especially stressful in a society like the United States, where energetically active, highly individualistic, and dynamically achievement-oriented values are paramount.

ILLNESS AS DEVIANCE

Because the occurrence and outcome of an illness are to varying degrees motivated, and because its institutionalization in the form of the sick role entails both moral and social role exemptions, it also constitutes a form of deviant behavior. It is not stigmatized in the same way that "sin" or "crime" are, and it is certified and approved as "authentic" in a way that malingering (the conscious or semiconscious simulating of illness) is not. But it is defined as an inherently negative, exceptional state, and the sick role includes the commitment to do everything possible to progress out of it. In this sense, it is what Parsons termed "a conditionally legitimated deviant" role.

If it becomes generalized in a population, illness also has the potential to develop into a more macroscopic kind of deviance, with serious implications for the functioning of whole groups, organizations, or institutional sectors of a society. Whether through the exemptions of illness or more defiantly motivated forms of passive resistance, the withdrawal of a critical mass of persons from a set of social activities can significantly impede or even stalemate them. Mindful of this, at the height of Soviet Russia's forced industrialization and collectivization of agriculture during the 1930s and 1940s, which was accompanied by increasingly severe labor discipline and regulation, the government instituted a number of controls over what sociologist Mark G. Field termed "the physician's function to certify illness." Field identified "two norms or indices readily available and understandable both to physicians and the medical bureaucracy" that were used as controls.

> The first index is that of temperature: patients who claim they are sick must show a temperature above a certain minimum. . . . This minimum varies with the necessities of production and the urgency of the situation. In periods of extreme emergency practically no one may be excused on this ground. . . .
> The second index (apparently less generally used) is the issuance of definite and limited norms of certificates to be granted in any one period. These norms, expressed in percentage of individuals on a physician's panel, may also be revised according to the situation. The doctor who consistently exceeds his norms will be called upon to explain his actions and may be admonished or punished unless he observes the quotas. . . . It was reported that during the industrialization drive there was a system of "socialist emulation or competition" organized among the physicians. This paralleled the one in vogue in industry in which individuals and factories were urged to challenge each other to reach higher production. In the medical field the physicians were ordered to compete to reduce to a minimum the number of days lost through illness and accidents. . . .[64]

Although it is hard to imagine a revolutionary movement organized around the theme "Sick persons of the world, unite!" under certain circumstances the en masse assumption of the sick role has social protest implications. This has been recognized and exploited in the "sick-in" strikes that have occurred in large American cities in recent years. It is significant that the groups participating in this quasi-legitimized form of passive resistance have often been engaged in public service jobs such as hospital employees, nurses, resident physicians, teachers, firemen, and policemen (with "the blue flu"). The sick role structure has provided a relatively respectable, nonaggressive way of expressing protest that is symbolically compatible with the service-orientation of their occupational roles.

To the extent that illness is a deviant role, it can also be said to have certain social control facets built into it: its negative valuation, its restrictions, and the rehabilitative process of therapy that the sick person is expected to undergo. Here the obligations of the sick role become involved.

SICK ROLE OBLIGATIONS

As Parsons delineated it, the sick role involves both conditionally granted exemptions and two sets of complementary and reciprocal obligations. The sick person is expected to define being ill as an unfavorable state and to do everything possible to return to health and healthy functioning. In Parsons's own words, "[I]f the case is sufficiently severe," this entails "seeking help from some kind of institutionalized health service agency. This seeking of help further includes the admission that being sick is undesirable and that measures should be taken to maximize the chances to facilitate recovery or, if the condition is chronic, . . . to subject it to proper 'management.'"[65]

The kind of "health service agent" who will be approached is influenced by social structural and cultural factors, as we have seen. For example, a middle-class American or Western European is likely to consult a biomedically trained physician; a Russian peasant, a "feldscher"; a Chinese peasant, a "rural medical worker" or a practitioner of traditional Chinese medicine; a Navajo Indian, a "hand trembler" and a "singer" as well as a "white doctor"; and a Zairean, both traditional and neotraditional "ngangas" in addition to Western-trained physicians, nurses, and medical assistants.

The establishment of a relationship with a health practitioner casts the sick person in the role of patient, whose primary responsibility now becomes that of cooperating with this expert in a joint effort to cure the patient's illness, or at least to control the symptoms and disease processes associated with it. In modern Western or Western-influenced medical systems, this obligation includes potential willingness to undergo a battery of diagnostic and therapeutic procedures, and to be admitted to the hospital, if it is deemed necessary, where the patient comes under the care of a complex team in a highly bureaucratic and increasingly technologized setting.

"ALTERNATIVE" PRACTITIONERS AND TREATMENTS

In the many societies of the world where modern Western biomedicine exists side by side with other culturally traditional ways of diagnosing and treating illness and maintaining health, a systematic "commuting pattern" between the multiple health/illness/medicine systems may be institutionalized. For example, as Navajo medicine man Scott Preston explained earlier in this chapter, Navajo patients characteristically go to Indian practitioners for certain health-related problems and to white doctors for others. One of the functions of the traditional Navajo "hand trembler" is to help patients to decide what kind of expert they should consult.

Utilizing the services of practitioners who offer explanations of illness and therapies that fall outside the orthodox armamentarium of biomedicine is not confined to contexts where two different cultures or subcultures meet. A striking instance of the extent to which patients seek the care of alternative practitioners and methods of treatment, and of the factors that lead them to do so, is to be found in the sphere of "cancer medicine" in present-day American society. So many patients (and their families) take recourse to what the American Cancer Society (ACS) terms "unproven cancer remedies," that an organizational unit of the ACS's Professional Educational division is specifically concerned with research and teaching on this phenomenon.[66]

A recent study by sociologist/psychologist Barrie R. Cassileth illuminates the complex patterns involved in the recourse to "new unorthodox cancer therapies" that appears to be gaining popularity in the United States.[67] Cassileth and her coinvestigators interviewed 304 patients being treated at a university cancer center, and 356 patients under the care of "unorthodox-therapy practitioners." They also obtained information on 130 such practitioners and 19 alternative therapy treatment clinics, including those that referred patients to the study. Cassileth and her colleagues found that:

> . . . patients who use unorthodox therapies are well educated, frequently asymptomatic, and are in the early stages of disease. Only 25% initiated alternative regimens while under active conventional treatment, and 40% of patients who had used both treatment types had discontinued conventional care after adopting an alternative therapy. Major factors associated with the use of unorthodox treatments included patients' belief that their cancer could have been prevented and therefore was now reversible by the same means, dissatisfaction with conventional practitioners and health care systems, and preference for nontoxic regimens and for an active role in treatment. . . .
>
> [S]ix types of unorthodox treatments emerged as commonest among patients studied. In descending order of frequency of use these included: metabolic therapy, diet therapies, megavitamins, mental imagery applied for anti-tumor effect, spiritual or faith healing, and "immune" therapy. . . .
>
> Sixty-five percent of patients received metabolic therapy from M.D.'s. . . . Self-care was practiced by 24% of patients on diet therapies, whereas over half were treated by naturopaths, homeopaths, nutritionalists, and lay affiliates of particular dietary approaches. . . . Megavitamin therapy was administered by physicians to 36% of patients, by chiropractors, 10%, and by patients themselves, 32%. . . . Over half of the patients [who received immune therapy] were treated by M.D.s, and approximately one third received immune treatment under the auspices of a practitioner who was neither a physician nor an osteopath. . . .
>
> Most patients spent under $1000 for the first year of unorthodox care, and 50% spent under $500. . . .
>
> Although unorthodox therapies differ by underlying concepts and treatment mechanisms they share a common perspective. Cancer and other chronic illnesses tend to be viewed not as disease entities but as symptoms of underlying dysfunction, disorder, or toxicity. Thus, treatments are geared toward improving the patient's own biologic and psychic capacity to counteract illness. Most patients find the internal logic and global, mind-body emphasis of this perspective intuitively correct and fundamentally appealing.
>
> Both the overall orientation and some of the specific practices associated with unorthodox therapies are consistent with the popular contemporary focus on physical fitness, proper nutrition, and improved mental attitude. The practices are also consistent at some level with conventional medicine's emphasis on environmental causes of cancer, [and] with established conclusions that "a number of dietary variables may contribute to the development of human cancers." . . .
>
> Intrinsic to the belief in unorthodox therapies is that conventional cancer treatments weaken the body's reserve, inhibit the capacity for cure, and misguidedly address the symptom (cancer) rather than the underlying systematic disorder. Nevertheless, only a small group of patients studied (8%) had refused to receive any conventional treatment, and 60% of patients who added unorthodox regimens remained on conventional therapy as well. The notion of noncompliance, traditionally used to describe patients who fail to follow physicians' orders, does not accurately encompass the behavior of this patient population. Most of these patients continue treatment as prescribed, and many physicians are supportive or neutral, if not actually involved in today's alternative therapies.[68]

THE SICK ROLE AND THE MEDICAL
PRACTITIONER-PATIENT RELATIONSHIP

Parsons characterized the "role relations between sick people and therapeutic agents" in all societies as "asymmetrical" in nature, entailing some degree of institutionalized "hierarchy" that can vary and change but that cannot be totally eliminated: "[W]ith respect to the inherent functions of effective care and amelioration of conditions of illness," he argued, "there must be a built-in institutionalized superiority of the professional roles, grounded in responsibility, competence, and occupational concern."[69] Parsons attributed the essential inequality of the practitioner-patient relationship to several factors. To begin with, there is what he called a "competence gap"[70] between the "health care agent" and those who seek his or her expert services. No matter how well educated patients may be, Parsons alleged, they do not have the basic scientific and clinical knowledge and training of a physician or the experience that comes from the fact that the physician "is typically caring for sick people as a full-time occupation."[71] Furthermore, in certain ways, the emotional and existential anxieties that people feel about their own actual or possible illness that they bring to the patient role are likely to short-circuit some of the medical knowledge and understanding that they ordinarily possess, and can more easily mobilize in nonpatient social situations.

In *Routine Complications*, her study of "troubles with talk between doctors and patients," sociologist Candace West provides "conversation-analysis" data that microdynamically document certain dimensions of the structured asymmetry in the doctor-patient relationship.[72] West's data consisted primarily of 532 pages of "transcribed two-party encounters" between eighteen physicians who were residents in a family practice center in the southern United States and their patients. She focused particularly on "turn-taking in doctor-patient dialogues"; questions and answers between doctors and patients; "medical misfires, mishearings, misgivings, and misunderstandings"; and "laughter and sociable commentary" in these "medical encounters." One of West's primary findings was that "overwhelmingly, physicians asked the questions. . . . [P]atients initiated only 9 percent of the 773 questions posed in [the] exchanges" that she recorded and analyzed.[73] As West astutely noted in her commentary, these patterns represent "a thoroughly interactional accomplishment. . . . [T]his order of affairs is not merely an outcome of patients' passivity nor of physicians' dominance. Rather, the dispreference we observed for patient-initiated questions is produced jointly by physicians and patients in the course of their talk with one another."[74] Especially interesting and revealing in this connection is the fact that the "systematic and asymmetric pattern"[75] of medical exchanges that West observed was due not only to the tendency of doctors to "advance questions which restrict patients' options for answers, but patients themselves stammer when asking questions of doctors. . . . [P]atients' infrequent questions to doctors were often marked by speech disturbances":

> Though some stutters preceded questions that may have been anxiety-provoking for patients, not all of them did. And while some stutters preceded patient reformulations of questions, other "reformulations" emerged as formulations of the same items that were stuttered. So, while repairs and reiterations exhibited no consistent patterns according to what, if anything, they "fixed," they did

provide considerable evidence of patients' difficulties "spitting out" their questions.[76]

Even more fundamental to the "asymmetrical hierarchy" in the practitioner-patient relationship than the "competence gap," Parsons contended, is what he called the health care agent's "fiduciary responsibility":

> The most general basis of the superiority of health agency personnel . . . and physicians in particular, seems to me to rest in their having been endowed with special responsibilities for the health of persons defined as ill or as suffering threats to their future health who have come under their jurisdiction. . . . [T]he physician has been institutionally certified to be worthy of entrusting responsibility to in the field of the care of health, the prevention of illness, the mitigation of its severity and disabling consequences, and its cure insofar as this is feasible. . . .
> [E]ssential to the implementation of fiduciary responsibility in this field . . . is the willingness of the person assuming such a role . . . to exercise such responsibility and to act within the limits of his prerogatives as a genuine trustee of the health interests of the patient population relative to whom he assumes responsibility. This is a component which goes beyond competence in the more technical sense. It involves an important component of moral authority, grounded in the common assumption of health care agents and sick people that health is a good thing and illness by and large is a bad thing, and that the balance should, insofar as it is . . . feasible, be altered in the direction of maximizing the levels of health and minimizing the influence of illness. It is in this connection that the health care agent performs functions of social control in the sense in which that concept is relevant to the emphasis on deviance and social control as part of the health care complex.[77]

In emphasizing the institutionalized "elements of inequality" in the doctor-patient relationship, its sources, and its functions, Parsons did not mean to imply that the patient is a supplicant, or that the role vis-à-vis the practitioner is a passive, supine one:

> I have already noted that it is erroneous, as some interpreters of my previous work in this area have maintained, to consider the role of the sick person, notably in the capacity of patient, who is positively related to health care agencies, as that of a purely passive object of manipulation or "treatment." Indeed, I should regard even the acceptance of such treatment as one type of active participation of the sick person. However, his activity very generally goes well beyond this. We might suggest that the level of activity is minimized for acutely ill patients, particularly when they are hospitalized and subject to the ministrations not only of physicians but of nurses and other hospital personnel. Even in these cases, however, some active participation in addition to merely accepting hospital treatment is generally involved. And, the less acute the mediate situation, the more likely it is that this participation will be substantial.[78]

As the foregoing indicates, there are extreme situations in which patients are so ill that they cannot interact meaningfully with the practitioner or take any responsibility for the decision-making and care that their treatment involves. But under

more usual circumstances, patients enter into an at least quasi-voluntary
with the practitioner and actively participate in the processes of diag
treating their medical problems.

Sociologist Anselm L. Strauss and research nurse Shizuko Fagerhaugh have
gone so far as to claim that in present-day American society, with its "prevalence of
chronic illnesses . . . that bring patients into contemporary hospitals [with] the technologies developed to manage them,"[79] "patients' participation in their own care"
should be "conceived . . . and recognized . . . as work."[80] For example, Strauss and
his coauthors argue that while patients with chronic conditions are in the hospital,
they and their kin are taught (usually by nurses) "the basics of technology (whether
drug, machine, or bodily monitoring)"[81] that will enable them to "work more or less
successfully at controlling symptoms and disease processes, and at carrying out
their regimens"[82] when they are discharged from the hospital.

How actively patients participate in their care, then, is not just a function of
their own personality traits and those of medical and nursing practitioners, or an artifact of an arbitrary, immutably fixed conception of their respective roles. It is also
influenced and modified by the type, severity, and incidence of the illness involved,
by the sorts of knowledge and technology that are applied to them, and by what are
defined as culturally appropriate patient and practitioner behaviors in various social
settings.

THE SICK ROLE AND CHRONIC ILLNESS

Talcott Parsons's contention that the sick role obliges the patient to do everything
possible to achieve "the goal of complete recovery" has frequently evoked the
criticism that it applies only to acute, curable illnesses. Although Parsons made it
more explicit in his later writings than in earlier publications, chronic as well as
acute illness was always a core referent for his conceptualization of the sick role.[83]
However, while acknowledging that "[t]here are many conditions which are, in any
given state of the art of medicine, incurable," he insisted that this "does not put
[them] in a totally different category from that of acute illness." Rather, Parsons
regarded the committed effort made by the patient with a chronic disorder to keep
his condition from deteriorating, to manage it and, if possible, to improve it, as the
functional equivalent of the obligation to try to get well. He alleged that "there is a
cost involved in this":[84] the inability to achieve the ideal goal of the sick role—complete recovery and graduation out of it—is often a source of strain for the patient
and practitioner alike. The tenacity of an illness or its worsening can raise problems
of competence, adequacy, and meaning that affect them both.

This perspective on the relationship between chronic illness and the sick role
was empirically documented and further developed in *Experiment Perilous*, a study
by the author of this text of a university hospital metabolic ward (F-Second). F-
Second's patients were ill with progressive and often fatal diseases that lay outside
the control of modern medicine, and were voluntary subjects for medical research
that might or might not aid their condition.[85] Fox discovered that one of the primary
mechanisms that this community of patients developed for coping with their illnesses was the "take up their bed" orientation. Although they could not hope to get
better, or in most cases even help to slow down the degenerative course of their ill-

nesses, the patients of Ward F-Second evolved and enforced patterns of behavior that obligated them to function as long and fully as they could, *as if* they were well, active, and productive. Though hospitalized and very ill, they struggled to remain ambulatory, to leave their beds whenever possible, in a wheelchair if not on foot, and they found "vocational" satisfaction in their collegial roles as research subjects for the physicians to whom their care was entrusted.

RECURRENT MISSTATEMENTS OF THE SICK ROLE

In light of the nuanced and developmental way in which Parsons formulated and reflected on the concept of the sick role—a concept that overshadows all others in the field of medical sociology—what accounts for the continuing appearance in the social science literature of reductionistic restatements like the following?

> The classic picture of the patient—whether painted by a discerning Dutch realist or more recently developed by Parsons with "sick role" imagery—is of an acutely sick person, hence temporarily passive and acquiescent, being treated by an active physician and helped by equally vigorous caretakers. That is hardly an accurate depiction of chronically ill persons except when rendered helpless during the most acute phases of an illness.[86]

Most such descriptions of the sick role are based exclusively on a reading of Parsons's early (1951) discussion of it in *The Social System*,[87] with no reference to anything else that he subsequently wrote on the subject. Even when considered within their own self-limited framework, these stubbornly reiterated summaries of the sick role are inaccurate accounts of what Parsons himself actually wrote. The persistence of these misinterpretations goes deeply into the sociology of sociology during the past three decades—its controversies and biases, ideologies and counterideologies—in ways that extend beyond the scope of this book.

It seems fitting, however, to end this chapter with observations on some of the changes that appear to be taking place in the sick role and in the doctor-patient relationship in American society, although the contours of these changes are still unclear, and available sociological commentary on them is largely speculative.

CHANGES IN THE SICK ROLE AND THE DOCTOR-PATIENT RELATIONSHIP IN AMERICAN SOCIETY

The exemptions of the sick role seem to be undergoing a complex and in some ways inconsistent set of modifications in American society. As jurist Nicholas N. Kittrie and sociologists Jesse R. Pitts and Philip Rieff pointed out, strongly influenced by the widespread diffusion of Freudian thought since the 1920s, a "continuing process of divestment" away from sin and crime models of deviance[88] toward "the medicalization of deviance"[89] and "the triumph of the therapeutic"[90] has been taking place. Fox has described this process in the following way:

> In an earlier, more religiously oriented era of a modern Western society like our own, some of . . . the kinds of attitudes and behaviors . . . that have come to be

defined as illnesses and regarded as belonging within the jurisdiction of medicine and its practitioners . . . were considered sinful rather than sick, and they fell under the aegis of religious authorities for a different kind of diagnosis, treatment, and control. In a more secular, but less scientifically and medically oriented stage of society than the current one, certain of these ways of thinking, feeling, and behaving were viewed and dealt with as criminal. Although sin, crime, and sickness are not related in a simple, invariant way, there has been a general tendency in the society to move from sin to crime to sickness in categorizing a number of aberrant or deviant states. . . . [This] evolution has been most apparent with respect to conditions that are now considered to be mental illness, or associated with serious psychological and/or social disturbances. These include, for example, states of hallucination and delusion that once would have been interpreted as signs of possession by the Devil, certain forms of physical violence, such as the type of child abuse that results in what is termed "the battered child syndrome," the set of behaviors in children which are alternatively called hyperactivity, hyperkinesis, or minimal brain dysfunction, and so-called addictive disorders, such as alcoholism, drug addiction, compulsive overeating, and compulsive gambling. . . . This . . . process . . . away from sin and crime as categories for abnormality, dysfunction, and deviance and toward illness as the explanatory concept has entailed what Peter Sedgwick calls "the progressive annexation of not-illness into illness."[91]

One of the societal consequences of the medicalization of deviance and its social control has been the extension of sick role exemptions to more people and to a broader range of attitudes and behaviors than in the past. In this respect, it has created a less stigmatizing and punitive outlook on certain forms of deviance, and introduced a quality of "therapeutic mercy" into the way that they are handled.

And yet, beginning in the 1960s this very medicalization has helped to set into motion a counter "de-medicalization" process. Uneasiness about the "power" and "control" exercised by a "dominant" medical profession, concern about the way in which applying the concepts of illness and therapy to an ever-widening gamut of attitudes and behaviors may be eroding the "right to be different," and criticism of the powerlessness, ostracism, dehumanization, and even "mortification of the self" that the label sick may imply, have been persistently voiced. One form that such reactions has taken is the application of an extreme version of labeling theory to illness:

> This . . . view emphasizes the degree to which what is defined as health and illness, normality and abnormality, sanity and insanity varies from one society, culture, and historical period to another. Thus, it is contended, medical and diagnostic categories such as "sick," "abnormal," and "insane" are not universal, objective, or necessarily reliable. Rather, they are culture-, class-, and time-bound, often ethnocentric, and as much artifacts of the preconceptions of socially biased observers as they are valid summaries of the characteristics of the observed.[92]

In this perspective, illness (above all, mental illness) is largely a mythical construct, created and enforced by the society, principally through the "professional dominance" of physicians and of hospitals that have "total institution" attributes.[93]

These critiques have not been confined to rhetoric. Concrete steps have been taken to declassify certain conditions as illness. One notable example was the American Psychiatric Association's decision to remove homosexuality from its official *Diagnostic and Statistical Manual of Mental Disorders.* A second example was the U.S. Supreme Court's ruling (*O'Connor* v. *Donaldson*) that mental patients cannot be confined in institutions against their will and without treatment if they are dangerous to no one and capable of surviving on the outside. This decision was one of a series of events that fostered the progressive "deinstitutionalization" of the mentally ill over the past three decades. A third example is the various actions that feminist groups have taken to contravene what they regard as the excessive readiness of the medical profession to "pathologize normal endocrinological events" that women experience, such as dysmenorrhea or nausea in pregnancy, and to make psychiatric syndromes out of some of their gender-associated personality characteristics and behaviors.

Important demedicalization elements are also present in the increased development of self-care in American society since the 1960s, with its emphasis on assuming personal responsibility for maintaining health and for managing one's own chronic illness condition. Both stress health, well-being, and living a "normal life," and how self-reliance and greater independence from biomedicine, physicians, and medical institutions can contribute to these desired states.

The coexistence of strong medicalizing and demedicalizing trends suggests that considerable ambivalence exists in the United States about how broadening the categories of illness and the sick role is affecting societal balances between exemptions and controls and rights and responsibilities. A striking legal expression of this ambivalence can be found in the "guilty, but mentally ill" verdict that a series of states have added to their statutes during the 1980s.[94] These provisions aim, "where warranted by the evidence," to "consider separately the issues of guilt, and the presence or absence of insanity," and to find some kind of middle ground between the verdicts of "guilty," "not guilty by reason of insanity," and "not guilty."[95] In effect, the concept of "guilty, but mentally ill" attempts to combine criminal culpability with sick role exemptions.

> Where the trier of fact determines that, at the time of the conduct charged, a defendant suffered from a psychiatric disorder which substantially disturbed such person's thinking, feeling or behavior and/or that such psychiatric disorder left such person with insufficient willpower to choose whether he would do the act or refrain from doing it, although physically capable, the trier of fact shall return a verdict of "guilty, but mentally ill." . . .
>
> [A] defendant found guilty but mentally ill, or whose plea to that effect is accepted, may have any sentence imposed on him which may lawfully be imposed upon any defendant for the same offense. Such defendant shall be committed into the custody of the Department of Correction, and shall undergo such further evaluation and be given such immediate and temporary treatment as is psychiatrically indicated. . . . The Commissioner shall thereupon confine such person in the Delaware State Hospital. Although such person shall remain under the jurisdiction of the Department of Correction, decisions directly related to treatment for his mental illness shall be the joint responsibility of the Director of the Division of Alcoholism, Drug Abuse and Mental Health and those persons at the Delaware State Hospital who are directly responsible for such treatment. The . . . residential treatment facility to which the defendant is committed . . . shall have the authority to discharge the defendant from the facility and return the defendant to the physical

custody of the Commissioner whenever the facility believes that such a discharge is in the best interests of the defendant. The offender may, by written statement, refuse to take any drugs which are prescribed for treatment of his mental illness; except when such a refusal will endanger the life of the offender, or the lives or property of other persons with whom the offender has contact.

A person who has been adjudged "guilty, but mentally ill" and who during his incarceration is discharged from treatment may be placed on prerelease or parole status under the same terms and laws applicable to any offender. Psychological or psychiatric counseling and treatment may be required as a condition for such status. Failure to continue treatment, except by agreement of the Department of Correction, shall be a basis for terminating prerelease status or instituting parole violation hearings.[96]

How uneasily and ambiguously criminality and illness are joined under these statutes was made clear in September 1986 when, for the first time in the country's history, a Delaware jury imposed the death penalty on a man who was found guilty but mentally ill in a murder case. This verdict raised such a host of novel and troubling questions that legal experts predicted it would eventually come before the United States Supreme Court.[97]

Perhaps the most salient and far-reaching alterations in the conception of the patient's role currently taking place in American society involve what Jay Katz eloquently terms "the respective rights, duties, and needs of physicians and patients in their intimate, anxiety-producing, and fateful encounters with one another.[98] These actual and incipient changes have crystallized around the convergence of public, legal, medical, and philosophical efforts to promote a greater degree of patient autonomy in the medical decision-making process in which doctor and patient are mutually involved. Greatly increased emphasis on the legal doctrine of disclosure and informed consent, and on the broader idea of giving patients a more participatory and authoritative voice in decision-making, has been a core component in these developments. In her article "From Informed Consent to Patient Choice," jurist Marjorie Maguire Shultz describes this process and some of the social, cultural, and biomedical factors that she believes have contributed to it:

> In the past several decades, . . . new developments have strengthened the argument that patient autonomy should receive more than pro forma respect. Advancing medical technology has greatly expanded the options available to the patient. Increased knowledge has heightened awareness of how much remains unknown. Debate and conflict within the medical community are widespread and public. Differences in experts' advice can often be resolved only on the basis of risk and value preferences. This medical uncertainty accentuates the need for professional advice, but it also strengthens the case for ultimate decision by the person whose life is directly involved.
>
> Medical choice increasingly depends on factors that transcend professional training and knowledge. . . .
>
> In the face of value pluralism, factual indeterminacy, and increasing options, patient autonomy has become a central principle of both popular and philosophical analysis of medical decision-making. Self-care and consumer movements have applied that principle, seeking to shift the balance away from professional dominance

and toward individual knowledge and control. Although medical traditions historically have downgraded patient autonomy, doctors, too, have begun to recognize
and accept patient demands for more information and control.

The law's response to pressures for greater recognition of patient autonomy
has been ambivalent. Existing rules repudiate the view that the mere hiring of a
doctor transfers all authority from patient to doctor. Yet full vindication of patient
autonomy interests would necessitate placing final authority regarding important
decisions in the hands of any patient having the capacity and the desire to exercise
it . . .[N]o such guarantee of patient autonomy is currently mandated by the law.[99]

It is not only the law that responds in an equivocal way to the issues and
phenomena surrounding patients' rights, autonomy, and their shared decision
making with physicians:

Many studies demonstrate that patients generally receive little information
about their diagnoses, laboratory tests, and medications and that they would prefer
to receive much more. However, studies on patient desire to make decisions give
conflicting results. Moreover, whether clinicians are able to assess their own
patients' preferences for information and decision making has not been determined.[100]

Mindful of these split and indeterminate results, Drs. William M. Strull, Bernard Lo, and Gerald Charles conducted their own research on the question, "Do
patients want to participate in medical decision making?" They administered questionnaires to 210 outpatients with hypertension (evenly distributed between a community hospital, a health maintenance organization, and a Veterans Administration
clinic), and to the 50 clinicians caring for these patients (41 physicians and 9 nurse
practitioners and clinical pharmacists). Strull, Lo, and Charles found that:

. . . outpatients with hypertension report receiving considerable information
about hypertension—more, in fact, than their clinicians report giving. Nevertheless, 41% of patients preferred receiving additional information about their illness.
A majority of patients also wanted extensive discussion of decisions about treatment; clinicians underestimated patient desire for such discussion in 29% of cases.
However, in actual decision making, patients reported playing a relatively passive
role, leaving the decision entirely up to the clinician in 63% of cases. Moreover,
only 53% desired to participate in such decisions. Fewer than one fourth of the
patients wished to make joint decisions with the clinicians. . . . Clinicians substantially overestimated both the amount of actual participation in decision making
reported by patients (in 48% of cases) and the amount of preferences for active
participation in decision making (in 32% of cases).[101]

Such patterns indicate that important changes in this sphere are still in
midstream and involve intricate matters of role redefinition, new relationships, and
fundamental values whose implications are not confined to medicine.

The subtlety of power-sharing in an ideal relationship between doctor and
patient must be acknowledged. Even patients who are clearly competent to make
decisions will suffer confusion and ambivalence. They will need guidance and

support of professionals and loved ones. Moreover, professionals are to a significant degree motivated by caring for others; we need them to continue to be. Respect for patients' autonomy should not cause doctors either to abandon compassion or to shed their responsibility for advising and caring for patients. But medical decisions depend upon moral values, economic considerations and risk preferences, as well as on medical expertise.[102]

If doctors could learn, and in turn teach their patients, that it is possible to sit down and reason together about the most important personal anxieties and fears that illness and its treatment engenders, then they could also point the way to living life not by submission but by mutual respect, with careful attentiveness to one's own and the other's rationalities and irrationalities. Living the life of medicine in such new and unaccustomed ways could extend the domain of reason and thus make doctors true healers to mankind. In the absence of such a commitment doctors only perpetuate and reinforce the alienation between man and man.[103]

In the next chapter we move from Jay Katz's vision of the ideal physician and his analysis of how far from realizing it we still are, to consideration of the profession of medicine, its relationship to health and illness in a society, and what sociologists have written—and not written—about it.

NOTES

1. J.C. Didier, "Illness: Physical Illness," *Sacramentum Mundi: An Encyclopedia of Theology*, 3 (1969), 98–100.
2. Illich is a laicized Roman Catholic priest who studied theology and philosophy at the Gregorian University in Rome and obtained a doctorate in history at the University of Salzburg. He served as an assistant pastor in an Irish-Puerto Rican parish in New York City. Subsequently, from 1956 to 1960, he was Vice-Rector of the Catholic University of Puerto Rico. He is the cofounder of the Center for Intercultural Documentation in Cuernavaca, Mexico.
3. Ivan Illich, *Medical Nemesis: the Expropriation of Health* (New York: Pantheon Books, 1976), pp. 132–35 and 175. Copyright Pantheon Books, a Division of Random House, Inc.
4. Ibid., p. 92.
5. René and Jean Dubos, *The White Plague* (Boston: Little, Brown and Company, 1952). See especially pp. 44–66.
6. Willy De Craemer, Jan Vansina, and Renée C. Fox, "Religious Movements in Central Africa: A Theoretical Study," *Comparative Studies in Society and History*, 18, no. 4 (October 1976), 472.
7. A recent example of the rediscovery of once-recognized syndromes is provided by the recognition of toxic shock syndrome as a complication of influenza and influenza-like illness. This syndrome, researchers believe is clinically similar to that described by Thucydides during the plague of Athens in 430 – 427 B.C. (Bruce Dan, "Toxic Shock Syndrome: Back to the Future," [Editorial] *Journal of the American Medical Association*, 257 (February 27, 1987), 1094–95.
8. Helene M. Cole and George D. Lundberg, eds., *AIDS From the Beginning* (Chicago: American Medical Association, 1986), p. xvii.
9. Samuel O. Thier, "Preface," *Mobilizing Against AIDS: The Unfinished Story of a Virus* (Cambridge, Mass.: Harvard University Press, 1986), p. vii.
10. *Mobilizing Against AIDS*, pp. 89 and 145. In addition to AIDS, outbreaks of a chronic mononucleosis-like syndrome have recently been reported in several regions of the United States. The search for possible causes of this syndrome is complicated by the fact that "the disease is still not well defined clinically, nor has it been described in any major review. Its

symptoms vary greatly, although the most striking are chronic severe fatigue lasting more than a year, and neurological problems." (Deborah H. Barnes, "Mystery Disease at Lake Tahoe Challenges Virologists and Clinicians," *Science*, 234 [October 31, 1986], 541–42).

11. Constance Holden, "Proposed New Psychiatric Diagnoses Raise Charges of Gender Bias," *Science*, 231 (January 24, 1986), 327-28.

12. From an unpublished talk by Lewis Thomas presented at the University of Cincinnati Medical Center, October 18, 1985, pp. 4–5.

13. René Dubos, *The Mirage of Health* (New York: Harper & Row, 1959), pp. 1–2.

14. Ibid.

15. This is the World Health Organization's definition of health, set forth at its 1956 meeting in San Francisco, California.

16. Charles C. Hughes, "Medical Care: Ethnomedicine," *International Encyclopedia of the Social Sciences*, 10 (1968), 87–93.

17. S. Jay Olshansky and A. Brian Ault, "The Fourth Stage of the Epidemiologic Transition: The Age of Delayed Degenerative Diseases," *The Milbank Quarterly*, 64, no. 3 (1986), 386–87.

18. From an unpublished talk by Scott Preston at the Fort Defiance Hospital on the Navajo Reservation, October 20, 1955. This talk occurred within the context of the Navajo-Cornell Field Health Research Project, organized jointly by the Navajo Tribe, Cornell University Medical College, and the U.S. Public Health Service in 1955, when the responsibility for the health of American Indians was transferred from the Department of the Interior to the Department of Health, Education and Welfare. The six-year project entailed close, first-hand working relations between medical scientists, health and medical professionals, and social scientists. The project's purposes included developing effective methods for the delivery of modern medical services to the Navajo; ascertaining the extent to which the knowledge gained would be applicable to others in similar socioeconomic circumstances; studying "discrete disease entities with particular reference to their possible shaping by Navajo culture"; and exploring whether "the sudden apposition of modern biomedical science and technology and the disease pattern of a 'nontechnologic' society could provide knowledge of value in the attack on contemporary U.S. medical problems."
See Walsh McDermott and others, "Introducing Modern Medicine in a Navajo Community," Part I, *Science*, 131 (January 22,1960), 197–205, and Part II, 131 (January 29, 1960), 280–87; Walsh McDermott, Kurt W. Deuschle, and Clifford R. Barnett, "Health Care Experiment at Many Farms," *Science*, 175 (January 7, 1972), 23–31; John Adair and Kurt W. Deuschle, *The People's Health: Medicine and Anthropology in a Navajo Community* (New York: Appleton-Century-Crofts, 1970); Kurt W. Dueschle, "Cross-Cultural Medicine: The Navajo Indians as Case Exemplar," *Daedalus*, 115, no. 2 (Spring 1986), 175–84.

19. Ronald C. Simons and Charles C. Hughes, eds., *The Culture-Bound Syndromes: Folk Illnesses of Psychiatric and Anthropological Interest* (Dordrecht, Holland: D. Reidel Publishing Company, 1985); Ronald C. Simons, "New Data on Susto" (Review Article), *Culture, Medicine and Psychiatry*, 10 (1986), 283.

20 Arthur J. Rubel, Carl W. O'Nell, and Rolando Collado-Ardón, *Susto, A Folk Illness* (Berkeley: University of California Press, 1984).

21. Ibid., p. 112.

22. Ibid., p. 6.

23. Ibid., p. 112.

24. Ibid., p. 7.

25. Ibid., pp. 8–9.

26. Ibid.

27. Ibid., p. 6.

28. Ibid., p. 114.

29. Ibid.

30. Ibid., p. 122.

31. Ibid.

32. Emiko Ohnuki-Tierney, *Illness and Culture in Contemporary Japan: An Anthropological View* (New York: Cambridge University Press, 1984), p. 1.

33. Ibid, pp. 56 – 60.

34. Ibid., p. 76.

35. Ibid.
36. Ibid.
37. Ibid., p. 78. (*Mizukō* = water child, or aborted fetus; *kuyō* = memorial service.)
38. Ibid.
39. McDermott and others, "Introducing Modern Medicine in a Navajo Community," Part II, p. 280.
40. Ibid., p. 281.
41. Earl L. Koos, *The Health of Regionville: What the People Thought and Did About It* (New York: Columbia University Press, 1954).
42. Ibid., p. 36.
43. Marvin K. Opler, "Cultural Differences in Mental Disorders: An Italian and Irish Contrast in the Schizophrenias—U.S.A.," in *Culture and Mental Health: Cross-Cultural Studies*, ed. Marvin K. Opler (New York: The Macmillan Company, 1959), 425–42.
44. Anne Parsons, *Belief, Magic and Anomie* (New York: The Free Press, 1969), Chap. 8.
45. Ibid., Chap. 6.
46. Mark Zborowski, *People in Pain* (San Francisco: Jossey-Bass, 1969). Zborowski's article based on this study, "Cultural Components in Responses to Pain," *Journal of Social Issues*, 8, no. 4 (1952), 16–30, is probably better known than his book, and continues to be reprinted in many anthologies.
47. August B. Hollingshead and Fredrick C. Redlich, *Social Class and Mental Illness* (New York: John Wiley and Sons, Inc., 1958).
48. This study was made before psychotropic drugs were developed, tested, marketed, and entered psychiatric therapy.
49. Charles Kadushin, *Why People Go To Psychiatrists* (New York: Atherton Press, 1969).
50. Ibid., p. 27.
51. Ibid., p. 15.
52. Ibid., p. 309.
53. Talcott Parsons, "Illness and the Role of the Physician," in *Personality in Nature, Society, and Culture*, eds. Clyde Kluckhohn and Henry A. Murray (New York: Alfred A. Knopf, 1948).
54. Talcott Parsons, *The Social System* (Glencoe, Ill.: The Free Press, 1951), Chap. X.
55. See, for example, Talcott Parsons and Renée C. Fox, "Illness, Therapy, and the Modern Urban American Family," *The Journal of Social Issues*, VIII, no. 4 (1952), 31–44; Talcott Parsons, "Definitions of Health and Illness in the Light of American Values and Social Structure," in *Patients, Physicians, and Illness: Sourcebook in Behavioral Science and Medicine*, ed. E. Gartley Jaco (Glencoe, Ill.: The Free Press, 1958), pp. 165–87; Talcott Parsons, "Some Theoretical Considerations Bearing on the Field of Medical Sociology," in his *Social Structure and Personality* (New York: The Free Press, 1964), pp. 325–58; Talcott Parsons, "Research with Human Subjects and the 'Professional Complex'" in *Experimentation with Human Subjects*, ed. Paul A. Freund (New York: George Braziller, 1970), pp. 116–51; Talcott Parsons, "Health and Disease: A Sociological and Action Perspective," in *Encyclopedia of Bioethics*, 2, (1978), 66–81.
56. Talcott Parsons, "The Sick Role and the Role of the Physician Reconsidered," *Milbank Memorial Fund Quarterly/Health and Society*, 53, no. 3 (Summer 1975), 257.
57. Ibid., pp. 259–60.
58. Renée C. Fox, "Medical Evolution," in *Explorations in General Theory in Social Science: Essays in Honor of Talcott Parsons*, Vol. 2, eds. Jan J. Loubser and others (New York: The Free Press, 1976), p. 781.
59. Parsons, *The Social System*, p. 440.
60. Ohnuki-Tierney, *Illness and Culture in Contemporary Japan*, pp. 191–93.
61. Renée C. Fox, "Medical Evolution," p. 775.
62. Renée C. Fox, *Experiment Perilous: Physicians and Patients Facing the Unknown* (Glencoe, Ill.: The Free Press, 1959), p. 132.
63. Bronislaw Malinowski, *Magic, Science, Religion, and Other Essays* (Glencoe, Ill.: The Free Press, 1948), p. 15.
64. Mark G. Field, *Doctor and Patient in Soviet Russia* (Cambridge, Mass.: Harvard University Press, 1957), pp. 165–67.

65. Parsons, "The Sick Role and the Role of the Physician Reconsidered," p. 262.
66. Working under the aegis of Diane J. Fink, M.D., head of the Professional Education section of the American Cancer Society, sociologist Helen E. Sheehan is currently responsible for this work.
67. Reprinted with permission from Barrie R. Cassileth and others, "Contemporary Unorthodox Treatments in Cancer Medicine: A Study of Patients, Treatments, and Practitioners," *Annals of Internal Medicine*, 101, no. 1 (July 1984), 105–12.
68. Ibid.
69. Parsons, "The Sick Role and the Role of the Physician Reconsidered," p. 271.
70. Parsons, "Research with Human Subjects and the 'Professional Complex,'" p. 127.
71. Parsons, "The Sick Role and the Role of the Physician Reconsidered," p. 269.
72. Candace West, *Routine Complications: Troubles with Talk Between Doctors and Patients* (Bloomington: Indiana University Press, 1984).
73. Ibid., p. 92.
74. Ibid., p. 95.
75. Ibid., p. 92.
76. Ibid., p. 94.
77. Parsons, "The Sick Role and the Role of the Physician Reconsidered," pp. 266 and 268.
78. Ibid., p. 270.
79. Anselm Strauss and others, *Social Organization of Medical Work* (Chicago: The University of Chicago Press, 1985), p. ix.
80. Anselm Strauss and others, "The Work of Hospitalized Patients," *Social Science and Medicine*, 16, no. 9 (1982), 977–86. This is also a central theme of their *Social Organization of Medical Work* (see especially Chap. 8, "The Work of Patients").
81. Strauss and others, "The Work of Hospitalized Patients," p. 983.
82. Ibid., p. 978.
83. Parsons, "The Sick Role and the Role of the Physician Reconsidered," p. 259.
84. Ibid.
85. Fox, *Experiment Perilous*.
86. Strauss and others, "The Work of Hospitalized Patients," p. 978.
87. Parsons, *The Social System*, pp. 428–79.
88. Nicholas N. Kittrie, *The Right to Be Different: Deviance and Enforced Therapy* (Baltimore: Johns Hopkins University Press, 1971).
89. Jesse R. Pitts, "Social Control: The Concept," in *International Encyclopedia of the Social Sciences*, 14 (1968), 381–96.
90. Philip Rieff, *The Triumph of the Therapeutic: Uses of Faith After Freud* (New York: Harper & Row, 1966).
91. Renée C. Fox, "The Medicalization and Demedicalization of American Society," in *Doing Better and Feeling Worse: Health in the United States*, ed. John H. Knowles (New York: W. W. Norton & Company, 1977), p. 11. Reprinted by permission of the American Academy of Arts and Sciences, Boston, Mass.
92. Ibid., pp. 17–18.
93. Among the most influential works in this criticism of medicalization and advocacy of demedicalization have been: Rick J. Carlson, *The End of Medicine* (New York: John Wiley and Sons, 1975); Michel Foucault, *The Birth of the Clinic*, trans. A. M. Sheridan Smith (New York: Pantheon Books, 1973); Eliot Freidson, *Professional Dominance: The Social Structure of Medical Care* (Chicago: Atherton Press, 1970); Erving Goffman, *Asylums: Essays on the Social Situation of Mental Patients and Other Inmates* (Garden City, N.Y.: Anchor, 1961); Illich, *Medical Nemesis*; Kittrie, *The Right to Be Different*; Ronald D. Laing, *The Politics of Experience* (New York: Ballantine, 1967); David L. Rosenhan, "On Being Sane in Insane Places," *Science*, 179 (January 19, 1973), 250–58; Thomas J. Scheff, *Being Mentally Ill: A Sociological Theory* (Chicago: Aldine Publishing Company, 1961); Howard Waitzkin, *The Second Sickness: Contradictions of Capitalist Health Care* (New York: The Free Press, 1983).
94. Delaware was the first state to pass a "guilty, but mentally ill" statute, in 1982. By Fall 1986 at least ten more states had adopted similar statutes. One of the major precipitating events for such

statutes was the fact that John W. Hinckley, Jr. was acquitted on the grounds of mental illness for the attempted assassination of President Reagan in 1981.

95. §3905, "Instructions on separate issues of guilt and insanity; instructions on verdicts," from the Delaware Law: Delaware Code Annotated, 1984, Cumulative Supplement, Chap. 4, Defenses to Criminal Liability, p. 11.

96. §408 and §409, "Verdict of 'guilty, but mentally ill'—Sentence; confinement; discharge from treating facility; parole; probation," from the Delaware Law: Delaware Code Annotated, 1984, Cumulative Supplement, Chap. 4, Defenses to Criminal Liability, pp. 15–16.

97. According to a *New York Times* article (October 12, 1986), the Delaware jury's decision was made in the case of Reginald N. Sanders, a 19-year-old dropout from college and the Marine Corps, who was convicted of killing John J. Butler, a 63-year-old businessman, in August 1985, two months after Mr. Sanders was released from the state mental hospital. Mr. Sanders had done yard work for Mr. Butler, who suffered from diabetes and heart problems and had an artificial leg.

98. Jay Katz, *The Silent World of Doctor and Patient* (New York: The Free Press, 1984), p. xiii.

99. Marjorie Maguire Shultz, "From Informed Consent to Patient Choice: A New Protected Interest," *Yale Law Journal*, 95, no. 2 (December 1985), 221–23. Reprinted by permission of The Yale Law Journal Company and Fred B. Rothman & Company.

100. William M. Strull, Bernard Lo, and Gerald Charles, "Do Patients Want to Participate in Medical Decision Making?" *Journal of the American Medical Association*, 252, no. 21 (December 7, 1984), 2990.

101. Ibid., p. 2993.

102. Shultz, "From Informed Consent to Patient Choice," p. 299.

103. Katz, *The Silent World*, p. 226.

CHAPTER 2

THE PROFESSIONS OF MEDICINE AND NURSING

SOCIOLOGY OF PROFESSIONS: THE STATE OF THE FIELD

Sociologists have written more about health professionals—especially about physicians—than they have about patients. Although the sociological literature on the medical and health professions is sizable, what it covers is highly selective in a number of ways. It is far more concerned with physicians than with nurses, and it pays scant attention to the range of occupational roles that are often termed the "allied health professions" (for example, physician's assistants, social workers, physical therapists, occupational therapists, pharmacists, dieticians, and so forth). The sociological studies and analyses concentrated on physicians are oriented around a relatively limited number of themes: notably, the "professional dominance" of physicians; their intellectual, ideological, and social "individualism"; their organized autonomy, authority, and power; their institutionalized sense of hierarchy; their management of medical uncertainty, mistakes, and failure; and their problems of "detached concern." Remarkably few first-hand studies have been made of the actual work situations of physicians and other health professionals, or of how they think, feel, and behave in these settings. Many of the studies that exist deal with physicians who are internists or psychiatrists, carrying out their daily round in the hospital during residency training.[1]

Despite these common and restrictive attributes of the literature, sociologists' views of professions in general, and of the medical profession in particular, are far from homogeneous. The sociology of professions is one of the most controversy-ridden areas of the discipline. To begin with, as Eliot Freidson has pointed out, a "definitional problem" regarding the identification of professions "has plagued the field for over half a century":

Much debate, going back at least as far as Flexner (1915), has centered around how *profession* should be defined—which occupations should be called professions and by what institutional criteria. But while definitions overlap in the elements, traits, or attributes they include, a number of tallies have demonstrated a persistent lack of consensus about which traits are to be emphasized in theorizing.[2]

One of the fundamental issues underlying this lack of consensus is the question of whether professions can and should be distinguished from other occupations. Some sociologists regard professions as analytically and empirically distinct types of occupations. Others view them as essentially indistinguishable from nonprofessional occupations; they tend to focus on "the process by which occupations claim to gain professional status,"[3] while eschewing a concrete definition of what a profession is. A more extreme, relativistic version of this perspective has exerted considerable influence on post-1960 sociological thought about professions. It is based on the assumption that the notion of a profession is a semi-mythic construct, created by the members of an occupation who "profess" to have special characteristics, qualifications, and responsibilities; they systematically persuade others that they do, and succeed in having these claims institutionalized in ways that accord them privileged rights and powerful authority.[4]

Sociologists (who not only write about labelling behavior, but also engage in it themselves) have attached a series of names to these divergent perspectives on professions. They have called the first approach (professional occupations can be objectively distinguished from nonprofessional ones) "functionalist," "structuralist," or "Parsonian." They have termed the second approach (professions are social constructs) a "negotiated order," "interactionist," or "Chicago school" outlook. Within this framework, there has been a notable tendency to ideologically label the functionalist orientation as static and conservative, and the negotiated order conception as dynamic, reformist, and potentially compatible with more radical thought. In fact, sociologists with a Marxist or radical view of professions have adopted and elaborated upon some of the key ideas in the negotiated order approach, and in the works of theorists in the Chicago tradition (especially Everett C. Hughes and Eliot Freidson).[5]

Achieving conceptual and empirical agreement in this field has been rendered all the more difficult by the historical change that has taken place in the outlook and ambiance of sociological writings on professions published since the 1940s and 1950s. Freidson characterizes this intellectual and ideological "shift" as follows:

[O]n the whole [the] dominant emphasis [of] . . . academic sociologists of the 1940s and 1950s . . . was on the special character of the knowledge and skill of the professions and on their special ethical or altruistic orientation toward their clients. This is not to say that they . . . were mere apologists for the professions. In the writings of virtually all of them we can find overt recognition and criticism of deficiencies in the performance of professions and most particularly of the degree to which economic self-interest rather than common good can motivate the activities of professionals and their associations. Nonetheless, the general tenor of their analyses has represented professions as honored servants of public need, occupations especially distinguished from others by their orientation to serving the needs of the public through the schooled application of their unusually esoteric and complex knowledge and skill.

In the 1960s, however, a shift in both emphasis and interest developed both in the United States and in the United Kingdom. The mood shifted from one of approval to disapproval, from one that emphasized virtues over failings to one that emphasized failings over virtues. The very idea of profession was attacked, implying, if not often stating, that the world would be better off without professions. Furthermore, the substantive preoccupation of the literature changed. In the earlier literature, the major scholarly writings focused primarily on the analysis of professional norms and role relations and on interaction with clients in work settings. While all writers acknowledged the importance of political and economic factors, they did not analyze them at length. The more recent scholarly literature, on the other hand, focuses on the political and cultural influence of professions, on the relation of professions to political and economic elites and the state, and on the relation of professions to the market and class system. . . .

Writers from the late 1960s on . . . emphasized . . . the unusually effective, monopolistic institutions of professions and their high status as the critical factor and treated knowledge, skill, and ethical orientations not as objective characteristics but rather as ideology, as claims by spokesmen for professions seeking to gain or to preserve status and privilege. The earlier effort to develop an analytically coherent definition of professions was attacked as merely apologetics on behalf of the status quo. . . . Instead of expertise, *power* became the key word for both academic and nonacademic writers on the professions. . . .[6]

In this intellectual and political climate, the idea of "profession-as-power" became hegemonic. A remarkably diverse array of social thinkers—including those of Marxist, "Chicagoan," and "Foucault-ian" propensities, and those concerned with "medicalization of deviance and society" issues[7]—portrayed professions as "monopolist . . . market groups" that used the knowledge they commanded to "gain wealth, power, and status from society"[8] for themselves and also to control how people think and act in critical and intimate areas of their lives. Brandishing the phrase "professional dominance," coined by Freidson in 1970[9] to refer primarily to "the relation of the medical profession to most other health care occupations in the division of labor,"[10] many of these authors went far beyond the circumscribed economic and occupational domination and monopoly that Freidson had in mind. They depicted a professional power that was sweeping in societal and cultural scope. Physicians were presented as the most powerful of powerful professionals in this enlarged sense of the term: dominating all other health care occupations that were obliged to work under their supervision and take orders from them; monopolizing access to health care through its gatekeeping functions; and "medicalizing" how people think about themselves and their problems.

The literature on the power of professions continues to flourish. But since the mid-1970s, another substantial body of writings about professions has been generated that contrasts sharply with writings during the 1960s–1970s. These commentaries assert that the professions are in decline, losing their once privileged position and power. Two sets of theories underlie these allegations.[11] One group of writers contends that a process of "deprofessionalization" is occurring whereby professions are losing the prestige, confidence, and trust that their clients and the public previously accorded them. In this view, a more educated, knowledgeable, questioning, and egalitarian-minded public is closing up the knowledge and status gap between professionals and clients who have become more discerning, critical, and assertive "consumers."[12] Drawing on Marxian theory, a second group of commentators claims that the professions are undergoing a process of "proletarianization," analogous to what happened to manual labor in industry during the nineteenth century.[13] They point out that there is a growing trend for professionals to become salaried employees in bureaucracies, rather than to be self-employed in individual practice as they were predominantly in the past. These writers argue that, as a consequence of this development, professionals are losing their economic independence and autonomous control over their increasingly routinized and "deskilled" work, and are becoming more and more subject to the control of management.

As the foregoing suggests, sociological thinking about professions is so nihilistic, so fraught with contradictions, controversy, and polemics, and so devoid of sound and systematic empirical data that one could conclude that there is no way to write a coherent, useful chapter on the profession of medicine that represents the current state of the field. I shall still attempt to do so, because there are certain characteristics of the occupational roles that are discussed by authors of all perspectives when the concept of profession is invoked.[14] I will first identify these common attributes and then examine the status and role of the American physician in these terms. From there, I will move on to consider nurses (the largest group of health-care professionals in the United States), the status-role components of nursing, and the relationship of nurses and nursing to doctors and medicine. Reference will be made to some of the changes that are occurring in nursing and medicine, and in the interface between them, including the way in which "broad social changes in sex roles and in women's conceptions of themselves"[15] are affecting a profession whose membership is as predominantly female as that of nursing.

PARAMETERS OF A PROFESSION[16]

Whether they consider professions to be presently waxing or waning, most sociologists would agree with Talcott Parsons's statement that the "development and . . . strategic importance of the professions" is one of the "most important change[s] that has occurred in the occupational system of modern societies."[17] Furthermore, irrespective of how they delineate the professional category and which traits they emphasize in defining it, sociologists also join Parsons in acknowledging that the "boundaries" of this group of occupations are "fluid and indistinct."[18] Different occupations and clusters of occupations are more accurately described as falling at a certain point along a continuum of professionalism, than as being either professional or not professional in an absolute sense. The appropriate question, then, is how professional one occupational role is compared to another, in relation to certain institutional criteria of professionalism against which both are evaluated. As already indicated, particular occupational roles may increase or decrease in professionalism from one historical period to another.

COGNITIVE CHARACTERISTICS: KNOWLEDGE, SKILL, AND MODE OF REASONING

Virtually all scholars and critics who have written about professions have emphasized their central relationship to the creation, transmission, mastery, and application of formal knowledge. To use Freidson's terminology, professionals are "agents or carriers of formal knowledge,"[19] whose work is conducted within a set of occupational roles for which a considerable degree of certified higher education is required. The extensive and intricate body of knowledge that training in a profession and its exercise entail is conceptual and theoretical in some respects, and empirical and factual in others. The *practicum* aspects of a profession also involve the learned application of specialized skills and techniques to the kinds of human activities and problem solving in which the field is engaged.

Learning the fundamental concepts, facts, and techniques of a profession and achieving validated competence in their use takes place through a prolonged process of education, training, and socialization. This process is "organized about that element of the modern cultural system ordinarily called the intellectual disciplines—the humanities, and the sciences, both natural and social."[20] It occurs in specialized professional schools which, in many modern societies, are located in universities and are part of the intellectual and social world of higher academia.[21] Who is admitted to professional schools, what their curricula are, how their student-trainees are examined and evaluated, and on what bases they are graduated into the profession, granted a degree, and, in certain professions, licensed to practice, are specified and controlled by these schools and the professions for which they are mandated educators.

Although the organized knowledge and technical skills that a person must acquire in order to achieve attested professional competence are not so esoteric that they are incomprehensible to nonprofessionals, they are sufficiently copious and complex to make it unlikely that such competence could be achieved by persons who do not undergo an extensive, organized process of professional education. What is more, in many professional fields, maintaining competence after formal training has been completed is a continuous challenge, largely because of the velocity with which the theory, knowledge, and technology of the disciplines involved change, expand, and progress.

The professions have tended to view themselves as guardians of the knowledge and skill that they dispense, with both the privilege and the responsibility of judging which aspects of what they know and can do (and of what they do not know and cannot do) they should explain to clients and the broader public. This discretionary, gatekeeping dimension of a profession can widen the technical competence gap between professional and client. The intellectual distance may be increased still further by the way that clients' anxieties about the problems for which they consult professionals may temporarily undercut the relevant knowledge they already possess, or diminish their capacity to absorb more.[22]

The kinds of expertise that clients seek from professionals and the feelings that they have about the matters that they bring to them are associated with another major set of characteristics that professions share: their distinctive relationship to the value and belief systems of the larger society in which they are embedded. Professions are occupations that deal with "serious" things, in the Durkheimian sense of the word. They are concerned with events and states of being that are considered to be of special moral and existential importance in the cultural tradition and the "collective conscience" of a society: for example, birth and death, health and illness, affliction, suffering and healing, enlightenment and ignorance, spiritual anguish and well-being, justice, the ordering of the relations of persons to one another and to public authority, and comprehension and control of the physical environment. This is one of the primary reasons given by professionals for not confining training to a sequence of "trade-oriented" courses that teach only specific skills and concrete empirical knowledge. Linking that specialized occupational training to a broader and deeper grounding in the society's intellectual and cultural tradition is considered essential to the development of professionals' ability to deal with the human condition concerns that are inherent to their work.

Professional education also emphasizes learning to reason, logically and lucidly, within the overarching framework of the field (the framework of differential diagnosis in clinical medicine, for example, or Socratic reasoning in the law). Standards of both intellectual and moral excellence are involved here, and thinking well analytically is regarded as basic to the professionals' ability to make informed, responsible, and judicious decisions about the "serious" questions that they treat.

The framework in which professionals learn to observe, analyze, judge, and decide not only provides them with an ordered way of bringing their knowledge and skill to bear on the problems and cases that they handle, but also of doing so with a built-in system for identifying and evaluating the uncertainty, risks, and limitations of alternative courses of action. In this somewhat paradoxical sense, "training for uncertainty"[23] is integral to a professional's knowledgeable and skilled competence.

VALUE COMPONENTS: SERVICE, COMMITMENT, AND "CALLING"

The fact that professions deal with human affairs of moral import is related to another of their core characteristics: their fiduciary, service-oriented nature. Professionals are expected to grapple with the problems entrusted to them in a manner that serves not only the needs of particular individuals and groups, but also the common good of the society. This capacity to serve others—to meet their human needs individually, interconnectedly, and as members of a larger community—is more than a matter of good moral character and high purpose. It is a form of competence vital to a profession. In many activities, in "such professions as social service, law, medicine, and the clergy," James M. Gustafson explains, "the effectiveness of one's work depends in a considerable measure on the qualities of interpersonal relationships that are developed [with clients]":

> . . . mutual confidence; recognition of aspects of the patient or client that are not fully articulated by him or her; metaphorically speaking, good peripheral vision so that the professional person can set the particular need or interest in the context of a larger and more complex whole. Such capacities are developed in professional schools through the kinds of technical information, concepts, and ways of thinking . . . indicated earlier. But they also involve a capacity for empathy—a putting of oneself in the place of the other so that one can both imagine and feel what the client's views of the circumstances are. Indeed, refined exercise of practical reasoning is developed in part through natural and cultivated human sensibilities and sensitivities and not simply through quantified, computerized problem-solving methods and techniques, as important as these are. In critical situations . . . this might even involve a sense of suffering with the client or patient, virtually adopting the client's anguish, while at the same time maintaining the perspective of the disinterested observer and external agent who takes into account the client's perspective while interpreting the circumstances from his or her professional one.[24]

These aspects of a profession ideally entail a high level of unstinting commitment to the work at hand and to intellectual, technical, and interpersonal excellence in carrying it out. They also involve trained accessibility and responsiveness to the problems, questions, and needs of petitioning others, and a conception of "the larger ends and purposes" the professional work serves—individually and collectively—that endows it with a "wide context of significance and meaning."[25] This is what Gustafson terms the "calling" dimension of a profession. He cautions, however, that a "'calling' without professionalization is bumbling, ineffective, and even dangerous,"[26] and that there are major social structural, as well as motivational "impediments" to developing, implementing, and sustaining a "sense of calling."[27]

In the present-day climate of change, criticism, and self-criticism that surrounds professions in American society, reference to a profession "as a vocation" (to use Max Weber's language) often takes the form of commentary on the *failure* of professionals and professionals-in-training to live up to the principles, responsibilities, and the "vision" that it involves.

The following excerpt from an article by a medical educator about what he considers the problematic attitude of "entitlement . . . pervasive in . . . the population of student physicians" (and "in today's society") is illustrative:

> "Entitlement" is a technical term that describes a sense of being entitled to attention, care taking, love, success, income, or other benefits without having to give anything in return. . . .
>
> [I]f medical educators do not confront this problem in their students, its effects can be pernicious. For one thing, there is the danger of a declining commitment to personal excellence as a duty to patients and the profession, especially when it involves personal sacrifices. In addition, if students avoid anxiety by looking outside themselves for the source of their professional or personal problems, they will be incapable of changing them. A more subtle concern is that clinicians who, when they are under stress, tend to think of their own comfort first, will find it difficult to tolerate and empathize with their patients' pain and uncertainty. Clinical judgment may even be affected if the physician is inclined to emphasize data that seem to make the task of explaining the illness easier while paying less attention to information that is disturbing or difficult to explain. When the ability to tolerate the discomfort of confronting, accepting, and overcoming one's own inevitable uncertainties and failings is endangered, it is difficult to evaluate patients thoroughly and objectively.
>
> Perhaps the best way to counteract entitlement is to demonstrate unentitled behavior that students can emulate. . . .[28]

The disinterested, *"vie serieuse"* commitment, service, and "calling" elements of a profession are more traditionally and solemnly enunciated in the codes of ethics and conduct and oaths that many professional occupations have formulated. The principal affirmations in professional codes and oaths include pledging to devote one's professional life to the service of humanity; making the welfare of clients the first professional consideration; respecting the secrets confided in the professional; not permitting "considerations of religion, nationality, race, party politics, or social standing" to affect one's professional "duty";[29] avoiding doing harm to one's own clients; and desisting from using professional knowledge in ways that are contrary to the concerns of humanity.

Professionals have been granted several kinds of institutionalized privileges. The bases for these privileges include types of knowledge and skill in which professionals are trained, the problems of personal and societal significance to which they are asked to apply their expertise, and the fact that, in their sphere of competence, they are entrusted with responsibility for the welfare of clients and the public more broadly. The first of these privileges are the various sorts of "credentialing" that professions exercise. In the United States, "two distinct methods of credentialing intermesh to form a larger system."

> One of the methods may be called occupational credentialing, whereby credentials are issued to individual members of occupations performing particular kinds of work. Licenses constitute the most conspicuous example of this method, though degrees, diplomas, and certificates of completion of a course of training are ubiquitous. The second method may be called institutional credentialing, whereby special credentials are issued to institutions that organize the production of particular kinds of services to the public, including the training or education of prospective members of an occupation. Charters, operating licenses, articles of incorporation, and accreditation are examples of the second method.[30]

Professionals use these formal mechanisms and a number of informal credentials, such as letters of recommendation from teachers, employers, colleagues, patrons, and clients, to establish and monitor the minimal criteria under which persons may enter and work in their occupations. They also reserve "at least a small number of positions in work organizations for those who possess those credentials."[31] As Freidson astutely points out, the positions set apart for credentialed professionals "are not solely those in which everyday work is performed."

> Positions are also reserved for teachers and researchers in professional schools and for those who supervise the everyday work of credentialed professionals and manage the organizations in which they work. This internal role differentiation aids professions in their efforts to maintain control over both their claimed knowledge and skill and the conditions under which they work.[32]

In addition, professionals have a certain amount of testimonial privilege. This privilege of not disclosing information confided to them in the context of the professional-client relationship is associated with the special nature of what professionals come to know about those who consult them. As part of their work, professionals not only have the opportunity, but also the right and obligation, to inquire into aspects of their clients' persons and lives that are intimate, private, and in some instances clandestine. This is particularly true of medicine, law, and the clergy. In American courts, these are the professions that have certain legally recognized privileges for confidential communications. As already indicated, maintaining confidentiality about what clients disclose to them is a central ethical principle in the code of most professions. This precept of "professional secrecy" (as it is termed in continental European societies) extends to information about clients discussed with colleagues as well as with nonprofessional others.

AUTONOMY AT WORK AND COLLECTIVE SELF-CONTROL

A final set of characteristics that mark professions off from other occupations is the considerable degree of discretion and autonomy that they wield at work and the complex system of formal and informal social controls through which professionals try to regulate their own individual and corporate behavior.

In this connection, I agree with Freidson that, although more professionals than in the past are now carrying out their work in formal organizations with bureaucratic features rather than being self-employed, they enjoy a much higher degree of "technical autonomy" in these settings than other categories of employees do. Furthermore, as credentialed professionals in such organizations, they have strategic authority and power over which services, resources, and goods made available by management their clients receive.[33]

The primary and most potent control that professionals exercise over themselves and each other emanates from the process of socialization that they undergo in the course of their long and demanding common training. This process, which transforms them from laypersons into professionals, entails both the acquisition of a large body of knowledge, skills, and distinctive modes of reasoning, and the internalization of shared attitudes, values, and patterns of behavior relevant to the work and occupational roles for which they are preparing. The "schooling" of professionals, then, involves what Emile Durkheim would have termed "moral formation," along with psychosocial and cognitive learning. In addition, it sets into motion a second mechanism of control that, at all stages in a professional career, continues to be a major device "for establishing a set of ideal [technical and normative] standards and encouraging compliance with them."[34] These are the sanctions of approval and disapproval, reward and punishment that are implicitly communicated and enforced through face-to-face interaction between colleagues. Built into these processes of socialization and sanctioning are a series of "occupational rituals"[35] that constitute another set of mechanisms by which a profession controls itself. These rituals are highly structured, periodically repeated collective experiences and exercises that dramaturgically express some of the most important intellectual, technical, and moral principles of the profession in a symbolic and ceremonial way.

The organizations and associations formed by professionals to represent, convoke, and serve their members have important social control and self-regulatory functions as well. By virtue of their bylaws and state statutes, some professional societies have the institutional authority to suspend and revoke as well as grant licenses to practice. Professional associations also have at their disposal an array of nonlegal means (for example, election to office, awarding of prizes) to honor particular members for exemplifying the profession's standards, or to dishonor those who violate them (censuring the offenders, removing them from office, cancelling their membership, and the like). Increasingly, professional associations encourage and provide various kinds of opportunities for continuing education to help members maintain and expand their competence. Many associations of health professionals require continuing education for periodic mandatory recertification. In recent years some professional organizations, such as medical societies and bar associations, have mobilized themselves to deal with what has come to be called "impairment": problems such as alcoholism, drug addiction, and emotional disturbance that undermine professionals' competence and imperil their clients, and that are assumed to result principally from the stresses and strains of professional work.

As already indicated, since the beginning of the 1960s the nature and effectiveness of the social controls governing the professions in American society have received growing attention from the professions themselves, from scholars, consumers and their advocates, and from the courts and legislative and regulatory bodies. This attention has involved questions about the justifiability of according so much autonomy to professions to regulate themselves, concerns about the adequacy of the ways in which professionals are actually doing so, and escalating demands for greater public accountability of professionals, including more control from without as well as from within. Sociologists have been prominent among those who have voiced the strongest convictions about the necessity of "external control mechanisms . . . for a socially responsible profession," on the grounds that "the consequences of its performances and power are too important to . . . outsiders for them to give up all control over their fate" by "leaving them to professionals."[36] Medicine has been singled out by sociologists and by other commentators, analysts, and critics "as the archetype of a 'powerful profession' that deals with matters of serious importance to our social as well as our individual well-being, and of the dilemmas and difficulties of adequately controlling such a profession."[37]

THE PROFESSION OF MEDICINE IN THE UNITED STATES

It has been estimated that there are roughly one-half million active physicians in the United States at the present time, engaged in a variety of medical roles. In contrast to certain Latin American and European societies, almost all physicians in the United States do full-time occupational work concerned with health, illness, and medical matters, chiefly the delivery of care. Despite the national trend toward employed rather than self-employed status, most physicians still work in their own offices. However, group practice has grown dramatically: between 1969 and 1980, the number of group practices increased by 36 percent, and the number of physicians participating in them more than doubled, from 40,000 to 88,300.[38] Both solo and group office units have become microcosmic parts of a larger, massively changing set of organizational structures on which they are highly dependent:

> Before World War II [health care] was largely a cottage industry composed of self-employed physicians working primarily in their own offices and sometimes sending their patients to hospitals where nurses and members of a few other health care occupations cared for patients according to the doctors' orders. It was, furthermore, financed largely by charitable contributions and by the patients themselves. And while it did require machines and other tools of the trade that even then were too expensive for individual physicians to own themselves and use in their offices—making physicians somewhat dependent on hospitals for access to capital equipment as well as beds and paramedical services—health care technology was not sufficiently developed to support a large manufacturing industry. . . . [I]n those days the role of government was essentially passive, protecting the institutions of health care by licensing, tax, and other laws, but remaining otherwise uninvolved.[39]

Today medical care is a large public matter involving patient, medical care system, insurance companies and government. The friendly doctor with a black bag making a house call and the patient visiting a simply equipped doctor's office have given way to for-profit and not-for-profit hospitals, tax-exempt bonds, third-party payments, premiums, reimbursements, benefit packages, health maintenance organizations, specialists, tests, technology, machinery, research, laboratories, and ever-rising costs. Our grandparents' financial or physical well-being, as they related to medical care, did not depend on the views of presidents, members of congressional committees, state legislators, or corporate executives. Today they do.[40]

The number of accredited medical schools in the United States grew from 86 in 1960 to 127 in 1986.[41] Admission to an American medical school is highly selective. In contrast to the policy of open enrollment practiced in many other countries, American medical school faculties choose who will be admitted to the study of medicine:

> This prerogative allows medical schools to admit men and women who, in the faculties' opinion, have the academic and personal qualities requisite for a career in a profession that provides vital services. . . . Criteria for selection include prior academic attainments, achievement on a standardized examination that assesses science knowledge and reading and quantitative skills, the views of college faculties about a candidate's academic abilities and personal qualities, and evidence of values and attitudes commensurate with a career of service in a helping profession. Most students who are admitted have been evaluated through personal interviews by one or more faculty members.[42]

What has been described as a "phenomenal increase" in the number of persons applying for admission to medical school began to occur in the United States in the 1960s, and continued into the mid-1970s. "The number of applicants to U.S. medical schools reached a historical peak in 1974 when 42,624 applied (2.8 applicants per position)."[43] By fall 1979, the total number of students enrolled in American medical schools had risen to a record high of 63,800. However, the number of applicants had begun to plateau, and a significant downward trend became visible. "By 1985 the number of applicants had dropped 23 percent to 32,893 (1.9 applicants per position)."[44]

Historically, most medical students have been white men of upper-middle class origins. This pattern persists. But one cardinal change in the social composition of medical students is certain to have a major impact on the future make-up of the medical profession: the rise in the number and proportion of women.

> During the 1950s and '60s there was a slow but steady increase in the percentage of women among the applicants, from 6 percent in 1950 to nearly 10 percent in 1969. Beginning in 1970 the curve turned upward abruptly, increasing its slope by a factor of 10. By the end of the decade, nearly 30 percent of medical-school applicants were women.[45]

Over the period 1974–1985, "male applicants declined 38 percent, while female applicants increased by 23 percent. In 1985 11,562 women applied for admission to medical school, and women constituted 33 percent [21,624] of the first year class."[46]

This demographic rapprochement between female and male medical students notwithstanding, the career patterns of women physicians in the United States still differ considerably from those of men. In proportion to their numbers, women have chosen pediatrics, psychiatry, anesthesiology, and pathology far more frequently, and surgery and the surgical specialties far less frequently, than have men. They have also been more inclined to practice in hospitals and other medical institutions with fixed-salary and fixed-hour arrangements. There are signs, however, that some of these patterns may be changing. For example, the percentages of women enrolled in residency training programs in psychiatry, pediatrics, pathology, and diagnostic radiology have decreased somewhat, while the percentages of women choosing family practice, obstetrics-gynecology, and general surgery have increased.

Despite the organized efforts made by medical schools and the Association of American Medical Colleges (AAMC) to recruit more "underrepresented minority students" (Blacks, Mexican Americans, mainland Puerto Ricans, and Native Americans), their numbers have remained low and relatively constant. According to the American Medical Association's Division of Medical Education, the total enrollment of minority students in American medical schools in the 1985–1986 academic year was 16.5 percent, of which 5.3 percent were black.[47] Minority students constituted only 9 percent of the 1985 entering class.[48] In the opinion of the AAMC, "the rising cost of medical education, the difficulties minority students confront in obtaining scholarships and loans, and reductions in class size threaten progress in minority enrollment."[49] Follow-up studies of minority physicians who have completed their training indicate that "when compared to nonminority graduates, they were significantly more likely to be in primary care, located in health manpower shortage areas, and serving poor patients."[50]

The cost of medical education has risen steeply, "driven substantially but not entirely by the rapid inflation of . . . the 1970s":

> This was reflected in tuitions and fees as well as in living expenses. From academic year 1974–75 to 1984–85, inflation-adjusted medical school charges increased by 113 percent at private schools and 95 percent at public institutions. Fewer students were able to meet these costs out-of-pocket, scholarship funds from federal sources dried up, and borrowing expanded rapidly. By 1985, the percentage of indebted medical students had reached 87 percent, with an average indebtedness of $29,943.[51]

There is some indication that this heavier debt burden, along with the high cost of starting in private medical practice, may be affecting the type of practice for which recent medical school graduates are opting:

> Traditional private clinical practice was chosen by 58% of the 1986 [graduating] class, down 7% from 1982. The rest expect to work in medical service organizations, including hospitals and group health maintenance organizations.[52]

The trend of declining numbers of medical school applicants, admissions, and graduates is expected to continue and to become more marked. Most medical schools have now capped enrollments or made small reductions in class size, in response both to the financial burdens they are carrying and to predictions of a future oversupply of physicians. Estimates of the prospective surplus of doctors have run as high as 70,000 physicians in 1990 and 145,000 in the year 2000.[53]

COGNITIVE CHARACTERISTICS OF MEDICINE

In its knowledge, skill, and mode of thought, and its ways of developing, transmitting, and applying them to matters of health and illness, medicine is a profession *par excellence*. Modern Western medicine encompasses a vast, intricate, continually changing and growing corpus of knowledge, drawn from congeries of biological, physical, and, to a lesser extent, behavioral scientific disciplines. Since World War II, it has evolved from a field whose primary scientific orientation emanated from anatomy, pathology, bacteriology, and physiology, to one in which biochemistry, biophysics, and pathophysiology became the paramount basic sciences. In this present era of what is often referred to as "the biological revolution," molecular biology (especially genetics), immunology, and neurobiology have become the foremost sciences, with transforming influence on the field's theory, knowledge base, and technical capacities.

Not only is modern medicine dynamically grounded in an aggregate of scientific disciplines, but it also commands a large battery of preventive, diagnostic, and therapeutic procedures, technologies, and drugs that range in complexity, innovativeness, and audacity from a regimen of bedrest and forced fluids to immunization; from a tonsillectomy and an appendectomy to cardiothoracic surgery, organ transplantation, and total artificial heart implants; from auscultation and percussion to the use of computed tomography (CAT) and position emission tomography (PET) scanners; and from digitalis and aspirin to psychotropic, anticancer, and immunosuppressive drugs.

Medicine has its own characteristic conceptual framework as well. Its underlying mode of thought is not simply the sum of its parts. Rather it is an emergent, eclectic product of the various disciplines on which it draws. Its way of reasoning is primarily scientific in nature. In its ideal-typical form, it entails the application of logico-rational thought to empirical phenomena that are assumed to have a direct or indirect relationship to health and illness. Probability reasoning predominates. Diagnoses are ruled out and ruled in, and treatment decisions arrived at according to a quasi-statistical, quasi-judgmental estimate of how likely a diagnosis is, given the signs and symptoms that a patient with certain attributes presents, of how dangerous it would be if a possible diagnosis were missed, even if it were not the most expected one, and of what the benefit/risk ratio for a patient might be if particular therapies were initiated or withheld. As the foregoing implies, the logic of clinical medical thought (and action based upon it) entails null hypothesis reasoning, with the highest priority given to unproving diagnoses that might be most serious for the patient before exploring diagnoses that might be more probable but less grave. In this sense, clinical medicine involves "fail-safe" reasoning, with built-in mechanisms intended to reduce errors of omission as well as of commission on the part of diagnosing, treating, and prognosticating physicians. Although in a cumulative and public health sense medicine deals with aggregates, and although its reasoning is guided by underlying principles and concepts, it proceeds on a case-by-case basis. Thus, it is continually confronted with the imperfect degree to which probability statistics and general precepts apply to a single individual, with all of his or her distinctiveness.

The process of medical education and training is demanding and protracted. In the United States undergraduate college education, four years of medical school, and graduate medical education (internship and residency), varying in length from three to seven years, are considered essential parts of the preparation of physicians for practice. Board examinations are given at different points along this continuum, culminating in those that are prerequisite for the practice of a specialty.[54] In addition, since the mid-1970s, "mandatory continuing education for physicians and other health professionals has become commonplace":

> Continuing medical education is required for relicensure, usually on a three-year cycle, in twenty-two states. The state medical associations in fourteen states require continuing education on a regular basis as a condition for maintaining membership in the association. Similarly, all medical specialty boards have endorsed the concept of voluntary recertification in their specialty, and have either initiated appropriate procedures or are developing them. One requirement for recertification is a specified level of participation in continuing medical education since last certified or recertified. Finally, the Joint Commission on Accreditation of Hospitals requires that hospitals provide continuing medical education opportunities for their professional staffs as a condition for accreditation. . . . [M]edical schools now represent the largest single provider of continuing education.[55]

VALUE AND MEANING DIMENSIONS OF MEDICINE

The concept of doctoring is an ancient one. Long, long before mankind had much in the way of scientific information or tools, wise men were singled out whose primary job it was to advise and treat their fellows.

From a scientific perspective in the twentieth century, we can well question the majority of potions, herbs, poultices, leeches and other "treatments" that doctors have imposed on their fellows through the centuries. . . . That leaves unaddressed, however, the question of what good doctoring is. . . .

Somewhere between Flexner[56] and the CAT scanner, we as a profession and we as a people have lost track of what good doctoring is. As each of you becomes a physician, this contradiction in one form or another will confront you. This, I submit, will be your own personal star war. . . .

If you lose your medical star war, what will happen? . . . Imperceptibly, you will cease to be a doctor and become a "doctoroid." A "doctoroid" is a bright young physician with good MCAT scores, good grades, excellent subspecialty electives, commendable national board scores, board certification in any one of a number of specialities, and an essential inability to deal with people or communities. A "doctoroid" sees its medical degree as a game of tennis—a hard-won personal skill to be used primarily for self-gratification. A "doctoroid" is well-to-do, dresses like a doctor, and behaves like a doctor, but it has no heart. . . .

The battle that we face is wholly different and, ironically, much more difficult than the one that was faced by our pre-Flexnerian colleagues. They had far less to master than we did and at the same time, they had far less to divert them from their mission of service than we do. A few basic skills and a great deal of bedside manner were all that they had to offer their patients. . . . [T]echnologies and opportunities . . . allow and even encourage us to lose our sense of people, patient, and community. . . .

It is not easy to be a good doctor today. It is not easy to work within the profession and maintain a sense of your humanity, your humility, and your commitment to service.

Doctoring is an old profession and a quintessentially human one. Your star war will be to keep it that way.[57]

The foregoing passage is excerpted from a speech that Dr. Fitzhugh Mullan delivered to the graduates of the College of Medicine of the University of Arizona in 1978. Dr. Mullan was then a physician in his 30s, well known to medical students as the author of *White Coat, Clenched Fist*. In this book, published two years earlier, he had told the story of his own experiences in medical school, internship, and residency, focusing particularly on "the nonmedical and nonscientific forces" that shaped his "political education as a physician," as a member of "a generation of young people in medicine who since the mid-1960s [had] consistently questioned the structure of American medicine . . . and collectively . . . labored to change it."[58] Mullan's "Medicine's Star Wars" address is an eloquent statement of the fact that the profession of medicine and the acts of doctoring consist of more than vast scientific information, high technology tools, certified advanced education, and virtuoso skill. It is an enjoinder to new physicians to recognize and live up to the moral obligations of the profession that they are about to enter. Without this commitment, Mullan affirms, a physician is a "doctoroid," not a doctor—a creature with the outer appearance but without the inner essence of a true medical doctor.

An authentic physician, Mullan affirms, does not regard his or her work as ordinary, as just a job like any other, or primarily as a means to achieve ego-gratification and personal success. Rather, the commitment is to human service—service to individual patients and to the community. The scientific, technological, and interpersonal knowledge and skills through which the physician renders this service ideally should be brought to bear on the problems of the people who come for care, with generosity, continuous availability, humanity, humility, and equanimity, and without prejudice or discrimination. Mullan appeals to his younger colleagues to be good doctors in these value-commitment and service aspects of their profession, while candidly admitting how hard it is to live up to these moral standards, and how often physicians actually fail to do so:

The first battle will be against the forces of complacency, laziness and fatigue. It will have to be fought almost daily during your career. The enemy will coax you to become insensitive, curt, greedy, prejudgemental, racist, rich, brusque, and thoughtless. It will attack late at night when you are on call, or after a weekend in the operating room, or in your office when the investment counsellor visits, or when you select a house, a car or a vacation plan.[59]

It is not only these physical, material, and motivational "temptations" and frailties that can "divert" physicians from the "mission" of doctoring, Mullan asserts, but paradoxically, the power and magnitude of the modern science and technology from which their technical competence derives.

What is there about health, illness, medicine, and doctoring that accounts for these extraordinary role-expectations? Here, the special relationship that medical work bears to the human body and psyche, to the human "story," and to what neurologist Oliver Sacks calls the "quintessential human condition of sickness" are centrally involved.

> My work, my life, is all with the sick—but the sick and their sickness drives me to thoughts which, perhaps, I might otherwise not have. So much so that I am compelled to ask, with Nietzsche: 'As for sicknesses: are we not almost tempted to ask whether we could get along without it?'—and to see the questions it raises as fundamental in nature. Constantly my patients drive me to question, and constantly my questions drive me to patients. . . .
>
> Hippocrates introduced the historical conception of disease, the idea that diseases have a course, from their first intimations to the climax or crisis, and thence to their happy or fatal resolution. Hippocrates thus introduced the case history of disease. . . . Such histories are a form of natural history—but they tell us nothing about the individual and *his* history; they convey nothing of the struggles of the person, and the experience of the person as he faces, and struggles to survive, his disease. . . . To restore the human subject at the centre—the suffering, afflicted, fighting, human subject—we must deepen a case history to a narrative or tale: only then do we have a 'who' as well as a 'what,' a real person, a patient, in relation to disease.[60]

These thoughts, questions and observations, and this conception of the patient's personhood, suffering, struggle, and "tale," belong to what might best be termed the existential or spiritual dimensions of doctorhood—the secularization of modern medicine notwithstanding.

The practice of medicine continually exposes physicians to "some of the most basic and . . . transcendent aspects of the human condition":[61] to birth, growth and development, sexuality, aging, mortality, and death; to the joys and sorrows, fulfillments and frustrations that are core to the quality of our lives; to the mysteries of our existence and identity; and to the most critical problems of meaning that we face—fundamental questions about the "reason" for pain and suffering, and above all, the "sense of total bewilderment and total anxiety about mortality"[62] with which we grapple:

> The ability of a physician, over a lifetime of practice, to deal with the human comedy, tragedy, and enigma inherent in medicine; to handle them personally, and on behalf of the patients and families he or she serves; to face the monotonous repetition as well as the amazing variety of the forms taken by the human condition; and to make sense of these happenings and of the struggling efforts they elicit from doctors and patients, requires far more than coping mechanisms.[63]

Something akin to James Gustafson's notion of the profession of medicine as a "calling"—of faith in the work of doctoring and belief in its relationship to "larger ends and purposes of human good"[64]—is ideally needed.

MEDICAL PRAYERS, OATHS, AND CODES OF ETHICS

The nature of medicine as a vocation and the special moral commitment that physicians are expected to make to its highest principles are expressed in the medical prayers, oaths, creeds, and codes of ethics under which the medical profession has functioned in numerous societies and various cultural traditions over the centuries:

> Medical prayers state a very personal commitment of the physician to his professional duty; oaths publicly pledge the new physician to uphold the recognized responsibilities of his new profession; and codes provide more comprehensive standards to guide the practicing physician.[65]

To this day, at their graduation from medical school, young American physicians ceremonially pledge themselves to live up to the ultimate values and basic precepts of doctorhood, usually in the form of the Daily Prayer of A Physician,[66] the Oath of Hippocrates or Maimonides, the Declaration of Geneva of the World Medical Association, or some variant of these. But in the United States, what is probably the most influential attempt to articulate the moral standards and rules of conduct that are supposed to guide physicians' professional behavior are the Principles of Medical Ethics of the American Medical Association (AMA), the national organization to which slightly less than half of U.S. doctors belong.

The AMA has had a formal Code of Ethics since 1847, the year in which the Association was founded. From the outset, the major axes of this code have concerned the relationship of physicians to patients, to fellow-physicians, to other practitioners of medicine, to the public, and to the society. The original code (significantly influenced by the Hippocratic tradition and by the treatise *Medical Ethics: Or, A Code of Institutes and Precepts Adapted to the Professional Conduct of Physicians and Surgeons*, published in 1803 by the eminent British physician Thomas Percival), was subsequently revised in 1903, 1912, 1947, and 1957.[67] The 1957 code of Ten Principles remained in effect for twenty-three years, until the summer of 1980, when the AMA's House of Delegates voted in a new set of seven principles.

The AMA Principles have consistently exhibited many classical traits of traditional codes of medical ethics. To begin with, although the AMA code has always been centrally concerned with the relations of patients to physicians as well as of physicians to patients, no nonphysicians have been directly involved in drafting its various versions. This is one of the ways in which the code continues to be paternalistic. It is based on the assumption that the physician—who is exhorted to provide competent, respectful, and compassionate care that will protect and benefit the patient—should play the dominant role in determining what actions will best advance the patient's as well as the doctor's interests.

Within this framework, the importance of the individuality of the doctor-patient relationship has been stressed by the code, along with maintaining professional secrecy as an integral part of that relationship. However much a "sacred trust" that confidentiality has been considered to be, until recently the code permitted the physician to reveal confidences in situations where the physician judged that divulgence would benefit the patient, irrespective of what the patient's opinion and wishes were about breaking confidence.

The pre-1980 versions of the AMA code were also restrictive and protectionistic in guild-like ways. They proscribed solicitation of patients and curtailed advertising; enjoined physicians to practice "a method of healing founded on a scientific basis" defined in a narrowly orthodox way; and prohibited physicians from associating professionally with anyone who violated this principle. Under this precept, chiropractors, for example, were considered to be members of an "unscientific cult." This judgment was maintained despite the fact that by 1979, chiropractors had attained licensure in every state in the United States; that over 23,000 chiropractors were treating more than eight million Americans for a wide variety of medical conditions; and that reimbursement for their services had been authorized by Medicare, Medicaid, Workmen's Compensation, many Blue Shield plans, and by other private insurance carriers.[68]

Its paternalism, individualism, and "guildism" notwithstanding, the AMA code has always been socially oriented. Moral philosopher Robert Veatch has pointed out that even older forms of the code emphasized that "the responsibilities of the physician extend not only to the individual, but also to society." In this regard the code was, and continues to be, "very different from the mainstream of international physician ethics with its exclusive commitment to the individual."[69]

The new AMA code of seven principles is more socially oriented than its predecessors. It accords top priority to the profession's relationship to society, affirming that "a physician must recognize responsibility to society, to patients, to other health professionals, and to self." It concedes that "the profession does not exist for itself; it exists for a purpose, and increasingly that purpose will be defined by society." It asks physicians to exhibit high respect for the law of the society. And it compels the physician "as a member of society" to "recognize a responsibility to participate in activities contributing to an improved community."

Contrary to what many physician and lay commentators on the 1980 code have implied, this accentuated social awareness and responsibility are not its most radical alterations. Rather, the code's most "revolutionary" aspects concern the recognition that it accords to the "rights of patients," and the way in which it makes respect for these rights mandatory, linking them to the physician's primary responsibilities. A vital part of the physician's respect for patients' rights, the code explicates, is the obligation to "deal honestly with patients." Furthermore, its statement about the safeguarding of patient confidences is stronger than in the past, and permits that confidentiality to be broken when it is in the interest of the patient as well as in the interests of society or required by law. This stands in dramatic contrast to the original code of 1857, which not only prescribed the responsibilities of physicians, but also unilaterally dictated the obligations of patients.

The monopolistic, guild characteristics of earlier AMA codes have been greatly reduced. As the initial report of the committee that reviewed the AMA principles put it: "The medical profession is no longer perceived as the sole guardian of public health, and consequently the traditional paternalism of the profession is in conflict with society."[70] A wide diversity of legitimate forms of medical practice is recognized. The physician is called upon to "utilize the talents of other professionals" and, except in emergencies, is granted the "freedom to choose whom to serve, with whom to associate, and the environment in which to provide medical services." The proscription against solicitation of patients in the 1957 code is dropped altogether.

The self-governing and self-policing principle of professional autonomy is maintained in the new code. But for the first time, "striving to expose those physicians deficient in character, competence, or who engage in fraud or deception" is associated with patient rights in general and the obligation to deal honestly with patients in particular, as well as with the responsibility to "uphold the honor" of the medical profession.

As the foregoing suggests, the older, more individualistic, paternalistic, self-determining, and protectionistic characteristics of the AMA code have not been eliminated, but impressive progress in that direction has been made. This evolution has come about partly as a result of the growing extent to which, since the 1960s, the American medical profession has not only found itself confronted with more independent, assertive, and critical patients, but has also become the object of collective pressures to change, ranging from consumer movement actions, to malpractice suits, to the passage of new rulings and laws. For example, the numerous antitrust suits against the AMA filed by chiropractors, and the Federal Trade Commission ruling that the AMA was using its ban on the solicitation of patients to restrain free competition among physicians, have played influential roles in certain of the modifications the AMA code has undergone. But, as will become more evident in subsequent chapters, the transformations in the code have come from within the medical profession as well, precipitated by changes in medical science, technology, education, organization, and practice, by a more questioning and self-critical outlook on the part of the profession, and by the influx into it of a new generation of physicians with new social attitudes.

MEDICAL SOCIALIZATION AND SOCIAL CONTROL

The American Medical Association as a professional organization, with its influential code of ethics and its largely conservative impact on issues like national health insurance, Medicare and Medicaid, professional competition, alternative modes of practice, and physician-hospital relations, is an important agent of social control inside the medical profession, and in health-illness-medical matters on the larger national scene. There is evidence, however, that in recent years the AMA has lost some of its professional and political influence. Its paid membership ranks have been declining, and its official stance on certain issues (such as chiropractic) has not prevailed or has been defeated.

The American medical profession exercises more significant modes of control over physicians and nonphysicians alike through defining and setting acceptable standards of medical care, deciding who is allowed to become a medical doctor (through its medical school selection and admissions policies and processes), and determining many aspects of practice. For example, the profession largely controls decisions about who can practice medicine and enter particular specialties and sub-specialties (through its influence over granting and revoking licenses and the composition, administration, and grading of National Board Examinations), and who can admit patients to given hospitals (through staff appointments and hospital privileges).

The most powerful and persistent form of control to which doctors are subject, and which they exert, is the medical socialization process that all American physicians undergo, especially during their medical school, internship, and residency years. In the next two chapters, this socialization process will be examined in analytic and empirical detail. Here, we will only identify some of the attributes of the intellectual, technical, and psychosocial training that physicians pass through that makes it so controlling of doctors in certain ways, and through them also controls their nonphysician colleagues and patients.

The medical educational and socialization process is long, intensive, and exacting. It is also a highly structured, uniform, and collective experience. All medical students pass through the same core medical school curriculum, and all physician-specialists the same postgraduate training required by their chosen field. Even more than the knowledge and skill that physicians acquire, the rites of passage and formative experiences that they undergo shape their attitudes in comparable ways that bind them together and set them apart from nonphysicians. The kinds of shared experiences that make the deepest common imprint on physicians are those that are most closely associated with birth, life, death, and the human condition; with the power and limitations of medical knowledge and skill; and with the distinctive prerogatives, responsibilities, and stresses of the physician's role. In this connection, certain highly patterned and symbolic events built into medical training have special, enduring, transmuting effects on the men and women who become physicians: for example, dissecting a cadaver in the anatomy laboratory, participating in an autopsy, performing venipunctures, doing pelvic and rectal examinations, delivering a baby, caring for a dying patient, "losing" a patient to death. These are among the key training experiences that physicians remember the most vividly and are most likely to associate with what progressively changed them attitudinally from lay persons into physicians.

An important part of the professional socialization process takes place indirectly and implicitly. This is particularly true of those facets of medical socialization that have to do with transmitting and enforcing physicianly attitudes, values, beliefs, and practices. By and large, the primary cognitive, scientific, and technical aspects of doctoring are conveyed more directly and overtly. But it is also true that attitudes, values, and beliefs are coded into the cognitive and technical material physicians learn.

In addition to the overall inclination for the psychosocial and ethical aspects of medical socialization to be hidden below the surface of the training process, a considerable part of it takes place silently. The silence is institutionalized, created and buttressed by a historical commitment to what psychiatrist Jay Katz has termed the "humaneness of services silently rendered."[71]

Thus, through the professional socialization process that they mutually undergo, physicians internalize common ways of thinking, perceiving, feeling, and acting in the realm of their work. This acquired and not totally conscious likeness and consensus make it more likely that physicians will respond to and deal with professional matters in similar if not identical ways—ways that they have been implicitly as well as explicitly taught. In turn, physicians' commonality is reinforced by the ingroup solidarity that the professional rites, rituals, and ordeals through which they pass help to create among them. The collective identity and consensus that physicians develop constitute a potent interpersonal as well as political force in their relations with lay persons and groups. It also contributes to physicians' convictions that they have special qualifications to govern and regulate themselves, individually and collectively, which those who have not undergone medical training do not possess.

The fact that so much of their psychosocial and ethical socialization takes place implicitly, silently, and preconsciously or unconsciously makes it difficult for physicians to be critically aware of their own professional attitudes and behaviors or to change them. Furthermore, their training in silence spills over into their relations with patients, increasing doctors' propensity not to talk freely with patients about their diagnosis, therapy, prognosis, and other important questions and decisions integral to their case.

These patterned interconnections between the ways that physicians are socialized and the modes of social control that they develop and employ are part of the "professional dominance" syndrome about which sociologists have written so much and so critically, with which the American public has become increasingly preoccupied and discontented, and of which the medical profession itself is slowly becoming more self-searchingly aware.

THE PROFESSION OF NURSING IN THE UNITED STATES

There is a pool of more than one million practicing nurses in the United States—a professional group twice as large as the estimated half-million active physicians. But whereas almost all physicians are engaged in full-time medically-related work, and most are in medical practice, there are many graduate nurses who are no longer practicing their profession. In sharp contrast to the imminent oversupply of physicians that is forecast, there is increasing concern about the unabating difficulties in recruiting and retaining a sufficient number of nurses to fill a wide range of important nursing jobs.

> For example, there are chronic vacancies for nurses in geriatric, psychiatric, coronary care, intensive care services, and other medical and surgical specialties in acute care hospitals, and in general duty nurses in many rural areas and urban inner city locations. Recruitment and retention problems are most acute for evening, night and weekend shifts. There are vacancies increasingly reported in staff and general duty nursing positions in nursing homes, often appearing to be related to specific geographical locations. Finally, there are reports of an increasing number of unfilled budgeted nurse positions in public health departments.[72]

The phenomenon of nurses temporarily or permanently not practicing is as complex as it is troubling. In a number of ways, it is associated with the most salient demographic characteristic that distinguishes the nursing from the medical profession. Nursing is overwhelmingly a profession of women (98.1 percent). One of the factors that have contributed to the discontinuities in nursing career patterns is the withdrawal of many nurses from professional activity after they marry and become mothers.

But the centrifugal pull of marriage and the family is neither the only nor probably the main reason for the exodus of nurses from the field. The fact that the economic rewards for becoming and remaining a nurse are so poor, in ways that are prototypical of "many of the limitations of women's occupations and women's changing career expectations," is a major source of frustration and discouragement to nurses of all age cohorts and levels of experience and status. It adversely affects their morale and acts as a deterrent to their "maintaining career commitments."

> The growing knowledge base and technical demands of nursing care and the plain hard work in terms of physical labor, night and weekend work hours, social

stress, and continuing responsibility are poorly remunerated in comparison to other occupations demanding similar levels of education, skill, and responsibility. The income gap between nurses and physicians, for example, has increased dramatically since 1945. After World War II, nurses' incomes were one-third of physicians' incomes, but by 1980 nurses were earning less than one-fifth as much as doctors. Moreover, the existing salary structures do not reward experienced, career-oriented nurses. Beginning nurses who are just out of school earn only slightly less than nurses with years of clinical experience. The loss of experienced nurses, partly a result of inadequate remuneration, leaves younger nurses without the support to cope with responsibilities that can easily overwhelm them.[73]

The social backgrounds of nurses also are quite different from those of physicians. A high proportion of nurses come from working-class and lower-middle-class families, rather than from the upper-middle-class milieux into which so many physicians were born. In addition, a much larger percentage of nurses than doctors are Catholic (and a substantial number are religious, active practitioners of their faith).

It is interesting to speculate on how these attributes of nursing—the fact that nursing is an occupational group composed primarily of women, largely of working- and lower-middle-class Catholic origins, many of whom have had short-term or interrupted careers—may have affected the overall professional status of the field. Do these characteristics of nursing contribute to the fact that it has lower professional status than medicine? This is a question that is rarely posed, either by doctors or nurses, and the social class and religious origins of nurses compared to doctors are hardly ever mentioned.

THE WORK, PROFESSIONAL STATUS, AND ROLE-SET OF NURSES

The occupation of a nurse is regarded as a less fully professional role than that of a physician. On a continuum of professionalism, nursing falls closer to what sociologists term "semi-," "quasi-," or "minor" professions than does doctoring. However, through active political lobbying, nurses have succeeded in getting their occupation shifted from the "semiprofessional" to the "professional" category of the U.S. Census.[74] Furthermore, the nurse's training, the nature of her work, and her occupational status are so closely interconnected with those of physicians that nurses stand apart from, and somewhat above, numerous "allied health professionals." For example, it is commonplace to speak of the medical and nursing professions, and of the doctor and nurse specifically and in conjunction with one another, when discussing patient care, and then to trail off into unnamed and undifferentiated reference to the "other" roles and jobs that are part of a modern medical team.

Unlike most other professions, nursing is usually conducted in "a very elaborate, highly technical division of labor among a number of occupations ordered both by specialization and authority":

> There is a hierarchy among occupations performing nursing and ancillary functions, with nurses superordinate to some and themselves subordinate to their own nursing supervisors. There is also a hierarchy in the overall division of labor, with members of the medical profession in the superordinate position.[75]

The complex, hierarchically ordered structures within which most nurses function are located in hospitals and nursing homes, their chief workplaces. In these contexts, the nurse is simultaneously an employee of the institution who is expected to abide by its policies and rules, an assistant to the physician whose orders relating to the patient's diagnosis and medical treatment plan she is expected to follow, and a primary patient caretaker and advocate.

The triple role-set confronts nurses with a cluster of structural strains. As a result of medical scientific and technological advances, the aging of the patient population, the increased incidence of chronic and degenerative diseases, and certain changes in patterns of medical practice, hospital patients are now more acutely ill than ever before, physicians not as continuously present in the hospital, and nurses are carrying more direct responsibility for patient treatment and care of greater technical and social complexity.

> The average length of a hospital stay has been reduced by 20 percent since 1970. More services can be given in a shorter period, and the diagnostic case-mix has shifted toward a sicker group of patients. The number of intensive care beds increased by more than 74 percent between 1972 and 1980. More complex technology, a greater need for services among hospitalized patients, and more difficult problems of coordinating the growing number of specialized personnel caring for patients put major responsibilities and stresses on nurses. These demands are exacerbated when physicians who have formal authority are absent from patient care settings because of other responsibilities and changing work habits.
>
> The number of hours worked by the average physician has declined from over 65 hours a week in 1943 to less than 50 hours a week in 1980. Moreover, most physicians spend less than two hours a day making rounds in the hospital. Thus, . . . there are extended periods during which physicians are not present in the hospital or easily accessible for direct consultation. Nurses are left with the continuing responsibility for acutely ill patients, but their authority to act in the absence of the physician has not been formally modified.[76]

The sustained nursing care of patients under these present hospital practice circumstances involves nurses in "many . . . tasks formerly regarded as solely those of physicians,"[77] such as monitoring cardiac arrhythmias, electrolytes, and blood gases, and administering intravenous medication. The "shifting interface" between nurses and physicians has created uncertainty, confusion, and some conflict about "the proper role for nurses and the relation of nursing functions to medical functions in the optimal care of patients."[78]

Part of the tension that exists between nurses and physicians derives from the character of the nurse-patient relationship. In their daily, hands-on, continuous care of patients, nurses deal with some of their most basic and intimate physical, emotional, and not infrequently, spiritual needs. They come to know patients in these outer and inner ways—especially how patients are reacting to and dealing with their illness and treatment. Nurses also have considerable contact with close members of patients' families. Under these circumstances, they often become identified with their patients as persons: with their feelings, values, relationships, life histories, and how these bear on what the hospitalized patient is experiencing. In fact, the nurse is ideally expected to do so, and to translate this identification into patient advocacy when it is called for:

. . . nurses are taught that their primary commitment is to the patient. The nursing ethos of the past, rooted in unquestioning obedience to the physician, has given way to an ethic of advocacy for the patient. The present American Nurses' Association Code for Nurses, for example, dictates that respect for human dignity and support of the patient's rights to self-determination are an integral part of nursing practice. Furthermore, when patients lack the capacity to decide, nurses are expected to act in their best interests, operating from a patient-oriented rather than a medically oriented perspective.[79]

As the foregoing suggests, this "commitment to the patient" may engender conflicts of loyalty and role responsibility for the nurse in her relationship to physicians in ways that can involve serious ethical problems and matters of conscience. Such conflicts were observed by pediatrician-sociologist Anthony Rostain in his ethnographic study of an intensive care nursery (ICN):

Nurses tend to develop strong attachments to their patients, acting as "surrogate mothers" to the infants during the weeks or months of close contact with them. Viewed by many parents as the "guardian angels" of their babies, nurses consider themselves patient advocates. They can become extremely protective if they perceive indifference or incompetence on the part of parents or doctors.

Nurses also provide continuity of care in the ICN and often function as intermediaries between the doctors and the family. This role becomes extremely difficult when the infant begins to deteriorate, especially if there are conflicts or unresolved differences of opinion between the medical team and the parents. Nurses may be asked to help persuade parents to follow medical advice which they themselves do not fully endorse. If they object, they may be criticized by physicians for becoming "too emotionally involved" with their patients. They may disapprove of the way parents or doctors are behaving, yet there are few avenues open to them for stating their grievances. This often leads to severe emotional distress and to strained work relationships in the intensive care unit.[80]

"What is the obligation of nurses when a decision that they believe to be morally wrong is made by someone else and they are ordered to implement it?" nurse E. Charlotte Theis asks.[81] Such conflicts are "an increasing source of moral anguish for nurses," she states, "particularly those practicing in intensive care units, nurseries for newborns, and nursing homes." The "anguish" is intensified by the fact that "the exercise of conscience by nurses is constrained by their obligation to other parties—physicians and employers—who are more powerful and have greater authority."[82]

HISTORICAL PERSPECTIVE
ON THE PROFESSIONAL EVOLUTION OF NURSING

The current state of nursing—its work and ethos, role responsibilities and rights, and its structural ambiguities and strains—can best be understood in historical perspective, with appreciation of the significant change and accelerating process of greater professionalization it has been undergoing.

One of the most significant concomitants of this process of increased professionalization is the relocation and upgrading of the formal training required for nursing. The primary form this has assumed is the gradual demise of hospital-based diploma programs and the increased assimilation of the education of nurses into colleges and universities. Over the period 1964 to 1978, for example, the number of hospital-based diploma programs dropped from 821 to 344; junior and community college associate degree programs grew from 174 to 677; and 155 more baccalaureate nursing programs in universities and colleges were established, bringing that total to 353.[83]

The founder and charismatic leader of modern nursing, of course, was Florence Nightingale, and it is through the hospital or diploma school that her system of training, ideology, and emblematic influence have significantly affected the American nursing profession. As sociologists Virginia L. Olesen and Elvi W. Whittaker point out:

> . . . the hospital or diploma school is often referred to as "the Nightingale system" . . . and most hospital schools of today could trace most of their lineage directly to the nursing school at St. Thomas's, London, designed and established by the lady herself. Indeed, the first schools in the United States opened in 1873 at Bellevue in New York, at the Boston Hospital Training School, and at the Connecticut Training School in New Haven, with Florence Nightingale . . . , by correspondence, involved in the act.[84]

The Nightingale system, embodied in the diploma school, has been predominantly oriented to "care at the bedside of the sick." Traditionally, the diploma school curriculum has emphasized the teaching of skills that the nurse must know in order to fulfill her caring function. Thus, the essential cognitive content of the training process was focused on the how-to-do-it aspects of nursing: the mastery of essential procedures and techniques and their clinical enactment.

The other major axis of the Nightingale/diploma school system is the importance it has attached to certain moral virtues, character traits, and personality attributes in the work of nurses, and in how they are selected and trained. Among the qualities that have been stressed are sobriety, honesty, truthfulness, trustworthiness, punctuality, quietness, orderliness, cleanliness, neatness, patience, cheerfulness, and kindness. The emphasis on these qualities grew out of Florence Nightingale's nineteenth-century efforts to overcome the problems of theft, uncleanliness, disorderly conduct, and alcoholism in many of the women of lower-class and underclass origins who were recruited into nursing. These virtuous traits and the significance accorded to them have been associated with the historic struggle of nurses to achieve respectability and recognition as women professionals, to evolve beyond the original "Sairy Gamp" image of nurses that Charles Dickens portrayed in his novel, *Martin Chuzzlewit*:

> She was a fat old woman, this Mrs. Gamp, with a husky voice and a moist eye, which she had a remarkable power of turning up and showing the white of it. Having very little neck, it cost her some trouble to look over herself, if one may say so, to those to whom she talked. She wore a very rusty black gown, rather the worse for snuff, and a shawl and bonnet to correspond. In these dilapidated articles of dress she had, on principle, arrayed herself, time out of mind, on each occasion as the present; for this at once expressed a decent amount of veneration for the deceased, and invited the next of kin to present her with a fresher suit of weeds. . . . The face of Mrs. Gamp—the nose in particular—was somewhat red

and swollen, and it was difficult to enjoy her society without becoming conscious of a smell of spirits.[85]

The uniforms and caps that the nursing profession and nursing schools developed toward the end of the nineteenth century were the very antithesis of Mrs. Gamp's dirty and worn black costume. They emphasized neatness and immaculateness, modesty and decorum, and they discouraged fashionable self-decoration or any sort of self-display. Garbed in starched white dresses, covered by starched bibs and aprons, wearing white or black oxford-type shoes, and white or black hose, their heads coiffed by white caps originally designed to cover the long, elaborately curled hair that was in mode during the late nineteenth century, nurses created and projected an image of themselves as ladylike women—pure, disciplined, responsible, and comforting—who were both "angels" and "soldiers of mercy." The influence of Christian religious orders in the pre-1850 history of nursing, of Florence Nightingale's military nursing experience during the Crimean War, and of Victorian, middle-class conceptions of womanhood, were all visible in these standardized uniforms. To this day (despite some of the modifications they have undergone, such as the introduction of white pants suits, more touches of color, and greater casualness about caps), nurses' uniforms incorporate and convey the same symbolic elements.

The Florence Nightingale Pledge, administered at capping and graduation ceremonies, is the nursing profession's equivalent of the Hippocratic and Maimonides Oaths taken by doctors. Like physicians, nurses solemnly promise to devote themselves to patients, to refrain from administering harmful drugs, to live up to the highest technical and moral standards of their profession, and to maintain professional confidentiality. But unlike physicians, until recently nurses also have pledged to live their lives in personal as well as professional "purity," and to faithfully assist doctors.

The kind of emphasis that nurses have accorded to practical skills, to personal values and virtues, to serving the hospital, and to obediently aiding the doctor stands in sharp contrast to the more intellectual, scientific, and technological orientation of the medical profession, its captain-of-the-ship conception of authority and responsibility, and its claims to autonomy. These differences in outlook reflect both the gender and the professional status differences between nursing and medicine.

Over the course of the twentieth century, and especially during the past few decades, American nursing has moved progressively away from some of the key attributes of its Nightingale cultural tradition, and in the direction of greater professionalization. Oelsen and Whittaker point out that this evolutionary trend has been relatively slow, not as deliberate as some nursing history accounts present it, and accompanied all the way by considerable ambivalence and conflicts.[86]

Gradually, diploma schools of nursing have been asserting and achieving a greater degree of independence from the hospitals to which they are attached—financially, administratively, educationally, and with respect to the nursing services that their faculty and students are expected to provide in the hospital. Although the applied, practicum aspects of nursing are still an important part of the training that students receive in these schools, much more basic science, theoretical material, and empirical knowledge that is not primarily skill-oriented has been introduced into the curriculum. The maternalistic and moralistic supervision by the school of all aspects of students' lives has been significantly reduced. Students' personal and interpersonal qualities continue to be emphasized (far more than in schools of medicine) and defined as central to the distinctive work of nurses and its intellectual, technical, and moral excellence. But increasingly, the tendency is for these dimensions of the nurse's role to be expressed in social science-influenced terms (personality attributes, interpersonal relations, group processes, and so forth), rather than in the form of ethical injunctions.

This evolutionary change in diploma schools has been accompanied by another development that has run parallel to it in certain respects, and in others has challenged the predominance and even the continuing appropriateness of such hospital school training. The education of nurses has moved progressively into college and university settings. Nathan Glazer suggests that this is part of a larger phenomenon: the trend over the last thirty years for a series of "minor professions" (such as social work, education, journalism, library science and administration, and urban planning) to seek to elevate their status to equal that of the "learned professions," like medicine and the law, "through the establishment of a basis in scientific knowledge and incorporation into a university."[87] For nursing, a benchmark event in this process was the publication of the position paper on education for nursing, prepared by the American Nurses' Association (ANA) Committee on Education and adopted by the ANA Board of Directors in September 1965:

> The education for all those who are licensed to practice nursing should take place in institutions of higher education [this paper declared]; minimum preparation for beginning professional nursing practice . . . should be Baccalaureate degree education in nursing . . . minimum preparation for beginning technical nursing practice . . . should be associate degree education in nursing; education for assistants in the health service occupations should be short, intensive, preservice programs in vocational education rather than on-the-job training. . . . [I]t is reasonable to expect that many diploma schools of nursing will participate with colleges and universities in planning for the development of baccalaureate programs; others will participate with junior colleges in planning for the development of associate degree programs.[88]

Since 1965, the trend in nursing education, away from diploma schools and toward colleges or universities, has accelerated. It is a development that has been especially threatening to nurses trained by diploma schools or affiliated with them, and a constant source of divisiveness in the nursing profession. Both the strong conviction that national nursing leaders feel about the necessity of at least a baccalaureate degree level education for the licensed registered nurse, and the tenacious resistance to the idea on the part of certain groups of nurses (along with many physicians, hospital administrators, and lay persons) are "audible" in the content and tone of the following recommendation by a prominent university nursing school dean:

> . . . the question of entry level education for nurses must be addressed in a planned and logical manner. The recommendation that the baccalaureate degree should be the entry level requirement for registered nurse licensure, with "grandparenting" of present license holders, is an idea long overdue. A planned phase-out of hospital schools must occur in the next few years. Most of the problems we presently face have been exacerbated by the unwillingness of nurses,

physicians, administrators, and the public to address this subject in a rational manner. As my viewpoint as a nurse educator may be seen as suspect, however, facts supporting this position may be enumerated briefly. To maintain continuity of employment, nurses require a career orientation rather than job training. Their education must provide possibilities for upward mobility. The patient public requires nurses able to synthesize knowledge from the physical and social sciences and act assertively on its behalf. Status problems affecting the present and future supply of nurses cannot be solved by the prebaccalaurate structure. Expanded role requirements in and out of hospitals can be prepared for at no less than the baccalaureate level. Hospital school graduates' participation in the nursing labor force is less than at any other educational level, and the present covert cost to the consumer of hospital school programs through third party support adds to hospitalization costs.[89]

In spite of persisting tension between diploma and university schools of nursing, and what sometimes seems to nursing leaders to be the "one step forward, followed by one step backward"[90] pattern in which nursing has dealt with this issue, especially in the past ten years, the preparation of nurses has undergone remarkable changes in the direction of a more liberal, intellectual, "higher" education.

[Since 1977] there has been a significant decline in the percentage of nurses whose basic educational preparation and whose highest educational preparation was a diploma in nursing. Among those employed in nursing the percentage of those whose basic preparation was in a diploma program declined from 71.4% to 59.6%. This was offset by increases in the percentage of nurses with associate degree and baccalaureate basic preparation, with the greatest rate of increase in those with associate degree preparation—from 13.7% to 21.2%. . . .

[T]he diploma graduates among the registered nurse population are on the average considerably older than the graduates from the other basic nursing educational programs. The median age of the diploma graduates was 44 years as compared to 31.5 years for the associate degree graduates and 30.2 years for the baccalaureate graduates, which provides additional evidence of the effect of the movement away from the diploma program to associate degree and baccalaureate programs as the entry into nursing. These data also suggest that the large decrease between 1977 and 1980 in the percentage of registered nurses coming from diploma programs will continue into the future. . . .

When all the formal academic nursing-related education of registered nurses is considered, it is seen that nearly three nurses out of every ten who were employed in nursing in 1980 had attained a baccalaureate or higher degree. In 1980 the *number* of employed nurses who held at least a baccalaureate degree was nearly 130,000 greater than in 1977. The 3-year increase in the number alone is equal to the *total* number of employed nurses who held a baccalaureate degree or higher in 1972. In 1952, the earliest year for which data on the educational preparation of nurses are available, fewer than one nurse in ten had a baccalaureate or higher degree.[91]

In turn, these trends in nursing education provided the preconditions and the impetus for the development of a new clinical role for nurses in ambulatory clinical care—that of the nurse practitioner. The first nurse practitioner program was initiated in 1965 at the University of Colorado, as a Commonwealth Fund-sponsored demonstration program designed to train nurses to give comprehensive well-child care in ambulatory settings, and to study the program's implications for an expanded, more autonomous, health care delivery-oriented definition of the nurse's role. In its original conception, the nurse practitioner combined elements from public health and pediatric nurse specialist roles.

The nurse practitioner experiment was supported initially by private foundations. In the 1970s, the federal government entered the picture with substantial funding, justifying their expenditures on the basis of what was then considered to be a shortage and geographical maldistribution of physicians. Numerous other programs were established to train a wider range of nurse practitioners, such as family, adult, school, obstetrics/gynecology, psychiatric, geriatric, and perinatal nurse practitioners. By 1979 an estimated 20,000 nurse practitioners had been trained in 104 master's programs and 133 continuing education programs, 90 percent of whom were practicing.[92] "The evolution of the nurse practitioner concept has . . . opened new, intellectually challenging career options for nurses outside of the restraining bureaucracy of the hospital, encouraged closer collaborative relationships with physicians, and developed new types of ongoing relationships between nurses and the public."[93] But in this era of a supposedly mounting oversupply of physicians, nurse practitioners are economically and politically embattled. They do not receive third party reimbursement, even by federal programs. They often find themselves in "confrontation with physicians in office-based practice who are concerned about declining office visits."

> There appears to be a growing backlash against nurse practitioners that is primarily economic in nature. Although the federal government has established antitrust laws to protect the rights of individuals or groups to pursue their chosen work, these laws will not preempt state nurse practice acts.[94]

There are many, including the founders of the nurse practitioner movement and its early nurse and physician participants who believe that nurse practitioners are a "potentially endangered species"[95] at this historical juncture. Nurse practitioners, their proponents feel, will have trouble surviving unless, in concert with the larger nursing profession, they develop their own "personal, institutional, and professional organization strategies to create an active (rather than reactive), funded, and well-oiled political machine."[96]

GIVING VOICE TO THE CULTURE OF NURSING

Finally, there is a less obtrusive way in which a small but significant group of the estimated .02 percent nurses who hold the doctoral degree[97] are currently working to identify, describe, and communicate "the uniqueness and richness" of what is "embedded in expert clinical nursing practice" that imbues it with "excellence and power."[98] In effect, these nurse-scholars are exploring and seeking to articulate the particular attributes of the "culture of caring" that constitute the essence of nursing: its practical and theoretical knowledge, values, beliefs, symbols, and patterns of ritual. One of the major thrusts of this undertaking entails breaking through what is regarded as the excessively "masculine" ethos of biomedicine, in ways that are intended to enlarge and humanize its perspective and enhance its healing expertise. Certain attributes of clinical nursing are emphasized and advocated in this connection: intuitive and holistic ways of knowing, cue sensitivity and other perceptual skills, creative searching, discretionary judgment, meaningful engagement in the clinical situation, and a feeling of identification with and relatedness to patients.[99] What is involved here is not only the "uncovering" of these qualities of effective and caring nursing, but also a move to document and further legitimize them. The goals are to improve and promote nursing and some of the culturally "feminine" conceptions on which its distinctive identity and "power" are declared to be based. From this development, outstanding "thickly descriptive" clinical ethnographies of the professional world and work of nursing are beginning to be written by nurses trained in social science that promise to enrich sociology and anthropology, as well as nursing itself.[100]

NOTES

1. Among the notable recently published books that break through these limited general characteristics of the sociological literature on the health professions are: Patricia Benner, *From Novice to Expert: Excellence and Power in Clinical Nursing Practice* (Menlo Park, Calif.: Addison-Wesley Publishing Company, Inc., 1984); Jonathan B. Imber, *Abortion and the Private Practice of Medicine* (New Haven: Yale University Press, 1986); Carole Joffe, *The Regulation of Sexuality: Experiences of Family Planning Workers* (Philadelphia: Temple University Press, 1986); and Toba Schwaber Kerson, *Medical Social Work: The Pre-Professional Paradox* (New York: Irvington Publishers, Inc., 1981).

2. Eliot Freidson, *Professional Powers: A Study of the Institutionalization of Formal Knowledge* (Chicago: The University of Chicago Press, 1986), p. 30. The reference contained in this quoted passage is to: A. Flexner, "Is Social Work a Profession?" *School and Society*, 1 (1915), 901–11.

3. Ibid., p. 30.

4. This perspective has much in common with the questions raised about the objective reality of disease by numerous social scientists and social critics in the 1960s and early 1970s. These scholars "emphasized that there is no simple and necessary relation between diseases in their biological and social dimensions," historian of medicine Charles E. Rosenberg explains. "Some ills have a well-understood physical basis; others, none that can be demonstrated. Meaning is not necessary but negotiated, the argument follows; disease is constructed not discovered. . . . Medical knowledge is not value-free to such skeptics but, at least in part, a socially constructed and determined belief system, a reflection of arbitrary social arrangements, social need, and the distribution of power. . . . This relativist point of view has sought to undermine not only the apparent objectivity of particular disease entities, but by implication, the legitimacy of the social authority wielded by the medical profession, which has traditionally articulated and administered these diagnostic categories." [Charles E. Rosenberg, "Disease and Social Order in America: Perceptions and Expectations," *The Milbank Quarterly*, 64, Suppl. 1 (1986), 34–35.] In this connection, Rosenberg cites the works of Michel Foucault, Françoise Delaporte, *Disease and Civilization: The Cholera in Paris, 1832* (Cambridge, Mass.: MIT Press, 1986), and Peter Wright and Andrew Treacher, eds., *The Problem of Medical Knowledge: Examining the Social Construction of Medicine* (Edinburgh: University of Edinburgh Press, 1982).

5. See, for example, Magali Sarfatti Larson, *The Rise of Professionalism: A Sociological Analysis* (Berkeley: University of California Press, 1977).

6. Freidson, *Professional Powers*, pp. 28–29.

7. See, for example, Jeffrey L. Berland, *Profession and Monopoly* (Berkeley: University of California Press, 1975); Peter Conrad and J. W. Schneider, *Deviance and Medicalization: From Badness to Sickness* (St. Louis: C. V. Mosby Company, 1980); Ivan Illich, *Medical Nemesis: The Expropriation of Health* (New York: Pantheon Books, 1976); Ivan Illich, *Toward A History of Needs* (New York: Bantam Books, 1980); Irving K. Zola, "Medicine as an Institution of Social Control," *Sociological Review*, 20, no. 4 n.s. (November 1972), 487–504.

8. Andrew Abbott, "Professions in America" (Review of Eliot Freidson's *Professional Powers*), *Science*, 234 (November 7, 1986), 766.

9. Eliot Freidson, *Professional Dominance: The Social Structure of Medical Care* (Chicago: Atherton Press, 1970).

10. Eliot Freidson, "The Reorganization of the Medical Profession," *Medical Care Review*, 42, no. 1 (Spring 1985), 13.

11. Freidson, *Professional Powers*, pp. 109–30 (Chap. 6); and also "The Reorganization of the Medical Profession."

12. See, for example, Marie B. Haug, "Deprofessionalization: An Alternate Hypothesis for the Future," *Sociological Review Monograph*, no. 20 (1973), 195–211; Marie B. Haug, "The Deprofessionalization of Everyone?" *Sociological Focus* (August 1975), 197–213; Marie B. Haug, "Computer Technology and the Obsolescence of the Concept of Profession," in *Work and Technology*, eds. Marie B. Haug and Jacques Dofny (Beverly Hills, Calif.: Sage Publications, 1977), 215–28.

13. See, for example, Larson, *The Rise of Professionalism*; Magali Sarfatti Larson, "Professionalism: Rise and Fall," *International Journal of Health Services*, 9 (1979), 607–27; Magali Sarfatti Larson, "Proletarianization and Educated Labor," *Theory and Society*, 9, no. 1 (January 1980), 131–75; Martin Oppenheimer, "The Proletarianization of the Professional," *Sociological Review Monograph*, no. 20 (1973), 213–27.

14. In his most recent work, *Professional Powers*, Freidson formulates his own perspectives on the "reality" and "power" of professions in a way that reconciles these different points of view for him and that stands apart from them. He uses "the idea of profession" as a "historic rather than an abstract, analytic concept," designating it a "folk concept"—a specifically American (and also English) "social category for distinguishing a group of occupations." (See especially pp. xii, and 35–36.)

15. David Mechanic and Linda H. Aiken, "A Cooperative Agenda for Medicine and Nursing," in David Mechanic, *From Advocacy to Allocation: The Evolving American Health Care System* (New York: The Free Press, 1986), p. 153.

16. In addition to the references cited in the previous notes, the following works significantly contributed to this section: Bernard Barber, "Some Problems in the Sociology of the Professions," *Daedalus*, 92, no. 4 (Fall 1963), 669–88; Bernard Barber, John J. Lally, Julia Loughlin Makarushka, and Daniel Sullivan, *Research on Human Subjects: Problems of Social Control in Medical Experimentation* (New York: Russell Sage Foundation, 1973); Bernard Barber, *The Logic and Limits of Trust* (New Brunswick, N.J.: Rutgers University Press, 1983); Howard S. Becker, "The Nature of a Profession," in *Education for the Professions*, ed. Nelson B. Henry (Chicago: National Society for the Study of Education, 1962), pp. 24–46; Howard S. Becker, *Sociological Work: Method and Substance* (Chicago: Aldine Pub. Co., 1970); Charles L. Bosk, *Forgive and Remember: Managing Medical Failure* (Chicago: University of Chicago Press, 1979); Rue Bucher and Anselm Strauss, "Professions in Progress," *American Journal of Sociology*, 66, no. 4 (January 1961), 325–34; Rue Bucher and Joan G. Stelling, "Characteristics of Professional Organizations," *Journal of Health and Social Behavior*, 10, no. 1 (March 1969), 3–15; Rue Bucher and Joan G. Stelling, *Becoming Professional* (Beverly Hills, Calif.: Sage Publications, 1977); A. M. Carr-Saunders and P. A. Wilson, *The Professions* (Oxford: The Clarendon Press, 1933); Amitai Etzioni, ed., *The Semi-Professions and Their Organization* (New York: Free Press, 1963); Eliot Freidson, *Profession of Medicine: A Study of the Sociology of Applied Knowledge* (New York: Dodd, Mead & Company, 1970); Eliot Freidson, "Professionals and the Occupational Principle," in *The Professions and Their Prospects*, ed., Eliot Freidson (Beverly Hills, Calif.: Sage Publications, 1973), pp. 19–38; Eliot Freidson, *Doctoring Together: A Study of Professional Social Control* (New York: Elsevier, 1975); Nathan Glazer, "The Schools of the Minor Professions," *Minerva*, XII, no. 3 (July 1974), 346–64; William J. Goode, "Encroachment, Charlatanism, and the Emerging Profession: Psychology, Sociology, and Medicine," *American Sociological Review*, 25, no. 6 (December 1960), 902–14; Mary E. W. Goss, "Influence and Authority Among Physicians in an Outpatient Clinic," *American Sociological Review*, 26, no. 1 (February 1961), 39–50; James M. Gustafson, "Professions as 'Callings,'" *Social Service Review*, 56, no. 4 (December 1982), 501–15; Everett C. Hughes, "Professions," *Daedalus*, 92, no. 4 (Fall 1963), 655–88; Everett C. Hughes, *The Sociological Eye: Selected Papers* (Chicago: Aldine-Atherton, 1971); Talcott Parsons, "The Professions and Social Structure," in Talcott Parsons, *Essays in Sociological Theory*, 2nd ed., rev. (Glencoe, Ill.: The Free Press, 1954), 34–49 [originally published in *Social Forces*, 17 (1939), 457–67]; Talcott Parsons, *The Social System* (Glencoe, Ill.: The Free Press, 1951), Chap. X; Talcott Parsons, "Research with Human Subjects and the 'Professional Complex'," in *Experimentation with Human Subjects*, ed. Paul A.

Freund (New York: George Braziller, 1970), pp. 116–151; Talcott Parsons and Gerald M. Platt, *The American University* (Cambridge, Mass.: Harvard University Press, 1973), especially Chaps V and VI; Talcott Parsons, "Health and Disease: A Sociological and Action Perspective," in Talcott Parsons, *Action Theory and the Human Condition* (New York: The Free Press, 1978), pp. 66–81 [revised version of the article appearing in *Encyclopedia of Bioethics*, 2 (1978), 590–99]; Wilbert E. Moore, *The Professions: Roles and Rules* (New York: Russell Sage Foundation, 1970); Eviatar Zerubavel, *Patterns of Time in Hospital Life: A Sociological Perspective* (Chicago: University of Chicago Press, 1979).

17. Talcott Parsons, "Professions," *International Encyclopedia of the Social Sciences*, 12 (1968), 536.
18. Ibid.
19. Freidson, *Professional Powers*, passim.
20. Parsons, "Professions," p. 536.
21. Parsons has pointed out that whereas in the English-speaking world, especially in the United States, the tendency has been for both teaching and research to be centered in the universities, in "continental Europe, especially the communist countries, the research function has more frequently been institutionalized in separate organizations usually called academies of science" (Parsons, "Professions," p. 536).
22. See the discussion of this facet of the "technical competence gap" between doctor and patient in Chapter 1, pp. 25–26.
23. Renée C. Fox, "Training for Uncertainty," in *The Student-Physician: Introductory Studies in the Sociology of Medical Education*, eds. Robert K. Merton, George C. Reader, and Patricia Kendall (Cambridge, Mass.: Harvard University Press, 1957), 207–41.
24. Gustafson, "Professions as 'Callings,'" p. 510. In the last portion of this quoted passage, Gustafson refers to what I have called "training for detached concern." See Harold I. Lief and Renée C. Fox, "Training for 'Detached Concern' in Medical Students," in *The Psychological Basis of Medical Practice*, eds. Harold I. Lief, Victor F. Lief, and Nina R. Lief (New York: Harper & Row, 1963), pp. 12–35. The concept of "detached concern" and the set of professional attitudes to which it refers will be discussed more fully in Chapter 3.
25. Gustafson, "Professions as 'Callings'," pp. 510 and 514.
26. Ibid., pp. 512–13.
27. Gustafson, "Professions as 'Callings,'" pp. 512–13.
28. Steven L. Dubovsky, "Coping with Entitlement in Medical Education," *New England Journal of Medicine*, 315, no. 26 (December 25, 1986), 1672–74.
29. This phrase is excerpted from the Declaration of Geneva of the World Medical Association. In the 1970s, some of the graduating classes of Stanford University Medical School chose to take their professional oath in the form of a version of the declaration that they modified for the occasion, rather than the more traditional Hippocratic or Maimonides oaths.
30. Freidson, *Professional Powers*, p. 64.
31. Ibid., p. 92.
32. Ibid.
33. Ibid., especially Chap. 8, "Professional Powers in Work Organizations." Freidson points out, however, that there is a structural paradox in the professional control of work in an organization. "Professional employees do have genuine privilege in being able to exercise considerable discretion in their work," he writes. "They are, furthermore, to a variable degree sheltered by a credential system. But they must do their work in circumstances that are shaped by the structure of the organization in which they work and by the resources made available to them by others" (p. 155).
34. Charles L. Bosk, "Social Controls and Physicians: The Oscillation of Cynicism and Idealism in Sociological Theory," in *Social Controls and the Medical Profession*, eds. Judith P. Swazey and Stephen R. Scher (Boston: Oelgeschlager, Gunn & Hain, Publishers, Inc., 1985), p. 43.
35. Charles L. Bosk, "Occupational Rituals in Patient Management," *New England Journal of Medicine*, 303, no. 2 (July 10, 1980), 71–76.
36. Barber and others, *Research on Human Subjects*, pp. 187–88.
37. Judith P. Swazey and Renée C. Fox, "Medical Sociology: The Profession and the Sociological Perspective," *Journal of the American Medical Association*, 247, no. 21 (June 4, 1982), 2960.
38. Council on Long-Range Planning and Development, American Medical Association, "Health Care in Transition: Consequences for Young Physicians," *Journal of the American Medical Association*, 256, no. 24 (December 26, 1986), 3387.
39. Freidson, "The Reorganization of the Medical Profession," p. 11.

40. Rashi Fein, *Medical Care, Medical Costs: The Search for a Health Insurance Policy* (Cambridge, Mass.: Harvard University Press, 1986), p. 2.
41. Association of American Medical Colleges, "Medical Education: Institutions, Characteristics and Programs: A Background Paper," September 1986, p. 1.
42. Ibid., p. 3.
43. Ibid., p. 4.
44. Ibid.
45. Arnold S. Relman, "Here Come the Women," *New England Journal of Medicine* (Editorial), 302, no. 22 (May 29, 1980), 1252–53.
46. Association of American Medical Colleges, "Medical Education," p. 4.
47. "AMA Insights," *Journal of the American Medical Association*, 256, no. 20 (November 28, 1986), 2805.
48. Association of American Medical Colleges, "Medical Education," p. 4.
49. Ibid.
50. Ibid.
51. Ibid.
52. John Walsh, "The M.D. Class of '86: Smaller, Deeper in Debt," *Science* (News & Comment Section), 234 (October 3, 1986), 21. Walsh is summarizing data collected by the AAMC.
53. These figures, derived from a forecast by The Graduate Medical Education National Advisory Committee, published in 1980, have been "criticized for conceptual and methodological reasons." They are cited with that caveat in Council on Long-Range Planning and Development, American Medical Association, "Health Care in Transition," p. 3387.
54. "In 1985, 97 percent of the graduates from U.S. medical schools entered residency programs; 86 percent intended to complete the education and training required for certification by a specialty certifying board." Association of American Medical Colleges, "Medical Education," p. 8.
55. Ibid., p. 9.
56. This is a reference to Abraham Flexner's *Medical Education in the United States and Canada* (New York: The Carnegie Foundation, 1910), the renowned "Flexner Report," which symbolically as well as historically and substantively ushered in the era of "scientific medicine" in American medical schools.
57. "Medicine's Star Wars: Will Doctoring Survive the Computer?" *The New Physician*, 28, no. 4 (April 1979), 22–24. Speech delivered by Fitzhugh Mullan, M.D., at the Convocation of the Class of 1978, College of Medicine, University of Arizona, May 19, 1978. Reprinted by permission of the author.
58. Fitzhugh Mullan, *White Coat, Clenched Fist: The Political Education of an American Physician* (New York: Macmillan Publishing Co., Inc., 1976), pp. x–xi.
59. Fitzhugh Mullan, "Medicine's Star Wars."
60. Oliver Sacks, *The Man Who Mistook His Wife for a Hat, and Other Clinical Tales* (New York: Summit Books, 1985), pp. xiii–xiv.
61. Renée C. Fox, "The Human Condition of Health Professionals," Distinguished Lecturer Series, School of Health Studies (Durham: University of New Hampshire, 1980), p. 12.
62. From a quoted statement by Woody Allen in Joseph Berger, "Some Films Are Finding Saints as Compelling as Sinners," *New York Times*, January 4, 1987 (Section 2), p. 6.
63. Renée C. Fox, "Components of Physicianly Competence," in *Social Controls and the Medical Profession*, eds. Judith P. Swazey and Stephen R. Scher (Boston: Oelgeschlager, Gunn & Hain, Publishers, Inc., 1985), pp. 228–29.
64. Gustafson, "Professions as 'Callings,'" p. 514.
65. Donald Konold, "Codes of Medical Ethics: History," *Encyclopedia of Bioethics*, 1 (1978), 162.
66. This prayer was formerly attributed to physician-philosopher Moses Maimonides, but is now believed to have been composed by another Jewish physician, Marcus Herz.
67. Konold, "Codes of Medical Ethics: History," 162–71; and Robert M. Veatch, "Professional Ethics: New Principles for Physicians," *Hastings Center Report*, 10, no. 3 (June 1980), 16–19.
68. Walter I. Wardwell, "The Future of Chiropractic" (Sounding Board), *New England Journal of Medicine*, 302, no. 12 (March 20, 1980), 688–90.
69. Veatch, "Professional Ethics," p. 18.
70. Ibid., p. 16.
71. Jay Katz, *The Silent World of Doctor and Patient* (New York: The Free Press, 1984), p. xvii.

72. Draft of a final report on the design for a two-year study of nursing and nursing education (Washington, D.C.: Institute of Medicine, National Academy of Sciences, 1980), p. 5.

73. Mechanic and Aiken, "A Cooperative Agenda for Medicine and Nursing," pp. 153–54. Reprinted with permission of The Free Press, a Division of Macmillan, Inc. Copyright © 1986 by The Free Press.

74. Freidson, *Professional Powers*, p. 58.

75. Ibid., p. 165.

76. Mechanic and Aiken, "A Cooperative Agenda for Medicine and Nursing," pp. 154–55.

77. Ibid., p. 155.

78. Ibid.

79. E. Charlotte Theis, "Ethical Issues: A Nursing Perspective," *New England Journal of Medicine*, 315, no. 19 (November 6, 1986), 1223. See *American Nurses' Association Code for Nurses, With Interpretive Statements* (Kansas City, Mo.: American Nurses' Association, 1985).

80. Anthony Rostain, "Deciding to Forgo Life-Sustaining Treatment in the Intensive Care Nursery: A Sociologic Account," *Perspectives in Biology and Medicine*, 30, no. 1 (Autumn 1986), 120–21.

81. Theis, "Ethical Issues: A Nursing Perspective," p. 1223.

82. Ibid.

83. *State Approved Schools of Nursing—R. N.* (New York: National League for Nursing, Annual Editions, 1965–1979).

84. Virginia L. Olesen and Elvi W. Whittaker, *The Silent Dialogue: A Study in the Social Psychology of Professional Socialization* (San Francisco: Jossey-Bass, 1968), p. 59. See Chapter II for an excellent sociohistorical treatment of the diploma-to-collegiate-school evolution of American nursing.

85. Quoted in Philip A. Kalisch and Beatrice J. Kalisch, *The Advance of American Nursing* (Boston: Little, Brown, 1978), p. 38.

86. Oleson and Whittaker, *The Silent Dialogue*, pp. 69–70.

87. Glazer, "The Schools of the Minor Professions," pp. 346–74.

88. "American Nurses' Association's First Position on Education for Nursing," *American Journal of Nursing*, 65 (December 1965), 106–11.

89. Claire M. Fagin, "The National Shortage of Nurses: A Nursing Perspective," in *Nursing in the 1980s: Crisis, Opportunities, Challenges*, eds. Linda A. Aiken and Susan R. Gortner (Philadelphia: J. B. Lippincott Company, 1982), p. 36.

90. Personal communication, Dr. Rheba de Tornyay, Dean, University of Washington, Seattle, School of Nursing, October 9, 1980.

91. Eugene Levine and Evelyn B. Moses, "Registered Nurses Today: A Statistical Profile," in *Nursing in the 1980s*, pp. 481–82. The data represented in this statistical profile are derived from 1977 and 1980 sample surveys of registered nurses. The 1977 survey was conducted by the American Nurses' Association, and the 1980 survey by Research Triangle Institute. The selection of the sample and the estimation of universe parameters were the same in both.

92. Loretta G. Ford, "Nurse Practitioners: History of a New Idea and Predictions for the Future," in *Nursing in the 1980s*, p. 243. (Loretta Ford is a nurse-founder of the nurse practitioner movement.)

93. Linda H. Aiken, "The Impact of Federal Health Policy on Nurses," in *Nursing in the 1980s*, p. 17.

94. Ibid.

95. Charles E. Lewis, "Nurse Practitioners and the Physician Surplus," in *Nursing in the 1980s*, p. 264. (Charles Lewis is a physician and professor of medicine who conducted the first randomized clinical trial of nurse practitioners in the 1960s.)

96. Ford, "Nurse Practitioners," p. 245.

97. Fagin, "The National Shortage of Nurses," p. 33.

98. Benner, *From Novice to Expert*, p. 2 and passim.

99. These attributes are identified and discussed in detail in Benner, *From Novice to Expert*, a book based on "descriptive research" through "a dialogue with nurses and nursing," that has played an important role in the developments I am discussing here and has become an authoritative text in the field.

100. See, for example, Zane Robinson Wolf, *Nurses' Work, the Sacred and the Profane* (Philadelphia: University of Pennsylvania Press, 1988).

CHAPTER 3

THE EDUCATION, TRAINING, AND SOCIALIZATION OF PHYSICIANS: MEDICAL SCHOOL

THE STATE OF THE LITERATURE

In the continually expanding social scientific literature on adult socialization, the process of becoming a medical professional, especially the "formation" of medical students and young physicians, has been a center of interest and concern. Interest in the education, training, and socialization of medical professionals was especially notable in the 1950s and early 1960s, when a number of landmark studies of medical socialization were undertaken by social scientists (psychologists and psychiatrists, as well as sociologists), encouraged by medical educators, and initiated and supported by certain foundations.[1] Publications based on this research continue to appear, and reference is frequently made to the concepts, methods, and findings of these studies in a variety of social scientific contexts.

However, from the mid-1960s into the 1980s, with some notable exceptions, a waning of such research has occurred. Sociologists dealing with adult socialization have turned their attention away from the making of a professional toward consideration of the stages in the human life cycle. The phenomenon of "mid-life crisis" and the process of aging are among the chief foci of these newer socialization studies.[2]

Why the relative decline of work on professional socialization has occurred is a study in itself, related not only to the current status, orientation and atmosphere of the social sciences, medicine, and various other professions, but also to larger societal trends.[3] The aging of social scientists along with the general population has contributed to the current preoccupation with middle- and old-age phases in the life cycle. Furthermore, some of the sociologists of professions and of medicine who have deflected their attention from studies of physicians have done so with a post-1960s conviction that socialization studies are not as significant, intellectually and scientifically, or as relevant to social criticism, policy, and change as research that deals primarily with economic, political, technological, organizational, and social stratification variables. As Samuel W. Bloom points out, beginning in the 1970s sociologists studying and writing about medical education changed their primary focus from interest in the psychosocial development of physicians-in-training to

> scrutiny of the bureaucratic nature of the organization of the modern medical center. . . . [T]he socializing agency as a social institution [became] the center of inquiry rather than the socializee. . . . Especially questions about power in the medical school—the analysis of power structure, decision making, and interorganizational relations in the . . . medical center—engaged sociological researchers.[4]

Foundations interested in medical education and care in the United States are now investing their resources in projects that deal with the cost, allocation, and regulation of medical care and its delivery; the prevention of illness and the maintenance of health; the health and medical care situations of particular groups in the population (among them the mentally ill, children, and the elderly); and ethical problems associated with advances in medical science and technology. Research on the men and women who do medical work, the socialization they have undergone, and the implications of this process for the technical and human quality of the care that they offer is not a part of foundations' current agendas.

Medical educators are concerned about many of the same issues that contributed to the physician socialization studies that they helped to foster in the past. These concerns and issues include the importance of developing values and attitudes in student-physicians "that promote caring and concern for the individual and for society" and the problem of teaching the psychological, social, cultural, and humanistic dimensions of health, illness, and medicine as effectively as biomedical knowledge and skills. They also involve the implementation of curriculum reforms that are appropriate remedies for these problems and deficiencies in the "general professional preparation of physicians whose practice environment and base knowledge in the next century will differ significantly from those of today." Medical educators express a sense of urgency about responding to these challenges, in order to prepare physicians for what they envision as a "twenty-first century" of far-reaching demographic, organizational, economic, and social change in the practice of medicine, as well as accelerating scientific and technological advance.[5] But despite their intense involvement in these socialization-relevant matters, medical educators are no longer inclined to invite sociological studies of becoming a physician, or of the curriculum changes and innovations they have initiated, as their predecessors did thirty years ago. Only occasionally do they "remember" that such studies were done in the past, or summon up findings from them that are pertinent to their present concerns. The data about medical education now being consistently collected are largely confined to demographic, manpower/womanpower, and academic history facts about medical school applicants and entrants and physicians in residency training.[6]

There is, then, a sharp discontinuity in the literature on the education, training, and socialization of medical professionals. As a consequence, there is much more detailed sociological information about medical schools, medical students and house staff (interns and residents) in the 1950s and early 1960s than in subsequent decades. This is especially problematic because of the significant amount of social and cultural change that has occurred since the 1960s in the milieu of medical education, the state of the medical profession, and in the outlook of the young men and women studying medicine. Daniel H. Funkenstein, the late Professor of Psychiatry and Consultant on Admissions at Harvard Medical School, characterized medical education as passing from the Scientific Era (1959–1968), to the Student Activism Era (1969–1970), into the Doldrums Era (1971–1974), and from there to the Primary Care and Increasing Government Control Era (1975–).[7] Whether or not one agrees with the time intervals and the specific characteristics of the successive periods that Funkenstein identified,[8] what is irrefutable is his claim that:

> During each of these eras, the social responsibility, the expectations of society toward physicians, the assignment of priorities in medicine, and the funding of careers changed. These changes had profound effects on the career choices of graduating physicians and were caused largely because of societal factors.[9]

There are also conspicuous gaps in the focus and content of the medical socialization research that has been undertaken and published. To begin with, as will be discussed in Chapter 4, there is a dearth of studies concerned with the socialization of physicians after their medical school and residency years. Little is known about what alterations occur in doctors' attitudes and feelings, values and beliefs, in their habits of mind and understanding, and in the way that they behave in practice, in different stages of their professional and personal life cycles. There is a substantial body of articles concerned with practicing physicians who are "impaired" (authored mainly by physicians, chiefly psychiatrists) that have appeared in medical journals over the past fifteen years.[10] However, these articles deal mainly with such extreme forms of impairment as alcoholism, drug abuse, depression, and suicidal tendencies, within a framework of analysis that only occasionally makes reference to "the distinctive . . . human condition content of medical work; what [physicians] experience in caring for patients; the particular stresses to which they are subject; the means they adopt and do not adopt for handling the stresses; . . . and what the consequences of their stress and coping patterns"[11] may be for their state of well-being and capacity to doctor.

Several other gaps exist in the literature on the socialization of health care professionals. Although the over one million practicing nurses in the United States outnumber the some 500,000 active physicians by more than two to one, relatively few published studies of their professional development exist. The two most renowned book-length analyses of the socialization of nurses are Virginia L. Olesen and Elvi W. Whittaker's *The Silent Dialogue* (1968) and Ida H. Simpson's *From Student to Nurse* (1979). They stand virtually alone. In fact, social scientists have studied the socialization of physicians almost to the exclusion of that of all other health professionals (physical and occupational therapists, medical social workers, dentists, pharmacists, and x-ray and laboratory technicians, among others).

The research on medical socialization that has been conducted is mainly concentrated on male medical students and house staff. This is partly due to the fact that when the key medical socialization research was done before the 1970s, women constituted only 9 percent of the entering medical school classes. Moreover, the social scientists who designed and carried out socialization research did not consider women in medical training sufficiently consequential or different from male students to take any special notice of them. Some studies of women medical students, interns, and residents are currently in process; however, they have not yet resulted in major publications.

The scarcity of studies on becoming a physician in schools other than American medical schools and teaching hospitals constitutes another gap in the social scientific work that has been done on medical socialization. The narrow scope of this research is a consequence both of the predominance of American sociologists in the field of medical sociology and of their unrecognized cultural provincialism. The only full-scale sociological work on becoming a physician in a society other than the United States is Judith T. Shuval's *Entering Medicine* (1980), a seven-year study of medical education in the Hebrew University and Tel Aviv Medical Schools of Israel. Despite the fact that Shuval identifies a number of distinctively Israeli characteristics of the medical schools, students, and educational/socialization processes that she examines, her book is culturally and cross-culturally thin. This is due not only to the fact that, as Shuval herself says, the curricular content of medical education in Israel, along with its dominant value system, are oriented to the United States, but also to her theoretical approach and research design, which draw heavily on American social science traditions.

Based primarily on the sociological literature, Chapters 3 and 4 present a descriptive analysis of the professional socialization of American physicians during their medical school years, their graduate or residency training, and, more briefly, during their years of practice. The substantial amount of data available for the 1950-1965 period will be supplemented by the more occasional sociological and other materials that exist for the late 1960s-80s and by my first-hand observations in medical educational milieux.[12] Some consideration of the continuing socialization of physicians during their years of practice also will be attempted.

The medical socialization processes, themes, and mechanisms that will be discussed in the greatest detail are the ones that receive the most attention in the literature. Notable among these are the attitude-learning sequences of "training for uncertainty" and limitation, "training for detached concern," and training in managing medical mistakes and medical failure. The "fate of idealism" and the propensity for cynicism among medical students and house staff, the "dehumanization" that they may undergo, and the forms of impersonality, structured silence, and evasion in communicating with patients (and with each other) that they may implicitly learn are the major thematic concerns invoked by social scientists. Sociologically and psychologically patterned silence, intellectualization and technicalization, detachment, medical humor, heroic activism, medical rituals, "scientific magic," and what Terry Mizrahi has identified as a "Get Rid of Patients (GROP) syndrome," are the ways of coping and coming to terms with the demands and stresses of impending physicianhood that are highlighted in the literature.[13]

BASIC CONCEPTS AND CONCEPTUAL ISSUES

When sociologists write about the socialization of physicians, they refer to the learning of attitudes, norms, self-images, values, beliefs, and behavior patterns, along with knowledge and skills, that are associated with becoming and being a doctor of medicine. Emphasis is placed on the part played by interaction with significant others, especially role models and reference groups. The learning process involved is generally depicted as one that teaches and enables physicians to fulfill their professional roles with relative competence and ease, and in ways that are compatible with social and cultural patterns that are latently as well as manifestly institutionalized in the medical profession. The socializing effect of medical school faculty, of senior residents and attending physicians in house staff training, of the peer group (the "little society," or subculture formed by medical students and by house officers), of nurses and other health personnel, and of certain landmark events and patients experienced en route to physicianhood have been especially emphasized by sociologists. Although they have taken note of the social backgrounds of medical students and physicians, by and large sociologists have not attempted to empirically document and systematically analyze whether, and in what ways, sex, social class, and ethnicity shape the attitudes, values, and aspirations that they bring to their medical training, or the differential impact that the process of becoming a doctor has upon them. The religious backgrounds and orientation of medical students, interns, and residents and what socialization-relevant import they might have are rarely mentioned.[14]

Sociologists, like most other observers of the medical educational process, including the men and women who undergo it, have been impressed by its powerful potential for altering the attitudes, values and beliefs, modes of thought, and behavior of the persons it trains. "The intensity and duration of medical education," says Charles L. Bosk, "marks it as one of the most distinctive forms of adult 'socialization' in our society, comparable only to what occurs at West Point . . . or in the seminary. Dissecting a cadaver, attending an autopsy, delivering a baby, witnessing a death—all are part of a unique set of tests, ordeals, and rituals designed to transform an ordinary person into a doctor."[15]

Although there is general consensus among sociologists about the intensity, duration, uniformity, and transforming impact of the medical socialization process, there is disagreement concerning its essential nature and the mechanisms, contexts, and sites chiefly responsible for its distinctive impact. One of the most basic differences in sociological perspective on this process is epitomized by the two major studies of becoming a physician that were conducted in the 1950s by the Columbia University Bureau of Applied Social Research (in the medical schools of Cornell University, the University of Pennsylvania, Western Reserve University, and the University of Colorado), and by the Sociology Department of the University of Chicago (at the University of Kansas School of Medicine).

Columbia University sociologists regarded the medical school as training "student-physicians," but University of Chicago sociologists saw it as training "boys in white."[16] The Columbia group was impressed with the extent to which the medical school years of training entailed "anticipatory socialization" for the role of physicians. In their view, the medical school curriculum and the experiences inherent in it made up an ordered continuum that progressively moved students toward physicianhood, attitudinally as well as scientifically and technically. In contrast, the Chicago group saw whatever socialization medical school effected as much more dissociated from becoming a physician. Rather, it seemed to them that the greater part of the training that students underwent entailed learning to adroitly play the student ("boy") role, so as to excel academically in ways that would enable them to master the vast amount of knowledge and the techniques they had to assimilate, earn them high grades and faculty evaluations, and make them eligible for the professionally critical award of a "good internship."

The differences between these two approaches to psychosocial learning that medical education entails were not confined to their contrasting conceptions of anticipatory socialization for being a physician and situational socialization for being a student. In several regards, the Columbia perspective on the socialization process attached greater importance to its latent content and influence than did the Chicago perspective. The attention of Chicago sociologists was focused on manifest learning experiences. These are interpreted in a highly rational and literal way, with particular attention to how much medical scientific knowledge and technical skill students had to acquire, their achievement-oriented competitiveness, the consequent stresses they faced, and the strategies they developed for coping and for keeping out of trouble with faculty. In this view, becoming a physician in more profound, less expedient senses was almost a luxury that had to be postponed until the hurdle of medical school was surmounted.

The Columbia sociologists did not ignore or minimize the magnitude of cognitive and technical learning that medical school education involved, but below its massive surface, they identified a sequence of experiences and layers of subliminal meaning common to students that had a powerful impact on them psychically and professionally. Among the deepest, most indelible of these shared experiences and meanings, they found, were those associated with what Fox has termed the "human condition" and "existential" aspects of medicine:

> Health, illness, and medical care are integrally connected with some of the most basic and the most transcendent aspects of the human condition. The conception of human beings; their birth, survival, and growth; their physical, emotional, and intellectual capacities and development; sexuality; aging, mortality, and death—the very quality of their lives—are core foci of health, illness, and medicine. . . .
>
> The experience of illness and the practice of medicine . . . summon up critical problems of meaning—fundamental questions about the "whys" of pain, suffering, accident, and *angst*; the limits of human life and death; and about their relationship to evil, sin, and injustice. . . .
>
> From the inception of their training and throughout their careers, . . . physicians are confronted with [these] implications of diagnosing, treating, and making prognoses about illness. Many of their encounters with patients entail primal physical activities that allow and oblige them to violate strong, even sacred, cultural taboos. . . . A paradoxical and potentially disturbing mix of the sacred and the profane is part of their work. . . . This kind of experience is epitomized in the anatomy laboratory and the autopsy room where medical . . . students learn about the structure and pathology of the human body by cutting into it and dissecting it. There they meet the mystery of life and the enigma of death in the form of a naked fellow human being who is laid out on a stainless steel table.[17]

Students did not often discuss their feelings about these dimensions of their medical school experiences or what they regarded as "milestone" events associated with them. But the "listening with a third ear" kind of participant observation that the Columbia fieldworkers conducted, the journals of their daily medical school activities, thoughts, and sentiments that a dozen students at Cornell agreed to keep for them, and the weekly sociological interviews with these student diarists all contained rich conscious and preconscious materials about the emotional and symbolic significance of these experiences and their rites-of-passage relationship to the progressive transformation of students into physicians.

Mature doctors' reactions to the details elicited by the Columbia sociologists also suggested that such cardinal events and their associations were enduringly imprinted in the collective memories and psyches of physicians. Even, and perhaps especially, certain sense-memories, like grasping the hand of the cadaver in the anatomy laboratory in order to dissect it or the characteristic organic odor of the body at autopsy—the "autopsy smell"—[18] were vividly recalled by physicians with something like the freshness and the feeling of a flash-back.[19]

The Chicago fieldworkers also obtained descriptive material regarding students' "strong feelings, fantasies," and the more latent, psychodynamic and sociodynamic processes that were a part of their socialization process. For example, they reported and analyzed a number of dreams about dissecting a cadaver in the anatomy laboratory. Even though the Chicago team had sufficient interest in such dreams to collect them, psychologist Daniel Levinson remarked, they consistently interpreted them "solely as a by-product of academic strain," in a way that was congruent with their self-limiting emphasis on more manifest aspects of "students' behavioral interaction and . . . their conscious ideas about the immediately impinging situation."[20]

In contrast to their Chicago colleagues, the Columbia sociologists also explored some of the latent respects in which the scientific and technical content of the medical school curriculum influenced the attitudes and outlook of medical students. They had a sociology of science interest in the modes of thought of the various medical scientific and clinical fields in which students were so intensively immersed, the current state of knowledge and non-knowledge of these branches of medicine, the techniques they employed, and the sociolinguistic characteristics of their scientific and technical vocabulary. They asked how these aspects of their training implicitly altered students' philosophical perspective on the human body and psyche, health and illness, and life and death in ways that affected their perspective on themselves and their patients and their relationships with colleagues, friends, and members of their families.

There was at least one other set of marked differences between the Chicago and Columbia approaches to the medical socialization process. The Chicago group—renowned for its interest in "disparities between aspirations and realities" in social life, its first-hand research on the sociology of deviance, and its insights into "cooling the mark" attitudes and behavior—found more evidence of these phenomena in the subculture of medical students than the Columbia group did. The Columbia study described the self-regulating "little society" of medical students as a straightforward, informal organization of peers that openly supported and reinforced values and norms that they and their faculty espoused. The social system formed by the students the Columbia team observed did not seem to have the same "undercover" characteristics portrayed by the Chicago sociologists. The Chicago group reported that their medical student world was one that presented a conformist public face to the faculty, while in private students not only collectively criticized some of the standards of excellence and etiquette, discipline, and self-discipline that the faculty expected them to meet, but also verbally advocated deviating from them.

Whether the dissimilarities in the Chicago and Columbia studies were more a reflection of the different conceptual and empirical assumptions that the two groups brought to their research or of differences in the environments of the medical schools that were the main sites of their fieldwork has not been resolved. Probably both sets of factors contributed to the disparities in the pictures of medical socialization that emerged from their inquiries. The University of Kansas School of Medicine studied by Chicago is a state-supported midwestern institution that had a relatively traditional curriculum and educational philosophy in the 1950s. Cornell University Medical College, where the greater part of the Columbia fieldwork was conducted, is a private Ivy League school that had a greater commitment than Kansas did to educational experimentation and innovation. In addition, as indicated, the contrasting premises, emphases, and angles of vision of the Chicago and Columbia schools of sociology varied sufficiently to account for some of the discrepancies in the ways that they perceived, reported, and interpreted the socialization of medical students. These medical education and socialization issues continue to be matters of academic debate and have also influenced the theoretical and methodological orientations of most subsequent studies of medical socialization.[21]

MEDICAL EDUCATION AND SOCIALIZATION IN THE 1950s

These differences notwithstanding, quite similar pictures of medical education and socialization in the 1950s emerged from the Chicago and Columbia studies. Students at medical schools throughout the country received their training under a system of modern medical education that had come to full maturity thirty years earlier. "By the 1920s," as physician-historian Kenneth Ludmerer has indicated, "the task of institution-building in [American] medical education had been completed":

> The new scientific and clinical subjects had been introduced at all the schools, as had the laboratory and clerkship. Permanent sources of financial support had been found; new laboratories had been constructed and equipped; teaching hospitals had been acquired; and an army of full-time faculty members had been assembled. In addition, state licensing laws . . . made certain that no proprietary school would be permitted to survive.[22]

Although American medical schools had grown "in size and bureaucracy," and had undergone periodic curriculum reforms, "these developments [were] only modifications of the existing system, not changes in the system itself. American medical education in its main outline [proved] remarkably durable."[23]

The medical curriculum of the 1950s was tightly and uniformly organized. It was arranged in what students referred to as a "lockstep" way, with little room for individual variation or choice. A sharp division existed between preclinical and clinical subjects and learning experiences. The first two years of training were unilaterally devoted to the preclinical or basic sciences: anatomy, physiology, biochemistry, pathology, pharmacology, and bacteriology, taught largely through formal lectures, voluminous texts, laboratory work with animals, the dissection of a human cadaver, participation in an autopsy, and the microscopic study of different types of animal and human tissue. Contact with live patients was sporadic and remote, largely confined to brief presentations to the entire medical school class by an instructor, generally to demonstrate some biological principle or phenomenon. It was not until the end of the second year, when students learned to take medical histories and conduct physical examinations in the physical diagnosis course, that they began to have more sustained and clinically oriented exposure to patients. The third year represented the "great crossing over" to the clinical phase of training. Both the third and the fourth years consisted mainly of a series of clinical clerkships on the in-patient services of the medical school's teaching hospitals (chiefly medicine, surgery, obstetrics, and pediatrics).

Students' collegial relationships to each other in the laboratory and clinical situations in which they worked unfolded within a structured set of arrangements that were as impersonally predetermined as the curriculum itself. By and large, medical students were alphabetically assigned to the small groups in which they performed most of their laboratory and clinical tasks: *A* s worked with *A* s, *Z* s with *Z* s, and so on.

The highly patterned, collective, and uniform nature of each phase of medical school training was reflected in students' characteristic dress and accoutrements.[24] Although they were not subject to any explicit dress code, students' self-presentation in each stage of their medical education was so similar that an observer could identify what year, and even what trimester they were in, by their attire and technical accessories. First-year students in the '50s tended to dress in long white laboratory coats, worn over khaki pants and sports shirts. They moved through the corridors of the medical school, arms laden with clipboards, notebooks, and atlas-like texts. In that era, when students spent all morning, Monday through Saturday, during the entire first year dissecting a cadaver in the anatomy laboratory, they emitted the faint but distinct odor of formaldehyde wherever they went. Toward the end of the second year, when they were beginning to see patients in physical diagnosis, students looked more freshly barbered, donned neckties and more formal (often grey flannel) trousers, and self-consciously carried unmistakably new, little black "doctors' bags." During the clinical clerkships of third and fourth years, the long white coats gave way to short jacket-length ones. Students pinned identifying name tags on their lapels, and, with conspicuous casualness, allowed their stethoscopes to hang out of their hospital coat pockets. Some fourth-year students, emulating the interns they would soon become, knotted a rubber tourniquet around one of their belt loops, as if they were perpetually "on call" to draw blood or start an intravenous infusion.

As the foregoing description suggests, the social backgrounds of medical students of the 1950s were as homogeneous as the curriculum that shaped them into physicians. The student body was mainly male, white, and upper-middle class, more Protestant than Catholic or Jewish. Most of the students were the sons of university-educated fathers, who were successful businessmen or professionals, including many physicians.

These students of the '50s were also unified in the kind of commitment they had made to medicine and in their outlook on it. By and large they were "early deciders" who claimed that they had "always wanted" to be doctors and who, by their freshman or sophomore year in high school, had made definite plans to undertake medical training. A sizable proportion of them had entered medical school from a liberal arts college major, which was favored by admissions committees at the time. Private specialty practice (with or without a part-time medical school affiliation) that included a large component of primary care was the career goal of the greatest number of students. Although oriented to "working directly with people" in general, and with the "individual patient" in particular, they tended to place greater emphasis on medical scientific competence in dealing with and solving patients' problems than on personal and interpersonal "art of medicine" considerations.[25]

The increasingly strong emphasis on medical science and technology notwithstanding, a "hands-on," master-clinician ethos prevailed among both medical students and faculty of the 1950s. The physical examination and the process of differential diagnosis were at once empirical and symbolic foci of this intellectual and value orientation, over which prevailed titanic, "clinician-and-teacher" role-model professors and chairmen, who still "walked the wards" in "classic Oslerian style."[26]

In certain medical schools the 1950s were also a time when various educational innovations were being tried. The most radically extensive changes were initiated by Western Reserve University's School of Medicine, where the traditional curriculum was razed and another progressively put in its place. The experiments in medical education clustered around a set of common themes. Organized attempts were made to close up the gulf that existed between the preclinical and clinical years of training, principally by designing opportunities for students to have earlier patient contact. Ways were also devised to introduce students to patients with "normal," commonplace health problems, such as those of uncomplicated pregnancy or everyday pediatrics, at the same time that they were being exposed to more extraordinary, enigmatic, heroic, and death-ridden dimensions of medicine through the anatomy laboratory, the autopsy, clinical pathology, and their first encounters with the "big medicine" of the hospital wards. Various methods of effectively conveying a more holistic conception of medicine and the physician's role were tried, with particular emphasis on the importance of psychological, social, and cultural factors in the genesis, symptomatology, and treatment of illness.

In the area of "comprehensive care" and teaching, efforts were made to incorporate more behavioral science (psychiatry, clinical psychology, sociology, and to some extent, cultural anthropology) and public health into the curriculum and upgrade the importance of the learning experiences in hospital outpatient departments (OPDs). This was based on the conviction that giving advanced medical students continuing responsibility for ambulatory patient care in an OPD setting was a practical and powerful medium through which they could be motivated and trained to take a more inclusive, humane, and socially aware approach to medicine. Finally, with the aim of decompressing and individualizing the medical curriculum, minor scheduling adjustments were made to modestly increase students' free and elective time. Although these reforms was intended to "liberalize" medical training, they were as collectively structured as the features of the traditional curriculum that they aimed to alter.

The medical curriculum of the 1950s was not only tightly organized and standardized; it also contained a remarkable degree of internal psychosocial logic. The learning sequences that it embodied unfolded in a systematic way, with each new step building on the ones that preceded it. This kind of order was a distinguishing feature of both the attitude learning and the cognitive learning that took place. Students were as methodically and cumulatively trained in certain attitudes, values, and norms as they were in biomedical knowledge and skills. This was so much the case that Fox was able to chart what she termed "a sociological calendar of the medical school": a detailed, chronological account of the entwined attitudinal and cognitive learning that students underwent inside and outside of the classrooms,

_..awries, wards, and clinics of their four years of medical training.[27] Such regularity in the socialization of medical students was all the more impressive because, to a significant degree, it was an unpremeditated and unrecognized consequence of the curriculum that was consciously planned and implemented by the medical faculty. A socialization substratum ran parallel to and below the surface of the cognitive aspects of the courses and clerkships. Latent messages and meanings were conveyed to students through the deep-structure content of the scientific and technical materials they learned, through their experiences in the classroom, laboratory, and clinical situations, and through the shaping influence of the formal and informal relations with faculty, patients, hospital staff, and with each other. One of the primary tasks that the social scientists involved in the socialization studies of the 1950s performed for medical educators was to uncover and identify the medical school contexts where students were undergoing professionally relevant attitude learning that the faculty had unknowingly arranged, and to which they were subliminally contributing.

The descriptive analyses of the socialization of American medical students in the 1950s written by sociologists are chiefly of two sorts: those that delineated the major sequences of attitude learning through which students moved; and those that focused on certain occurrences in the process of medical education that students regarded as signal events (such as their first autopsy, the first time they took a patient's history and did a complete physical examination, their neophyte attempts to draw blood from patients, and the first birth and death that they witnessed). These two sorts of cross-sectional analyses converged. On closer inspection, what the students experienced as "milestone" happenings entailed the coming together of several different strands of attitude learning in ways that had strong emotional, symbolic, and rites-of-passage significance for them.

The 1950s studies concentrated on certain attitude learning sequences; training for uncertainty, certainty, and limitation, training for detached concern, training in teamwork, and training in the allocation and management of scarce time figured prominently among them. The "fate of idealism" was followed through medical school: that is, the process by which students came to temper their Olympian medical standards and professional value-commitment with "reality-situation" factors of which they gradually became aware. There was also considerable interest in how students learned to deal with the competitive, achievement-and-success dimensions of their medical school experiences, and in how they reconciled such self-interested aspects with the more disinterested, collectivity-oriented professional obligation to devote themselves to the welfare of patients. Students' training in medical ethics and responsibility (rather narrowly and specifically conceived) and their development of a "professional self-image"—an internalized sense of their own doctorhood—[28] were other centers of attention.

An interesting dialectical process of attitude-learning emerged from these focused studies. A good deal of the socialization that took place in medical school seemed to entail the blending of counterattitudes: uncertainty with certainty, detachment with concern, idealism with realism, self-orientation with other-orientation, and active responsibility and meliorism with humility and the ability to desist. Various of the attitude-learning trajectories involved a "midway" phase in which students appeared to have temporarily *over*-learned one of a set of counterattitudes. At a certain point in their third year of medical school, for example, many students behaved with exaggerated "certitude," complained of feeling "emotionally numb," and sounded more "cynical" than "idealistic." By the end of the fourth year these overdetermined modes of feeling and acting receded. Most, if not all, students seemed to have arrived at something like a dynamic equilibrium between ostensibly "incompatible" clusters of attitudes, values, and norms, which they had progressively learned to combine into more "consistent and stable patterns of professional behavior."[29] (Whether such contrapuntal patterns of learning are characteristic of other professional and adult socialization contexts as well, and why, are questions that were not raised by the social scientists who conducted these medical school studies or by those who have read what they published.)

MEDICAL EDUCATION AND SOCIALIZATION IN THE 1950s: TRAINING FOR UNCERTAINTY

Perhaps the best known and most frequently cited sociological analyses of attitude-learning sequences that students underwent in the medical school environment of the 1950s are those that delineated the processes of training for uncertainty and the training for detached concern. These accounts documented the non-random nature and the latent psychosocial logic of medical student socialization in that era. They identified some of the crucial events and pivotal experiences inherent to that socialization and the attitudes and behavior patterns that students developed in response. The uncertainty and detached concern parameters of the physician's role and development have been reinvoked and reexamined in many post-1950s sociological studies of doctors and also of nurses and other health professionals.

As outlined in the original study by Fox, training for uncertainty consisted of the flow of medical school experiences that successively and cumulatively taught students to perceive medical uncertainty, to recognize and acknowledge some of its implications for the role of physician and for the well-being and security of patients, and to develop shared, patterned ways of coping with its meaning and consequences, as well as its *de facto* existence.[30]

Students were faced with three basic types of uncertainty as they advanced from one phase of the curriculum to another: the uncertainties that originated in their incomplete mastery of the huge and rapidly growing body of concepts, facts, and skills that modern Western medicine encompasses; the uncertainties that stemmed from the gaps, limitations, and ambiguities that also characterize this impressive corpus of medical knowledge and technique; and the uncertainties that grew out of difficulties in distinguishing between personal ignorance and ineptitude, and the instrinsically imperfect, enigmatic, and tentative properties of medicine itself. Their neophyte state of knowledge and of self-confidence made it especially difficult for students to discern where their own uncertainty left off and that of the field of medicine began.

Gross anatomy, the course that initiated students into medical school, played a cardinal role in confronting them with the realization that, no matter how well-informed and competent they might become, their mastery of all that is known in medicine would never be complete. This was rendered more dramatic for them by their year-long experience of dissecting a human cadaver in the anatomy laboratory. The finitude of their cadaver, and the seeming infinitude of the "blueprint of the body" facts that anatomy represented and that they were expected to learn, came together for the students in ways that both heightened and reified their sense of the "enormity" of medicine and the impossibility of commanding it all.

Second-year pharmacology, their introduction to the state of knowledge of medical drugs and the reactions of well and sick animals and humans to them, epitomized for students the uncertainties associated with the incompleteness rather than the fullness of medical knowledge. The lack of a general overall theory of drug action, the related difficulty of predicting how a given individual would respond to a particular drug or drug combination, and the ubiquity of side effects impressed students with the fact that "there are so many voids" in medical knowledge that the practice of medicine sometimes seems largely "a matter of conjuring . . . possibilities and probabilities."

The third kind of uncertainty—that of distinguishing between personal limitations and those of medical science and technology—became salient for students in physical diagnosis, the course that bridged their preclinical and clinical training. As they learned examination, observational, and history-taking methods and techniques essential to detecting and defining the nature of patients' problems, students often found themselves questioning how much of their "trouble . . . hearing, feeling or seeing [was] personal," and how much of it had to do with "factors outside of themselves"—with "the faults of the field, so to speak."

The range of course-related experiences bearing upon students' training for uncertainty was as broad as it was systematic. Throughout the curriculum, students were repeatedly exposed to experiences that furthered this aspect of their attitude learning. In the clinical years, for example, the several forms of medical uncertainty that they encountered were enhanced for them by their increasing contact with patients and their developing sense of professional responsibility. As students' awareness of their impending doctorhood grew, their sense of urgency about the "necessity of knowing enough to do justice to our patients" also increased. They came to regard their "gaps in knowledge" and "unsureness" as more serious than in earlier stages of their training.

Threaded through their preclinical and clinical years in ways that both magnified and consolidated their training for uncertainty were the various contexts and guises in which students encountered death. These included dissecting a cadaver in anatomy, witnessing and contributing to the death of some of the laboratory animals on which they worked in their basic science laboratories ("sacrificing" these animals, as the students euphemistically and ironically put it), observing several autopsies, examining post-mortem tissue specimens in clinical pathology, and meeting terminally ill and dying patients. Students were astonished and disquieted to learn that, although death is an ultimate and finite certainty, it is also more elusive and mysterious than they had supposed. Whether death will occur in a given case, when it will come to pass, and what causes it, students discovered, are questions that often cannot be easily or categorically answered. Furthermore, they began to see that the relationship between the physician's knowledgeable and skillful intervention in a patient's condition and the ability to forestall or prevent the patient's death was more tenuous than they had assumed.

There was a structured discontinuity in students' experiences during the preclinical and clinical years that also significantly contributed to their training for uncertainty. What students described as an "experimental" and "philosophy of

doubting" outlook characterized the first two years of medical school. F
basic science teaching that they received was the explicit and implic...
that an irreducible amount of uncertainty is inherent to medicine. They learned u...
uncertainty is "legitimate" and "inevitable," that it is fortunate as well as regrettable
because it can lead to new medical scientific knowledge and understanding, and
that, in any case, it is best handled by openly admitting that it exists and openly
grappling with it.

Although this systematic doubting was not suspended in the clinical years,
students began to learn more about some of the undesirable consequences of
"doubting too much." The realization began to dawn that however cognizant
physicians may be of the indeterminate aspects of a case, they must sufficiently
commit themselves to some diagnostic and therapeutic hypotheses to take clinical
action. Furthermore, although patients may regard a physician's willingness to
admit uncertainty as a reassuring indicator of candor and integrity, too great a display of unsureness may alarm them or undermine their confidence and trust. These
insights were absorbed by students and tested in some of the novice doctor-patient
relationships they formed during their third and fourth years of medical school. By
the time they reached graduation, Fox concluded, most had achieved some balance
between Hamlet-like doubting and its opposite extreme, super-certitude.

Based partly on their own observations of psychiatric residents and graduate
physicians in practice, sociologist Donald Light and psychiatrist Jay Katz have
made two amendments to the training for uncertainty sequence that Fox described.
Light contends that "as clinical responsibilities grow, training for uncertainty becomes training for control." This "shift," he claims, is discernible "in Fox's
materials, as medical students take on more clinical work in their last two years."[31]
Katz suggests that some of the medical students' ways of coping with the stresses of
uncertainty reported by Fox (and that she also observed in her study of doctors on
Ward F-Second, a metabolic research unit[32]), are collective defense mechanisms
that are as conducive to a "*disregard of uncertainty*" in "actual clinical encounters,"
as they are to "keeping these uncertainties in mind . . . struggling [with them] . . .
and acknowledging them to patients."[33]

The coping mechanisms discussed by Fox and Katz, which allowed students
to mute their awareness of medical uncertainty and moderate their anxiety about it,
were even more apparent in the training for detached concern through which they
learned to handle their feelings in dealing with the highly evocative aspects of medical work.

MEDICAL EDUCATION AND SOCIALIZATION IN THE 1950s: TRAINING FOR DETACHED CONCERN

Ideally, the detached concern dimension of the physician's role entails the ability to
bring objectivity and empathy, equanimity and compassion into a supple balance
with one another—combining and recombining them in ways that are compatible
with the delivery of competent, sagacious, and humane patient care. Like their training for uncertainty, students' training for detached concern unfolded with impressive orderliness, developing chiefly through the impact of certain curriculum
experiences.

It began, as much attitude learning did, in the anatomy laboratory. There students encountered death, the evanescence of personhood, nudity, and anonymity in the form of their cadaver—a human body that they were allowed and obliged to cut apart and examine in minute detail. Students maintained that most of the time the "very dead" appearance and texture of the cadaver helped to shield them against the full emotional realization that the body on which they were working was once a human being. However, when they dissected the hands, face, and genitalia, the "humanness" of the cadaver "asserted itself" to a degree that they found disturbing. Students' intense scientific engrossment in learning anatomy and in performing well in the laboratory (with the intellectualization and technicalization that this absorption entailed) and the death-ridden erotic and gallows humor in which they engaged were their chief ways of handling the undercurrents of feeling that these aspects of the dissection brought to the surface.

Students worked with live laboratory animals in many of their other preclinical courses. The anatomy laboratory had given them some emotional and technical preparation for manipulating and cutting into a body. Because of the animals' nonhuman status, students were less prone to react to them with the sort of primal anxiety that the cadaver had aroused in them. Nevertheless, they felt disquietude over the fact that the animals were alive, moved, bled, and sometimes were "sacrificed" on the "altar" of their learning.

The first autopsy in which students participated in their second medical school year had major import for their training for detached concern.[34] Students reported that the autopsy reminded them of the anatomy laboratory in a number of ways. In the autopsy, however, they found themselves confronted with death as "recent life," with the chastening realization, as one student put it, that "on the wards of learning, and throughout our professional careers, some of our patients will die." Despite the anticipatory socialization that they had received through their prior work on the human cadaver and on live laboratory animals, students were profoundly affected by the autopsy. Once again, intellectualization, technicalization of the learning tasks at hand, and their strong motivation to "do well" and "act professional" helped students to manage their feelings. But in this setting, by tacit agreement, they dealt with their deepest emotions in mutual silence. ("You don't bare your heart about the autopsy. . . . You sort of sit on the lid of your feelings.") Conspicuously absent were the macabre humor with which students had responded to death in the anatomy laboratory and the easy verbalizing and vigorous discussion in which they engaged in other shared medical school situations.

Later in the second year, in preparation for the approaching clinical phase of their training, students began to practice certain procedures on themselves and on their classmates. For example, they both carried out and were subjects for urinalyses, glucose tolerance tests, capillary punctures, venipunctures, auscultation, percussion, blood pressure determinations, nose and throat swabs, fluoroscopy of the gastrointestinal tract, typhoid vaccinations, and personal and psychiatric case histories. This phase of their experience and development was notable for the collective state of hypochondriasis that it elicited. "We are now in the process of contracting the diseases we are studying," a student explained, "in order to develop emotional immunity to them."

In a sense, the cadaver, the laboratory animals, the deceased person on the autopsy table, and the classmates on whom students worked were all "pre-patients."

It was not until the end of the second year, chiefly in physical diagnosis, that students began to have face-to-face contact with "real patients." The process was very gradual, beginning with short, task-delimited group visits to hospitalized patients chaperoned by instructors. Gradually, these patient contacts were lengthened, came to include more interaction and responsibility, and were no longer flanked by supporting clusters of classmates and faculty supervisors. Finally, the momentous day arrived when the medical student "soloed," taking a patient's entire medical history and carrying out a complete physical examination without the presence or aid of anyone else.

Certain aspects of the history and physical examination embarrassed the students, challenging the tenuous professional composure and smoothness of manner they were just beginning to assume. Intimate and potentially erotic aspects of the clinical tasks they were learning to perform (such as taking a sexual history, examining a woman's breasts, doing a vaginal or pelvic examination, palpating a man's testicles, carrying out a rectal examination), along with any sort of "very emotional reaction" by a patient, were likely to be disturbing to students. At this point in their training, most of them were struggling to manage their own overabundance of concerned feelings and to achieve greater detachment.

The clinical years of medical school were organized around interviewing and examining patients. Although students gained more skill and poise in these activities, particular kinds of patients were likely to make them feel anxious, frustrated, or sad. Very sick children, mentally ill patients, alcoholics, "hostile, uncooperative" patients, elderly and dying patients confronted students with problems of suffering and vulnerability, communication and compassion, mortality and meaning that were profoundly unsettling to them.

Somewhere in the course of the third year, students' difficulties in relating to patients shifted from what they had previously experienced as too much concern to that of too much detachment. They were no longer so preoccupied with how to manage excessive emotion as they were troubled about what had happened to their former capacity to respond feelingly to patients and their predicaments. This was a period that students apprehensively described as a time of "emotional numbness." In part, they were disquieted by the greater capacity for professional detachment that they had newly developed. In part, they were reacting to a state of "feelingless-ness" that resulted from their tendency, at this point in their training, to push their strong emotions about a variety of medical situations below the surface of their consciousness. The "numbed" interlude was a relatively short one. By the time students reached their senior year, they had progressed beyond the stage of hyperdetachment to a new level of integration that enabled them, more comfortably and effectively, to blend objectivity and equipoise with compassionate concern.

MEDICAL EDUCATION AND SOCIALIZATION IN THE 1950s: EPISODIC SOCIALIZATION EXPERIENCES

Medical students of the 1950s also shared a number of episodic experiences that systematically shaped their conceptions of the physician's role. At Cornell University Medical College, for example, in the springtime of their third year, students took a course in infectious disease at the Willard Parker Hospital, located further downtown than New York Hospital where the medical school was situated. Arrayed in their short white coats and carrying their little black bags, students often hitchhiked between the two hospitals. Cars stopped for them with notable frequency. Many drivers praised their student passengers for their choice of a noble profession and for the hard-working, self-abnegating way in which they were studying to become physicians. Often these chauffeurs went on to contrast the pristine dedication of medical students with the more tarnished behavior of mature physicians—their inaccessibility, impersonality, the high fees they charged, and so on. At the end of the morning, over lunch, students discussed both their experiences in the clinic and their conversations with the persons who had given them lifts. It was in an automobile and in the hospital cafeteria, then, that students learned from an assortment of lay people and from each other how they and the profession they were entering were seen by the public.

As part of their Public Health course, students spent a day watching school doctors and nurses at work. They were struck by the fact that the technique used here to give the children their immunization shots was not identical with the one that they had been taught. When students questioned the doctor about this, he explained that his method had developed as a response to most children's fear of needles. He assured the students that the technique they had learned was the "right" one, but that his modification hastened the injection and short-circuited the children's anxiety without exposing them to any significant added risk. When students discussed incidents like this with one another, they concluded that they were learning that "real medicine can be good medicine."

Third-year students also had an eight-week course in animal surgery, rotating in the roles of surgeon, assistant surgeon, anesthesiologist, and nurse as they carried out increasingly complex operative procedures on laboratory dogs. Students brought to this task the middle-class, American, egalitarian notions of teamwork with which they had entered medical school. They were surprised and chagrined to discover that the type of peer group collegiality to which they were accustomed, and in which they believed, "did not work well" when they were cast in the role of surgeon. Too much consultation with their teammates about what they intended to do made it difficult to meet the simulated operating room schedule. It also endangered the welfare of their dog-patient, who had to be maintained for a more extended period under anesthesia, with his surgical wounds exposed, while the student-surgeon democratically sought colleagues' opinions. As a consequence of their trial-and-error experiences as role-playing surgeons, students reluctantly decided that there were other than arbitrary, purely temperamental reasons why surgeons had to act "authoritarian," "like a captain of a ship," when making decisions, giving orders, and taking responsibility for their own and their team's actions.

Such critical incidents, which occurred throughout medical school training, were spin-offs from the formal curriculum. They were highly patterned events, structured by the content, context, and sequence of the course work, by the social system of the medical school, and especially by how "the little society of medical students" interpreted them. To a striking degree, these incidents were neither planned nor recognized by the faculty. Their socialization impact derived largely from their collective nature, and from the informal ways in which they were experienced and discussed by medical students, quasi-independently of their teachers.

CHANGES IN MEDICAL SCHOOLS AND MEDICAL STUDENTS IN THE 1960s AND EARLY 1970s

The 1960s ushered in what Daniel Funkenstein has termed the "Scientific Era" of medical education and Robert H. Ebert calls "the peak of the era of experimental medicine."[35]

> The founding of the National Institutes of Health and the National Science Foundation, the launching of Sputnik, and passage of the National Defense Education Act profoundly altered all education. Society, government, foundations, students, and medical schools gave research their highest priority, and vast sums of money became available. . . .[36]

> The only question asked by Congressional committees with an overview of NIH was—what could you do if you had more money? By the mid-1960s, medical schools and teaching hospitals had every reason to be optimistic. . . . Many of the research training programs sponsored by the NIH included clinical experience in a subspecialty as a legitimate adjunct to training for research, it being argued that clinical knowledge of a field was essential if one were to engage in clinical research. . . . With support from NIH, most university hospitals developed strong subspecialty divisions in various clinical departments, and this inevitably led to an expansion of subspecialty patient care. . . . Between 1960-61 and 1970-71, full-time clinical faculty increased by 167 percent (from 7,201 to 19,256) while the number of medical students increased by only 45 percent (from 21,379 to 30,084). . . . [T]he size of the clinical faculty had little to do with the needs of medical students, but was related . . . to the demands of the research laboratory, graduate training, and the specialty practice of medicine.[37]

In the mid-1960s, as part of his program for the "Great Society," President Lyndon Johnson persuaded Congress to pass legislation that created Medicare and Medicaid. Medicare and Medicaid benefitted not only the patient recipients but also medical schools and teaching hospitals, providing funds that helped them to augment their clinical practice, divisions, and departments. More medical schools became university affiliated, embedded in expanding academic medical centers that increasingly included a consortium of hospitals and a cluster of health-related professional schools. Several additional academic medical centers were built in the 1960s, further enlarging the national capacity to educate physicians. The clinical training of students and house staff in these centers was focused on severely ill patients with complicated, often unusual disorders, and was in the charge of full-time clinical faculty, usually specialists, who stressed the importance of advanced technology and clinical investigation in the understanding and management of disease.

New "community-based" medical schools also made their appearance in the 1960s, many of them unaffiliated or loosely affiliated with a university. In part, they constituted "a pedagogic (and political) reaction to an era of burgeoning science and technology in medicine." In contrast to traditional academic medical centers, they emphasized "primary care, secondary care, and extensive exposure to successful community practitioners."[38]

The students admitted to medical school at the beginning of the 1960s were selected from a pool whose numbers had declined since the 1950s. Funkenstein attributed this drop in applicants to the low birth rate twenty-one years earlier (during World War II) and to the then current enthusiasm about basic scientific research, which was drawing students away from medical school into graduate school science programs. According to Funkenstein, a greater number of the students who entered university medical schools such as Harvard were bioscientifically oriented than in the past, partly because there was a "dramatic increase in the scientific preparation of all students," and partly because admission committees showed a preference in this direction. The students characterized by Funkenstein as more "biosocially" inclined, with interpersonal service and social science and psychological interests and abilities, were increasingly being attracted to the field of psychiatry. For bioscientific and biosocial students alike, the full-time medical academician and subspecialist, with a large component of research in his work, displaced the private practitioner as a role model.[39]

In Ebert's view, one of the most important curriculum changes initiated during the early 1960s was the emphasis on pathophysiology as an introduction to clinical medicine. This involved full-time clinical faculty in teaching what had previously been regarded as the "almost exclusive domain of the preclinical faculty." First- and second-year medical students now had more contact with clinicians than in the 1950s, predominantly with physicians who were theoretically and practically grounded in the basic sciences. This kind of integration of the preclinical and clinical facets of medicine was reinforced by the repercussions of the "biological revolution." As more molecular and cell biologists became "the popular recruits in basic science departments, the . . . medical schools had to depend [more] on full-time clinicians to share the teaching of organ physiology, anatomy, bacteriology, and pharmacology."[40]

In the second half of the 1960s, the confident serenity of the "Scientific Era" of medical education was shattered. Suddenly (or at least it appeared sudden to medical educators) a wave of students crested in medical schools throughout the country whose appearance, rhetoric, and behavior were drastically different from those of their predecessors. The following excerpts contain the essence of the surfacing of this new generation of medical students:

> The year was 1966 and beards were still considered by many to be the domain of those they chose to call hippies. Facial hair was clearly a coming commodity among young people, and two classmates sported nicely trimmed beards through the first year and a half of medical school. We speculated a good deal about what would happen if they didn't shave before they started Physical Diagnosis. . . . The stage was set for a challenge. One of my hirsute colleagues avoided the problem by shaving, while the other held his ground. Sure enough, in the second week of the quarter he received a terse note from the Dean of Students requesting him to shave. The news of the demand spread quickly through the class, angering many people. . . .
>
> Looking back on it now, the SWAB (Save WAller's Beard) campaign seems amusing but hardly political. . . . After a week or two of debate, during which time Waller stalwartly refused to take a razor to his now-famous face, some two-thirds of the class signed the SWAB petition *requesting* [italics the author's] permission

of the medical school for Waller to remain as he was. . . . Eventually the issue was referred to the chief of the first clinical service on which Waller was scheduled to work, Internal Medicine. . . . The question was raised in a departmental meeting and reportedly caused an angry debate. . . . Allegedly the . . . professor . . . ended the discussion saying, "Beards, schmeards, if the boy knows his medicine he'll pass. That's all there is to it."

. . . Waller kept his beard. . . . The class was elated by the victory and I personally felt that we had struck a blow for human, or at least medical, liberty.

Today, in honesty, I am not so sure. The SWAB campaign was, at that time, profoundly political for me. Waller's beard was a symbol of departure from the medical style that was oppressive and exclusionary. The fight to save it represented not just a battle for individualism, but an effort to liberalize a tight and arbitrary medical norm. For me, beards had become an insignia. They indicated resistance to blind tradition and thoughtless authority. Beards were in themselves political and the sign of a political person.[41]

To the Editor: As Stanford students who have taken issue in the past with Dr. Kriss's views on [the physician's way of dressing], we should like to reply to his Sounding Board article [Joseph P. Kriss, "On White Coats and Other Matters," *New England Journal of Medicine* 292: 1024–1025, 1975].

Having argued that the white coat is not prerequisite to a good doctor-patient relation, we should like to indicate why we might choose not to wear one. Dr. Kriss states that the white coat is easily identifiable. We agree. We feel that in the eyes of many the white coat identifies its wearer as a member of the medical professional hierarchy. A white-coated provider of care high in the hierarchy is supposed to be regarded by the patient and by other health workers as a more competent source of care and information than workers lower in the hierarchy. . . . [W]e would prefer that the patient learn to judge the abilities of each health worker on his or her own merits, rather than to learn to rely on the potentially misleading symbolism of the white coat, and that nonphysician health personnel learn to regard themselves as equal members of the health-care team. . . .

Dr. Kriss . . . finds it disrespectful for students "to dress inappropriately" during a patient presentation. Since we have shown that we disagree with his view of what is appropriate dress, we believe that if respect is to be "mutual and based on trust," it must include a willingness on his part to trust us to make our own decisions about how we present ourselves to patients.

We as students are genuinely concerned with improving the quality of our relations with patients, faculty, and other members of the health-care team. We cannot improve these relations without changing them somewhat. We hope that these changes can be accomplished in the spirit of mutual trust and respect.

Ken Newgard
Bill Rollow
Leslie Walleigh
and 72 Other
Medical Students[42]
Stanford, CA

To the Editor: The almost incessant drumming against the medical profession is largely of our own making. The aloofness and detachment of many members of the profession is, time and again, wrapped in the cloak of "dignity." . . .

[W]e must continue to touch our patients. The touch is, after all, a variation of a modicum of healing—viz., the laying on of hands. . . . [L]et's tell the patient that we care, and we're glad to reach out, literally, to touch. It does not require an act of another world to offer sympathy, courtesy, cheerfulness, laughter or concern to those who seek us out. And, I suspect, in the last analysis, not only would our patients feel better, but so would we. A tremendous amount of stress can be lifted from our lives if we would simply be what we started out to be back in college: sympathetic people, working to help distressed patients, honestly, courageously, daily—and to hell with dignity.[43]

Each year that I was Dean of the Harvard Medical School, I met with the entering first year students, and in September 1968 at such a meeting there occurred a small incident that I have never forgotten, for it was to presage a sudden and in some ways frightening change in the medical school. While making some benign welcoming remarks, I was suddenly interrupted by a young woman who demanded to know why she and her classmates had to provide some information asked for by the AMA. I said it was to provide demographic information about physicians in training that added to a national database. She responded with some harsh words about the AMA, but the class remained quiet, and I continued my remarks. This young woman had been a student activist at Radcliffe College, and I was to meet her later in Harvard Yard when, in April 1969, University Hall was occupied by the SDS. . . . One might have expected the distant Harvard Medical School in Boston to be immune from this disruption in Cambridge, but one of the reasons given for the occupation of University Hall was the purchase, by the Harvard Medical School, of housing adjacent to the Peter Bent Brigham Hospital which was to be razed in order to build the new Affiliated Hospital. A medical student body that until April 1969 had seemed totally committed to scientific medicine suddenly changed, and now expressed concern for the Roxbury tenants who would be evicted by an oppressive medical school in order to build a teaching hospital remote from the needs of the people. And so began what Funkenstein called the era of "student activism." [44]

This seemingly abrupt and turbulent period of social challenge and social change in American medical schools coincided with the upsurge of student protest on college and university campuses throughout the country. It continued into the mid-1970s, graduating with the medical students into their internships and residencies, and abating, without disappearing, at the end of the Vietnam War.

That same period marked the beginning of a decade of rapidly escalating numbers of college students aspiring to become physicians. This trend peaked in the academic year 1974-1975 when, despite the expansion in size of medical school classes and number of American medical schools, there were almost three applicants for every first-year medical school place. During the 1970s, with the help of unprecedented support for medical education from the federal government, the number of medical schools increased from 101 to 126, and their total student enrollment more than doubled, rising from 30,084 to 63,800.[45]

The growth included a notable increment in the number and percentage of women and minority student applications and admissions to medical school. The 1964 Civil Rights Act, the adoption of a resolution on equal opportunity by the Association of American Medical Colleges (AAMC) in November 1970, and Title IX of the Educational Amendments of 1972, along with attitude changes engendered by the civil rights and women's movements, all contributed to these developments.

With the exception of Funkenstein's Harvard Medical School-centered studies, we have almost no social science research on this era in American medical education, when the composition and the attitudes and values of students appeared to change so markedly. Nothing like the first-hand socialization studies of the 1950s existed in the late 1960s and early 1970s to record and analyze these historic social phenomena. One of the only descriptive accounts of the "new" medical student published by a sociologist was the ideal-typical portrait assembled by Fox out of her own observations and field notes. Because of its singularity, it seems appropriate to reproduce most of it here:

> Despite the efforts being made to recruit young persons into medical school from minority groups and nonprivileged social class backgrounds, the new medical student is still likely to be a white middle-class man. He arrives in medical school garbed as he was in college—in blue jeans or modishly colored sports slacks and tieless shirt. His hair is long, though usually not unkempt, and he may have grown a moderate beard. When he begins to see patients, he often starts wearing a tie and sometimes a jacket. He may also cut his hair on the short side of long and shave more closely.
>
> Although he is fiercely intent on being accepted by a medical school, unlike his counterparts in the 1950s, the new medical student is generally a "late decider." It is not uncommon for him to have committed himself to becoming a doctor in the second half of his college career. . . .[H]e worked hard and competitively as a college student in order to earn the very high grade-point average that made him eligible for admission to medical school. He is aggressively achievement-oriented, but deplores it in himself, his classmates, his teachers, the medical profession, his parents, and American society generally. As engaged as he is by medicine, he wonders continually whether it is really his "vocation." The "on call twenty-four hours a day" demands associated with the traditions and responsibilities of many branches of medicine contribute to these doubts. For he is concerned about what this kind of relentlessness may do to his person, his relationships to patients and colleagues, his family life, and his capacity to participate in the cultural, civic, and recreational activities that he considers healthy and humanizing, as well as pleasurable.
>
> Such a student is likely to have come to medical school with declared interests in fields like community medicine, public health, family medicine, psychiatry, and pediatrics (the latter, he feels obliged to explain, because it is "holistic" medicine and entails caring for "new and future generations"). In the end, these may not be the fields that he will actually enter. But they express the interpersonal, moral, and societal perspective on physicianhood that he brings with him from college. He is actively committed to such humane and social goals as peace, the furtherance of civil rights, the reduction of poverty, the protection of the environment, population control, and improvement in the "quality of life" for all.

He extends the principles that underlie these commitments to medicine and the role of doctor. In his view, health and health care are fundamental rights that ought to be as equitably distributed as possible. For this reason, as he sees it, the physician should not only care for the psychological, social, and physical aspects of his own patients' illness; he should have a "genuine concern for the total health of mankind." He should take initiative in dealing with some of the factors at work in the society that adversely affect health and keep the medical care system from functioning optimally to maintain and restore it. Although the doctor's social dedication should be universalistic, the new student believes, he has special obligations to those who are disadvantaged or deprived.

The new medical student is also staunchly egalitarian in his conception of the doctor and of the doctor's relationship to patients and to non-physician members of the medical team. The student disapproves of "all-knowing" or "omnipotent" attitudes and behavior on the part of physicians. ("The doctor is not a king . . . a high priest . . . or a technological master who can control or dominate all.") He maintains that physicians should approach patients "as human beings" with "respect for their feelings and opinions," rather than as "diseased specimens" or persons incapable of understanding their own medical condition and the treatment prescribed for it. Ideally, a collegial and "non-authoritarian" relationship with patients ought to be developed, one that is "honest," "open," and non-manipulative. ("The physician should reach people through conversation that is not like that of a salesman. . . . He should have open communication with patients . . . and hide as little as possible from them.") "Integrity [and "authenticity" that are] emotional and moral, as well as intellectual, is basic to this relationship, too. It entails more than being honest and consistent in what one says and does: it is actively critical and self-critical, involving the "questioning of self, colleagues, teachers, physicians and the intentions of the institution."

A "detached concern" model of relating to patients is not one that the new medical student admires or would like to exemplify. Rather, he places the highest value on feeling with the patient. Although he recognizes the need for maintaining some objectivity in this relationship, he does so with regret. For him, he says, to feel is to be human and compassionate; it dignifies and heals; and the more one feels, the better. However scientifically and intellectually inclined he may be, the student believes that it is all too easy to distance oneself from patients (and from one's own humanity) by approaching the problems for which they seek the doctor's aid in an overly conceptual and technical way. He considers "direct experience" . . . to be the method *par excellence* by which the physician should learn and come to understand. It allows him to maintain close contact with patients and "reality" and also to seek knowledge and truth that go beyond the passive acceptance and mastery of what is handed down to him by past generations. ("We are experiencing physical diagnosis in relative virginity. . . . We still don't know the 'rules of the game' and are therefore likely to violate them in worthwhile ways.")

Finally, although the new medical student would not downgrade the importance of training, knowledge, skill, and experience for competent physicianhood, he also insists that the doctor's values, beliefs, and commitments are a critical part of his ability to help patients, reform the health care system, and "improve society." ("Ethical, moral, and social issues are a base on which a superstructure of scientific knowledge should be built, rather than the over-Flexnerian tradition in which scientific schema formed the base. . . .") And so the physician must be more than just a "good human being." He must also concern himself with the "philosophical" problems of life and death, suffering and evil, justice and equity, human solidarity, and ultimate meaning in which his chosen profession and the human condition are grounded.

This is the at once critical, activist, and meditative ideology [and] world view that the new student brings to medical school. How predominant it is, whether it will prevail, whether in interaction with the medical school environment and the social climate of the seventies it will produce a new type of physician, time, the professional socialization process, and, one hopes, studies of it, will eventually tell.[46]

Many faculty members reacted to the appearance of such students with a complex mixture of astonishment, admiration, bewilderment, skepticism, anxiety, and indignation. Above all, they were ambivalent. Were medical students really as "new" and ardently committed to sociomedical change as they looked and sounded? Or were their blue jeans and beards, their "anti-white coat" sentiments and behavior, their "revolutionary" speech and action no more than a fashionably fierce and idealistically youthful phase through which they were passing? Medical educators were not only split among themselves in their response to this question; they were also split *within* themselves. Irrespective of which position they took, their continual questioning implicitly acknowledged that the students with whom they were confronted were sufficiently different from those to whom they were accustomed to warrant a great deal of faculty discussion.

During this era of student activism, faculty also expressed considerable doubt about the role that the medical school, its curriculum, and its teachers played in the socialization of medical students:

> The changing attitudes of students had an impact, and some members of the medical faculties were sensitive to the events in the outside world and were sympathetic to social change. . . . But it should be remembered that it was the force of external events, not internally generated ideas, that caused these changes in the internal environment.[47]

To some degree, such denial of the impact of medical education on the ideas and attitudes of medical students constituted a defense mechanism on the part of the faculty. Perplexed by the generation gap that yawned between them and their students, buffeted by students' criticism of "The Medical School Establishment" and their rebellious actions against it, the faculty found a certain protection in claiming that their only educational influence on students was a strictly biomedical one, and in disavowing responsibility for whatever the outlook and conduct of the new generation of physicians currently in medical school might turn out to be.

Despite this tendency to verbally play down their effect on students and on practice, medical educators made a number of significant changes in the curriculum in the late 1960s and early 1970s. These were designed to prepare students to actively promote and participate in the development of a high-quality, reasonably priced national system of health care that was more equitably distributed, accessible, and socially sensitive. In part, these alterations in curriculum were organized attempts to meet the criticisms of the vociferous "new" medical students, and also those of the American public who, in this period of far-reaching social and cultural change, was beginning to define medical care as a "right" rather than a "privilege."

Steps were taken to loosen and diversify the "lockstep" medical curriculum. Both elective and free time were expanded. Multiple tracks were created, establishing a variety of patterns in which students could proceed through medical school in accordance with their present interests and future plans. A number of M.D.-Ph.D. programs were instituted that allowed students to combine advanced training in different medically relevant fields. A required core curriculum was set into place whose primary *raison d'être* was to integrate the various basic sciences with each other and with clinical training. Departments and programs of community medicine, social medicine, preventive medicine, and family medicine were founded. Students were given opportunities for fieldwork and practicum experiences outside the walls of academic medical centers, with the express aims of acquainting them with more than "ivory tower" medicine, familiarizing them with the health and medical care delivery problems of disadvantaged groups in the society, and developing their general ability to think of health, illness, and care in a social system framework. Some of these extramural experiences were originally started by students and subsequently adopted for credit by the faculty. Greater emphasis was placed on the role of behavioral science in training physicians to improve the overall system of health care delivery, as well as their individual relations with patients. The earliest courses in "bioethics" were launched. These went beyond medical etiquette and specific "dos and don'ts of doctorhood" to consider the ethical and moral dimensions of medical decision-making, especially problems associated with the use of certain biomedical advances (such as life support systems, birth technology, the implantation of human, animal, and artificial organs, and genetic engineering), human experimentation, informed voluntary consent to research or treatment, the proper definition of death, and the humane treatment of the dying. Many medical schools also replaced their traditional grading systems with a pass-fail type of evaluation, in an effort to discourage aggressively self-interested competition and status anxiety among students.

Looking back on this era, when he was a medical student and house officer, Dr. Fitzhugh Mullan tried retrospectively to interpret it:

> During most of the sixties, and part of the seventies, I assumed that I was part of a revolution. My sense and definition of that revolution developed and changed over time, but throughout, I anticipated that some sort of new order was being established in society in general, and that I specifically was involved in the retooling of medicine. Furthermore, I took the groups that I worked with to be the institutions of the revolution and fully expected them to survive and grow. . . .
>
> Now I find myself asking what happened? My simple assumptions of the past years have not held up well in the mid-seventies. . . . I can briefly rekindle the simple belief in . . . the "Movement," as we so often and so imprecisely called it, . . . or change, or revolution, that we shared. Yet today, that belief seems dated to me, naive, simplistic, unserviceable, and I am left wondering, what really happened? Was there a revolution? What was accomplished? Was I a revolutionary? And toughest, who am I now? . . .
>
> I suspect that my dental friend would be satisfied with the predictions that he had made about my future in 1967. To him, it would seem, reasonably enough, that I have settled down to the relatively staid personal and professional life that

he foresaw. I don't think his prophecy has been fulfilled as simply or completely as it might seem. Significantly, my butcher doesn't really believe I'm a doctor—at least not a doctor as he and many Americans understand a doctor. . . . For him, it was the way in which I practiced medicine that made me suspect. For others, it might be my beliefs or my style of dress or my political allegiances. But for many people I have not been, and am not a doctor in the old mold. That, more than any single reform or innovation, has been my experience and my offering as I have grown up in medicine.[48]

Mullan's questioning, doubting, critical, and self-critical style of reflection is pervaded by the spirit of the times of which he writes, in a way that continues to distinguish him from what he refers to as "a doctor of the old mold." Medical schools and medical students have not totally reverted to a pre-1960s model, any more than Dr. Mullan himself has. Nevertheless, the mid-1970s to mid-1980s period brought another set of far-reaching changes in medical education, the men and women undergoing it, and the larger medical system and society of which they are part, which marks it off from the idealistically expectant social tumult of the period that preceded it.

CHANGES IN MEDICAL SCHOOLS AND MEDICAL STUDENTS IN THE MID-1970s TO MID-1980s

If possible, there are even fewer sociological publications concerning medical schools, medical students, and their professional education and socialization during this decade than those that deal with the 1960s, nor are there likely to be more, for one is hard-pressed to identify any relevant sociological research that is currently "in the field." The absence of inquiry is not only regrettable because of the theoretical and empirical discontinuity in sociological work that it represents. From a historical point of view, it forfeits the opportunity to record and analyze the social changes taking place in the men and women being recruited into medicine and in those training them, in terms of the manifest and latent content and impact of the medical school curriculum, the structure and orientation of academic medical centers, and the organization and outlook of the profession and practice of medicine more broadly. Although these changes are less flamboyant and quite different from the "white coat, closed fist" type of the 1960s, they are probably altering the face of American medicine in more far-reaching and irrevocable ways.

The 1976-1986 period has seen a number of modifications in the size and composition of the medical student body. At the start of this period there was a great deal of lamenting by medical educators over the way that the unprecedented numbers of applicants to medical schools were straining the admissions machinery of many institutions to the breaking point, increasing their tendency to automatically screen out those whose grade point averages and science scores on the standardized Medical College Admissions Test (MCAT) fell below a quite high level. There was also much complaining by students and faculty about the so-called "premedical syndrome" that seemed largely to result from this deluge of medical school aspirants and its influence on medical college admissions policy. The "premed syndrome" was the ironic term for a series of "signs and symptoms" purportedly displayed by many college undergraduates ferociously determined to enter medical school: aggressive competitiveness, self-interested pursuit of grades, narrow minded overspecialization, high anxiety, and more than occasional incidents of academic dishonesty.[49] The atmosphere created by this syndrome was seen as antipathetic to the development of humanistic and humane physicians and, as Dr. Lewis Thomas wrote in an influential article, as destructive to liberal arts education more generally:

> The influence of the modern medical school on liberal arts education in this country over the last decade has been baleful and malign, nothing less. . . . [If something is not done to change the situation] all the joy of going to college will have been destroyed, not just for the growing majority of undergraduate students who draw breath only to become doctors, but for everyone else, all the students, and all the faculty as well.[50]

Not only do "some of our brightest and most sensitive young men and women graduate from some of our finest universities without getting a college education," a medical school dean asserted, but, in addition, too often they carry the "warped values" they have developed as undergraduates into medical school, where "more competition and more examinations" reinforce, refine, and augment them.[51]

In the 1980s, both the number of applicants and of new entrants to medical schools began to decline. According to American Association of Medical Colleges (AAMC) statistics, the 1985–1986 applicant pool decreased by 8.7 percent from 1984 to 1985. The total number of students admitted to first year medical school classes and total medical school enrollment also declined modestly.[52] The distressed concern about the "morbid experience" and "sorry condition" of "premed" and entering medical students did not vanish, but it abated somewhat.[53]

Before the downward trends became apparent, the seemingly endless rise in the numbers of students interested in medicine masked a steady and significant decline in the proportion of several subgroups of medical students. The number of black and other minority students entering medical school had increased rapidly during the 1960s and early 1970s, the period of the strongest medical educational commitment to affirmative action. However, in the decade from 1974 to 1983, black and minority students accepted into United States medical schools fell from 10 percent to 8.8 percent of first year new entrants, even though the number of black and minority applicants increased during this time, and the acceptance rates for nonminority applicants rose.[54] Less recognized than this decline in minority students was the sharp drop that had also taken place in the number of men applying to medical school. Medical educators privately acknowledge that the great increase in women applicants and entrants covers over the fact that male applicants have diminished by as much as 50 percent in many medical schools.

The medical school at present, then, is one with many more female and significantly fewer male and minority students than in the "activism era" of the late 1960s and early 1970s. It is also an institution with a quietly descending number of student applicants and entrants. This decrease is due partly to a shift in college students' interests and career aspirations, and partly to a discreet policy of incrementally reducing the size of entering first-year classes that medical educators have set into motion. This latter step has been taken in response to two interconnected developments. First, the government ended its capitation allowance for each student admitted to medical school. These funds were granted in the 1970s to increase the size of medical school classes and provide start-up costs for new medical schools, out of a conviction that the medical educational system was training too few physicians and too many specialists. Second, this short-lived government program helped to create a "crisis of success," so that a projected national surplus of 25,000 to 50,000 doctors by 1990 was anticipated.[55]

We know very little about the effect that these compositional changes in the student body are having on the ambiance of the American medical school, or what their consequences may be for the medical socialization process. There is some psychodynamically oriented research, such as the ongoing longitudinal study of the physical and psychological health concomitants of "stress and adaptation in medical students," that psychiatrists Malkah T. Notman, Patricia Salt, and Carol C. Nadelson are conducting at Harvard and Tufts medical schools, which provides suggestive though fragmentary data.[56] In their analysis of the interview and questionnaire responses of 261 first-year students, these researchers found no significant sex or minority group status differences in the overall number or intensity of stresses that students reported, although women were more prone than men to identify and discuss what they considered to be the physical and emotional symptoms of stress that they were experiencing. There were both sex and minority group differences in the sources of stress perceived by students. For example, women students reported more stress than the men in the areas of schoolwork and living conditions; minority group students reported more stress from schoolwork than nonminority group students.

The progressive increase in the number of women students in medical schools, along with the critical mass of women who achieved professional status in medicine in the 1970s and 1980s, has focused attention on a set of issues highly relevant to the value climate and the emotional atmosphere in which both men and women students and house staff are presently being trained. Will the significantly greater presence of women alter the predominant influence of "masculine" attitudes, modes of expression, interaction patterns, coping mechanisms, and life styles that are embedded in the scientific and professional ethos of medicine and in the long and powerful process of socialization that physicians undergo? As historian Regina Markell Morantz-Sanchez reminds us, this is by no means a new question. It was raised but not solved in the nineteenth century when, on the wave of an earlier period of feminism, women entered medical schools and the medical profession for the first time. "One can hope only," she writes, "that at least some of the concerns that they brought to medical practice in the past—an emphasis on human care and a concern for the profession's responsibility to the community—will occupy center stage in the practice of medicine once again."[57] "It is probably too soon," she concludes, to "make any predictions about the prospective role of women physicians or about the possible results of their increasing numbers within the profession," particularly whether it "will result in a general reorientation of professional values."[58] Certainly, however, this is a phenomenon that sociologists as well as historians should closely watch and study.

However important the demographic changes in the medical student population may prove to be, they constitute only one item in a list of major developments that are affecting the socialization environment of the 1980s medical school. An inventory of pertinent developments would include the following:

1. *Intense preoccupation with the dramatic rise in the cost of medical care in the United States over the past twenty-five years.*

2. *Increasing emphasis on "cost containment" and its elevation to the status of a moral as well as a practical categorical imperative.* Beginning in the 1970s, *the establishment of cost-containment educational programs* for medical students, physicians in residency training, or both.[59]

3. Partly as a consequence of the *diagnosis-related-groups (DRG's) system of payment* for hospital care that has been instituted and the resulting shorter lengths of hospitalization, much *briefer and shallower opportunities for medical students to have contact with in-patients.* "The recent extensive alterations in hospital financing have aggravated the problems involved in teaching clinical medicine in hospitals. For example, because patients are being admitted and discharged as quickly as possible, there is little time for reflective study and learning by students and physicians, and sometimes no time to make the patients as comfortable as possible."[60] As in the 1950s era of comprehensive medical care and teaching programs, *educators are "looking again at whether teaching in ambulatory-care settings might provide a good alternative."*[61] Thirty years after such teaching in outpatient clinics programs was launched and subsequently failed, for somewhat ironic reasons it may now represent "an idea whose time has finally come."[62]

4. *A greatly increased number and proportion of very old persons among hospitalized patients, who are chronically ill and often severely disabled physically and/or mentally.* This is a consequence of the aging of the American population, and the progressive frailty and deterioration of health with age, especially of the "old old." "The elderly average more than twice the rate of hospital admissions and hospital days per year of those under 65 years. Moreover, the use of hospital services by the elderly increases as they age. For example, the rate of hospital admissions of persons aged 75 and over is 51 percent higher than that of persons aged 65 to 74, and their rate of hospital days is 70 percent higher."[63] Although medical students' contact with in-patients during their years of clinical clerkships may be shorter than in the past, they are exposed to more very sick, very elderly patients than any other cohort of American medical students ever has been.

5. *The continuing development of high-technology medicine, with its powerful diagnostic, polytherapeutic, and life-sustaining capacities*; its dominion in university hospitals and academic medical centers, where medical students are largely trained; its relationship to the life-and-death ethical and existential dilemmas facing modern medicine, epitomized by the centrality of intensive care units in such teaching hospitals.

6. *Escalating public and medical professional concern about ethical issues associated with advances in biomedical science and technology and their use in the delivery of medical care.* Beginning in the 1970s, the inclusion of bioethics courses in most American medical schools,[64] often displacing or eclipsing courses in psychiatry and social science, called "behavioral science" in medical schools of the 1950s and 1960s.

7. A new trend, in the 1980s, to offer *humanities courses in medical school*—courses in literature, art, and sometimes music, as well as in bioethics. The premise of these courses is that the humanities provide a needed counterbalance to the overweening emphasis on science and technology in medical education, and that they have the potential of more sensitively and deeply attuning physicians-in-training to the human condition of their patients and its relationship to their own. From the 1950s into the 1980s, American medical schools moved from psychiatry to behavioral science to bioethics to the humanities, in their perennial search for a curriculum to more effectively develop students' understanding of the emotional, cultural, and so-

cial dimensions of human behavior in sickness and health, and foster in them the kinds of humane attitudes and values conducive to this understanding.

8. *The distancing and in many instances the virtual absence of senior faculty members from clinical teaching.* Medical school deans, department chairmen, and professors are pulled away from teaching by their absorption in organizational, administrative, and governance functions, and by their obligation to bring sufficient funds into the medical center to help support themselves, their departments, their divisions and their teams through the monies that they generate in patient care and via research grants.[65] *House staff, particularly residents, have always been among the primary teachers of medical students; in the mid-1980s, this is even more true.* In any case, by and large, *the pre-1960s role-model professor has vanished.*[66]

9. A systematic, though largely unintentional *downgrading of the value of skilled, direct, patient-oriented clinical observation in making diagnoses, formulating prognoses, and evaluating therapy.* This neglect of clinical phenomena results from the current tendency to rely on "the 'hard' data of morphology and laboratory tests" to obtain what is believed to be the most objective kind of scientific information,[67] and from the medical faculty's diminished involvement in bedside teaching.

Clinical skills are no longer actively taught. A casual pass is made in the course on physical diagnosis, but students are not observed talking to patients or examining them. We are training future physicians who have never been observed to elicit a history or perform a physical examination—not in second-year physical diagnosis class, not in third-year clinical clerkships, and not during house officership. And lo! the various specialty boards have abandoned the practice of observing candidates as they take a history and perform a physical examination. Is it any wonder that clinical skills are lost? That little reliance is placed on information so obtained? That tests and "numbers" take precedence?[68]

10. *A generalized state of demoralization on the part of medical faculty in the face of certain trends and changes in the organization, economics, status, and outlook of the medical profession.* Predominant among the matters that trouble faculty (and also their colleagues in practice) are:

The explosion of health care costs; the various fixed, prepayment and prospective payment systems for medical care that have evolved in response to escalating costs; the reduction in hospital bed occupancy and the loss of income for medical centers and practitioners that are in part consequences of these developments.

The rapid growth of explicitly for-profit entities in health services—the investor-owned corporation. Concern about the "coming of the corporation," or "medical-industrial complex"[69] turns around the question of whether "such organizations which have to produce a satisfactory return on stockholders' investments, [will] become excessively commercialized at the expense of quality of care, education, research, access to care for the indigent, and the fidiciary responsibilities of physicians."[70]

What is felt to be a *malpractice crisis*: the greater number and larger medical malpractice claims being filed; rapidly mounting insurance premiums; problems of obtaining professional liability insurance; the ways in which the malpractice situation may be altering practice patterns (including stopping practice altogether in certain fields like obstetrics); fundamental disquietude over whether the incidence of negligence by physicians is much higher than in the past and if so, why; distress over the possible relationship between the malpractice "epidemic" and an erosion of public esteem for and trust in the medical profession.

11. *The informal communication of the medical faculty's troubled and disheartened state of mind to medical students*, who are already concerned about how these and other changes in American medicine will affect their experiences, opportunities, and accomplishments as physicians.

> I have been dean for student affairs at Harvard Medical School for eight years. It is my responsibility and privilege to listen to medical students and to support their personal and professional development. What they have been telling me this year troubles me. It is exemplified by a recent encounter with a third-year student.
>
> The student was distressed. What had sustained him through the preclinical years was the anticipation of learning patient care. Now he had earned the right to wear a white coat and enter the wards. What he had encountered had discouraged him profoundly. The problem was . . . his interaction with his teachers. Once the formal teaching rounds were over, they talked only about the problems they faced. . . . Medicine, they said, was no fun any more. If students were included in the conversations, the faculty reminisced about the good old days, which neither they nor the students would ever see. They wondered aloud whether they would choose medicine if they had it to do over again.
>
> I have heard perhaps a dozen similar stories from students doing clerkships at some of Boston's leading teaching hospitals. But the lamentations about the woes afflicting medicine are hardly limited to teaching faculty. . . . All this hits students hard because they are already worried about the indebtedness they are incurring, particularly in view of the stories about the doctor glut, declining incomes, and the increasing competition for residency positions. They fear that their debts will force them to choose specialties on the basis of anticipated earnings rather than intrinsic interest. Indeed, some, in the role of tutors for premedical students, have begun to dissuade the college students they advise from choosing medicine, because they consider the prospects to be so bleak.[71]

Very similar student patterns are discernible in a small questionnaire-based study conducted at a quite different kind of medical school, at the University of Minnesota–Duluth, which is committed to training family physicians for rural practice. The 97 percent of the first- and second-year students who responded to this inquiry expressed many reservations about the way that American medicine was developing and their own professional relationship to it:

> A majority of the students were "extremely" concerned about the type of practice climate that would exist by the time they would enter practice [and] . . . had already "seriously" questioned their decision to become physicians . . . influenced by their concerns about the ways in which medicine was changing. Two categories of answers dominated the students' concerns about the future of medicine: loss of autonomy and inadequate financial rewards. Of these two, financial considerations emerged as the paramount concern. . . . The one exception to students' rather consistent emphasis on financial concerns was the low ranking given to "inadequate financial rewards" in affecting their views of medicine . . . as

a desirable profession. . . . The second major finding . . . was that the s[...]
quently reported that their present and future decisions about specialt[...]
practice location, and practice type had been and would continue to be inf[...]
by their concerns about changes in the organization and financing of medical[...]
The direction of this shift was consistently from a smaller to a larger practice co[...]
munity, from a solo or partnership to a group (or from a smaller to a larger group)[...]
and from a generalist to a more specialist practice.[72]

12. *A new wave of attempts to reform the medical school curriculum is taking place,*
precipitated by the revolutionary advances in medical science and technology, the
metamorphoses of the content, organization, and mode of delivery of medical care,
the concomitant value and policy problems that are occurring, and the anomie-like
reactions to them.

> The Panel respects the degree of change and innovation already under way. . . .
> However, it is urgent that considerably more be done to adapt the general profes-
> sional education of students in medicine to the changing circumstances already ap-
> parent or emerging for the future. The Panel does not choose to invoke the hysterical
> hyperbole of crisis; nor do we wish to impugn the high quality of much that is being
> done. . . . [But] Panel judges that the present system of general professional
> education for medicine will become increasingly inadequate unless it is revised.[73]

> Last May . . . the Faculty of Medicine gave its approval to the dean and a
> group of professors to create an experimental curriculum. . . . Instead of merely
> tinkering with course requirements or shifting hours of instruction from one sub-
> ject to another, the authors of the program have begun by making a fresh appraisal
> of the knowledge, skills, and attitudes that physicians today and tomorrow need to
> possess. On this foundation will be built an entirely new curriculum. Not only will
> it seek to alter what students learn; it plans sweeping innovations in the methods
> by which they are taught. . . . Stirrings of change are evident elsewhere in the
> United States. . . . This . . . has not come about by chance. Many forces have com-
> bined to alter the body of medical knowledge, the way in which doctors practice
> their craft, and the system of delivering health care services in this country. It is
> only natural, then, that educators are starting to wonder how they should respond.
> As yet, the outcome is hard to predict. Like ancient China, medical education has
> experienced many assaults from the outside world without undergoing substantial
> change. Even so, I believe that pressures have now reached such a point that basic
> reforms are likely to occur.[74]

As we shall see in the next chapter, the current socializing experiences of interns and residents—young doctors in the house staff phase of their training—are
even more directly and significantly affected by all these sociomedical changes and
incipient changes than are those of medical students, and by the anxious, disheartened, and bewildered reactions of the mature physicians who are their supervisors.

NOTES

1. See Howard S. Becker and others, *Boys in White: Student Culture in Medical School* (Chicago:
University of Chicago Press, 1961); Daniel H. Funkenstein, "The Learning and Personal
Development of Medical Students, Reconsidered," *The New Physician*, 19, no. 9 (September

ınkenstein, *Medical Students, Medical Schools and Society During* the Career Choices of Physicians 1958-1976 (Cambridge, Mass.: ıy, 1978); Kenneth R. Hammond and Fred Kern, Jr., *Teaching* (Cambridge, Mass.: Harvard University Press, 1959); Milton J. 's Doctors (New York: Appleton-Century-Crofts, 1964); Harold ·dynamic Study of Medical Students and Their Adaptational ," *Journal of Medical Education*, 35, no. 7 (July 1960), 696– ？eader, and Patricia L. Kendall, eds., *The Student-Physician:* ...e *Sociology of Medical Education* (Cambridge, Mass.: Harvard _¬, 1957); George E. Miller, *Teaching and Learning in Medical School* ...ıge, Mass.: Harvard University Press, 1961); Stephen J. Miller, *Prescription for Leadership: Training for the Medical Elite* (Chicago: Aldine Publishing Co., 1970); Emily Mumford, *Interns: From Students to Physicians* (Cambridge, Mass.: Harvard University Press, 1970).

2. Jeylan T. Mortimer and Roberta G. Simmons, "Adult Socialization," *Annual Review of Sociology*, 4 (1978), 421–54.

3. Samuel W. Bloom, "The Sociology of Medical Education: Some Comments on the State of a Field," *Milbank Memorial Fund Quarterly*, XLIII, no. 2 (April 1965), 143–84; "Socialization for the Physician's Role: A Review of Some Contributions of Research to Theory," in *Becoming A Physician: Development of Values and Attitudes in Medicine*, eds. Eileen C. Shapiro and Leah M. Lowenstein (Cambridge, Mass.: Ballinger Publishing Company, 1979) 3–52.

4. Bloom, "Socialization for the Physician's Role," p. 16.

5. *Physicians for the Twenty-First Century*, Report of the Panel on the General Professional Education of the Physician and College Preparation for Medicine (Washington, D.C.: Association of American Medical Colleges, 1984), passim.

6. Both the *Journal of Medical Education* and the *Journal of the American Medical Association*, in its Annual Report on Medical Education in the United States, publish such statistics each year.

7. Funkenstein, *Medical Students, Medical Schools and Society During Five Eras*, especially Chap. 2

8. It is my own first-hand impression that what Funkenstein describes as the Student Activism Era lasted more than one year, beginning around the mid-1960s and not ending until the mid-1970s. Funkenstein's twenty-five years of research on medical students, particularly the way that they choose their careers, ended in the 1970s. As he would recognize, the 1980s constitute still another era.

9. Funkenstein, *Medical Students, Medical Schools and Society During Five Eras*, p. 11.

10. See the annotated selected bibliography on impaired professionals (including attorneys, judges, and clergy, as well as physicians) in *Social Controls and the Medical Profession*, Judith P. Swazey and Stephen R. Scher, eds. (Boston: Oegleschlager, Gunn & Hain, Publishers, Inc., 1985), pp. 231–50.

11. Renée C. Fox, "The Human Condition of Health Professionals," Distinguished Lecturer Series, School of Health Studies (Durham: University of New Hampshire, 1980), p. 33.

12. As a member of the Columbia University Bureau of Applied Social Research team that undertook studies in the sociology of medical education in the 1950s, I spent four years as a participant observer at Cornell University Medical College in direct fieldwork contact with the medical socialization process. Since that time I have been continually engaged in teaching, observing, and interviewing premedical and medical students and house officers, and have regularly visited and lectured in medical schools throughout the country, where I have had considerable contact with medical students and house staff. I have kept a fieldworker's record of many of these experiences.

13. The concepts "training for uncertainty," "training in detached concern," and "scientific magic" were coined by me. The concept "fate of idealism" is Howard S. Becker's. Everett C. Hughes pioneered studies of "mistakes at work"; Charles L. Bosk is the chief sociologist to have developed this concept in a medical (surgical) socialization and professional self-control framework. Physician-psychoanalyst Jay Katz has made the most important contribution to understanding the social and psychological dynamics of the silence surrounding the doctor-patient relationship. See Renée C. Fox, "Training for Uncertainty," in *The Student-Physician*, eds. Merton, Reader, and Kendall, 207–41; Harold I. Lief and Renée C. Fox, "Training for 'Detached Concern' in Medical Students" in *The Psychological Basis of Medical Practice*, eds. Harold I.

Lief, Victor F. Lief, and Nina R. Lief (New York: Harper and Row, 1963), 12–35; Renée C. Fox, "The Sociology of Modern Medical Research," in *Asian Medical Systems: A Comparative Study*, ed. Charles Leslie (Berkeley: University of California Press, 1976), 102–14; Howard S. Becker, "The Fate of Idealism in Medical School," *American Sociological Review*, 23 (February 1958), 50–6; Charles L. Bosk, *Forgive and Remember: Managing Medical Failure* (Chicago: University of Chicago Press, 1979); Jay Katz, *The Silent World of Doctor and Patient* (New York: The Free Press, 1984); and Terry Mizrahi, *Getting Rid of Patients: Contradictions in the Socialization of Physicians* (New Brunswick, N.J.: Rutgers University Press, 1986).

14. Medical schools and residency programs do not ask applicants to identify their religious background. This is a safeguard against allowing religion to influence their admissions policy in any way, as it did in an earlier historical era. However, it does not explain why sociologists have not attempted to collect their own data on this subject. Two notable exceptions to this pattern are the data on medical students' religious values at the beginning of the freshman year and at the end of the senior year, reported by Gordon W. Allport, Philip E. Vernon, and Gardner Lindzey in *Study of Values. A Scale for Measuring the Dominant Interests in Personality*, 3rd ed. (Boston: Houghton-Mifflin Company, 1960); and John Colombotos and Corinne Kirchner's *Physicians and Social Change* (New York: Oxford University Press, 1986), which examines the relationship between medical students', house staff's, and practicing physicians' social backgrounds (religion included), their professional characteristics, and their attitudes.

15. Charles L. Bosk, "The Doctors," *Wilson Quarterly* (Spring 1980), p. 81.

16. Howard S. Becker and others, *Boys in White;* Merton, and Reader, and Kendall, *The Student-Physician*.

17. Fox, "The Human Condition of Health Professionals," pp. 12–14.

18. Renée C. Fox, "The Autopsy: Its Place in the Attitude-Learning of Second-Year Medical Students," in Renée C. Fox, *Essays in Medical Sociology: Journeys Into the Field* (New York: John Wiley & Sons, 1979), p. 58.

19. Fox, "The Human Condition of Health Professionals," p. 21.

20. Daniel J. Levinson, "Medical Education and the Theory of Adult Socialization," *Journal of Health and Social Behavior*, 8, no. 4 (December 1967), 254–56.

21. See Bloom, "Socialization for the Physician's Role," and Renée C. Fox, "Is There A 'New' Medical Student?: A Comparative View of Medical Socialization in the 1950s and the 1970s," in Fox, *Essays*, pp. 78–101.

22. Kenneth M. Ludmerer, *Learning to Heal: The Development of American Medical Education* (New York: Basic Books, 1985), p. 256.

23. Ibid., p. 255.

24. For a fuller description of the sociological atmosphere of medical education in the 1950s, see Fox, "Is There a 'New' Medical Student?" especially pp. 81–92.

25. Funkenstein, *Medical Students, Medical Schools and Society During Five Eras*, passim.

26. Paul B. Beeson, "The Changing Role Model and the Shift in Power," *Daedalus*, 115, no. 2 (Spring 1986), 83–97.

27. Robert K. Merton, "Some Preliminaries to a Sociology of Medical Education," in *The Student-Physician*, eds. Merton, Reader, and Kendall, pp. 46–47. Donald Light later developed a "sociological calendar of psychiatric socialization," building upon the concept and the unpublished sociological calendar of the successive phases of medical school training that I developed for the Columbia University Bureau of Applied Social Research project in the 1950s. See Donald Light, "The Sociological Calendar: An Analytic Tool for Fieldwork Applied to Medical and Psychiatric Training," *American Journal of Sociology*, 80, no. 5 (March 1975), 1145–64; Donald Light, *Becoming Psychiatrists: The Professional Transformation of Self* (New York: W. W. Norton & Co., 1980), Chap. 5.

28. Mary Jean Huntington, "The Development of a Professional Self-Image," in Merton, Reader, and Kendall, *The Student-Physician*, pp. 179–87.

29. Merton, "Some Preliminaries to a Sociology of Medical Education," pp. 72–76.

30. The analyses of "training for uncertainty" and "training for detached concern" in this chapter are drawn heavily from the précis contained in Fox, "Is There A 'New' Medical Student?" pp. 83–88.

31. Light, *Becoming Psychiatrists*, p. 282.

32. Fox, *Experiment Perilous*.

33. Katz, *The Silent World*, p. 173.
34. Fox, "The Autopsy," passim.
35. Robert H. Ebert, "Medical Education at the Peak of the Era of Experimental Medicine," *Daedalus*, 115, no. 2 (Spring 1986), 55–81. Reprinted by permission of *Daedalus*, Journal of the American Academy of Arts and Sciences.
36. Funkenstein, *Medical Students, Medical Schools and Society During Five Eras*, p. 12.
37. Ebert, "Medical Education at the Peak of the Era of Experimental Medicine," pp. 61–63.
38. Christopher C. Fordham, III, "Changing Medical Education—The New Schools" (Editorial), *New England Journal of Medicine*, 301, no. 13 (September 27, 1979), 719–20.
39. Funkenstein, *Medical Students, Medical Schools and Society During Five Eras*, pp. 12, 18–22.
40. Ebert, "Medical Education at the Peak of the Era of Experimental Medicine," p. 65.
41. Fitzhugh Mullan, *White Coat, Clenched Fist: The Political Education of an American Physician* (New York: Macmillan Publishing Co., Inc., 1976), pp. 20–2.
42. Ken Neward and others, *New England Journal of Medicine* (Letters to the Editor), 293, no. 11 (September 11, 1975), 564–65.
43. Wallace J. Mulligan (Navajo Nation Health Foundation, Ganado, AZ), *New England Journal of Medicine* (Letter to the Editor), 293 no. 11 (September 11, 1975), 564. Like the letter from the Stanford medical students cited above, this letter was written in response to Kriss's article "On White Coats and Other Matters."
44. Ebert, "Medical Education at the Peak of the Era of Experimental Medicine," pp. 69–70.
45. Ibid., p. 73.
46. Fox, "Is There A 'New' Medical Student?" pp. 78–101.
47. Ebert, "Medical Education at the Peak of the Era of Experimental Medicine," p. 71.
48. Mullan, *White Coat, Clenched Fist*, pp. 215 and 222.
49. Peter Conrad, "The Myth of Cut-throats Among Premedical Students: On the Role of Stereotypes in Justifying Failure and Success," *Journal of Health and Social Behavior*, 27 (June), 150–60.
50. Lewis Thomas, "How to Fix the Pre-Medical Curriculum," *The Medusa and the Snail* (New York: Bantam Books, 1980), 113–16. This essay originally appeared in the *New England Journal of Medicine*, 298 (1979), 1180–1.
51. Richard H. Moy, "Critical Values in Medical Education," *New England Journal of Medicine*, 301, no. 13 (September 27, 1979), 695.
52. Association of American Medical Colleges, *Annual Report 1984-85*, "Students," *Journal of Medical Education*, 61, no. 3, suppl. (March 1986), 249.
53. Moy, "Critical Values in Medical Education," p. 695.
54. Steven Shea and Mindy Thompson Fullilove, "Entry of Black and Other Minority Students Into U.S. Medical Schools," *New England Journal of Medicine*, 313, no. 15 (October 10, 1985), 933–40.
55. Derek Bok, "Needed: A New Way to Train Doctors," *Harvard Magazine* (May-June 1984),. 34.
56. Malkah T. Notman, Patricia Salt, and Carol C. Nadelson, "Stress and Adaptation in Medical Students: Who Is Most Vulnerable?" *Comprehensive Psychiatry*, 25, no. 3 (May/June 1984), 355–66.
57. Regina Markell Morantz-Sanchez, *Sympathy and Science: Women Physicians in American Medicine* (New York: Oxford University Press, 1985), p. 361.
58. Morantz-Sanchez, *Sympathy and Science*, p. 7.
59. John M. Eisenberg and Sankey V. Williams, "Cost Containment and Changing Physicians' Practice Behavior: Can the Fox Learn to Guard the Chicken Coop?" *Journal of the American Medical Association*, 246, no. 19 (November 13, 1981), 2196–97.
60. Gerald T. Perkoff, "Teaching Clinical Medicine in the Ambulatory Setting: An Idea Whose Time May Have Finally Come," *New England Journal of Medicine*, 314, no. 1 (January 2, 1986), 27.
61. Ibid. [italics added]
62. Ibid., p. 31.

63. A. A. Scitovsky and A. M. Capron, "Medical Care at the End of Life," *American Review of Public Health,* 7 (1986), 61–62.

64. In 1986, 95 medical schools had an ethics or human values program, compared with 12 schools in 1971. Albert Jonsen, Address at Annual Meeting, American Association of Medical Colleges, Oct. 26-29, 1986; reprinted in *Medical Educators* 62 (1987), 95–99.

65. Robert G. Petersdorf and Marjorie P. Wilson, "The Four Horsemen of the Apocalypse: Study of Academic Medical Center Governance," *Journal of the American Medical Association,* 247, no. 8 (February 28, 1982), 1153–61.

66. Beeson, "The Changing Role Model," p. 90.

67. Alvan R. Feinstein, "On Blind Men, Elephants, Spectrums, and Controversies: Lessons From Rheumatic Fever Revisited" *Journal of Chronic Diseases* (Editorial), 39, no. 5 (1986), 341.

68. Ludwig W. Eichna, "Medical-School Education, 1975-1979: A Student's Perspective," *New England Journal of Medicine,* 301, no. 3 (September 25, 1980), 731. This article is based on Dr. Eichna's four years as a full-time medical student at Downstate Medical Center, which he undertook after he retired in July 1974 from the chairmanship of the Department of Medicine of that institution. He underwent this second stint of medical school education, including taking all the examinations required, to better identify, analyze, and communicate the problems that underlay the course and results of medical education, with which he had become increasingly dissatisfied as a physician/medical educator/chairman.

69. Arnold S. Relman, "The New Medical-Industrial Complex," *New England Journal of Medicine,* 303, no. 17 (October 23, 1980), 963–70; Paul Starr, *The Social Transformation of American Medicine* (New York: Basic Books, Inc., 1982), pp. 420–49; Bradford H. Gray, ed., *The New Health Care for Profit: Doctors and Hospitals in a Competitive Environment* (Washington, D.C.: National Academy Press, 1983).

70. Bradford H. Gray and Walter J. McNerney, "For-Profit Enterprise in Health Care: The Institute of Medicine Study," *New England Journal of Medicine,* 314, no. 23 (June 5, 1986), 524.

71. Carola Eisenberg, "It Is Still a Privilege to Be a Doctor" *New England Journal of Medicine,* 314, no. 17 (April 24, 1986), 1113–14.

72. Frederic W. Hafferty and James G. Boulger, "A Look by Medical Students At Medical Practice in the Future," *Journal of Medical Education,* 61 no. 5 (May 1986), 364–66.

73. *Physicians for the Twenty-First Century* (Introduction by Steven Muller), pp. xii–xiii.

74. Bok, "Needed: A New Way to Train Doctors," p. 32.

CHAPTER 4

THE EDUCATION, TRAINING, AND SOCIALIZATION OF PHYSICIANS: RESIDENCY AND PRACTICE

SOCIALIZATION OF INTERNS AND RESIDENTS: 1950s INTO THE 1980s

In contrast to the discontinuities in the sociological literature on medical students, the studies of the socialization of interns and residents that have been published span a thirty-year period, extending from the mid-1950s to the present. Although the number of such studies is limited, taken as a whole they provide a "thickly descriptive"[1] account of this "journeyman apprenticeship"[2] phase of a young physician's career. These are the years of residency or graduate medical training, as a member of a hospital's house staff. Under the authority and supervision of older attending physicians, the young, modestly salaried doctor takes major, twenty-four hour, on-call responsibility for patients—their admission to the hospital, their medical history and examinations, the diagnosis of their medical problems, the prescribed therapy and care that they receive, and their eventual discharge or death. The largely first-hand research that has been devoted to this professional socialization period encompasses a diverse cross-section of internships and residencies that train for a number of specialized branches of medicine (internal medicine, surgery, psychiatry, and obstetrics and gynecology), on a variety of services, situated in different types of university, community, and public hospitals.

In addition to sociological monographs, the available literature includes a stream of published articles, essays, and letters about the experiences of house staff, written by physicians, some with appreciable social science training, that regularly appear in major American medical journals. By and large, these publications focus on the high level of stress and fatigue and the intricate role dilemmas that the residency years entail. There is another, related genre of literature about house staff that has considerable sociological interest. These are the provocative, confessional, usually very critical and self-critical books by physicians who have recently emerged from this training, of which Fitzhugh Mullan's autobiographical *White Coat, Clenched Fist*, and the semifictive *House of God*, by the pseudonymous Samuel Shem, are prime examples.[3]

The year of internship, followed by two to four years as a resident (depending on the specialty), all agree, is the "true vocational training period."[4] It is during this time that young physicians achieve greater mastery of general and specialized medical knowledge and skill, and directly experience the technical and ethical parameters of medical decision-making. Residency is also the time when they consolidate their acquisition of professional attitudes and values, crystallize their professional identity, and commit themselves to the particular field of medicine in which they will practice, including how, where, and with whom they will practice it.

The sociological studies of internship and residency treat many of the same socialization themes as those dealing with medical students and medical schools. Notable among these are training for uncertainty, detached concern, control and self-control, responsibility, and the handling of mistakes at work. However, more intensively and extensively than the medical student/medical school studies, the literature on the house staff stage of professional training deals with its ritual aspects, especially its associated rites of passage and occupational rituals. Other major themes include the social structure and cultural ambiance of the teaching hospitals and the medical, psychological, and social characteristics of the patients for whom house staff are responsible in these settings; the complexity of the simultaneously collegial and subordinate role of house officers and attending physicians—particularly the fact that although they are the primary patient caretakers, it is the attending physicians who are the ultimate clinical decision-makers; and the social system and world-view of the "total institution" subculture formed by the house staff.

Most sociological accounts emphasize how stressful the years of internship and residency are, and they explore the deleterious effects this high level of stress can have on the physical, mental, and emotional state of these young physicians and on the way that they feel about and treat patients.

> The critical years of internship and residency in internal medicine during which freshly minted MDs are thrown into the trenches as the first line of defense against disease and trauma constitute the transition period between medical school and practice. . . . It is a traumatic period of learning in the chaotic atmosphere of the emergency rooms as well as in the erudite symposia sponsored by the attending faculty physicians. Interns and residents . . . are continually faced with the "nuts and bolts" of everyday patient management as well as theories and diagnoses of rare and poorly understood diseases. The years of house staff training provide the crucible in which the professional consciousness of the doctor is forged. It is a baptism by fire into the practice of hospital-based and clinical medicine to which doctors must submit themselves in order to become fully certified members of their profession.
>
> It is also a period of first employment. They are paid to provide services to large numbers of indigent patients and, increasingly, to middle-class ones as well.

In much of their work, they are treating the poor, the victimized, the homeless and the wretched. . . . Additionally, they themselves believe that they have been degraded; they lose control over their personal lives, which become dominated by work. They become easily exploitable labor, working extremely long hours for a modest salary. After being seniors in medical school, . . . they are plummeted to the bottom of the physician hierarchy. . . .

Even though there is the promise of future rewards . . . such degradation breeds resentment. In their isolated subculture they manifest resentment for nearly everyone with whom they come in contact; however, it is the patient who becomes a major target for the young doctors' disgruntlement.[5]

Despite the scope and detail of the sociological works on internship and residency, they have several crucial gaps. They mention, but do not explore, the relations of interns and residents with nurses, other health professionals and hospital personnel, patients' families, and with their own families[6] and nonmedical friends —the nature of these relationships, what happens to them during the prolonged and demanding house officer training process, and what role they play in the orientation, content, and outcome of this stage of doctorhood. Nor are there studies available of the comparative experiences of women and men house staff or of whether, and if so how, the great increase in the numbers and the felt presence of young female physicians is affecting the interns' and residents' subculture.

SOCIALIZATION IN INTERNSHIP

Two major sociological studies of the learning experience and impact of internships exist in the published literature: Emily Mumford's *Interns: From Students to Physicians*, and Stephen J. Miller's *Prescription for Leadership: Training for the Medical Elite*.[7] The primary data collection for these studies took place in the late 1950s and early 1960s, at a time when almost all interns were men, and prior to the eruption of the period of social protest and challenge by American medical students and house officers that occurred at the end of the sixties. As the titles of the two books suggest, these studies had contrasting though interrelated goals. Mumford's research was focused on medical internship at a community hospital and a university hospital, with the express purpose of describing and analyzing the patterned similarities and differences between them. Miller's study dealt exclusively with a so-called "elite internship," located on a unit of a city hospital, renowned for its academic medical research, that was run by a prestigious medical school.[8]

The assumptions about socialization on which the two research studies were based also diverged. Mumford's conceptual framework closely followed the Columbia University-Bureau of Applied Social Research premises about the "anticipatory socialization" import of young physicians' experiences, the continuities and discontinuities that these experiences represented, their latent as well as manifest influence, and their possible long-term professional significance in shaping individual and collective doctorhood:[9]

The internship stage of training [Mumford wrote in the introduction to her book] offers a nearly perfect example of potentially effective adult socialization. The beginning physician is introduced and moved into patterns of behavior with his colleagues and with patients in an emotionally charged atmosphere. His encounters and experiences there can reinforce and protect some of the commitments he began to form in medical school. Or he can face a series of frustrations, reality shocks, and contradictions, as well as escape routes that provide alternatives and possibly rationalizations for altering the commitments. The years of house-staff training often provide a physician's first personal encounter, his initiation rites, in medicine. For some, these years are also the last chance the medical profession has to exert direct, sometimes round-the-clock, and near-exclusive influence or control.[10]

Miller cleaved to the University of Chicago's more situationally specific, "negotiated order" perspective on medical socialization, with its emphasis on pragmatic, expedient, "learning the ropes," and "coping" behavior:

> My study of a Harvard internship [Miller stated] is aligned with the [Chicago] study of the University of Kansas [Medical School], and so identifiable by the assumption underlying the analysis presented: . . . that the internship is an apprenticeship conducted in the hospital, an organization which poses specific problems that must be resolved by interns before they are permitted to practice medicine or go on to further training for a variety of careers in the medical profession. . . . [It] is an apprenticeship for fledgling physicians so they may learn medicine by actually providing patient care under the supervision of more experienced physicians . . . in an organization whose explicit purpose is not the education of physicians but the provision of . . . care. . . . Interns face a problematic situation, requiring them to determine how to satisfy the purpose of an internship and do the work that will serve the purpose of the hospital. The demands of work are . . . an obstacle that must be overcome before interns resolve the problems inherent to the situation. They must learn where things and people are, the implications of rank and privilege, the expectations of those with whom they must work and who are permanent members of the organization. Further, they must learn what the rules are, which rules can or must be broken, which followed to the letter. The failure to learn these things necessary to do the work they are assigned may preclude learning anything else. They must, before they learn anything else, learn the ropes.[11]

Mumford's well-designed, comparative study integrated several waves of field observations with questionnaire-derived qualitative and quantitative data. It was the first to describe and analyze how the social system and social networks, history and cultural tradition, and the value orientation and value climate of the particular hospitals in which graduate physicians train affect the "ideals," "standards," and "behavior and professional communication patterns," out of which they "create their own different constructions of a way of life in medicine." It is a classic work, unreplicated to this day.

> The fresh start implicit in the first day of internship is associated with great expectations [Mumford writes]. Practically no one enters this phase of a medical career planning to become careless of scientific standards or treatment. But each hospital throws the spotlight on certain aspects of the intern's work and leaves some work relatively protected against visibility or supervision and thus potential-

ly subject to neglect. In this process each hospital provides selective reinforcement for some ideals and some of the intern's initial commitments, and each hospital allows some leeway around some other ideals. These factors can vary markedly in different learning environments, and they condition which ideals, which standards, and which behavior and professional communication patterns are most consistently reinforced and accepted by the graduate physician. . . . The pressures and possibilities each hospital [offers] its interns daily, and the hospital's hopes for its interns provide some of the material for them to create their own different constructions of a way of life in medicine.[12]

In a key chapter entitled "The First of July in Two Hospitals," Mumford enables us to accompany two physicians on their respective first days at University Hospital and Community Hospital, where each is beginning his year of internship. Characterizing the ethos surrounding internship at University Hospital as "joining a proud company," and that of Community Hospital as entering "a friendly place," she proceeds to show in ethnographic detail how the experiences, atmosphere, and "directions that were implied this first day in each hospital would be repeatedly confirmed"[13] as the year unfolded. In another evocative chapter devoted to a case study of "The Medical Chart," Mumford demonstrates how the greater importance attached to chartwork in University than in Community Hospital is symbolically and substantively indicative of the two hospitals' different value emphases, styles of interaction, media of communication, and modes of socializing newcomers.

Essentially, University Hospital is an urban, medical school-affiliated, academically oriented, and tradition-conscious institution. It has a formal, hierarchically-ordered, team-structured, professional atmosphere, a commitment to "graduated specialization" and "advancing knowledge" through teaching and research, and a preference for "interesting" patients—defined as those whose complex or unusual biomedical conditions furnish good teaching and learning opportunities for house staff and attending physicians. Community Hospital is a much smaller institution, dedicated to the health care of the suburban town in which it is located. It has a flexible, informal milieu, encourages "individual initiative," and defines "interesting patients" in a pluralistic fashion—including those who are "interesting persons" or who have psychological problems, as well as those with biologically intriguing conditions.

The hospital unit on which Miller's study of interns is set has many of the attributes of Mumford's University Hospital, with an even more "proud tradition" of medical research and academic prestige. Based on his field observations and *in situ* interviewing, Miller describes what it is like to be an intern in this setting, tracing out the stages that interns go through as they grapple with the responsibilities and demands of this house officer year, and try to come to terms with them. At the outset, Miller finds, they tackle the arduous, overwhelming amount of work that internship entails by trying to "get everything done":

> They stay at the hospital until all hours of the night, examining patients, carrying out medical procedures, doing laboratory tests, and writing it all down in patients' charts. Early the next morning they are back, finishing last-minute chores before another day begins. As if this pace weren't grueling enough, they try to do all their academic work as well, though they may sleep through some of the lectures and conferences.[14]

They are surprised not only by how much there is to do, but also that it involves "nursing, laboratory, and administrative, as well as purely medical, tasks" ("scut work," as they commonly refer to it) that have little relevance to their future careers.[15] The "initial perspective" that interns develop during the first weeks is that no matter how hard the work is, or peripherally relevant to the diagnosis and treatment of patients' illnesses, it is all their responsibility, and they must find a way to do it. Assistant residents play a key role in "fostering the interns' whole hog attitude toward responsibility."[16] In the "doing everything" phase, interns give up all their leisure time and activity, sacrifice family life, and sleep very little. This eventuates in a collective physical and psychological crisis, marked by sleep deprivation, out of which evolves a new "operating perspective organized around the idea of clinical experience."[17] Having decided that it is not possible to do everything that supposedly is their responsibility, interns now focus their major attention and energy on taking care of patients, from which they feel they can learn the most medicine. They cut back on the time and effort devoted to academic activities, such as conferences, seminars, less interesting rounds, and reading, defining these as less important. Despite the new circumscribed definition of their work, and partly because of it, interns are more intent than ever on having responsibility for patient care. Miller observes that the interns' quasi-competitive determination not to relinquish patient care responsibility to residents, their immediate superiors in the hospital hierarchy, "has a great deal to do with [their] maintaining a high level of [clinical] effort."[18]

Miller underscores the fact that the interns' development of a strategy for coping with their situation and of rationalizations to support it is part of a social learning process that is "determined" by the hospital in which their training program is embedded—an institution that is organized primarily for the purpose of providing service to patients, and only secondarily to teach interns and other medical personnel. He emphasizes the acquisition of managerial, "learning the ropes" skills, especially learning to "tactfully exploit superiors and subordinates," a technique, Miller alleges, that they continue to use throughout their training whenever there are problems to solve that "require improvisation and diplomacy."[19]

According to Miller, this "maximizing clinical perspective" phase of socialization lasts for the rest of the internship year. However, in reanalyzing Miller's data, Light found two more stages of development:

> After six months, the interns felt they had learned all they could from maximizing clinical experience, and they took on the more depressing perspective of merely Pushing Through to the end of the year. This continued for about three months, when the interns began to learn from the teaching staff how to discern the unique and subtle aspects of largely routine cases so that they acquired the perspective of Learning from Each Patient.[20]

To a degree, Miller's description of the stresses of internship coincides with the accounts of its rigors that "have been catalogued over the years in a variety of biographical and anecdotal formats, including books that range from scholarly surveys to best-selling novels,"[21] and also numerous medical journal articles. These writings confirm Miller's findings that, although the entire house officer period, from internship through residency, contains many intense and stressful experiences, it is the first year that is fraught with the most pressure and strain.[22] However, compared with the more recent publications on "the distress of internship,"[23] Miller's study appears to *underestimate* the amount and range of difficulty these young physicians face and the adverse effects it can have on the quality of their medical reasoning, the skill with which they perform such technical tasks as reading and interpreting electrocardiograms,[24] their ability to relate to patients in a concerned, compassionate and insightful way, and on their emotional health and personal lives.[25]

The articles that have been appearing in the 1980s mention sources of stress not treated by Miller:

> The intern must, for the first time, assume responsibility for difficult and emotionally charged problems involving such issues as death, sexuality, and disability. Mature behavior is demanded of residents, whose maturation has often been delayed by their intense commitment to premedical and medical education. New responsibilities of marriage and parenthood may be encouraged, financial pressures from accumulating debts may intensify.[26]

This literature also suggests that the hardships of the house officer years may have increased since the late 1960s, when Stephen Miller conducted his field research:

> Before the late 1960s the resident's job ["resident" is used here to include internship] routinely involved more patient contact and included many procedures that are now performed by technicians and nurses. Clerical responsibilities, coordination of consultant activities, dictation of complicated discharge summaries, and scheduling of procedures is the "scut work" of the 1980s. None of these activities yields even the meager interpersonal satisfaction that performing laboratory tests, starting intravenous lines, or drawing blood (the "scut work" of the 1960s) used to give residents. Taking patient histories has become more complicated as hospitals admit larger numbers of elderly, chronically ill patients with multiple complex past hospitalizations. The fear of malpractice suits has created anxiety among residents who believe that their inexperience will be responsible for lawsuits. The factual knowledge base that residents are expected to command is far greater than that of two decades ago; thus, they are more afraid that they will harm a patient because they do not know an essential fact and are more anxious about their preparation for specialty board examinations. . . . The salaries of residents have increased substantially over the past two decades, but as in all American households, purchasing power (in 1967 dollars) has actually fallen, after a brief increase in the mid-1970s. . . . The effects that increasing debts from the high costs of medical education may have on residency training—by creating greater pressures to moonlight and thereby further lengthening the work week—are not yet clear.[27]

The newer publications on internship and residency highlight the degree of sociological ambivalence that physicians in practice and medical educators feel about the hardships of this period of training, and how their shared ambivalence contributes to the institutionalized persistence of these hardships. Despite the widespread professional recognition of the negative and even "hazardous" side effects of the "ordeals" of internship and residency, physicians' memories of this phase of their training "are generally positive, and surviving the internship takes on an almost ritualistic meaning. The intensity of experiences is remembered favorably

. . . making it difficult to generate much enthusiasm for change."[28] The passionate, often defensive and angry responses of many physicians to an editorial essay by Norman Cousins are particularly instructive in this respect. "[T]o what extent do the burdens placed on the interns come more under the heading of hazing than conditioning?", Cousins asked. "Does hazing of this sort reflect credit on the profession? Is it really necessary?" He ended his piece by stating his conviction that, "The custom of overworking interns has long since outlived its usefulness. It doesn't lead to the making of better physicians. It is inconsistent with the public interest. It is not really worthy of the tradition of medicine."[29] Among what the editors of *JAMA* referred to as the "avalanche of . . . commentary" that the *Journal* received in response, a sizable number of the letters from physicians supported the ardors of the internship and the rites of passage on moral grounds that "aspiring physicians should be prepared to undergo a reasonable degree of hardship in their ascent to a profession built on a tradition of personal sacrifice. Since medicine is dedicated to healing and the alleviation of human suffering, the training of physicians should emphasize the subordination of their personal comforts and perquisites."[30]

The dissimilarities between Miller's description of the stresses of internship in the late 1960s and early 1970s and those written in the 1980s by nonsociologists (largely physicians) seem largely attributable to changes that have occurred in the sociomedical environment of interns, both inside and outside the hospital. The net effect of some of these changes appears negligible. For example, "although few training programs now require being on-call every other night [as was formerly the case], the work week for most interns and residents still exceeds 80 hours."[31] At its 1987 annual meeting, the American Medical Association recognized that "the time had come to address the historical pattern endured by generations of physicians: long hours and little sleep." In an "overwhelming vote," the AMA delegates called for a prompt study and report on how the "exhausting and often onerous" schedule of residents and their supervision by senior physicians affect the quality of patient care. The AMA's effort to develop its own guidelines on these aspects of residency training was triggered in part by legal action against New York Hospital for a patient's death, allegedly due to "repeated mistakes" by fatigued and unsupervised house staff, and by the wide media coverage of this case. Professional action, the AMA hopes, will avoid "improper" legislative or administrative regulation of the schedules, work load, or supervision of house staff.[32]

On the other hand, the changes in the hospital patients for whom interns care—their personal and social attributes, as well as their medical problems, and the impact that they have on house staff (factors that Miller did not examine)—do make a significant difference. The growing incidence of AIDS patients—with their devastating medical complications and mortality and with the complex emotional, social, and ethical issues that surround their disease and care—is the most dramatic new dimension in the nature of residency training for physicians, and in the work of caregivers generally, at many teaching hospitals. Ethnographic accounts of caring for AIDS patients, studies of the anxiety and stress experienced by residents and other health care workers, and special education and support programs developed by hospitals are a new and growing part of the literature on residency training.

The question of whether the present-day professional and personal situation of interns is more difficult than it was in the past is not easy to resolve. The impression that the "distress of internship" may have increased is to some degree an artifact of the greater legitimacy now accorded to talking about these difficulties, the intellectual and emotional "impairments" and even breakdowns in young physicians to which they can lead, and the distancing and brutalizing effects that the structural strains of internship can have on the kinds of relationships house staff form with patients. The fact that a group of house officers undertook a study of "the intern and sleep loss," whose findings punctured the heroic, medico-moral myth that the physician who is highly committed to the vocation can physiologically overcome the side effects of extreme fatigue, and that it was published in the prestigious *New England Journal of Medicine*[33] epitomizes this new legitimacy. It also represents a continuing heritage from the "tell-it-like-it-is," "authenticity" convictions of the "new" medical students and house officers who burst upon the academic medical scene in the social protest and social reform era of the late 1960s to early 1970s.

SOCIALIZATION IN RESIDENCY

The studies of residency are the richest in the sociology of medical education literature. Part of the reason for this is the shared assumption on the part of social investigators that residency has become "the summative statement of [the physician's] professional identity."[34] Charles Bosk argues that it has "replaced medical school" in this regard. He attributes this change to the fact that since the 1950s, when "the major research on student socialization in medical school was completed," the "occupational destinations" of physicians have become more heterogeneous and specialized. "Norms now crystallize around specialties," and it is in the residency phase of training that one "learn[s] what it is to be a physician by learning to think, act, feel like a specialist."

> If, on an individual level, residency shapes attitudes about care at a more macrolevel, residencies shape the overall structure of medical work, sorting the graduates of medical schools into the twenty-three diploma-granting specialties, and then sorting them again into niches within a specialty. Residencies provide different career opportunities for those within them. Some pave the way for academic careers. . . . Other residencies introduce younger physicians to an area's medical community and allow them to seek opportunities within a local market. In the short run, residency training determines what work one does, with whom, and under what conditions. In the long run, it is a substantial factor determining what kind of professional one becomes.
>
> During training a resident learns a field's basic clinical problems, its treatment for them, and its philosophy of care. Beyond this, the resident learns a specialty's style, flavor, and way of doing things; the graduate medical student acquires the specialty's personality.[35]

A consideration of five book-length sociological works on residency provides a cross section of the extant literature, spanning a range of specialties and training milieux from the 1970s to the early 1980s. These works deal with a number of the key medical socialization phenomena and themes with which sociologists have been regularly concerned, approaching the empirical study of residents and residency with a variety of theoretical, methodological, and sociophilosophical assumptions:[36]

Donald Light, *Becoming Psychiatrists: The Professional Transform(* York: W. W. Norton & Co., 1980).

Charles L. Bosk, *Forgive and Remember: Managing Medical F* University of Chicago Press, 1979).

Diana Crane, *The Sanctity of Social Life: Physicians' Treatment of Critically Ill Patients* (New York: Russell Sage Foundation, 1975).

Diana Scully, *Men Who Control Women's Health: The Miseducation of Obstetrician-Gynecologists* (Boston: Houghton-Mifflin Company, 1980).

Terry Mizrahi, *Getting Rid of Patients: Contradictions in the Socialization of Physicians* (New Brunswick, NJ: Rutgers University Press, 1986).

Although Donald Light's *Becoming Psychiatrists* is a detailed ethnographic account of the professional socialization that occurs in a specific type of residency—psychiatric training in an elite, psychoanalytically oriented program—it is the most comprehensive of the five works. Light's concrete aim was to "examine what kinds of people choose to become psychiatrists, how their training experience alters their sense of illness, treatment, and responsibility, how they cope with suicidal patients, and how they overcome the uncertainties of their work."[37] His larger intent was to study "what happened to residents during their transformation from regular physicians to psychiatrists"[38] in a way that would contribute to a more general theoretical and empirical understanding of the nature of professional socialization and its effects.

Although Light was educated in a University of Chicago-shaped sociological tradition, his perspective on professional medical socialization comes closer to the Robert K. Merton/Columbia University/Bureau of Applied Social Research approach than the "negotiated order," "situational socialization" outlook of the Howard Becker/Chicago view. Professional socialization, he writes, "is more than learning roles of situational adjustment":

> [C]ertain aspects of a person's identity and life patterns are broken down (desocialized) so that a new identity can be built up. While the person actively participates in the process and to some degree negotiates the terms of his or her new identity, this activity serves more to coopt the person into using the concepts, values, and language of those in power. Conversion occurs through the stages of moral transformation which intensify trainees' commitment to the professional community. . . . [T]he greater the trials undergone, and the more active the commitment required, the more likely the new identity will be sustained.[39]

Light developed the "sociological calendar" as a device for condensing the field materials he collected at University Psychiatric Center, and for analyzing the manifest and latent socialization of psychiatric residents in this setting as a social process in socially structured time. Through his calendrical analysis, one can see the primary focus of the resident's concern and energy move progressively from "managing patients" (one month), to "doing therapy" (two months), to "countertransference" (five months), to "knowing the unconscious" (nine months), to finding and developing their own "individual style" (twenty months). As residents move along in the three-year training period toward a new professional identity, changes take place in their ways of understanding and dealing with various work-related issues, such as therapeutic models and techniques, the physician's relation to nonmedical staff, and the nature of the doctor-patient relationship. In the dynamic unfolding of their doctor-patient relations, for example, residents shift from "rescue fantasies" (attempts to "cure" patients), to trying to make patients responsible for managing themselves, to the view of patients as responsible for work in therapy. The "final ideal" that they reach in their second residency year is that of patients able to care for themselves who are also motivated to work hard in therapy. Light found that the chief phases of socialization occur in the first year of residency. The second year is the time when residents work principally with outpatients and nonpatients, when they deepen their commitment to analytic psychotherapy (some by undertaking a personal analysis), and when their sense of competence and mastery grows appreciably. In the third year (the elective programs period of their training), residents sort themselves out as they make professional choices that lead them down diverging specialty, subspecialty, practice, and career paths.

In his treatment of the residents' daily round of diagnosing and managing patients, being supervised in psychotherapy, and participating in case conferences, and the cognitive, psychological and social learning these experiences entail, Light singles out treating suicide as the rite of passage par excellence. The suicide of a patient, he indicates, is the supreme ordeal for psychiatrists-in-training, because it symbolizes fallibility and "failure" in a manner that casts doubt on their own and the field's professional competence and worth. He portrays the "suicide review"— the formal conference at which this event is retrospectively discussed—as "a tribal ritual intended to bury the case and reaffirm the professional standards that may have been shaken."[40] Light sees "the beliefs and rituals" that are evoked by the special problems of dealing with suicide as "reflect[ing] on all psychiatric work."[41]

The ritual reaffirmation of "how fine psychiatry and psychiatrists" are that takes place in connection with suicide is closely related to the two major sets of socialization themes that Light finds woven into the whole sequence of psychiatric residency: training for uncertainty and control, and training for omnipotence. He uncovers a cluster of unanticipated, largely negative consequences of the process of learning to deal with uncertainty and maintain control over their environment that the residents undergo, among which various forms of "overcontrol," grandiosity, and institutionalized narcissism figure prominently.

In reviewing *Becoming Psychiatrists*, Charles Bosk was struck by the resulting occupational self-centeredness and conceit and their clinical implications:

> The young psychiatrists Light describes are as a whole curiously unreflective about the legitimacy of their entitlements as psychiatrists. There are precious few moments in this ethnography when residents display appropriate humility. By and large these psychiatrists seem a very vain lot; the older psychiatrists who are their teachers have taught them to be obsessed by questions about their own performance. Light identifies the occupational vanity of psychiatrists in terms of the social forms it takes (storytelling, interviewing, case presentation), all of which are artifacts of the psychoanalytical model. In psychiatry, residents learn to substitute elegant explanations for effective results; the critical performances are those that publicly display skill at interpretation, regardless of what happens to the patient.[42]

Light is aware that his study of a famous psychodynamically based residency program depicts the end of an era in American psychiatry. The field is no longer so dominated by the model and the "mandarins" of psychoanalytic psychiatry. Rather, a number of alternative biological, behavioral, cognitive, and systems-analysis paradigms are competing for ascendancy in the profession. Biopsychiatry now prevails in academic departments and centers, although most practicing psychiatrists are still physicians who were trained in residencies like the one observed by Light. He would be the first to advocate that continuing studies be made of the way these shifts are affecting the socialization of psychiatric residents, with what consequences for them, their specialty, their patients, and medicine and medical education more generally.

Charles L. Bosk's epigrammatically titled book, *Forgive and Remember*, is based on an eighteen-month-long participant observer study of two services of the surgical training program of the elite, urban, academic "Pacific Hospital": the Able service, a "high research–low clinical orientation unit," and the Baker service, a "high clinical–low research orientation unit." Bosk's aim is to portray and analyze how surgeons are taught and learn to "detect, categorize, . . . sanction, and/or neutralize"[43] what he alternately calls "error," "mistakes at work," and "medical failure." He also provides an ethnographic account of "the ordinary and extraordinary rites, rituals, and practices which comprise the everyday life of surgeons."[44] Such meetings as attending and work rounds, case conferences, grand rounds, and mortality and morbidity conferences, Bosk points out, are not only scientific and technical events; they are "occupational rituals that allow physicians to dramatize, to teach, and to remind themselves and their colleagues of their sense of what it means to be a physician.."[45] In addition, they are media of social control, employed to keep error at a minimum. Bosk found an elaborate system of informal, ritually structured professional controls built into the socialization processes, work routines, and collegial relations of the surgical services, which contradict the assertions made by some sociologists that the medical profession lacks "mechanisms for either individual internal control or colleague control."[46]

Bosk's decision to study a group of surgeons "to determine how error is detected, categorized, and punished"[47] among senior physicians and physicians-in-training was guided by his assumption that certain characteristics of surgery were likely to highlight the occurrence of medical error, its technical and moral implications, and whatever mechanisms of accountability exist for dealing with it:

> [T]here are qualities peculiar to the practice of surgery that make surgeons the most appropriate object of our study. . . . These features are the precise and definitive nature of surgical intervention—its visibility, the expectation of success that surrounds this intervention, and the relatively short time frame in which outcomes are known. All of these make surgeons more accountable than their colleagues in other specialties.[48]

Bosk had hypothesized that because of the different emphases of the Able and Baker surgical services and the different leadership styles of their attending physicians, their ways of identifying, classifying, and redressing errors would also be different. He found instead an "underlying uniformity" on the two services that "formed a unique *gestalt*."[49]

A basic component of this *gestalt* was the strong distinction made between technical and moral errors. What was regarded as technical errors, Bosk came to see, involved "failure to apply correctly the body of theoretic knowledge on which professional action rests." Moral errors entailed "failure to follow the code of conduct on which professional actions rests." Moral errors were "more often the subject of serious social control efforts" than technical ones. In the hierarchical world of surgery of Pacific Hospital, on both Able and Baker services, senior physicians placed great emphasis on how junior physicians, in the residency phase of their training, reacted to and handled error once it was discerned. The failure of a resident to "route problems properly because of professional pride or the failure to confess error and admit shortcomings," were regarded as moral rather than technical errors—a serious breach of "good faith" that signified the inability or unwillingness of a young surgeon to acknowledge the "underling status."[50] A technical error committed by a resident whom attending physicians considered to be competent was viewed as "innocent" and "blameless" if it had the following characteristics:

> The resident quickly recognizes the problem; the resident seeks appropriate help for it by informing the attending; the resident appears to have learned a "lesson" from the entire experience; and most important, the resident has not made the same mistake before on this rotation. Errors with these characteristics are seen as part of the educational process. They allow attending and resident to take the role of teacher and student respectively. The misadventure is reviewed retrospectively, the technical or judgmental error that led to the untoward result is identified, and a generalizable lesson is extracted from the whole sad experience.[51]

Moral errors, however, were seen as blameworthy and were subject to swift, stern, and publicly humiliating punishment if:

> The resident failed to recognize a problem sufficiently early or attempted to cover the mistakes up; the resident failed to seek appropriate help; the resident failed to improve performance over successive trials; and the resident had made the same mistake previously on the same service. Errors with these characteristics are not viewed as part of the ordinary educational process. Rather, they signal that a resident fails to possess the skills or honor the commitments that lifelong practice in a specialty requires. When such mistakes occur, attendants often approach residents, eager to punish. Public dressing-downs are not uncommon.[52]

It is largely through a highly structured but subtle "system of . . . give-and-take," embedded in the different kinds of rounds that occur on a surgical service, that the "routine surveillance" of residents takes place. Within the confines of rounds, attending physicians "evaluate house staff, regulate performance, and identify deviant house staff—those who cannot meet the demands of a surgical career."[53]

Bosk singles out two sets of rituals, woven into the social controls established by attending rounds, that play an important dramaturgic and symbolic role in the everyday surveillance process. The first are "[h]orror stories: grotesque catalogs of all the things that can go wrong in treating patients." They are "moral parables, an element of the oral culture of medicine that remind all that healing is a difficult business that must always be done with care."[54] Horror stories are recounted both by attending and surgical residents. "Putting on the hair shirt," the second major ritual that Bosk identifies, is strictly confined to attending physicians. It is a "prerogative of status" that is enacted in the Mortality and Morbidity Conference:

> Attending surgeons publicly abase themselves before an audience of their colleagues and subordinates. They publicly claim that they made mistakes in the handling of the case. They put on the hair shirt, as the argot of surgery has it.

When an attending puts on the hair shirt, he points out to the group what lessons he learned from treating the patient; he explains why he might better have followed some other course of action; and he urges all to consider the case before acting on similar cases in the future.[55]

Normative mistakes by surgical residents were taken with great seriousness, and an impressively nuanced and forceful system of sanctions and rituals existed to deal with them. However, Bosk found that the long-term socialization and social control "message" that physicians-in-training received about these matters was a mixed one. The same sorts of errors that were felt to be "calamitous" when made by residents were "disattended" when made by senior surgeons. Furthermore, close monitoring ended once residency training was completed, and normative mistakes and issues became a private matter, surrounded by professional discretion, tolerance, and silence. The post-residency surgeon was assumed to have internalized the standards of the profession and to have acquired the learned capacity and the achieved right to be self-regulating.

Bosk concluded that the major unintended consequence of the surgeons' long, intricate process of socialization for dealing with medical error is that, in the end, it conveys the sense that the normative mistakes that seemed so grave when one was a resident are not so serious after all, and "need not concern physicians outside of residency too greatly."[56] Most failing residents secure positions in other training programs, because whatever collective sanctions they received during their training are "unremembered," if not completely forgiven, once the training period is over. Corporate collegial control is outbalanced by the degree to which "the profession equates professional and individual controls"[57] once the surgeon graduates from residency.

Diana Crane's *The Sanctity of Social Life* is based on her extensive study of physicians' attitudes and values regarding the treatment of critically ill and dying patients, and of how doctors behave in the face of the difficult moral as well as medical issues that surround decision-making under these life-and-death circumstances. Crane's book is not primarily concerned with the socialization of resident physicians, but one of her key findings has an important bearing on the shaping influences that a residency can have on how a young physician, in this stage of training, thinks, feels, and acts about such serious treatment decisions.

The major instrument of her research, carried out in winter 1970–1971, was a questionnaire mailed to a stratified sample of resident and attending physicians in neurosurgery, pediatric heart surgery, pediatrics, and internal medicine, at American hospitals differing in affiliation, governance, prestige, and size. Over 3000 physicians either returned questionnaires or were interviewed by Crane. In addition, the charts of all critically ill in-patients in a particular university hospital during 1969 were systematically examined to ascertain what treatments they did and did not receive.

The central findings of Crane's research turn around her discovery that physicians were inclined to use what she terms a "social definition" of life, death, and the treatable patient, one that attached great importance to the patient's capacity for interaction, and to the symbolic meaning as well as the physiological role of the brain and brain function in this connection:

> Evidence from the present study suggests that physicians respond to the chronically ill or terminally ill patient not simply in terms of physiological defini-

tions of illness but also in terms of the extent to which the patient is capable of interacting with others. The treatable patient is one who can interact and who has the potential to interact in a meaningful way with others in his environment. The physically damaged salvageable patient whose life can be maintained for a considerable period of time is more likely to be actively treated than the severely brain-damaged patient or the patient who is in the last stages of terminal illness. The brain-damaged infant is also defined as untreatable by many physicians since he lacks the potential to establish social relationships with others.[58]

Crane's data were collected considerably before the current medical and societal debate about deciding to forego life-sustaining treatment. Her research was done at the very beginning of the emergence of American bioethics—a little more than two years after the Harvard Medical School Ad Hoc Committee published their criteria for defining brain death, before the brain death statutes that now exist in numerous states had been passed, some five years before the case of Karen Ann Quinlan, and more than a decade before so-called Baby Doe cases erupted onto the public scene. Historically and sociologically, then, the results that she reported and her interpretation of them antedate and anticipate these more recent developments.

Within the framework of the overall consensus that she found among physicians concerning social and medical considerations in decisions to treat critically ill patients, Crane observed a number of patterned responses that distinguished house staff from more senior doctors. Particularly in prestigious hospitals affiliated with medical schools, residents were "very likely" to be more active in their treatment of gravely ill patients than attending and private physicians were inclined to be. They seemed to form a normative subculture of their own. This was especially notable on internal medicine services, Crane felt, where senior residents had the most influence on the house staff's socialization for such decision-making:

> In internal medicine, the process of socialization appears to be delegated by the senior physicians to the senior residents whose activities in this area are the most intensive. The role of the attending physicians who go on rounds with the house staff is attenuated by the fact that they perform this role for only one month at a time. In addition, individualism appears to be the norm. Young physicians tend to disclaim that they are influenced by older physicians in these matters. The relative absence of controversy among them, however, seems to suggest that intensive contact with a small group of senior residents does lead to the development of a fairly consistent point of view toward these problems, at least in the prestigious departments in which these interviews were conducted.[59]

In a 1985 article, William Winkenwerder, Jr., then a senior medical resident in an elite academic institution, presented a more complex analysis than Crane's of the social structural and value conditions under which house staff are confronted with "the care of critically ill and dying patients" and of their socialization impact.[60] He is especially concerned about situations in which residents experience "conflicts of conscience" between their own ethical principles and the treatment decisions made by attending physicians to whom they are subordinate:

> Residents are fully licensed to practice medicine, but they are not totally autonomous. They have heavy responsibilities in patients' care, but they are not independent in making many decisions. They are usually the primary caretakers,

but usually not the ultimate decision makers. Their job clearly is one of many ambiguities and contradictions as well as great uncertainty. Such a complex role
makes it difficult to answer questions regarding residents' rights and responsibilities, particularly in situations of moral dilemma. . . .

Little attention has been paid to the issue of whether residents are always
bound to the decisions of their attending physicians, and whether it may ever be
appropriate for residents to decline to participate in the life-sustaining care of
patients on ethical grounds.[61]

In contrast to Crane, Winkenwerder recognizes the powerful and legitimate
influence that attending physicians have in the group process by which decisions
about treatment are made in teaching hospitals:

The ultimate responsibility for making decisions has always rested with attending physicians. This arrangement is legally sound and it provides for a unified
plan of action. The opportunity to oppose an attending physician's or team's
decision, even in the form of abstaining from care, has the potential, albeit small,
of bringing the walls of authority down. All of us would agree with the illogicality
of allowing every physician to unilaterally invoke his preference, but do we have a
mechanism for dealing with more serious conflicts of moral opinion, especially
since they are so value driven and wrapped in uncertainty?[62]

Again in contrast to Crane, Winkenwerder sees the most serious conflicts arising in
cases where it is the attending physician, rather than the resident, who wishes to actively treat a critically ill patient.

That such conflicts and dilemmas, centering on the statuses, roles, and
relationships of attending and house staff physicians, have a continuing socializing
effect on young physicians is attested to by Dr. Winkenwerder's own troubled
memories of being obliged by senior physicians to try to keep certain terminally ill
patients alive or to resuscitate them. This is further confirmed by some of the letters
to the editor written in response to his article by other young physicians several
years beyond their residency, who also "look back on [this] experience" with what
they hope is "some perspective." One of the most interesting of these letter writers
raised the following question:

In reading Dr. Winkenwerder's article, I wondered how long the interval
was from the experience he describes and the writing of the article and if time has
changed his feelings on the issue. . . .While I agree with his suggestions, I feel
that time and experience are valuable teachers and wonder whether when Dr.
Winkenwerder is the attending physician faced with a similar dilemma, he will act
as his attending physician did or as he would have as a house officer.[63]

Dr. Winkenwerder's reply lucidly stated where he stood in the ongoing medical and
moral socialization process in which he and his peers were engaged:

Dr. Light's final question in difficult to answer. I have not faced a similar
situation yet. Since it is not a question of who is right or wrong, my approach
would be to avoid drawing sides and to search for areas of mutual agreement about
the problem. If there were still irreconcilable differences of opinion, I would allow

the resident to remove himself from the case, providing that continuing on the case constituted a clear compromise of his ethical values and that being off the case would not jeopardize the patient's care. The attending physician must still bear final responsibility.[64]

As the title of Diana Scully's book announces, the intent and style of *Men Who Control Women's Health* distinguish it from the works of Crane, Bosk, and Light. The tone of the book is ideologically and morally indignant. It aims to mobilize political outrage and action through a behind-the-scenes sociological view of what residents in obstetrics and gynecology explicitly and implicitly learn during this formative period of their specialty training.

Scully's comparative participant observation study is located on the obstetrics and gynecology services of an elite private hospital and a public one. It starts with the categorical assumption that wherever obstetrician-gynecologists are trained, they are "miseducated" to develop "skills and attitudes that are at variance with the health care needs of women." The fields of obstetrics and gynecology are treated in a monolithic way, as if they were both under the dominion of surgery. No consideration is given to the differences between them, to the structural strains that may result from the fact that they are paired and combined, to such nonsurgical aspects of this dual specialty as infertility, fetal medicine, and "women's wellness" programs, or to the controversial "doctors' dilemmas" described by Jonathan B. Imber[65] that surround what he terms "obstetrical family planning" (treatment for infertility and fetal monitoring) and "nonobstetrical family planning" (abortion and sterilization).

The obstetrical-gynecological work for which residents are trained is depicted by Scully as narrowly, almost exclusively confined to learning to use two primary tools—the forceps and the scalpel—in a fashion that encourages physicians to regard their patients as surgical learning objects, and that prepares them for self-servingly conning their future patients into undergoing unnecessary surgery. She alleges that the culture and psychological makeup, as well as the membership of obstetrics and gynecology, are overwhelmingly masculine, and that the field has attracted an uncommonly large number of men who are fundamentally ambivalent or hostile toward women, with a strong need to exert power and control over them. Inexplicably, given her strong feminist convictions, she does not consider the implications of the fact that a growing number of women physicians are now choosing this specialty.[66]

Scully has observed and recorded suggestive field materials on the residency world of obstetrician-gynecologists, including some of their distinctive in-group language and occupational rituals. However, in sharp contrast to the kinds of in-depth interpretive analysis of such phenomena that Light and Bosk attempted in their ethnographic studies of psychiatric and surgical residencies, Scully deals with what she saw and heard in a literal, absolutist way. The ironic, self-mocking connotations of some of the vocabulary that obstetrician-gynecologist residents use and the emblematic and social control dimensions of their rituals seem to escape her. Even more striking and significant is the absence in her work of any allusion to the medical uncertainty, moral ambiguity, ethical conflict, and the physical, psychological, and social stress that are so prominent in the other studies of socialization in residency.

In the end, Scully's book is principally interesting as an example of the genre it represents: a thinly empirical, post-1960s, social movement-oriented work of militant social criticism.

Terry Mizrahi's *Getting Rid of Patients* is the most recently published study of the socialization of physicians in their house staff years. As such, it reflects the changed and changing conditions in medical education, medical science and technology, and the delivery of health care under which graduate medical training is now occurring. Mizrahi is more systematically conscious of the "mediation of larger societal forces" and their influence on the house officer socialization process than the previous authors cited.[67] In part, this is a consequence of the professional background and motivation that she brought to her research:

> My interest in physician training and the doctor-patient relationship resulted from my background in health care policy and the consumer health movement. I wanted to understand more about the dynamics of the so-called health crisis and in particular to understand the role of physicians in shaping and perpetuating the American health care system. I chose to scrutinize internal medicine because it is the largest and one of the most prestigious specialties.[68]

She is especially interested in social reforms that would bring about "more humanistic health care" directed to "the good of patients," breaking through our "two-tier system of medical delivery" in which, as she sees it, "those who cannot pay are abused and those who can pay get less than what they pay for."[69] Its critical and activist origins notwithstanding, the book is less polemical and political in tone and content than Scully's.

Mizrahi's research, conducted in the late 1970s and early 1980s, spans the three-year training program in internal medicine at a large southern university medical center, "Southern Area Medical School (SAMs)." The program had a good reputation, though it was regarded as less competitive than more academic university centers. It emphasized clinical rather than research aspects of medicine and was what the house officers considered a "big city hospital" program compared to smaller community hospital internships and residencies. During her study, the proportion of women on the predominantly male, virtually all-white house staff increased from 5 to 20 percent; the attending physician faculty remained all-male and all-white.

Using participant observation, in-depth interviews, and self-administered questionnaires as her primary methods, Mizrahi focused her inquiry on the effects of residency training on the doctor-patient relationship, particularly on the etiology, structure, dynamics, and consequences of what she terms the "Get Rid of Patients" (GROP) perspective that the house staff develops. Her research also included a follow-up study of a random sample of 26 former house staff members five or six years beyond their residency.

From the outset it becomes clear that the SAMs house staff has its own particular and powerful culture, and that they, rather than the attending physicians, are the main socializers of interns and residents. In contrast to the continuous teaching presence of faculty on the surgical services of Pacific Hospital (studied by Charles Bosk) and their close monitoring of residents' clinical activities, the medical attending physicians at SAMs are conspicuously absent, distant, and "discounted" by house staff. The alienated autonomy of house staff vis-à-vis faculty that Mizrahi describes coincides with the accounts of "the house officer's changing world" that have been appearing in medical journals:

> Teaching hospitals are also moneymaking hospitals. The faculty has little time and often little inclination to teach. Attending rounds are made to ensure third-party payments. There are no monetary rewards for teaching, and teaching won't get faculty members promoted. Many big city hospitals, the former bastions of house-staff training, either have closed or are in difficult financial straits. Academic and clinical faculty members don't have time to give to these foundering behemoths. The house-staff members are given, and assume, more and more responsibility. As a result of this increased responsibility and of the decrease in the faculty's time for and interest in teaching, the house staff has become more and more independent. The faculty and the house staff have become estranged. Everyone is busy taking care of patients or doing research. House officers have role models but few heroes.[70]

Because of these conditions, Mizrahi shows, even before young physicians begin their stint as interns, they have been significantly influenced by the attitudes, values, and behavior of house staff who taught them as medical students:

> They had spent the last two years of their clinical hands-on [medical school] training principally in the company of, and being taught (hence socialized) by, interns and residents. Their daily activities had generally been supervised by house staff, not by attendants, who were usually not as accessible or available.[71]

It is principally from house officers, Mizrahi claims, that medical students receive "anticipatory socialization to a negative doctor-patient relationship"[72] that primes them for the GROP outlook and behavior patterns that they adopt during house officer years. The "GROP perspective," Mizrahi contends, is the salient principle around which the house staff organizes its work and its culture. Through her identification of the impious in-group language that interns and residents use when they talk about patients, she invokes the stressful and fatigue-ridden, anxious, hostile, and angrily embattled GROP atmosphere within which their care of patients proceeds:

> The conditions of labor [of the house staff], including the overwhelming workload, the degraded status of many of the patients, the necessity of jockeying for beds, the paperwork, the scut work, the fears—the actuality—of making mistakes under what seemed to them like battle conditions, all served to lower [their] regard . . . for the subjectivity of the patients and for themselves. . . .[73]
>
> The terms the internal medicine house staff used to describe their experience were those applicable to combat. They portrayed themselves, figuratively and literally, as doing battle. The patient, the embodiment of a recalcitrant and impenetrable system, many characterized as the ultimate enemy. . . . Their collective descriptions of patient-related encounters included such violent and aggressive terms as "hits," "crashing and burning," "under fire," "getting killed," "time bombs," "trainwrecks," "killers," "under the gun," "going down the tubes"—all of which connoted siegelike, assaultive circumstances. . . .[74]

"Gomers," "hits," "trainwrecks," "turkeys," "scumbags," "dirtbags," "crocks," "garbage," "junk," "SHPOS" (*s*ub-*h*uman *p*ieces *o*f *s*hit) were terms repeatedly used to characterize patients. . . . [T]he peer culture supported such skills as "GROPing," "turfing" (guarding your territory against the incursion of new patients), and "dumping" (finding a reason to get a patient assigned to another service). The peer culture valued this GROP orientation because it allowed for the release of pent-up anger and hostility, served to intimidate abusive patients, and conferred upon those who GROPed skillfully a certain amount of status and esteem from peers.[75]

Mizrahi describes an array of structural strains to which the house staff is subject that contribute to the GROP process: patient overload and shortages of beds; limitations in the placement of patients; cost-containment policies; the obligation to do everything possible to effectively diagnose and actively treat all medical problems, no matter what the limiting conditions; the iatrogenic side effects of these very interventions in this era of potentially harmful as well as powerfully beneficial high-technology medicine; and conflicts that house staff experience between their heavy responsibility for patient care and their desire and obligation as physicians-in-training to look to patients as sources of learning.

Their learning-versus-care conflicts, combined with the fact that they have so many patients to treat in a short amount of time, are a primary source of the two systems for classifying patients that house officers have evolved. One is based on the dichotomous distinction between the "interesting" and the "uninteresting" patient. The so-called interesting case epitomizes the desirable patient from an educational point of view. The second consists of a continuum from "ideal" to "despised" patient:

> The ideal patient corresponded roughly to the characteristics of the middle class: intelligent without questioning the doctor's judgment, clean, deferential, helpful, cooperative, and so forth. The despised patient was one defined in the subculture as an abuser: a self-abuser, system abuser, house staff abuser or some combination. Such patients were frequently labeled with slang terms reflecting derision and contempt.[76]

In turn, these categories influence whether or not patients are "GROPed" by the house staff, how unreservedly, and with the use of what strategies (transferring patients to another service or another hospital, discharging them as soon as possible, passing them along to "subordinates" such as social workers, ancillary staff, or medical students, or mentally and psychologically withdrawing from involvement with certain patients).

In most regards, Mizrahi's findings closely parallel those of another study of the "backstage," informal labeling of patients by house staff. Deborah B. Liederman and Jean-Anne Grisso, young physicians with social science training, carried out a small intensive inquiry into what they called "the gomer phenomenon" among internal medicine house staff in an elite northern university hospital.[77] To reach an understanding of which patients were defined as "gomers," how they differed from other patients, and the meaning of this labeling, junior residents supervising inpatient services at University Hospital were asked for the names of gomer patients on their service in December 1979 and January 1980. They matched the final gomer sample of 18 patients with a matched control sample of 18 general medical patients selected at random from computerized hospital records. After a close review and content analysis of all these charts, they conducted informal group interviews with house officers to learn how the residents perceived and explained their use of the term "gomer."

Unlike Mizrahi, Liederman and Grisso found that "gomer is neither a class-linked nor race-linked pejorative term," nor one that is "applied merely to malinger-ing, self-destructive patients."[78] But in every other respect, their interpretation of "gomerism" coincides with Mizrahi's analysis of "GROPism." They insightfully conclude that:

> [G]omers were patients whose illnesses and management posed special frustrations for resident physicians. Gomers suffered irreversible mental deteriora-tion; their illnesses were complex and intractable; they were unable to resume nor-mal adult social roles; and they had no place to go upon discharge. . . .
>
> [T]he gap between the myth of omnipotence of technologic medicine and the realities of gomer patients on the wards—becomes starkly visible to young physicians in the early stages of professional socialization. Although the recourse to informal labeling of patients may be construed as a breakdown in defenses, . . . it may also be viewed as one mode of coping with the enormous physical and emo-tional demands placed on housestaff.
>
> On another level, gomerism signals major points of stress in the system, situations that involve peculiarly modern social and medical dilemmas as well as universal existential problems. Modern high-technology, interventionist medicine not only makes possible, but frequently appears to dictate, intervention in patients whose illnesses were merely passively observed by doctors only decades ago. Yet in some patients, . . . medical intervention is to no avail, or even harmful.
>
> The gomer patient, who deteriorates in the hospital, whose illness is unlike-ly to be significantly improved by medical treatment, who has no concerned fami-ly to place him in a meaningful social network and confer personhood as opposed to mere patienthood upon him, confronts resident physicians with . . . profound threats to their ideals of themselves as physicians. . . .
>
> It is significant that the use of a private internal language is largely con-fined to physicians in residency training, that is, to idealistic and ambitious young persons in a transitional phase in their careers. . . . Senior physicians tend not to use terms like gomer perhaps because . . . [they] are not "front-line," that is, they are not required to care for the difficult hospitalized patients in the inten-sive, minute-to-minute way required of housestaff. More important, their ex-perience has tempered and made more realistic their expectations of medicine and of themselves. . . .
>
> Another difference between senior physicians and house staff is that the latter are formally still at the learning stage. . . . House staff are compelled by the nature of their position as trainees to judge patients in terms of their learning value. . . . Gomers are rarely, if ever, interesting cases.[79]

Terry Mizrahi's unique follow-up study of a number of former SAMs house of-ficers permits us to see how situationally specific or enduring their residency socializa-tion proved to be. Experience with the patients at SAMs seems to have played a determining role in the practice settings and types of careers in internal medicine that these young physicians selected. Their career decisions were "based as much on their aversions to aspects of internal medicine practice as on the positive components of the specialty." The majority of former house staffers were what she terms "system defenders," who had entered subspecialty private practice and were doing quite well, although they were working harder than they anticipated." Those whom she calls "system perpetuators" were in academic practice in either general internal medicine or one of its subspecialties, and they were feeling some disgruntlement because of "bureaucratic politics and the pressures exerted upon them." One "system rejector" had chosen a specialty "removed from prolonged patient care—emergency medicine." There were also three "system distorters, who saw themselves as pursuing medicine to the point of financial independence, at which time they would retire or pursue other interests."[80] By and large, however, most were satisfied with the training they had received and comfortable with the medical and financial success they were experiencing, although they saw themselves as "one of the last generations of doctors who are 'free' professionals." They viewed the changes occurring in American medicine— "more regulation from outside, a surplus of doctors, a decline in income"—as harbingers of the profession's incipient demise.[81]

It is remarkable how distant these physicians already felt from their internship and residency years. They vividly recalled the sleep deprivation they had undergone, and they did not deny that "the GROP perspective" had characterized their house officer days. Although they conceded that the house officer experiences had been temporarily dehumanizing and had taken a serious toll on their lives during that period, they looked back on the system through which they had passed as inevitable, necessary, effective, and "worth it." Ironically, they were inclined to view the younger physicians who succeeded them as house staff as "rude, abrupt, [and] uncaring," and both to resent and morally disapprove of the "dehumanized way" in which these interns and residents treated some of their patients.[82] Compared to their former SAMs selves and the present house staff physicians, these doctors now had broader conceptions of competent internal medicine and good patient care. They accorded a higher priority to their relationship to patients than they had in their house staff days, including the psychosocial and environmental factors that they had denigrated when they were still interns and residents.

Mizrahi concludes her book with a key medical socialization question: "Will physicians-in-training regain their humanism, if not idealism, in their permanent 'real' career settings?" For the physicians in her study, she replies, the answer to that question is a "qualified yes":

> Private practitioners are concerned about . . . the "whole" patient because they are competing in what they perceive to be a highly competitive marketplace. Their outlook is more humanistic than that of the house staff because for the most part their patients pay them directly or indirectly for their services, are closer to them in social rank, and share a similar value system. Academic practitioners treat their patients more humanistically than house staff because they have little responsibility for their primary care, leaving that to the new house staff, and can choose their own patients more carefully.[83]

The medical, organizational, physical, economic, psychological, social, cultural, and educational conditions under which house staff work remain as they were. They continue to foster dehumanizing, GROP attitudes and behaviors toward "the thousands of patients across this country under the collective care of house staff," Mizrahi concludes.[84]

THE SOCIALIZATION OF PHYSICIANS IN PRACTICE

Research on doctors in practice and on the socialization effects of professional and extraprofessional experiences upon them is conspicuously scarcer than studies of how medical school and residency influence the intellectual and sociopsychological development of physicians. To some extent, this discrepancy is due to the fact that it is easier and less ethically complicated for social scientists to gain access to academic medical settings than to other medical milieux. In addition, study of the continuing socialization of physicians in practice has been unintentionally deterred by the two major sets of assumptions about medical socialization that have influenced most of the work done in this field. On the one hand, social scientists have supposed that the most profound changes in attitudes, values, and behavior patterns take place during the strong, homogenizing process of socialization that is built into physicians' years of training. One of the unstated side effects of this assumption has been the tendency to minimize or overlook the continuing socialization of physicians after their years of formal education and training are completed, and to collectively view doctors as unchanging. On the other hand, social scientists have insisted on the important effect that the work setting has on the professional outlook and performance of practicing physicians, as well as on those still in training. However, they have emphasized the situational importance of the physician's work environment in a way that has systematically played down whatever enduring socializing effects the work place may have on the doctors participating in it. In this perspective, physicians "are portrayed almost as social chameleons, responding only to the direct and immediate pressures of one environment after another."[85]

An exploration of the scant literature yields up a corpus of studies of the technical medical performance of physicians in practice conducted in the 1950s and 1960s by Dr. Osler L. Peterson and others who were associated with or influenced by him; several qualitative articles published in the 1960s by psychiatrist Gerald L. Klerman and psychologist Daniel J. Levinson on promotion as a "phase in the personal-professional development" of psychiatrists; Eliot Freidson's qualitative study of professional social controls in a comprehensive, prepaid, health maintenance organization-type medical group, begun in the early 1960s and published in the mid-1970s; Mizrahi's follow-up case study of a small number of physicians five to six years after their house staff training; Jonathan B. Imber's field study of how the obstetrician-gynecologists in private practice in a particular community think and feel about abortion and how they deal with it; and John Colombotos and Corinne Kirchner's large-scale interview and mail questionnaire research on how physicians' attitudes toward political and health care issues vary and change, spanning the 1960s and 1970s.[86] Mizrahi's, Imber's, and Colombotos and Kirchner's books were published in 1986. In the light of the meager past record, the availability of three such works at once is promising, all the more so because some of the socialization-in-medical-practice patterns that they independently identify are similar.

Although Osler Peterson's ground-breaking research on general practice in North Carolina became a model for a number of other like studies, its bearing on whether and how physicians' experiences in practice change their outlook and behavior is quite limited. Peterson and a team comprised largely of internists evaluated the way that a sample of 90 internal medicine/general practitioners in different rural and urban milieux conducted their practices in the "natural" settings of office, hospital, and home. The physician behavior studied was narrowly confined to basic physical diagnosis and treatment skills, such as taking a clinical history, doing a physical examination, utilizing laboratory tests, and prescribing medication. Their quality of performance was judged according to the patterns and standards espoused and formally taught by medical schools and academic medical centers. The most intriguing and often cited finding of this study was the ostensible decrease in relationship between performance in medical school and in practice. Some correlation was observed in physicians aged 28-35, but after age 35, the relationship became insignificant. Furthermore, a curious kind of rapprochement between physicians in the over-35 age cohort occurred: those whose level of performance in medical school had been relatively weak appeared to have steadily improved their average performance in practice, whereas the technical quality exhibited in practice by physicians who had done well in medical school seemed to have declined.

Samuel Bloom offers an interesting sociological interpretation of these crisscrossing results: "It was as though the situation—the culture—of the practicing profession took over the major influence on the practitioner, functioning to equalize the total group and reduce their earlier differences." As Bloom points out, no attempts were made by Peterson and his collaborators to discern the degree to which the diagnostic and therapeutic behaviors learned by these physicians in medical school were feasible and appropriate in their North Carolina practice settings, or to investigate what factors might have contributed to the alterations in physicians' professional behavior that they observed.[87]

One clue to these unexamined questions is suggested by another result of the Peterson study: the fact that little association was found between the excellence of medical work, as judged by the internist-researchers, and patient approval, as implied by the income of the physician. This calls to mind Eliot Freidson's well-known distinctions between client-dependent and colleague-dependent practice.[88] In a client-dependent (usually solo) practice, Freidson indicates, it is the patients' conceptions of their needs and their own lay referral system that chiefly determine the flow of clients physicians see and their level of economic success, rather than the opinions, standards, and referrals of fellow physicians. Thus, when there are conflicts between what Freidson calls the "lay tradition" of patients and the "professional tradition" of doctors, client-controlled physicians are inclined to give greater priority to doing what will attract and please patients than to their colleagues' norms of professional excellence or their esteem.

Klerman and Levinson's theoretical discussion of a composite case study of a psychiatrist promoted to director of a community health center looks upon such an advancement to executive responsibility, in the career of any professional, as a "transition that affects [a person's] . . . total life picture." They approach this advancement within an analytic framework that "draws upon the multiple perspectives of societal and organizational change as well as upon those of individual personality and career development."[89] Klerman and Levinson are sufficiently impressed with the major psychological and social changes in a person's state that such an event involves—in social psychic structure and "role self identity"[90]—to view it as entailing a major process of new socialization. They delineate what they consider to be the five resocialization phases through which an individual progressively moves in the course of anticipating, being nominated for, accepting, assuming, and getting established in the executive position of director.

Eliot Freidson's *Doctoring Together* is the only first-hand study of a group practice in the literature. It provides a detailed picture of what medical work is like, and how it is socially controlled in a "model medical group, deliberately set up . . . by physicians who were better trained than average . . . to be as close as possible to the ideal of liberal medical reformers."[91] Included in this ideal conception was the high and continuous degree to which a physician's work could be surveilled and governed by the other physicians in the group. Freidson's central findings concerning the ways in which these physicians actually regulated their own and their peers' work, in a setting where every precondition supposedly existed for collegial self-monitoring and control to flourish, bear directly on the question of how much and what kind of influence the organization and value commitment of a medical practice can have on doctors' attitudes and behavior.

Freidson concluded that despite its "ideal" characteristics, the group practice he studied did not in fact operate as a "collegium" that was "a truly responsible self-governing body."[92] Using Pitts and Crozier's concept of a "delinquent community," he went so far as to characterize the "professional community" of this medical group as one in which its "norms and practices" were such as to both draw all members together defensively in a common front against the outside world of the laity and, internally, to allow each his freedom to act as he willed."[93] Freidson attributed the reluctant, temporizing, and evasive fashion in which these physicians exercised social control over their work, especially their "avoidance of confrontation," to habits of action developed in solo, entrepreneurial practice that they carried into group practice, and that shaped the characteristics of the particular system of enforcement they established:

> [In solo practice], just as the fee barrier was an impersonal mechanism that discouraged patients from demanding services the physician did not want to give while relieving him of the necessity of confronting the patient and refusing the service, so was the solo referring mechanism a device by which the physician could sever relationships with a colleague who had given offense without having to confront him directly and complain about his offenses. . . . While the medical group clearly lacked such "automatic" methods of denying service and suspending cooperative work relations, the etiquette of nonconfrontation appropriate to circumstances in which these automatic methods existed nonetheless persisted. The outcome in many instances was a veneer of cooperation underneath which were stored memories of offenses never directly expressed or resolved. . . . Some effort to sanction the other by avoiding work relations was made, but ultimately it was impossible in the medical group. Closed-panel practice cannot survive if only popular or nonoffensive physicians are referred to; the workload of consultants in the same specialty would become impossibly unequal. . . . Avoidance of cooperation also was impossible for physicians in the same specialty, who had to cover each other on emergency duty. . . . [O]ffenses did arise which seemed too impor-

tant to simply ignore. Rather than confront an individual whom one could not merely avoid, however, one instead made efforts to "work around" the offender.[94]

Freidson describes how the physicians in the group "neutralized" the formal authority of the administration through their qualms about employing it and their unwillingness to grant it legitimacy. On balance, the medical group was "more a mock bureaucracy than a functioning" one,[95] and physicians were left to govern themselves in an informal collegial manner. However, according to Freidson, this informal system of collective professional control did not work very well either:

> [A] series of interpretive screens were interposed between the practicing physicians and their awareness and perception of the performance of their colleagues. The interpretive rules led to normalization of actions that by lay standards could be called "mistakes" and so functioned to reduce the universe of what could be perceived as poor performance requiring control. In turn, the rules of etiquette limited the way the universe of performance could be viewed by others. And . . . should poor or otherwise objectionable performance pass through all these screens and be perceived, public, formal, and deliberately systematic methods of control were rejected on the basis both of propriety and of imputed effectiveness.[96]

In the end, Freidson claimed, because of the "failure" of the largely private and personal sanctions that physicians deployed, the administration played a far greater role in the process of social control in the medical group than the doctors did, in spite of the limitations that existed on its formal authority:

> Social control was . . . left to often unwilling officials, and its exercise was pushed into the underground of administrative discretion by the reluctance of the collegium to participate in the process. . . . [T]he importance of [the administration's] role was the direct outcome of the abdication of the collegium from exercising the effective self-government that it insisted was solely its own legitimate function.[97]

"[B]elow the purview of formal accounting procedures," Friedson concludes, "at the level of concrete, everyday work, a systematic but uncodified set of habitual understandings and conceptions shared by the participants sustains a process of social control which permits, and even encourages, performance undesired by formal plans."[98]

Seen in the light of his previous work, Freidson's conclusions are both predictable and puzzling. On the one hand, they are compatible with his "professional dominance," "organized autonomy" perspective on the medical profession and his prior conviction that, "even if the profession were to undertake more systematic modes of colleague supervision or review of work performance, its operation of such settings is not likely to be as effective as it can be and, if the profession's claim is taken seriously, as effective as it should be."[99] On the other hand, he implies that the "flaws of professional autonomy" are not only more conspicuous and complex in a group than in a solo practice, but that they are also greater. What is more unexpected is that Freidson, who has been a leading situational-theory advocate of the position that "socialization does not explain some important elements of professional performance half so well as does the organization of the immediate work environment,"[100] attached such persistent importance to the deeply internalized "set of habitual understandings and conceptions" that the physicians in the group practice he observed presumably brought with them from individual practice and their prior medical training. In fact, as Bosk has recognized, "Freidson's group seems to be the apotheosis of the socialization system" that he described in *Forgive and Remember*—a system that had the unintended consequence of making "individual conscience . . . the measure of all things," and "other sources of criticism . . . just so much meddling."[101]

Jonathan Imber's *Abortion and the Private Practice of Medicine* is based on two rounds of intensive personal interviews (in 1978 and 1981) with all but one of the 26 obstetrician-gynecologists who practice in "Daleton," a northeastern American city of about 100,000 persons. It is a singular study of how an entire community of practitioners, individually and collectively, regard a procedure for which doctors are the sole legal providers, but which "continues to occupy a controversial place in American life."[102] Imber presents an illuminating analysis of the array of factors that have influenced the differing convictions that Daleton's obstetrician-gynecologists hold about abortion and the stances they have taken about requests for it. Underlying the picture that emerges of "the doctor's dilemma"[103] in this situation and the "expedient [and] anguished . . . inconsistencies in physicians' rationales"[104] for dealing with abortion is a multivariant and dynamic conception of how their personal and professional socialization progressively brought them to the stand they have taken.

Daleton physicians' attitudes and practices regarding abortion, and their practice choices more generally, were influenced by their age, religious background and beliefs, when and where they received their medical training, their specialization within obstetrics and gynecology, the stage of their career, the structure and community context of their solo or group practice, and by their own families, particularly the attitudes of their wives.[105]

In this latter connection, Imber gives a nuanced account of how the interaction between their wives' outlook and the changed context of their medical practice altered the attitudes of younger practitioners in Daleton toward abortion and their willingness to perform it. A number of these doctors had done their residency post-1973, after the *Doe* v. *Bolton* and *Roe* v. *Wade* companion decisions handed down by the U.S. Supreme Court had liberalized the abortion laws. As a consequence, in their house staff years, abortion was "considered a legitimate and important part of becoming an obstetrician-gynecologist."[106] Not only had they acquired experience in carrying out abortions, but in some of the residency programs in which they trained, there was considerable pressure to perform them. Upon coming to Daleton, where "the move into private practice permitted a much broader discretion about what to do,"[107] the "youngest and most skilled technicians of abortion" among them responded to the fact that the "demands for abortion could [now] be met by someone else,"[108] and purposely chose to discontinue their clinical work with it. "Their wives figured prominently in their reasons for avoiding the procedure as much as possible."[109]

Imber highlights one other major set of factors that had a socializing impact on the agreement or refusal of Daleton's obstetrician-gynecologists to perform abortions. Even if they were disposed to do first-trimester abortions, most of these doctors were unwilling to undertake second-trimester abortions because of the medical and surgical challenges, uncertainties, and risks they entailed. Imber's recognition of these biomedical factors, and the way that a community of practitioners reasoned about and reacted to them, is a rare exemplification of Bosk's enjoinder to "take the sociology of knowledge of modern medicine seriously, the better to see how the nature of a particular cognitive realm structures values, attitudes, and practice."[110]

The consequence of these various influences and the interplay between them was that although the number of requests for abortion was large, the number of abortions performed in Daleton by obstetrician-gynecologists in private practice was not great, compared to those done in clinics outside the community. In effect, "however unintentionally," these physicians had "resisted . . . the institutionalization of abortion."[111] By "taking refuge"[112] in private practice in this way, they had made abortion clinics that "were known for not refusing requests"[113] the logical alternative to the constraints they had placed on the right of a woman to have the procedure done. Although they themselves had engendered this situation, the obstetrician-gynecologists of Daleton felt troubled by the medical and moral implications of what they had unwittingly brought to pass.

The assumptions about the socialization of physicians in practice that are implicit in Imber's analysis are congruent with the explicit "conceptual framework of socialization"[114] that undergirds John Colombotos and Corinne Kirchner's studies of the attitudes of physicians toward political and health care issues presented in *Physicians and Social Change*:

> In this book, the idea of socialization is extended to neglected nonclinical topics, namely political issues and changes in the organization of health care, and to neglected sources of socialization. The latter include both early pre-training experiences, as reflected in . . . physicians' *professional* characteristics, such as their practice setting and specialty. Thus, physicians' social and professional characteristics are viewed as indicators of socialization experiences that make for variations in physicians' attitudes. . . . Historical events are also viewed as socialization experiences. . . . While physicians' social and professional characteristics point to experiences according to their location in the social structure, their age-generation and their exposure to historical events point to experiences according to their location in the historical process.[115]

The Colombotos/Kirchner data are drawn mainly from two large telephone interview and mail questionnaire research projects: a longitudinal study of a stratified sample of physicians in private practice in New York State covering the periods before the passage of Medicare (1964 and 1965), and after its enactment (1966, 1967 and 1970); and a more broad-ranging survey of the personal, sociopolitical, and professional influences on the outlook of a national sample of senior physicians, interns, residents, and medical students conducted in 1973.[116] The intricate findings of these well-conceptualized and methodologically sophisticated investigations are not easy to summarize. The following are the results of this research that have especially instructive implications for evaluating and enriching the different approaches to the socialization of physicians at various stages in their personal and professional life cycle that are represented by the works discussed in this chapter:

- Colombotos and Kirchner found doctors were more heterogeneous and less uniformly conservative, resistant to change, and opposed to modifications in the organization of health care than either the public or they themselves generally supposed.

- Although more conservative politically than the general population, substantial portions of physicians held liberal views. A considerable number supported a role for government in health care; a majority favored "some form" of national health insurance; more than half believed a small group practice of three to five physicians was "likely to lead to the best medical care"; over 80 percent favored peer reviews in hospitals, and as many as 50 percent in doctors' offices. Nearly two-thirds of the physicians responded that they would hire a nurse-practitioner or a physician's assistant, but there was wide variation in the duties that physicians were willing to delegate to such persons. Though not surprisingly, the customary fee-for-service mode of reimbursement was agreeable to three-quarters of the physicians; fixed fees under a national health insurance plan were also acceptable to a large percent (nearly two-thirds), and capitation to a fourth of them, while only 14 percent found an annual salary acceptable.

- Physician attitudes were characterized by considerable "pluralistic ignorance." Particularly notable is the significant degree to which they underestimated the support of their colleagues for some form of national health insurance.

- Certain "early nonprofessional sources of socialization" had an important effect on physicians' attitudes toward "more diffuse issues, such as broad political leanings," and "government-in-medicine views." Thus, physicians differed strongly and persistently in both their past and current political views according to their religious and ethnic background, in ways that corresponded to their counterparts in the general population.

- However, the same type of relationship between the socioeconomic origins of physicians and their political attitudes did not seem to be present. The very slight political differences according to socioeconomic background that had existed when they first entered medical school appeared to fade with time and subsequent professional experiences.

- The social background characteristics of physicians were largely unrelated to their health care attitudes toward such matters as group practice, peer review, medical division of labor, task delegation, methods of physician reimbursement, and prepayment mechanisms. But some of the professional characteristics of physicians that Colombotos and Kirchner consider to be "sources of [doctors'] later socialization" (such as "work setting" and, to a lesser degree, specialty) influenced both physicians' health care attitudes and their political and government-in-medicine views.

- The authors interpret these foregoing patterns as relevant to the theory of professional socialization in two ways: as indicative of the fact that physicians' prolonged, intensive training does not obliterate all the effects of their early background on their professional attitudes, behaviors, and careers; and also of the potent impact that the immediate pressures of the social settings in which physicians currently work have on their present attitudes.

- Certain generational differences between older and younger physicians showed up in the survey, primarily with regard to political and government-in-medicine issues. Among medical students and house staff, there were "sharp, incremental, and consistent differences," according to their year of training. Those more advanced in their training took more conservative positions on these issues than those in earlier stages of their training. In contrast, among senior physicians, although the younger were more likely than the older to hold liberal views, the differences were much smaller and not consistently incremental. The "liberal shift" among medical students and house officers appeared to be short-lived, since by the mid-1970s they were more conservative than their predecessors.

• Below the surface of these apparently minor and passing generational shifts, a much more significant, far-reaching, and enduring set of transformations seem to have been occurring in the ideology of the American medical profession, antedating the 1960s and continuing to the present. The influence of historical, or what Colombotos and Kirchner call "period" changes, is most visible in their case study of the effects of the passage of Medicare on physicians' attitudes and behavior. Even before it was enacted, physicians were already beginning to adjust to it as "an anticipatory fait accompli." Shortly after Medicare was passed, but before doctors had much experience with the program, almost three-quarters of them were in favor of it. As they experienced Medicare in action, they became strong supporters and defenders of it. In turn, this progressive change in attitudes toward Medicare had positive spin-off effects on physicians' attitudes toward certain closely related issues: their acceptance of health care as a right, their willingness to accord a great role for the federal government in the field of health, and their increased recognition of the inadequacy of medical care for poor people in American society. However, what did *not* change were their attitudes toward Medicaid, their general political and economic-welfare ideology, and their views about more apolitical professional matters of group practice, peer review, and medical division of labor.

Throughout the complex and careful analysis of the range of general and specific attitudes that they examined, John Colombotos and Corinne Kirchner have threaded their underlying assumption that these attitudes are influenced by the socialization of physicians and their professional norms and ideologies on the one hand, and by the social processes of self-selection and self-interest on the other. They identify a series of conceptual, methodological, and empirical questions that their approach to the socialization of physicians has raised, and they present these as an agenda for future work, to which they encourage social scientists to respond.

Their invitation is an appropriate note on which to end this chapter.

NOTES

1. This is a phrase coined by anthropologist Clifford Geertz in his essay, "Thick Description: Toward an Interpretive Theory of Culture," in Clifford Geertz, *The Interpretation of Cultures: Selected Essays* (New York: Basic Books, 1973), pp. 3–30.
2. Rosemary Stevens, *American Medicine and the Public Interest* (New Haven: Yale University Press, 1971), p. 379.
3. Fitzhugh Mullan, *White Coat, Clenched Fist: The Political Education of an American Physician* (New York: Macmillan Publishing Co., Inc., 1987); Samuel Shem, *The House of God* (New York: R. Marek Publishers, 1978). The popular television show, "St. Elsewhere," with its docudrama qualities, closely resembles this kind of "presentation-from-the-inside" genre of literature.
4. Stevens, *American Medicine and the Public Interest*, p. 380.
5. Terry Mizrahi, "Getting Rid of Patients: Contradictions in the Socialization of Internists to the Doctor-Patient Relationship, *Sociology of Health & Illness*, 7, no. 2 (July 1985), 214–35. See also Terry Mizrahi, *Getting Rid of Patients: Contradictions in the Socialization of Physicians* (New Brunswick, N.J.: Rutgers University Press, 1986).
6. To my knowledge, there is only one published sociological study of the spouses of physicians: Martha R. Fowlkes, *Behind Every Successful Man: Wives of Medicine and Academe* (New York: Columbia University Press, 1980).

7. Emily Mumford, *Interns: From Students to Physicians* (Cambridge, Mass.: Harvard University Press, 1970); Stephen J. Miller, *Prescription For Leadership: Training for the Medical Elite* (Chicago: Aldine Publishing Company, 1970).

8. Miller also did several weeks of comparative fieldwork in a suburban general hospital in order to address himself to the question: "Is an elite internship different?" See *Prescription For Leadership*, pp. 208–26.

9. Mumford's qualitative study of internship in these two hospitals was launched in 1958 when she was working as a research assistant at Columbia University's Bureau of Applied Social Research (BASR). It was part of a larger national study of the learning process that interns and residents undergo, funded by the Commonwealth Fund. The study also included follow-up data on interns and residents who had previously been medical student respondents in the Columbia/BASR medical school socialization project.

10. Mumford, *Interns*, pp. 1–2. Reprinted by permission of Harvard University Press.

11. Miller, *Prescription For Leadership*, pp. 229–33.

12. Mumford, *Interns*, pp. 36, 68.

13. Ibid.

14. Miller, *Prescription For Leadership*, p. 183.

15. Ibid., pp. 184–85.

16. Ibid.

17. Ibid., pp. 189–202.

18. Ibid.

19. Ibid., p. 234.

20. Donald W. Light, "Medical and Nursing Education: Surface Behavior and Deep Structure," in *Handbook of Health Care and the Health Professions*, ed. David Mechanic (New York: The Free Press, 1982), p. 464; Donald W. Light, "The Sociological Calendar: An Analytic Tool for Fieldwork Applied to Medical and Psychiatric Training," *American Journal of Sociology*, 80, no. 5 (March 1975), 1149–51; Light cites pp. 200–201 and p. 238 of Miller's book to support his claim that these two other stages of socialization are implicit in the field materials reported in *Prescription For Leadership*.

21. Barry Blackwell, "Prevention of Impairment Among Residents in Training" (Editorial), *Journal of the American Medical Association*, 255, no. 9 (March 7, 1986), 1177.

22. Jay W. Smith, William F. Denny, and Donald B. Witzke, "Emotional Impairment in Internal Medicine House Staff: Results of a National Survey," *Journal of the American Medical Association*, 255, no. 9 (March 7, 1986), 1155–58.

23. Jack D. McCue, "The Distress of Internship: Causes and Prevention," *New England Journal of Medicine*, 312, no. 7 (February 14, 1985), 449–52.

24. Richard C. Friedman, J. Thomas Bigger, and Donald S. Kornfeld, "The Intern and Sleep Loss," *New England Journal of Medicine*, 285, no. 4 (July 22, 1971), 201–3.

25. Smith, Denny, and Witzke, "Emotional Impairment in Internal Medicine House Staff."

26. McCue, "The Distress of Internship," p. 449.

27. Ibid., pp. 450–51.

28. Ibid.

29. Norman Cousins, "Internship: Preparation or Hazing?" *Journal of the American Medical Association*, 245, no. 4 (January 23/30, 1981), 377.

30. "Internship: Physicians Respond to Norman Cousins," *Journal of the American Medical Association*, 246, no. 19 (November 13, 1981), 2141–44. The quotation is taken from Norman Cousins's resumé of and response to these recurrent themes ("Norman Cousins Responds," p. 2144).

31. McCue, "The Distress of Internship," p. 449.

32. Christine Hinz, "Scheduling, Supervision of Residents to Be Examined," *American Medical News*, July 3–10, 1987, p. 9; Ronald Sullivan, "New York Moves to Cut Sharply the Hours of Doctors in Training," *New York Times*, May 31, 1987, p. 1.

33. Friedman, Bigger, and Kornfeld, "The Intern and Sleep Loss."

34. Charles L. Bosk, "Professional Responsibility and Medical Error," in *Applications of Social Science to Clinical Medicine and Health Policy*, eds. Linda H. Aiken and David Mechanic

(New Brunswick, N.J.: Rutgers University Press, 1986), p. 465. Copyrigh
The State University. Reprinted with permission of Rutgers University Pre:

35. Ibid.

36. Two other first-hand, book-length sociological studies of residency that sh
tioned here, although they will not be reviewed in this chapter: Rue Buch(
ing, *Becoming Professional* (Beverly Hills, California: Sage Publications, 1! _____ ...... Laub
Coser, *Training in Ambiguity: Learning Through Doing in a Mental Hospital* (New York: The
Free Press, 1979).

37. Donald Light, *Becoming Psychiatrists: The Professional Transformation of Self* (New York:
W.W. Norton & Co., 1980), pp. x–xi.

38. Ibid., p. 239.

39. Ibid., p. 327.

40. Ibid., p. 215.

41. Ibid., p. 210.

42. Charles L. Bosk, "The Tribal Rites of Specialists in Training," *Hastings Center Report*, April
1981, p. 44.

43. Charles L. Bosk, *Forgive and Remember: Managing Medical Failure* (Chicago: University of
Chicago Press, 1979), pp. 6 and 16.

44. Ibid.

45. Charles L. Bosk, "Occupational Rituals in Patient Management," *New England Journal of
Medicine*, 303, no. 2 (July 10, 1980), 71–72. See the discussion of these "occupational rituals,"
and especially the "putting on the hair shirt" ritual described by Bosk in Chapter 4 of *Forgive
and Remember*.

46. Bucher and Stelling, *Becoming Professional*, pp. 281–2. In this connection, Bosk also cites:
Bernard Barber and others, *Research on Human Subjects: Problems of Social Control in Medi-
cal Experimentation* (New York: Russell Sage Foundation, 1973); Diana Crane, *The Sanctity of
Social Life: Physicians' Treatment of Critically Ill Patients* (New York: Russell Sage Founda-
tion, 1975); Eliot Freidson, *Doctoring Together: A Study of Professional Social Control* (New
York: Elsevier, 1975); and Bradford H. Gray, *Human Subjects in Medical Experimentation: A
Sociological Study of the Conduct and Regulation of Clinical Research* (New York: John Wiley
and Sons, 1975).

47. Bosk, *Forgive and Remember*, p. 27.

48. Ibid., p. 29.

49. Ibid., p. 13.

50. Ibid., p. 180.

51. Bosk, "Professional Responsibility," p. 466.

52. Ibid.

53. Bosk, *Forgive and Remember*, p. 84.

54. Ibid., p. 103.

55. Ibid., pp. 138–39.

56. Bosk, "Professional Responsibility," p. 468.

57. Ibid.

58. Crane, *The Sanctity of Social Life*, p. 199.

59. Ibid., p. 135.

60. William Winkenwerder, Jr., "Ethical Dilemmas for House Staff Physicians: The Care of Critically Ill and Dying Patients," *Journal of the American Medical Association*, 254, no. 24
(December 27, 1985), 3454–57.

61. Ibid.

62. Ibid.

63. Susan E. Light, "Letters," *Journal of the American Medical Association*, 255, no. 22 (June 13,
1986), 3113.

64. William Winkenwerder, Jr., "Letters: In Reply," *Journal of the American Medical Association*,
255, no. 22 (June 13, 1986), 3114.

65. Jonathan B. Imber, *Abortion and the Private Practice of Medicine* (New Haven, Conn.: Yale
University Press, 1986).

). In this connection, in order to explore some of the more subtle ways in which gender may play a part in the approach of men and women physicians, historian Regina Markell Morantz-Sanchez did an intriguing comparative case study of obstetrical and gynecological care at the female physician-run New England Hospital for Women and Children for the period 1873–1899, and Harvard's male-run Boston Lying-In for the period 1887, using a systematic sequential sample of case records. She found a "rough parity" between the therapeutics of male and female physicians with regard to the complication rates and frequency of forceps use. However, with regard to medication, male Boston Lying-In physicians followed "an objective model," prescribing drugs according to physical symptoms, whereas women physicians dispensed medication or supportive therapy "for less codifiable and nonphysical reasons." Another noticeable difference was that the women physicians at the New England Hospital entered much more information on patients' charts. In addition to an account of actual treatment, they provided more data than male physicians at Boston Lying-In did on patients' medical backgrounds and their social status. Furthermore, New England Hospital sought a different kind of patient from the Boston Lying-In: the "worthy poor." Morantz-Sanchez concluded that "men and women doctors acted alike in most therapeutic situations, but for very different reasons and with meanings both different to themselves and their patients." (Regina Markell Morantz-Sanchez, *Sympathy and Science: Women Physicians in American Medicine* (New York: Oxford University Press, 1985), pp. 225–31 and 363–7.)

67. Terry Mizrahi, *Getting Rid of Patients: Contradictions in the Socialization of Physicians* (New Brunswick, N.J.: Rutgers University Press, 1986), p. 168. Copyright © 1986 by Rutgers, The State University. Reprinted by permission of Rutgers University Press.

68. Ibid., p. 173.

69. Ibid., p. 172.

70. Joseph E. Hardison, "The House Officer's Changing World," *New England Journal of Medicine*, 314, no. 26 (June 26, 1986), 1714.

71. Mizrahi, *Getting Rid of Patients*, p. 28.

72. Ibid., p. 166.

73. Ibid.

74. Ibid., pp. 32–33.

75. Ibid., p. 41.

76. Ibid., p. 167.

77. Deborah B. Liederman and Jean-Anne Grisso, "The Gomer Phenomenon," *Journal of Health and Social Behavior*, 26 (September 1985), 222–32.

78. Ibid.

79. Ibid.

80. Mizrahi, *Getting Rid of Patients*, p. 170.

81. Ibid., p. 163.

82. Ibid., p. 162.

83. Ibid., p. 171.

84. Ibid., p. 172.

85. John Colombotos and Corinne Kirchner, *Physicians and Social Change* (New York: Oxford University Press, 1986), p. 76.

86. Osler L. Peterson, Leon P. Andrews, Robert S. Spain, and Bernard G. Greenberg, "An Analytical Study of North Carolina General Practice, 1953–1954," *Journal of Medical Education*, 31 (December 1956), part 2; Fremont J. Lyden, H. Jack Geiger, and Osler L. Peterson, *The Training of Good Physicians: Critical Factors in Career Choices* (Cambridge, Mass.: Harvard University Press, 1968); Gerald L. Klerman and Daniel J. Levinson, "Becoming the Director: Promotion as a Phase in Personal-Professional Development," *Psychiatry*, 32, no. 4 (November 1969), 411–27; Freidson, *Doctoring Together*; Imber, *Abortion and the Private Practice of Medicine*; Colombotos and Kirchner, *Physicians and Social Change*.

87. Samuel W. Bloom, "Socialization for the Physician's Role: A Review of Some Contributions of Research to Theory," in *Becoming a Physician: Development of Values and Attitudes in Medicine*, eds. Eileen C. Shapiro and Leah Lowenstein (Cambridge, Mass.: Ballinger Pub. Co., 1979), pp. 34–37.

88. Eliot Freidson, "Client Control and Medical Practice," *American Journal of Sociology*, 65, no. 4 (January 1960), 374–82; Eliot Freidson, *Patients' Views of Medical Practice: A Study of Sub-*

scribers to a Prepaid Medical Plan in the Bronx (New York: Russell Sage Foundation, 1961), Chap. 10.

89. Klerman and Levinson, "Becoming the Director," pp. 411–12.
90. Ibid., p. 426.
91. Eliot Freidson, *Doctoring Together: A Study of Professional Social Control* (New York: Elsevier, 1975), p. 14. Copyright 1975 by Elsevier Science Publishing Co., Inc. Reprinted by permission of the publisher.
92. Ibid., p. 258.
93. Ibid., pp. 214–15.
94. Ibid., pp. 243–44.
95. Ibid., p. 105.
96. Ibid., p. 205.
97. Ibid., p. 239.
98. Ibid., p. 259.
99. Eliot Freidson, *Profession of Medicine: A Study of the Sociology of Applied Knowledge* (New York: Dodd, Mead & Company, 1970), p. 366.
100. Ibid., p. 89.
101. Bosk, "Professional Responsibility," p. 470.
102. Imber, *Abortion and the Private Practice of Medicine*, p. 125.
103. Ibid.
104. Ibid., p. 128.
105. Only one of Daleton's private practitioners of obstetrics and gynecology was a woman at the time that Imber did his study.
106. Imber, *Abortion and the Private Practice of Medicine*, p. 73.
107. Ibid.
108. Ibid., p. 75.
109. Ibid., p. 71.
110. Bosk, *Forgive and Remember*, p. 189.
111. Imber, *Abortion and the Private Practice of Medicine*, p. 76.
112. This is a leading concept in Chapter 6 of Imber's book.
113. Imber, *Abortion and the Private Practice of Medicine*, p. 69.
114. Colombotos and Kirchner, *Physicians and Social Change*, p. 182.
115. Ibid., pp. xii–xiii.
116. For a detailed description of the sampling designs, methods and instruments of data collection, and the measures and scales used in these studies, see Colombotos and Kirchner, *Physicians and Social Change*, pp. 4–5, 138–40, and 203–40.

CHAPTER 5

THE HOSPITAL: A SOCIAL AND CULTURAL MICROCOSM

The hospital stands at the center of the ensemble of institutions that are integral to modern medicine. In this era of hospital architecture, it is likely to be a substantial, vertical presence on the landscape—a building or complex of buildings that was expanded and built upwards as the hospital developed scientifically, technologically, and organizationally. In an advanced modern society like that of the United States, the hospital is the principal "house" within which medical diagnosis and therapy, patient care, clinical research, and the first-hand training of nurses, physicians, and other health professionals take place. It is also an important economic entity whose capitalization, expenses, and costs have reached proportions of national concern.

The centrality of the modern hospital is not only attributable to its scientific, technological, and financial contours, its table of organization, and the array of explicitly medical functions that it performs. Its more-than-medical significance and some of its distinctive features are associated with the particular ways in which it is linked to the larger society and culture.

The hospital is a microcosm shaped by structures and networks, ideas and images, values and beliefs of the society and culture that both surround and pervade it. In this respect, it is no different from other social institutions. But the hospital also has a more singular relationship to society and culture—one that is allegorical in nature. A hospital is a highly symbolic world, intimately and powerfully connected to the "hardest surfaces" of social and cultural life and to its most "deep-lying" dimensions.[1] It incarnates and calls forth essences of our collective existence in some of their most perplexing, painful, illuminating, and uplifting forms.

Many writers, artists, social critics, and reformers have found the hospital to be a living social, moral, and spiritual metaphor. As participant observers in a "magic mountain" tuberculosis sanitorium[2] and a tumor-ridden "cancer ward,"[3] novelists Thomas Mann and Aleksandr Solzhenitsyn experienced and portrayed two sequestered, disease-centered communities that provided insights into the human spirit and the political as well as philosophical good and evil of the surrounding societies. Poet Amy Clampitt saw and felt it this way:

I write from the denser enclave of the stricken,
eight stories up, a prairie *gratte-ciel*.
Above the valley floor, the bell tower
of a displaced Italian hill town listens, likewise
attentive to the mysteries of one Body.
If the two salute, it must be as monks do,
without gesture, eyes lowered
by the force of gravity. Between them,
down among the car parks, tree shapes
stripped twig-bare appear to bruise
with tenderness, illusory as sea anemones.
There is no wind. For days
the geese that winter in the bottomland
have been the one thing always on the move,
in swags of streaming fronds, chiaroscuro
sea blooms, their wavering V-signs
following the turnings of one body.
Where are they going?
                    Down in the blood bank
the centrifuge, its branched transparent siphons
stripping the sap of Yggdrasil
from the slit arm of the donor, skims
the spinning corpuscles, cream-white
from hectic red. Below the pouched pack
dangled like a gout of mistletoe, the tubing
drips, drips from valve to valve to enter,
in a gradual procession, the cloistered
precincts of another body.
                    Sunset, its tinctured
layerings vivid as delirium, astonishing
as merely to be living, stains the cold
of half a hemisphere. The old
moon's dark corpus, its mysteries
likewise halfway illusory, tonight sleeps slumped
on the phosphorescent threshold of the new.[4]

To Florence Nightingale, as historian Charles Rosenberg has indicated, the hospital was "not only a dismaying reality, but also a didactic microcosm illustrating the interdependence of health and order in the larger world."[5] Sociologist Erving Goffman depicted the hospital as an "asylum" that epitomized the most "encompassing" and "total" of institutions in our Western society.[6] In his view, the hospital, along with institutions as ostensibly diverse as monasteries and convents, army barracks and boarding schools, jails and prison camps, was a "forcing house," with the enveloping, systematic power to "strip," "mortify," control, and alter "the self" of the persons who came to reside within it.

A very different image of the hospital-as-asylum is conveyed by surgeon-essayist Richard Selzer. Recalling his last visit to Honorio Delgado, a hospital in Peru, he writes:

> What a far cry it is from my sleek and spanking hospital in New Haven—all glass and prestressed concrete. And yet, so like. A hospital is only a building until you hear the slate hooves of dreams galloping upon its roof. You listen then and know that here is . . . an inner space full of pain and relief. Such a place invites mankind to heroism. For us, Honorio Delgado has become an instrument with which to confront life, a rock that stands firm against the incessant lapping of fate. . . . Tomorrow we leave Peru carrying with us the pathetic belief that the way to heal the world is to take it in for repairs. One on one. One at a time.[7]

This chapter will be concerned with the kind of sociocultural world that the hospital constitutes. It will identify and examine major social and cultural attributes of a hospital, reflecting on their implications for the universe of the hospital itself and for the society and culture of which it is a part. The modern, Western, American hospital will be the primary empirical and analytic referent. Attention will be focused on the contemporary forms that the modern hospital has assumed. Underlying this present-day perspective, however, is historical awareness that the modern American hospital, "with its trained nursing staff, well-equipped laboratories, and operating room facilities, its emphasis on organization and cleanliness, and a patient clientele drawn from all social classes dates only from the 1880s,"[8] and that the imprint of the hospital's previous history is still upon it.

"To most observers," historian Charles Rosenberg comments in his study of the rise of America's hospital system,

> The twentieth-century hospital seems an inevitable, if perhaps imperfect institution, one that grew unavoidably out of the interaction between social necessity and an emerging technical capacity. But despite this aura of inevitability, both logic and history emphasize that the American hospital's development has been contingent. Its history reflected a mixture of policy and drift, of change which grew out of the complex interaction between technical innovation, social attitudes, demographic and economic realities, and—finally—the crystallizing aspirations and values of an increasingly self-conscious medical profession. The hospital's functions and boundaries were negotiated in the past and are being renegotiated today; that history reflects choices not made, as well as those pursued.[9]

It will not be taken for granted that, in the 1980s, a wide spectrum of persons make up the population of hospital patients, that the hospital is so predominant in the care of the sick, or that most Americans are born and die in a hospital. While granting the role that medical scientific and technological progress and the evolution of the medical and nursing professions have played in these developments, the chapter will seek a broader sociological understanding of the hospital's dominion in matters of sickness and health.

Some attention will be paid to a number of significant changes that American hospitals are undergoing, and what their long-term consequences are likely to be. In this connection, two seemingly antithetical phenomena will be examined: the "dehospitalization" movement, and the development of large investor-owned hospital corporations. The growing emphasis on cost containment in the delivery of medical care and its implications both for hospitalization and dehospitalization also will be considered.

Although the chapter focuses on American hospitals, it will include some observations on how the modern hospital looks and feels when it is located in other Western or non-Western societies and cultures. These comparative materials serve as safeguards against an ethnocentric perspective on the hospital, and provide insights into which features of the modern hospital seem to be present no matter what its societal and cultural milieu, and which are more specifically Western and American.

THE HOSPITAL AS BUREAUCRACY

The modern hospital is a bureaucracy. This is one of its most conspicuous characteristics, recognized (and frequently lamented) by all who enter and exit from its portals—patients, visitors, professional staff, technicians, administrative, clerical, and housekeeping personnel, volunteers, delivery persons, messengers, vendors, police, clergy, and undertakers—who move through the hospital in a continuous day-and-night procession. To a pronounced degree, the hospital displays many of the attributes of a bureaucracy that were delineated by Max Weber.[10] It is a rational organization with an elaborate, systematic division of labor and a high degree of specialization of expertise, responsibilities, rights, and authority, whose manifold statuses, roles, and offices are structured according to a principle of hierarchy, and governed by impersonal rules and rule-like norms.

However, the hospital differs from the Weberian paradigm in several basic respects. It is an organization with a certain division in its lines of administrative and occupational authority. Although the unusually large number of professionals in a hospital are subject to administrative jurisdiction, they define, evaluate, and control their own work primarily on the basis of technical and moral standards of competence. In this regard, they retain and exercise considerable autonomy.[11] The hospital functions, then, on two bases of authority—administrative and professional—with a certain amount of built-in strain and potential conflict between them. This strain is cushioned and negotiated by the intermediary of administrators, who are health professionals or who have had special professional training in health care administration. The functioning and governance of the hospital also is premised on a number of parallel lines of professional authority. Each of the numerous professional groups in the hospital has its own department and set of services, with varying amounts and styles of control over its specialized work and that of the semiprofessionals and nonprofessionals under its supervision.

The two principal chains of side-by-side professional authority in the hospital are those of physicians and of nurses. The aspects of nurses' work that concern the diagnosis, treatment, and care of patients are conducted under the explicit orders of physicians. These orders have the added force of being formulated and recorded in writing, and they are legally as well as morally and organizationally binding. In this crucial respect the doctor-nurse relationship is a powerfully superordinate-subordinate one. But the nursing division of a hospital has its own independently managed hierarchy, which is not staffed by physicians or subjugated to them. In this corporate sense, doctors do not simply tell nurses what to do, and nurses do not simply comply with doctor's orders. Furthermore, all hospital matters associated with nursing are administered and regulated by the nursing service itself. As nursing has evolved from its earlier "handmaiden-to-the-physician" role, and achieved fuller professional status, it has also acquired greater autonomy in relationship to the medical profession, which is visible in the formal organization of a hospital. Yet, both inside and outside the hospital, the collegial and organizational relationship between the professions of medicine and nursing is far from equal, and it is fraught with both old and new sources of tension and ambiguity.[12]

BUT WHAT KIND OF BUREAUCRACY?

In many of its subdivisions, the organization of a hospital resembles that of other bureaucratic enterprises. For example, inspecting a hospital's table of organization reveals that, like nonhospital bureaucracies, it has top-level boards of directors and managers and divisions devoted to operations, financial management, accounting, budgeting and payroll, operations, systems and management data processing, development, legal affairs, public relations, information and reception, security, plant operation, office services, records, housekeeping, maintenance, food services, personnel health, and so forth.

However, there are particular features of such hospital tables of organization that distinguish them from those of other bureaucratic establishments. As is to be expected, the hospital has a series of medical and nursing divisions, each of which deals with a specialized sphere of the wide range of diagnostic and therapeutic fields and procedures of which modern medicine is composed. In addition, the hospital has organized areas of operation concerned with such things as admissions and discharge, chaplaincy or pastoral services, volunteers and auxiliaries, and transport—meaning moving people, substances, equipment, and messages back and forth inside the hospital, as distinct from transportation to and from the hospital via ambulance, which is also a special division of the hospital.

The extent to which a hospital is organizationally geared to the ever-present possibility of emergency is apparent in the number and diversity of services devoted to it, such as the emergency department, trauma, resuscitation, and critical and intensive care. The fact that a great many of a hospital's medical and surgical activities entail working intimately on the human body in ways that involve removing and replacing vital bodily fluids and organs is organizationally reflected in formal committees such as those concerned with tissues, transfusion, anesthesia and blood gas, and transplant. The risks, hazards, and harm that patients' illnesses and treatment may pose for patients, staff, and the public, and the degree to which the hospital is preoccupied with clinical safety, are also represented in its formal structure by committees such as infection control and radiation safety, and by the institutionalization in some hospitals of roles like that of risk manager.

Other special characteristics of the hospital and its organization are apparent in committees that are termed credentials, therapeutic standards, quality assurance, utilization review, protection of human subjects, and ethics. These have to do with the scientific, technical, clinical, and moral standards that health professionals are expected to meet, with their credentials and license to practice, and with the hospital's legal and ethical responsibility to monitor and regulate its professional personnel in these regards. Ethics committees and committees for the protection of human research subjects emanate from public concern about problems associated with the powerful means that modern medicine now wields in caring for illness, prolonging life, and conducting clinical research. Through quality assurance and utilization review committees, hospitals try to deal with the intense cost-containment pressures to which they have become subject in the past decade: to find rationally effective and socially acceptable ways of reducing medical care costs without diminishing the quality of patient care.

The authoritative influence of physicians in many of a hospital's subdivisions and committees is still dominant. Yet it is also notable that a larger and wider cross section of nonphysicians (including persons whose occupations fall outside the health field) are now members of the hospital's committee structure and have a considerable impact on the processes of deliberation and policy shaping that occur in these contexts. Furthermore, the management and functioning of the hospital is increasingly affected by outside regulatory agencies, governmental legislation, business interests, and by the actions and reactions of the general public, not the least of which is the ever-mounting spiral of medical malpractice suits.

HOSPITAL RULES: THE CASE OF POST-MORTEM PROCEDURES

As indicated, in common with other bureaucracies, the hospital is "a continuous organization bound by rules."[13] Such an abstract statement about its rule-governed nature, however, does not capture the essence of the hospital—those attributes that endow it with its "hospital-ness." A suggestive way to identify some of the more distinctive characteristics of the hospital-as-bureaucracy is to look more closely at the substantive focus and content of particular sets of hospital rules. What are these rules about, manifestly and latently? And are there other institutions, medical or nonmedical, bureaucratic or not, that have similar rules, with comparable meanings?

For this analysis, a striking example are the rules that describe and regulate how the bodies of patients who die in the hospital should be prepared, labeled, and transported to the morgue. The rules that we will consider are those of a particular metropolitan, university-affiliated, not-for-profit hospital. They were issued by the hospital's division of nursing and its transport service department, and co-signed by an associate administrator nurse in charge of patient support and therapeutic services and by the director of the transport services. Revised numerous times over the years, the latest version was sent to all patient units and patient transport under the authority of the associate administrator of nursing, to officially announce and explain how, "effective Monday, May 2, 1983, responsibility for the disposition of deceased patients will rest jointly between Nursing and Transport Services." The rules were elaborated in sufficient detail to cover fifteen single-spaced typed pages. They consisted of five sections: "Post-Mortem Care: Nursing Responsibilities; Viewing of the Deceased in the Chapel; Infection-Control Practices; Transport of Deceased Patients; Supplemental Procedure: Viewing Bodies; Procedure for Transporting Deceased Patients." The stated purposes of the meticulously spelled-out procedural rules in this document were: "to provide respectful care of the deceased; comply with documentation standards; provide patients' significant others with the opportunity for grieving; and, when applicable, to prevent the spread of infection or possible radioactive contamination in hospital personnel and morticians." Key passages from these rules include:

   I. Notifications
      A. Notify physician who will declare time of death, call or speak to family or responsible person, request permission for autopsy and fill out autopsy permission form, if applicable, and death notice. The physician also fills out two copies of the death certification *unless the death involves the Medical Examiner's Office.* . . .
      B. Notify Clinical Director or Evening/Night Coordinator about death.
      C. Notify Transport Services who will make arrangements for a transporter to bring morgue litter to the unit to transport body to morgue. Be sure to specify the time the transporter's service will be required.
  II. Prepare body for viewing by patient's significant others.
      A. Body may stay on unit only for a maximum of two hours after death.
      B. Clean and replace false teeth immediately.
      C. Close eyes and mouth. Place folded towel under chin if necessary.
      D. Clean body and change linen as necessary.
      E. Place body in dorsal recumbent position with one pillow under head.
      F. Remove extraneous equipment from room, e.g., crash cart, I-Med pump, 02 equipment, etc.
      G. If there is to be an autopsy, or if it is a Medical Examiner's case, leave *all* tubes in place, including I.V.'s, Foley catheters, nasogastric tubes, etc. . . .
      H. Insure patient has identi-band on wrist.
      I. Have ice water, cups, Kleenex, and chairs available in room for patient's significant others.
      J. Insure privacy and encourage significant others to be alone with patient for about 20 minutes before interrupting them.
 III. Gather patient's clothing and valuables being certain to check all closets, drawers and bedside table.
      A. Remove all jewelry including wedding ring. If ring cannot be removed manually, see Ward Manual for ring removal procedure.
      B. Give clothing and valuables to significant others, if present. . . .
 IV. Documentation:
      A. Record in the Nurse's Record:
         1. Date and time of death
         2. Physician who was notified
         3. Physician who declared patient dead
         4. Whether significant others were notified and/or in attendance
         5. Disposition of patient's clothing and valuables
      B. Complete death notice (RN signature).
   V. Prepare body for transport to morgue. (See page three for care and labeling of infected patient's body and body of patient with radioactive substances)
      A. Obtain a Shroud-Pac containing a plastic shroud sheet, cotton chin straps, two cellulose pads, three identification tags, three 36" ties, and two 60" ties. Also obtain four ABD pads.
      B. Stamp unmarked side of the pads using Addressoplate. Write in time of death using *Eastern Standard Time.*
      F. Place plastic shroud under patient. . . .
      G. Fold shroud sheet as shown in illustration in package.
      H. Tie shroud at head and feet with 60" ties and attach second identification tag.
      I. Request transporter to bring morgue litter into the room.

J. Transfer patient from bed to morgue litter with the help of transporters.

K. Give death notice and two copies of the death certificate to the transporter. These documents are delivered to the Information Desk. (Between 9:30 p.m. and 7:00 a.m., the two copies of the death certificate are placed in the drawer marked "death certificates" at the Information Desk and the transporter takes the death notice to the Telephone Room.)

VI. Policy

Opportunity for family members to view the body of the deceased in the Hospital Chapel shall be provided, when requested, in accordance with the procedure described below.

VII. Purpose

The purpose of this policy is to respect the request of the family unable to be present at the time of death and to whom viewing of the deceased is highly significant to their well being. . . .

VIII. Transport

When you are transporting a deceased patient you should wear rubber surgical gloves. . . . Each time a body is transported to the morgue, litter should be wiped down in the morgue area with alcohol prior to returning the litter to its original location. The alcohol and paper towels can be found in the drawers of the desk. Dispose of the towels by placing them in isolation trash can located under the desk. After wiping down the morgue litter, remove the rubber gloves and place them in the isolation trash can.

Transport the body along one of the designated routes. These routes travel through the least populated areas of the hospital in an attempt not to upset patients or visitors. When transporting the body move swiftly and quietly. Do not stop to talk with other employees or discuss the task that you are carrying out. Attempt to move swiftly but do not treat the patient in a careless manner. Use the same care that you would use in transporting a live patient.

IX. Final Tasks

The morgue is located in the basement. . . . You will be met by a Security Officer or an Information Services representative along with another messenger. The door to the morgue room will be unlocked. . . .

Now select a drawer to place the body in. There are nine (9) drawers into which bodies can be placed. A tag on the outside of the drawer means that the drawer is occupied. Always try to use the waist-level drawers first. . . .

Both messengers should now move the patient from the morgue litter to the drawer tray. In moving the patient always keep in mind the principles of body mechanics that you have been taught. . . . Take care to be gentle in moving the patient. . . .

When you return the morgue litter, sign the log book, and note the time you returned the litter. . . . Return to the Transport area and report to the Dispatcher. At this time the Dispatcher should record the name of the second messenger involved in the move and the time the messenger arrived back at the transport office.

In form and in style, these rules are prototypically bureaucratic. The language in which they are set down is logico-rational, technical, legalistic, impersonal, and precisely matter of fact. Minutely specific actions are detailed within a framework that emphasizes hierarchy, division of labor, responsibility and accountability, order, propriety, efficiency, exactitude, caution, coordination, labeling, record-keeping, timing, and time. This codified inventory of procedures has all the core characteristics of the rules in any modern bureaucracy. And yet these rules are not like all bureaucratic others.

They are rules that chronicle as well as dictate the sequelae of a hospital death. As such, they concern the inevitability and the mystery of human mortality and the special relationship of medicine and medical institutions to the life cycle—particularly to birth and death, and also suffering and survival.

However standardized and secularly professional the statement and enactment of these procedures may be, pronouncing a patient dead, cleaning and arranging the body for viewing, shrouding it, transporting and accompanying it, and readying it for burial are inherently sacred, anciently religious tasks (latently influenced, in the case of an American hospital, by the society's Judeo-Christian tradition). Calling it "post-mortem care," or using plastic shrouds instead of Biblical linen winding sheets to wrap the body, does not expunge its sacral character.

These death-precipitated hospital activities also entail a great deal of work that is dirty and fraught with the danger of contamination and pollution. This is true symbolically as well as literally, because it is work that involves intimate contact with death and the human body in ways that touch deep, primal feelings of repugnance and fear, and that violate strong cultural taboos. But the entire post-mortem hospital sequence is protected and purified by the norms of asepsis, prudence, and respectful discretion that prevail over it.

Although written out in hospital manuals, self-consciously executed by hospital personnel, and recorded and documented in each of its phases, this whole process is part of the covert life of the hospital. Its full significance is hidden behind the technicalization and bureaucratization of the post-mortem procedures and the depersonalized vocabulary in which they are phrased. It is deliberately kept away from the view of all but the hospital personnel who participate in it by the swift, quiet motions with which it is carried out, by the body coverings, designated routes, subterranean locations, locked doors and compartments that are used, and by the silence that surrounds it. Not even all the professional members of the hospital staff are fully aware of everything that ensues following the death of a patient. For example, many physicians are not cognizant of the details of post-mortem care that nurses administer. Furthermore, the chief actors in the process—the responsible physician, nurses, chaplain, transporters and messengers, security officer, and the information desk clerks—do not talk about it. Their silence is procedurally recommended, for the sake of decorum, out of respect for the deceased and family members, and with the intent "not to upset" patients and hospital visitors. It also seems to provide both professional and nonprofessional personnel with a shield that insulates them from the full emotional impact of the continual occurrence of death in the hospital and the grimly solemn work that is associated with it.[14]

OF THE HOSPITAL, THE MILITARY, AND THE RELIGIOUS

The treatment of death is one among many possible examples of how the distinctive work of the hospital and the moral, existential, and medical implications of what takes place within it affect its social system structurally and atmospherically. The hospital is organized around health and illness, life and death, pain and injury, accident and emergency, the perils of human existence (including the hazardous side effects of medical and surgical treatment), and a wide range of individual and social human problems that have come into the orbit of medicine. In these respects, it has a certain affinity with military organizations, on the one hand, and religious institutions, on the other.

It is not fortuitous that, like members of the military, the personnel of a hospital are dressed in uniforms that identify who they are in terms of their type of work, their departmental affiliation, and their rank in the hierarchy. Their apparel represents more than the external mark of the highly differentiated and stratified hospital bureaucracy. It is also relevant to the underlying emergency dimension of a hospital and to the imperatives of mobilization and coordination that this entails. A hospital is a collectivity that is perpetually geared to respond to medically urgent and dangerous situations. It must be able to rapidly assemble many diversely trained persons and set them into orderly, synchronized, composed, and efficient action. Uniforms facilitate this process, because they are visible, portable, functionally specific markers that quickly, silently, and officially indicate the category to which each hospital worker belongs, and what he or she is competent and authorized to do.

Hospitals are related to religious institutions in a number of ways. Among the historically earliest hospitals of the West were those created by the Episcopate of the Catholic Church at the Council of Nicea in 325 A.D., where the Bishops instructed that hospitals be established in every cathedral city. The institutional creation of hospitals grew out of the spiritual/humanitarian Christian tradition of *caritas*, the care of souls, and of healing. At the time of the Crusades, in the twelfth and thirteenth centuries, hospitals became hospices as well, offering hospitality, sanctuary, and spiritual ministrations, along with physical care to those who arrived at their doors. Monks and religious brothers and sisters were the primary hosts and caretakers. Those who were received and tended in church hospitals were largely the poor and incurably ill.

Although hospitals have undergone major metamorphoses over the centuries, a considerable number of them still function under religious auspices (in American society, mainly Catholic, Protestant, and Jewish). Furthermore, virtually every hospital, no matter how secular its orientation, has a chapel or a meditation room on its premises and a chaplaincy service as part of its organization.

But independently of whether a hospital is sectarian or denominational, has a chaplain on its staff, or has set aside a place for prayer, religiously resonant experiences and questions are an integral part of its life. This is because, as we have emphasized, it is a place where people are born—where they enter the world; where suffering and pain of all sorts—physical and psychic, moral and spiritual—are concentrated; where anxiety, sadness, anguish, bewilderment, anger, and fear are pervasive; where care and caring abide. Comfort, hope, trust, and faith exist too, and healing, recovery, and even cure occur. Hospitals also are places where every form of human aloneness, woundedness, disorientation, and misery is assembled and laid bare, along with the ravages of human violence. And it is a place where, in the end, dying and death come to pass—the place where most people exit from the world.

In the hospital the comedy and tragedy of human existence, its nobility and its ignominy, lie close to the surface, are juxtaposed, and intermingle. Not only do people's life-stories begin and end here, but they are elicited and revealed, in all their sameness and variety, while the overseeing, "central clock that is found in practically every hospital unit,"[15] ticks neutrally and endlessly on. A microcosm like this teems with the basic religious problems of meaning, order, direction, identity, relatedness, good and evil, justice and mercy, that our lives and our deaths represent and contain. Irrespective of the degree to which they are acknowledged and responded to as such by patients, families, and hospital personnel, these religious essences are always present in the hospital's "denser enclave."[16]

THE HOSPITAL AND THE BODY

Whatever empirical and analogic connection the hospital may have to other institutions, there is at least one respect in which it stands apart from them. This singularity resides in the hospital's relationship to the conscious and unconscious, living and dead human body.

The body is at the absolute center of the hospital's medical work and also a good deal of its nonmedical activity. In the name of prevention, diagnosis, therapy, and care, the body is unclothed. It is touched continually by many pairs of hands, including private, highly connotative regions, orifices, and cavities of the body that are ordinarily touched only in the most intimate personal relations and contexts. This handling of the body involves certain ungentle and even assaultive procedures, ranging from percussing and hammering various bodily sites to the hard pounding that cardiopulmonary resuscitation entails.

The body is persistently under observation in the hospital. It is intently looked at, listened to, felt, and asked about; its input and output are recorded and measured; the odors it emanates are systematically noted. Even some of the simpler, more innocuous modes of clinical observation, such as listening for heart sounds with a stethoscope or inspecting the interior of the eye with an ophthalmoscope, are more intrusive than those permitted in everyday, nonmedical contacts. As medicine and its technology have advanced, the hospital has increasingly become the locus of powerfully penetrating machines, such as computed tomography (CAT) and positron emission tomography (PET) scanners that look and hear into the deepest and smallest recesses of the body. Computer-assisted monitoring devices scrutinize, trace, and analyze complex physiological processes inside the body. These machines watch over patients' bodies and produce copious data about them, making it possible for physicians and nurses to closely observe patients at a distance, away from the bedside.[17]

Many of the diagnostic and therapeutic actions conducted in the hospital involve taking substances from patients' bodies—blood, urine, mucus, secretions of various kinds. Other interventions call for putting substances on or into their bodies—pharmacological and biological materials, radioactive matter, electric currents, physical devices, prostheses, and artificial and transplanted organs. This whole battery of examinations and treatments require still other, invasive ways of working on the body: the administration of injections and intravenous infusions, connecting the body to machines via tubing inserted into it and, above all, conducting surgery on and within it.

In surgery, the body is anesthetized. Different layers of unconsciousness are induced. Vital bodily processes are temporarily suspended or taken over for a time by machines. The body is opened and cut into: "wounded," to use the terminology of surgeons themselves. After the layer upon layer of dissecting inward of which the operation consists is completed and all the other forms of surgical cutting, tying, arranging, attaching, grafting, and implanting have come to an end, the process is reversed. Incisions and body structures are sutured—sewn back together with a great variety of needles, surgical stitches, and thread or other materials—until the body is once again "closed up," as the surgeons say.[18]

The so-called post-mortem care that is administered to the bodies of deceased hospital patients has already been described in some detail. When permission is granted for an autopsy or when one is legally required, the recently dead body undergoes a searching pathological examination that combines attributes of anatomical dissection with those of major surgery.[19]

There is so much bodily movement of patients, on rolling stretchers and in wheelchairs, from one place to another in the hospital, that it creates a stream of traffic. Patients are moved to and from "specialized machine areas, where machines are used to do tests, monitor the course of diseases, or provide treatment." They are also moved "according to the acuity of disease, from acute to intermediate rehabilitation wards or back to acute and intermediate wards as their condition changes."[20] When death occurs, as we have seen, patients' bodies are conveyed from the clinical areas of the hospital to the morgue—in some instances, with intermediary stops at the chapel and the autopsy room. Bodily products, most notably blood, plasma, serum, and urine, also are carried through the hospital corridors, traversing out-patient and in-patient services, clinical laboratories, and the blood bank.

Under no institutional "roof" in society other than the hospital is the human body handled and worked on in all these ways.

HOSPITAL TIME

The unending activity of a hospital, with its organized shifts, rotations, and rounds, takes place within a highly structured and regulated temporal order.[21] The distinguishing characteristics of its time frame are closely related to the social and cultural, as well as the practical and technical, nature of a hospital.

A great deal of significance is accorded to time and timing in a hospital, particularly as indicated and measured by the clock. Events and actions that are defined as important are not only verbally recorded; they are temporally registered as well. For example, as we have seen, the time that a death occurs in the hospital is "declared" by the physician, entered in the nurse's record, and written on the identifying labels and documents that accompany a deceased patient to the morgue. When the morgue litter is returned, the transporter notes the time in a special log book, and when the transporter and the second messenger arrive back at the Transport Office, the time is again entered in a hospital record by the Dispatcher. The times that medications are administered to patients are officially recorded in their charts by the nurses who dispense them.[22] The narrative chronicling of what was done in the course of a surgical procedure, dictated post-operatively by the surgeon in charge and entered into the patient's chart, is still another documented set of acts that is punctuated by references to time: when the operation began, when each of its key phases occurred, and what its total duration was.

Although a premium is placed on how rapidly a piece of surgery is performed, an operation that takes many hours because of the extraordinary skill that it requires or the gravity of the patient's condition has special prestige. In other types of hospital work as well, positive or negative value is attached to duration—to "how long" a task takes. In turn, this is related to the emphasis placed on promptness in the daily round of the hospital's scheduled activities—the many delays and the prolonged waiting that so frequently occur in hospitals notwithstanding.

Much of the regular, everyday work of the hospital proceeds in fixed schedules of various sorts, patterned according to the status categories of the personnel carrying it out, their roles, and the types of activity involved. Thus, as described in Chapter 2, nurses work in shifts on a given service, whereas house officers rotate periodically among various services. Physicians are on call; nurses usually are not. The group of physicians in most hospitals who make the earliest ward rounds are surgical residents, who characteristically appear on the floor by 6:00 A.M. "so that they can be scrubbed, capped, gowned, and ready to operate on their first patient at precisely 8:00 A.M."[23] Nurses take patients' vital signs (temperature, pulse, and respiration) at four-hour intervals. They may administer some medications *pro re nata* (p.r.n.—according to circumstances, or when needed); but a great many of the medicines that they dispense have been prescribed by physicians with particular time intervals attached—for example, every four hours or q.q.h. (*quoque quarta hora*).[24] These medication cycles are consolidated and coordinated so that on each service, and throughout the hospital, patients receive their medications at the hospital's standardized medication times.

On all in-patient units, specific hours are also designated for waking patients, serving them meals, admitting their visitors, and for putting patients to sleep at what is institutionally defined as the end of their hospital day.

In several respects, hospital time, so tightly scheduled within its own parameters, is imperfectly synchronized with time outside the hospital. Virtually every patient is struck by how early one is awakened in a hospital for vital signs to be taken, as the nursing night shift ends and the morning shift begins; by the difference between hospital and home mealtimes (for instance, supper at 5:00 p.m. in the hospital); by how scheduled tests and procedures and their requisite conditions (for example, fasting) can alter the sleeping, waking, eating, and visiting time patterns of normal social life; and how surgery or a critical phase of illness can subjectively project a patient beyond time.

As already indicated, in East Coast American hospitals, the activities that ensue around the care and disposition of bodies of deceased patients are all recorded in Eastern Standard Time, even during the Daylight Savings time season of the year. In an analogous fashion, as Zerubavel has noted,[25] nurses and doctors usually refer to the central clock on each hospital unit, rather than to their own watches, when they arrive at work, go on duty, begin a round, start a report, leave the floor for a meal, or go off duty. Central clock time is common, authorized hospital time, related to but not necessarily identical with individual, personal watch time, or with what the clocks and watches outside the hospital say. It is a "collective representation of the sociotemporal order of the hospital"[26]—an order that reflects and expresses the hospital's physical and social functioning and its medico-moral significance.

The time structure of a hospital is influenced by biological and sociological factors: by the metabolic processes and rhythms of the human body that must be taken into account in medical diagnosis and treatment (as, for example, in the spacing of medication); and by the requisites of assigning and coordinating the large numbers of different kinds of specialized personnel who make up the work force of the hospital bureaucracy.

Looked at in a broad perspective, the time frame of the hospital also rests on certain moral assumptions about its reason for being and the import of what it does. The hospital is one of a relatively few organizations and services in American society that operate around the clock, seven days a week, 365 days a year. Its ceaseless functioning, as Zerubavel points out, is based on the essentially moral conviction that matters pertaining to health and illness are so serious, and medical and nursing services for patients so indispensable, that a hospital should never close its doors. The principle of "continuous coverage" has been institutionalized in the hospital.[27] Its incessant cycle of work is organized so that, although individual doctors and nurses are not on duty or on call all day, every day, and every unit and office does not function twenty-four hours a day, the hospital as an entity never stops its work or even temporarily shuts down. The emergency ethos of the hospital is integral to the principle and fact of continuous coverage. It rests on the practical and moral assumption that a medical emergency is an ever-present possibility to which it is imperative to respond.

HOSPITAL RITUALS

To a significant degree, many rituals are embedded in the schedules, procedures, and practices of a hospital. Among these, Bosk has identified what he calls the "occupational rituals" that are inherent to such meetings as attending and work rounds, case conferences, grand rounds, and mortality and morbidity conferences, at which physicians discuss the problems of making a diagnosis and prescribing treatment for their patients.[28] These meetings involve more than intellectual, scientific, and technical exchanges about patient management. Built into them, Bosk shows, are ceremonial patterns of behavior that "allow physicians to dramatize, to teach, and to remind themselves and their colleagues of their sense of what it means to be a physician," and that "assist them in managing uncertainty, making treatment decisions, and evaluating outcomes."[29] Theatrical ritual is present in the medical gallows humor and the hyperrealistic "horror stories" about what can and does go wrong in the treatment of patients. A more latent and technicalized form of ritual is encoded in the structure and style of the medical discourse that physicians use on these occasions: for example, in their probability reasoning, their hedged assumptions, Socratic teaching, and in their "decisions not to decide."[30]

The dramaturgic dimensions of such occupational rituals are vividly illustrated by what Bosk terms the "putting on the hair shirt" aspects of mortality and morbidity conferences, in which senior (attending) surgeons publicly and ceremonially "abase themselves" before their peers and subordinates. Attendings do three things when they put on the hair shirt: they claim that they made mistakes in the handling of the patient's case under discussion, explain why it might have been better to take some other course of action, and note that lessons have been learned. Beyond these explicit communications, a number of more latent messages are conveyed by the hair shirt ritual:

> . . . for the superordinate, putting on the hair shirt only emphasizes the surgeon's charity, humanity, and the scope of his wisdom. . . . It allows him to express guilt without being consumed by it. . . . At the same time, it communicates to subordinates that no one is perfect; it models for them the proper expression of

guilt and teaches them to accept that such accidents are an inevitable, unfortunate, and intractable part of professional life.[31]

Renée Fox has observed comparable, but more sequestered and ironic, rituals among research physicians who have the dual, often conflicting responsibility of caring for seriously ill patients and conducting clinical investigations upon them. Within the confines of this type of research group, at meetings held privately inside their laboratories and conference rooms, gallows humor flourishes, as does another complex ritual that Fox has termed their "games of chance."[32] In this context, physicians take bets on such solemn medical matters as the diagnosis or prognosis of a patient's illness and the impact of therapy; on the outcome of particularly important laboratory tests or risky experiments on their patient-subjects; and on whether a particular patient will live or die:

> On one level, [the game of chance] is a collective way of "acting out" the chance elements that are inherent to medical science and practice. It is also a way of "acting on" them, for it involves a group of medical professionals in a game-like contest, in which they pit their knowledge, experience, skill, and powers of reasoning and prediction against the unknown, adventitious, hard-to-control factors in the diagnostic, therapeutic, and prognostic aspects of medical work. "Winning" the bet, by "guessing" right, represents a symbolic mastery of these chancy forces, and a schematic victory over them. The wagering is fundamentally ironic in nature: It mimics probability reasoning-based medical scientific thinking, and it is playfully structured around the premise that what physicians . . . know and do not know, what they can and cannot do, and how their interventions affect patients— all have much in common with a game of chance. At the same time, the betting behavior is self-depreciatory and self-mocking, depicting supposedly professional medical expertise and action as highly speculative, full of guesswork and gambles, and fraught with luck. . . . Finally, the game of chance is both a protest and a petition. It is a ritualized way of declaring that what medical professionals know and can do for patients, and whether or not their patients get better or worse, live or die, *should* have more order and meaning than the throw of the dice or the turn of the roulette wheel.[33]

In addition, Fox has identified various celebrative rites of passage that physicians and nurses create for hospital patients. One of the most common of these is a party to mark the anniversary of having undergone a risky surgical procedure, particularly if the patient was perilously ill at the time, and the procedure involved was experimental. In the 1950s, on the hospital ward that she studied, Fox saw parties like this given for patients who had undergone the removal of their adrenal glands for malignant hypertension or terminal cancer of the prostate and who had survived for one year. In the 1960s and 1970s, she observed many comparable anniversary celebrations for patients who had received organ transplants, particularly heart transplants. Often, these were called "birthday parties," recognizing patients' one-year (or more) survival, and what was deemed their "rebirth" and "new life."[34]

The cardinal activities of hospital nurses and the daily cycle within which they are carried out are also laced through with ritual. In her ethnographic study of nursing rituals in an adult medical unit of a large urban hospital, Zane Wolf[35] has minutely detailed how the ritual elements in nurses' change of shift report, medicine administration, admission and discharge of patients, medical aseptic practices, and post-mortem care link nurses to each other, to the distinctive duties and traditions of their profession, to the sociotemporal order of hospital life, to the bodies and the medical and human condition of patients, and to their "coming in," "staying in," and "going out."[36]

Richard Selzer has vividly described how the universe of surgery inside a hospital pulsates with ritual:

> A stillness settles in my heart and is carried to my hand. It is the quietude of resolve layered over fear. And it is this resolve that lowers us, my knife and me, deeper and deeper into the person beneath. It is an entry into the body that is nothing like a caress; still, it is among the gentlest of acts. Then stroke and stroke again, and we are joined by other instruments, hemostats and forceps, until the wound blooms with strange flowers whose looped handles fall to the sides in steely array.
>
> There is sound, the tight click of clamps fixing teeth into severed blood vessels, the snuffle and gargle of the suction machine clearing the field of blood for the next stroke, the litany of monosyllables with which one prays his way down and in: *clamp, sponge, suture, tie, cut.* And there is color. The green of the cloth, the white of the sponges, the red and yellow of the body. . . .
>
> You turn aside to wash your gloves. It is a ritual cleansing. One enters the temple doubly washed. . . .
>
> I must confess that the priestliness of my profession has ever been impressed on me. In the beginning, there are vows, taken with all solemnity. Then there is the endless harsh novitiate of training, much fatigue, much sacrifice. At last one emerges as celebrant, standing close to the truth lying curtained in the Ark of the body. Not surplice and cassock but mask and gown are your regalia. You hold no chalice, but a knife. There is no wine, no wafer. There are only the facts of blood and flesh. . . .
>
> The operating room is called a theatre. One walks onto a set where the cupboards hold tanks of oxygen and other gases. The cabinets store steel cutlery of unimagined versatility, and the refrigerators are filled with bags of blood. Bodies are stroked and penetrated here, but no love is made. Nor is it ever allowed to grow dark, but must always gleam with a grotesque brightness. . . .
>
> In the room the instruments lie on trays and tables. They are arranged precisely by the scrub nurse, in an order that never changes, so that you can reach blindly for a forceps or hemostat without looking away from the operating field. The instruments lie *thus!* . . .
>
> And what of the *other*, the patient, you, who are brought to the operating room on a stretcher, having been washed and purged and dressed in a white gown? Fluid drips from a bottle into your arm, diluting you, leaching your body of its personal brine. . . . Soon a man will stand over you, gowned and hooded. In time the man will take up a knife and crack open your flesh like a ripe melon. . . .
>
> What is it, then, this thing, the knife, whose shape is virtually the same as it was three thousand years ago, but now with its head grown detachable? . . .
>
> At last a little thread is passed into the wound and tied. . . . The tempest is silenced. The operation is over. On the table, the knife lies spent, on its side, the bloody meal smear-dried upon its flanks. The knife rests.
>
> And waits.[37]

Inside the hospital communities created by patients, out of their shared predicament of illness, treatment, and separation from the "world outside," ritual abounds, too—much of it unknowingly corresponding to the ritual practices of nurses and doctors. (Later in this chapter, the "small society" of hospital patients will be discussed more fully.)

Hospital rituals have common referents, whether they occur among physicians, nurses, or patients, in the conference room, auditorium, laboratory, operating room, or on a clinical unit or ward. These rituals cluster around problems of uncertainty, risk and limitation, detached concern and grace under pressure, and of meaning and order in hospital life. They involve the human comedy, tragedy, and mystery associated with illness and medicine, and a curious mix of the sacred, profane, and blasphemous, the traditional and the modern. Rituals also embrace the importance and efficacy of scientific and technical expertise and the seriousness of hospital work. Rituals address the practical and moral necessity of striving to realize the highest professional and human values, and to achieve consensus and solidarity before all the difficult situations and decisions that doctors, nurses, and patients mutually face.

Some hospital rituals, such as medical rounds and conferences, are cognitively, technically, and morally didactic. Others, like "the game of chance," are permeated by "scientific magic": "essentially magical ways of behaving that simulate medical scientific attitudes and behaviors, or that are hidden behind them, and that help physicians and nurses to face problems of uncertainty, therapeutic limitation, and meaning by 'ritualizing their optimism' (as anthropologist Bronislaw Malinowski would have put it)."[38] Still others, especially those that involve closeness to death or cutting into the human body, have religious overtones. All the rituals are empirically and symbolically related to essential features of what a hospital is, does, stands for, and evokes. As such they provide physicians, nurses, and patients with collective ways of thinking and feeling about what the hospital asks of them, and of actively coping with it.

HOSPITAL LABELS AND SIGNS

The world of the hospital is not only structured by rules, procedures, and schedules, and pervaded by symbolism and ritual; it is also filled with labels and signs. Virtually all hospital equipment, furniture, and supplies are marked with the name of the hospital and the service to which they belong. Medical drugs are labelled with their name, content, indications, and contraindications. Hospital personnel and patients are labelled, too. Employees and staff wear pins with their own and their department's name printed on them, and identification badges bearing their personal photograph. The white hospital coats of medical staff are often embroidered with the name of the hospital, the service with which the wearer is affiliated, and if he or she is a person of high professional rank in the hospital bureaucracy—for example, a chief of service, or a senior attending physician—that individual's name may be embroidered on the coat as well.

The importance of correctly identifying a patient at all times during hospitalization is codified in hospital policy manuals, detailing responsibilities and procedures for the use of identification bracelets, identification plates to emboss on all medical record forms, and medical record numbers. Patients are officially tagged with a plastic identification bracelet as part of the admissions process. The names of the hospital, the patient, and the patient's physician are imprinted on this bracelet, along with the patient's date of birth, sex, and medical record number. The bracelet remains on the patient's wrist throughout the entire period of hospitalization. It is routinely consulted by personnel caring for or transporting patients whose capacity to identify themselves is impaired by sedation, anesthesia, disorientation, unconsciousness, or coma, and as a check in a variety of situations, such as the administration of medications, where an error caused by treating the "wrong" patient might have serious clinical consequences. Newborn babies in the nursery have their names spelled out on the beaded bracelets placed around their wrists (blue for boys, pink for girls). Many of the young resident physicians working on the obstetrics service use the same alphabetical baby beads to affix their own names to their stethoscopes. At the other end of the life spectrum, deceased patients are ushered out of the hospital with identification tags tied onto their right toe, their shroud, and their personnel belongings.

The omnipresence of signs on the walls and doors of the hospital is equally striking.[39] Their quantity and the nature of their messages infuse the hospital with a depersonalized, "Alice in Wonderland/Through the Looking Glass"/"Big Brother Is Watching You" atmosphere all its own.

One cluster of signs is informational and directional, telling people where they are in the hospital, where to go (and where not to go), and how to get there. Another group of signs spells out hospital rules, regulations, procedures, and policies of various sorts: for example, visiting hours, fee schedules and hospital charges, obligatory aseptic practices for visitors to the isolation unit, a declaration of the hospital's "policy not to discriminate in the acceptance, placement, transfer or treatment of patients on the basis of race, creed, color, national origin, or sex," regulations of the Department of Health of the state in which the hospital is located, and so forth. Still other signs are admonitory and/or exhortative:

Danger. Oxygen in Use. No Smoking.

Biohazard. Admittance to Authorized Personnel only.

Surgery. Restricted Area. No one permitted beyond the red line without scrub suit, or dress cap and boots. This is MANDATORY.

Please Keep This Door Closed At All Times.

No Admittance at This Time. Babies are Feeding.

No Admittance, Coronary Care.

No Fresh Flowers Admitted in This Patient Area.

No Smoking in Patients' Rooms.

For Your Protection, Hospital Safety Codes Prohibit Personal Televisions.

This plethora of labels, tags, and signs throughout the hospital is related to its special characteristics. The hospital is a public facility through which a vast amount of human traffic continually moves, among whom are ambulatory patients and visitors unfamiliar with the premises who need help in finding their way. It is also a large, complex bureaucracy within which hundreds of employees, engaged in hundreds of different roles, circulate and carry out the sorts of work that make it important for them to be quickly and accurately recognized by each other, and by patients. The fact that the hospital is a relatively open, around-the-clock, public place that is supposed to be available at all times to help anyone in medical need brings many distraught and confused people into its orbit, with pronounced problems of orientation and identification. Characteristically, the physical layout of a hospital through which this human mass flows and wanders is bewildering: multi-layered and labyrinthine, reflecting the intricacy of the hospital's social structure, the requisites of its technology, and the accretive, historical process by which most hospitals have developed, adding on space and facilities as they evolved. For these several reasons, there is need for many signposts and "I.D." markers inside the hospital.

The powerful modes of diagnosis and treatment that the modern hospital uses have potential side effects and hazards that could have serious consequences for patients, staff, and others filing through the building each day. Medical and surgical interventions must therefore be managed with skill and caution. Safeguards must also be established and enforced to protect patients rendered physically or emotionally vulnerable by their illness and treatment, and that will facilitate rather than impede their recovery. Most of the admonitory signs in the hospital concern these clinical dangers and obligations, and the prudence and vigilance that competent and responsible hospital-based medicine calls for. In such a populous and in many ways impersonal institution as a modern hospital, mistakes and misidentifications that could have serious biological, psychological, and social consequences are ever-present possibilities. Many of the tags and labels that patients and personnel wear are designed to forestall such untoward happenings, to protect the hospital against liability as well as to keep patients, staff, and employees from undue harm. The numerous "No Admittance" and "Restricted Area" signs that cordon off certain places in the hospital are part of the fail-safe, protective dimensions of hospital life. At the same time, they circumscribe some of the closed-to-the-outside-world areas of the modern Western hospital that make it a total institution-like enclave, despite its public, open-24-hours-a-day characteristics.

THE INNER WORLDS OF THE HOSPITAL

The enclosed and restricted spheres of the hospital derive from still another of its major characteristics. The hospital is an encompassing social system, interlarded with many smaller social systems. Although these mini-worlds inside the hospital exist side by side and interact with one another, they are sufficiently different and mutually insulated to maintain separate existences.

A whole series of such subcultural worlds have been formed by the great variety of occupational groups who work within a hospital. We know little about them sociologically. The few past studies that have been made of the hospital lives of doctors and nurses mainly concern the shared professional learning and socialization experiences that they undergo (such as the works discussed in Chapter 4). Recently, a number of articles have been published by residents that describe and analyze some of the special challenges and problems faced by house staff working in American hospitals in the 1980s. They deal candidly and feelingly with such phenomena as the "distinctive ethical dilemmas faced by residents in caring for critically ill and dying patients,"[40] the "impact of the acquired immuno-deficiency syndrome (AIDS) on medical residency training,"[41] and the painful frustrations that house officers experience in caring for the many hospitalized, often elderly patients, who suffer from "chronic disabling problems . . . [with] gradual deterioration in mental function, . . . that lead neither to death nor cure, but to the new twentieth-century institution, the nursing home."[42] Some of these articles provide penetrating glimpses of the "private culture and language" that residents develop "in the setting of the acute care, technologically-oriented hospital"—for example, their informal labeling of certain patients as "gomers," and what Leiderman and Grisso term the whole "gomer phenomenon" of which it is a part:

> In an era in which the goal of medical care has become cure, even though only a few decades ago relief and comfort were acceptable ideals for physician and patient alike, it is little wonder that patients with refractory problems are particularly troubling to the house staff. For overworked, young physicians, the seemingly inexorable decline of patients whose humanness, in their often confused and combative states, may be difficult to perceive represents failure which underscores the impotence of modern medicine. Gomer image and lore captures the universal human fears of illness, intellectual decline, loss of autonomy, and aging as well as the doctor's frustration that modern medicine which promises to do so much, too often fails to deliver its promise.[43]

Some of the newer studies of nursing authored by nurses with social science training look deeply into the values, beliefs, and meanings, as well as the knowledge and skills that are "embedded in actual clinical nursing practice."[44] In so doing, works like Zane Wolf's study of nursing rituals[45] or Patricia Benner's monograph on "excellence and power in clinical nursing practice,"[46] "uncover" and articulate aspects of the care-oriented culture of hospital nurses that are coded into their technical expertise.

But, by and large, we do not have more holistic, social scientific descriptions and analyses of what it is like, and what it feels like, to be a physician or a nurse at work in a hospital. There is nothing in the sociological or anthropological literature, for example, that is comparable to Peggy Anderson's *Nurse*,[47] an ethnographically-based semifictionalized recording of the thoughts, feelings, and experiences of a head nurse in a general hospital located in a large American city; or Samuel Shem's picaresque portrait of the clinical "adventures" of a group of residents in a comparable reality-based hospital that he satirically calls the "House of God."[48] We seem to leave such accounts to novelists and science writers.

Sociologists have virtually never studied the occupational communities formed within the hospital by so-called "other members of the medical team." They have paid no attention to paramedical personnel, domestic, maintenance, transport, and administrative and clerical employees of the hospital. Some of these groups of workers function from within distinctive subcultures of their own that have been shaped by their common ethnic backgrounds, the neighborhoods in which they live, and the labor union to which they belong, as well as by the work that they share in the hospital. For this reason alone, these hospital echelons are sociologically interesting. What is more, no matter how well-staffed with medical and nursing professionals a modern hospital may be, it could not function without all these other workers in whom sociologists have never shown any real interest.

However, social scientists have produced an impressive array of studies of the social worlds of hospital patients, vividly and systematically analyzing both their separateness from and interconnection with the worlds of the hospital staff. These studies are ethnographic in nature. They are more frequently set in mental hospitals than in hospitals that care for physical illness, and more likely to have been conducted in the period extending from the 1940s to the early 1960s, than in the 1970s and 1980s. Their researcher-authors are anthropologists, psychiatrists, and psychologists, as well as sociologists.[49]

Irrespective of the sort of hospital in which they were located (university, private, governmental), or the type of service on which they were focused (psychiatric, medical, surgical, or more specialized units like an oncology or a research ward), certain common patterns have emerged from these studies of the collective existence of hospitalized patients. In every case, an intricately fashioned, highly structured "small society"[50] of patients was found to exist. These were patient communities with their own systems of statuses and roles, values, beliefs, and norms, symbols and rituals. They had their own vocabulary, including a language of silence, and both formal and informal processes of socialization, stratification, and social control.

Patients also formed clubs, particularly under the circumstances of long-term hospitalization, like the sewing circle established by five women patients on one of the wards in the mental hospital that Stanton and Schwartz studied,[51] or the Adrenalectomy Club, founded and organized by the male patients with end-state hypertensive cardiovascular disease who underwent this experimental procedure on the metabolic research ward studied by Fox.[52] (The first patient to have his adrenal glands removed was President of the Adrenalectomy Club; the second, Vice-President; and the third, Secretary-Treasurer. When the President died, the Vice-President did not succeed to the presidency: the office was left vacant.)

In all the hospital milieux studied, the social systems that patients created and maintained were centered on their shared situation of illness and hospitalization, its problems and stresses, and the ways of coming to terms with their predicament that they mutually devised, taught each other, and enforced. In several respects, these were hidden communities. They were sufficiently subterranean to be invisible and inaudible to most of the hospital staff. Many of the deeper feelings of patients were cryptically expressed, coded into the special language, humor, and symbolism with which they communicated with each other. Their patient world tapped into and was part of what William Caudill termed the "covert emotional structure" of the hospital.[53]

In subliminal, largely unconscious ways, the collective life of the patients was exquisitely sensitive to what was occurring inside the communities of the doctors and nurses responsible for their care. On Ward F-Second, the metabolic research unit studied by Fox,[54] for example, a mirror-image relationship existed between the team of research physicians and their patient-subjects. The two groups of men, faced with severe common stresses—great uncertainty, limitations, hazard, and death—independently and interdependently arrived at comparable ways of making sense of them, enduring them, and actively coping with them. For Fox, the pathos of this inadvertent commonality of the patients and their doctors was one of her most important findings.

The classic accounts of "mood sweeps" and "collective disturbances" in the psychiatric hospitals studied by Stanton and Schwartz and by Caudill[55] reveal a comparable kind of below-the-surface, interactive relationship between the social systems of patients and of staff, "usually operat[ing] outside of the specific awareness of the individuals . . . participating in it."[56]

We shall now turn our attention to hidden disagreement about any aspect of patient management, for we found that the fact that disagreement was covert was itself a matter of surprising importance. Accompanying it was a syndrome of difficulty in the group almost as clear as the clinical symptoms of acute appendicitis in the individual. . . .

Patients who were the subject of such a covert disagreement showed a clinical change so very frequently that it seems probable all were affected to some extent, even though many did not show a pronounced or important change. . . .

All patients who were the center of attention for the ward for several days or longer during the period of study were the subjects of such a covert disagreement. The most striking finding was that pathologically excited patients were quite regularly the subjects of secret, affectively important staff disagreement; and, equally regularly, their excitement terminated, usually abruptly, when the staff members were brought to discuss seriously their points of disagreement with each other. . . .

The collective disturbance is also primarily an institutional phenomenon. . . . In our experience, an acute crisis was always preceded by a period of less acute partial disorganization among the staff: "contagion" did not arise out of the blue, but out of recognizable conditions. These were manifested in obvious ways, once the relevant data was brought together. Errors in technique were more frequent: doors were left unlocked, messages were forgotten, and so forth. Absenteeism increased, with a consequent loss of support for both patients and other staff members; much of the absenteeism was clearly due to functional illness related to difficulties in working. Staff members were preoccupied with the problems of other staff members—which meant turning their attention away from the patients so that still less effective staff time was left for patient care. During such periods, experienced staff members often could and did predict that "something is going to happen." . . . [57]

What the patient communities observed but did *not* put into words was as ordered and regulated as what they did express, and as latently influenced by the subliminal sentiments and behaviors of the hospital staff. This is movingly exemplified by the kind of structured silence that prevailed in the "private worlds" of children dying from leukemia that Myra Bluebond-Langer entered through her study of terminally ill children on the pediatric ward of a midwestern teaching hospital. In this context, the strictest kind of "mutual pretense"[58] was practiced:

[T]he terminally ill children knew they were dying before death became imminent. What remains unclear, however, is why they kept such knowledge a secret. The few admissions of awareness, made to nonstaff and nonfamily members, were often couched in symbols with vague references. . . . Their consistent impenetrable silence in the face of ultimate separation and loss requires an explanation, which lies in understanding the social order of which the children were a part and their reasons for preserving that order. . . .

The children lay before their caretakers as members of society unable to remain members. There they all were: children with futures to be molded; parents charged with this responsibility; medical practitioners trained to cure. Leukemia now threatened everyone's ability to fulfill their socially defined roles. Moreover, it threatened their ability to carry on social interaction. . . .

Interaction could take place as long as everyone acted as if they still had their social roles. It could be maintained as long as the children, parents, and medical practitioners fulfilled the social obligations and responsibilities necessary for the maintenance of those respective roles. . . .

Everyone could retain their identity and membership in society, except those who did not practice mutual pretense; they were ostracized and abandoned. . . . No one seemed to know this better than the terminally ill children; for they practiced mutual pretense unto death.[59]

THE HOSPITAL IN CULTURAL AND CROSS-CULTURAL PERSPECTIVE

The sociological portrait of the modern hospital developed in this chapter is based on observations made in American medical settings. Without consideration of what the hospital and the hospitalization experience are like in other societies in which contemporary biomedicine is also practiced, the distinctively American and Western features of what has been presented are not apparent. This is all the more true, anthropologist Emiko Ohnuki-Tierney reminds us, because of the "widely held assumption today . . . that biomedicine is 'scientific,' and therefore 'objective,' thus, 'culture-free,'"[60] rather than recognizing that "the theories and practices of biomedicine undergo transformation in each recipient society."[61] In this light, the hospital is not only embedded in the culture and society of which it is an integral part; in many empirical and symbolic ways, it is a microcosm of that culture and society.

Although there is a sizable literature on the cultural context of organizational structure and process, the vast majority of social science studies of modern complex organizations are concerned with factories and business firms of various kinds. In comparison, relatively few sociological studies of the hospital as an organization have been carried out,[62] and even fewer have been developed in a cultural or cross-cultural framework. Until the recent growth of corporate medicine in the United States, sociologists had the unstated and unexamined tendency to assume that the hospital is a less strategic organization in a modern society than an industrial enterprise, and that even when it functions as a not-for-profit organization, it is a Weberian-type bureaucracy like any other. Sociologists have acknowledged that the historical, social, and cultural factors that have shaped the development of hospitals and of health care systems in different societies are not obliterated or universalized by processes of modernization. But they have been inclined to suppose that the hospital and "the basic pattern of practice in modern society [are] increasingly dominated by the imperatives of the emerging technology, the objective pattern of morbidity in the population, and growing public expectations which are a world phenomenon."[63]

There are some studies that constitute notable exceptions to this trend. In the 1950s, a few anthropologists interested in the role of social and cultural factors in mental health and illness and in what constituted a "therapeutic milieu" did some exploratory first-hand research in non-American psychiatric hospitals. Their findings were highly suggestive of the deep-structure significance and the tenacity of societal culture patterns in creating a collective atmosphere in these hospitals and in shaping social interaction within them. The patterns they observed were strikingly different from those characterizing American mental hospitals at the time.

Anne Parsons, for example, spent three months on a mixed-diagnosis, female ward in the Provincial Hospital of Naples, Italy, observing the social structure of that unit and comparing it with what she had seen and heard in her intensive studies of comparable psychiatric hospital settings in northeastern United States, and briefer studies in England.[64] She found "the ward society" of the Neapolitan hospital to be one in which there was "perpetual motion and activity and interpersonal exchange of a diffuse and present-oriented nature." It contrasted sharply with "the chronic wards of old-style American and English hospitals: the museum atmosphere or the quality of anomie, i.e., removal from the stream of social organization and events is almost totally lacking in Naples."[65]

> I saw a number of fights between patients, usually of a verbal nature but not infrequently ending in blows, hair-pulling, etc., so that patients had to be separated by nurses. In such cases, one or both patients are bound at the wrist and ankle so as to be held to one of the stone seats in the courtyard, which is the center of patient life. Thus punishment did not cut the patient off from social interaction, as does the seclusion more commonly used in the United States. Such fights appeared to give rise to line-ups between nurses and other patients. Each patient would try to defend her honor, casting all of the insults, in which Neapolitan dialect is so rich, at the other. . . . Quarrels between nurses also sometimes result from quarrels between their favorites. On the disturbed ward . . . the frequency of patient quarreling is far higher so that the place is continually in an uproar. . . .
>
> In comparison with the American state hospital, I felt that highly elaborate delusions and individual ways of expression were minimal. . . . In particular, there was far less of a tendency towards the elaboration of paranoid systems in which the hospital or doctors were held responsible for all of the patients' difficulties than in the American hospital. . . .
>
> [T]reatment and recovery, and thus illness, were seen according to two principal norms: that one should eat and not worry. In fact mental illness often seemed to be defined as being thin and recovery as gaining weight. . . .
>
> [O]ne of the most important characteristics of the intra-patient society [is] that it is present-oriented. In this it differs radically from the patient societies of American psychotherapeutically-oriented hospitals where patient discussions are a means by which therapeutic insights are discussed, tested, and consolidated. Rather the [Neapolitan] patient society can be seen as a perpetual interchange which is based on immediate feeling states and immediate reactions to others rather than the exchange of biographical materials seen as distinct from the present context. . . .[66]

Parsons connected the behavioral patterns that she observed inside the hospital with certain attributes of southern Italian/Neapolitan culture. She emphasized the social saliency and strength of the family and the way that it followed the patient into the hospital through frequent visits full of the diffuse conversation and interaction of familial relationships in the "outside world" (including "the family's stuffing food down the throat of the unwilling patient"). She also noted that "impersonal bureaucracy [was] conspicuously missing in southern Italy . . . even within the context of those formal organizations which do exist," so that although "the mental hospital [was] such a formal organization and by necessity [had] some rules, its spirit [was that of] a giant network of informal ties" in which particularized contacts and pleading were important. In addition, Parsons cited the low degree of job specialization in relatively nonindustrialized Naples as conducive to the comparative ease and success with which patients could transplant their occupational activities into the work program of the hospital.[67]

Anthropologist William Caudill's observations of Japanese psychiatric hospitals in the 1950s revealed many fundamental attributes of Japanese society and culture, interwoven with the Western influences on their administration and treatment that Japanese psychiatrists trained in Europe or the United States brought to their work. The social structure of the Japanese hospital, Caudill reported, was "tighter" and control was "more hierarchical" than was generally true for hospitals in the United States. Like so many other aspects of Japanese society, the hospital was organized in terms of a "family model," as well as a principle of hierarchy. This "firm control within a family model" structured the relations between doctor and patient, which were "clearly, if benevolently, authoritarian," and also "more relaxed and friendly" than in American psychiatric hospitals. The "rhythm of the on-going life" in a Japanese hospital seemed different from that of an American hospital. Although disturbances occurred, "violence and emotion tended to erupt quickly and to be dissipated shortly thereafter." There was less sustained tension, as well as less violence on the wards of Japanese than American psychiatric hospitals.[68]

Western medical influences notwithstanding, very little emphasis was placed on psychodynamics and psychotherapy. Morita therapy, an indigenous Japanese form of treatment with roots in Zen Buddhism, played a particularly important role in the hospital. This therapy does not emphasize the obstructive, pathological aspects of the patient's problem as Western psychotherapy does, or encourage systematic self-examination and introspection. Instead, Morita therapy focuses on breaking the cycle of what is considered to be the patient's hypersensitive relationship to the social and natural environment, by stressing the curative effects of nature, the constructive effects of manual labor, and the importance of the attitude of "acceptance." After a first stage of treatment that consists of complete bed rest for four to seven days, followed by a period in which the patient begins to communicate with the doctor through a diary on which the physician comments in writing several times a week, the patient is put to work doing simple manual tasks with the intent of bringing him or her into contact with nature.[69]

Caudill also made a special study of the institutionalized role of *tsukisoi*, which is unique to Japanese hospitals.[70] This is a type of female nurse who serves as an all-encompassing personal attendant to a hospitalized patient, in a way that represents and extends family care. *Tsukisoi* specialize in different categories of physical and mental illness, and they are employed in general as well as psychiatric hospitals. The highly particularized, emotionally and physically intimate, around-the-clock care that these women provide, its unsparing tenderness and the self-sacrificing power over the patient that it entails, are infused with "Japanese-ness" in ways that Caudill associated with the "mothering" role of women in the Japanese family.

In the 1960s, sociologist William A. Glaser conducted a more macroscopic, comparative study of general hospitals, which he developed within a cross-national, organizational framework, focusing particularly on the relations between the hospital and religious, family, and economic institutions. The scope of his research was ambitious. It consisted of interviews, observations, and a review of pertinent literature in sixteen countries (England, Sweden, the Netherlands, West Germany,

France, Switzerland, Spain, Italy, Greece, Poland, the Soviet Union, Turkey, Cyprus, Lebanon, Egypt, and Israel). *Social Settings and Medical Organization: A Cross-National Study of the Hospital*, published by Glaser in 1970,[71] contains a myriad of facts and tentative findings about hospitals in these different countries, plus codified sets of empirical propositions about the relationship between various societal attributes of religion, family, and economy, and a series of organizational characteristics of hospitals. Because Glaser's book is such an encyclopedic and formalistic one in which, as he himself states, "the generalizations often . . . outrun the data,"[72] it defies summarization. Above all, it represents a massive agenda for research in comparative organizational sociology, with the hospital at its center, that by and large has not been further pursued.

In 1984, two books were published that contain rich and reflective field data on the hospital and hospitalization in the People's Republic of China and in Japan: *The Chinese Hospital*, by Gail E. Henderson and Myron S. Cohen, and *Illness and Culture in Contemporary Japan*, by Emiko Ohnuki-Tierney.[73] Through both explicit and implicit comparison with hospital settings in the United States, these two works highlight the culturally specific "American-ness" and "Western-ness" of many attributes of hospitals in this society that are too often thought to be inherent to biomedical science and technology, and to the process of modernization more generally. One of the common patterns that emerge from these recent studies of Asian hospitals, as they did from the earlier cross-cultural observations by Caudill and Parsons, is that even in hospital settings outside the United States where advanced modern medicine of Western origins is practiced, patients' family members, and also to some degree their kin-like associates, friends, and representatives, continue to care for them in important ways. As Ohnuki-Tierney puts it, "care of the sick is not transferred completely to the hospital" in Japan, even when patients are hospitalized.[74] These findings support the hypotheses of Talcott Parsons and Renée Fox in a 1952 article, that the "removal of much of the treatment of illness from the family" in the United States is "attributable to something more than the technological developments of modern medicine."[75] Parsons and Fox suggested that the pronounced degree to which care of the sick is relinquished by the American family and delegated to professional others and the hospital is associated with certain social, cultural, and psychological features of the American urban family type, and its particular strengths and vulnerabilities. The characteristics that they singled out were the small, isolated, emotionally intense nature of the American kinship unit, its exclusivity, the high affective demands placed upon it and each of its members, its emphasis on individualism and independence, and its relatively sharp segregation from other social institutions and arenas of activity in the society.

The Chinese Hospital is based on the five months in 1979–80 that sociologist-Sinologist Gail Henderson and her physician-husband Myron Cohen, a specialist in infectious diseases, spent living and working at the Second Attached Hospital of Hubei Provincial Medical College (a tertiary-care facility) and its *danwei*, or work unit. It is a unique and fascinating medical sociological study in many regards. Certain of Henderson and Cohen's observations on hospital patient/ward staff/family/work unit attitudes and relationships have special relevance to sociological phenomena and issues that have been discussed in this chapter:

> Does the sick person in China adopt the traditional passive role of obediently accepting treatment? Or does the patient (still under the influence of Cultural

Revolution rhetoric) enter into an egalitarian or even challenging relationship with the medical staff? As our observations of the *danwei* had led us to expect, politics was less important than traditional social norms. . . .

Tinghua was used often [by the ward staff] to describe desired patient behavior; it translates as "do as you are told," "be obedient," literally, "listen to what is said." Most commonly, *tinghua* is used to describe children who obey their parents. . . .

Not surprisingly, this authority relationship between practitioner and client is accompanied by the assumption that the less the patient knows, the better. If one believes that a patient gets better by behaving well, then the recovery will proceed even more quickly if the patient is not "upset" by concerns relating to the illness. If a physician needs to discuss a patient's case, it is the relatives who are consulted, not the patient. . . .

[T]his . . . does not imply that [patients] were completely at the mercy of the ward staff. . . . [P]atients on the infectious disease ward exhibited a rather impressive amount of information about and understanding of their disease processes. Although patients were forbidden to see their hospital charts, each patient carried a booklet with a summary of the medical history; and each patient, whether uneducated peasant or sophisticated urbanite, could rattle off the events in his or her case, medications, laboratory tests, and indicators of illness. With this accumulated information and the opinions of friends and relatives, they formed an evaluation of their medical care. Patients seemed surprisingly well versed in Western as well as Chinese modes of things. . . .

Chinese patients' sense of confidence as they attempt to understand and evaluate their medical treatment is further bolstered by a national policy that encourages self-education in all spheres. . . .

The second patient resource is the use of indirect voice in decision making and in conflict resolution. . . . [W]hen problems with a patient arise or an important decision must be made, physicians are unlikely to deal directly with the patient; instead, they contact the patient's relatives. Informed consent in China involves the family and the unit, not the individual. Friends, relatives, and work unit leaders act on the patient's behalf, so that the patient need not deal directly with the medical personnel. . . .

Often the nearest kin sleeps in the bed next to the patient and helps provide nursing care. . . . Whether they are actually on the ward or not, however, relatives are a force with which the medical staff must contend. . . . Physicians are justifiably wary of the complaints of relatives, which can cause problems with their own leaders. . . . [T]he patients' work unit leaders can serve not only as potential advocates but also as final arbitrators for disputes between patients and those who provide medical care.[76]

The conceptions of illness, medicine, and therapy that are institutionalized in this hospital, its definitions of the roles of patients, doctors, nurses, health aides, family, and *danwei* leaders, and the structure and tenor of the relationships between them are quintessentially Chinese. They are a blend of Marxist-Leninist, Maoist, Confucian, Taoist, Buddhist, and Western ideas, values, beliefs, norms, and organizational patterns. Nowhere is this more apparent than in the carefully calligraphed lists of rules, regulations, duties, virtues, and service slogans that are posted in the hospital's wards and nursing stations.[77] Like those observed by Fox and Swazey on the Critical Care Unit of another Chinese hospital—Tianjin's First

Central Hospital—where they did a month of participant observation in the summer of 1981, these rules and aphorisms seem to be "as neo-Confucian as they are Maoist, and more of both than they are Marxist or Leninist."[78]

Anthropologist Emiko Ohnuki-Tierney has written an exquisite descriptive analysis of Japanese hospitalization as "a cultural system" and as a "social drama."[79] She developed this analysis from fieldwork in 1979 and 1980 in the Kobe-Osaka-Kyoto region of Western Japan (the Keihanshin area), among middle-class urban Japanese. It is centered on hospitalization either for the treatment of a physical illness or for an operation.

More vividly and powerfully than any of the other writings discussed in this chapter, Ohnuki-Tierney's anthropological view of the hospitalization process shows how deeply embedded it is in the culture and society of which it is part:

> By studying the hospitalization process, we can learn a great deal about Japanese culture and society and about the actual interactions of individuals involved in the process. Conversely, we can never really interpret the hospitalization process without a thorough understanding of Japanese culture and society. Hospitalization in Japan is by no means a universal experience involving simply the biomedical treatment of a disease. Rather, it is a Japanese experience, *mutatis mutandis.*[80]

Her account not only illuminates that Japanese experience, but also highlights some of the peculiar features of what it is like to be hospitalized in the United States:

> In the United States, where the sovereignty of the individual is sacred, the patient role ironically denies individualism, at least symbolically. It begins with admission to a hospital, when an individual must discard such traces of personal identity as personal belongings, including clothes. People must change to nondescript sterile gowns, and wear wristbands as identification, and assume a new identity as a "patient."
>
> In sharp contrast, the patient role in Japan reinforces individual identity, as well as each patient's identity as a social persona. This is indeed ironic, since Japanese culture is not known for its emphasis on the individual. In Japan, where one must usually wear a uniform from kindergarten all the way through high school, and formerly through the university, hospital patients use their own nightwear. . . . Nightwear is one of the most welcome gifts to a patient, chosen especially by those who know the patient well. Attractive nightwear is thought to cheer the patient. The patient must change this clothing often, since it gets soiled, or symbolically polluted, by the sick body more quickly than usual. Extra nightclothes ease the work for the family, which usually is in charge of laundering them, and also make the patient presentable to visitors. . . .
>
> To ascertain the feelings of health professionals on this matter, I described the American admission process and the use of hospital gowns to a group of eight doctors. Their negative reaction was just as strong as that of nonprofessionals. One doctor in his mid-fifties, who was once the head of a medium-sized hospital but was now in private practice, said that if a Japanese hospital decided to enforce such a rule, people would bring suit against this abrogation of human rights, and it would be all over the front pages of the newspapers.[81]

The nurses whom Ohnuki-Tierney interviewed also objected to the idea of instituting the use of hospital gowns. As one head nurse vehemently stated, "at least when they are ill," people should be able to choose their personal attire.

According to Ohnuki-Tierney's description, the Japanese custom of having a personal introduction to a doctor is very important to patients about to enter the hospital. It is "a means by which patients and their families choose the doctors, rather than being chosen by them. It also helps to establish a personal, [human] relationship between the two."[82] The average length of hospitalization in Japan—42.9 days—is the longest in the world. Hospital patients retain their kinship identity, as well as their individual identity, chiefly through the continued participation of the family in their care. Family members attend to their personal needs and their intimate bodily functions, provide meals for them, receive visitors, and make lists of the gifts that they bring in anticipation of the return gifts that must be sent after the patient's recovery. The custom of *mimai* (visits to the patient bearing gifts with symbolic meaning) "sustains the identity of the patient as a social persona."[83] In addition to close family members, more distant relatives, friends, and colleagues at work are all expected to visit patients, and to offer gifts:

> New nightwear, soap, cologne, and other items are chosen as gifts because of their power of symbolic purification. Most importantly, food that embodies the energy of nature receives the primary focus. Thus, hospitals allow or even expect the patient's family to feed him/her good food, and have long visitation hours so that visitors can bring food. . . . The third type of gift is flowers. Flowers are pleasing to the bedridden patient, and the flowering process suggests growth and the vigor of nature. However, there are a number of taboos in choosing flowers. The most important is to avoid giving potted flowers, since the roots suggest a metaphor for the patient having roots in the hospital and never being discharged.[84]

Ohnuki-Tierney not only connects this combination of features that characterize Japanese hospitalization to fundamental aspects of Japan's culture and its underlying world-view; she goes further than that. She contends that "hospitalization experience in contemporary Japan . . . demonstrate[s] how Japanese culture and society have powerfully transformed the underlying concepts and practices of biomedicine, which was originally introduced from the West, and has been highly acclaimed by the Japanese as the epitome of superior Western science and technology."[85] Thus, although the care delivered in the modern Japanese hospitals that she studied is "biomedical," it is not Western. It has undergone "Japanization" in its underlying concepts and in its delivery modes.[86]

As the hospital customs described indicate, the Japanese consider illness to be a state of bodily imbalance that must be righted through a long rest, "called *ansei* (peace and tranquility"),[87] from which the lengthy hospital stay in Japan partly stems. "In addition to rest, the most important methods of treatment are the removal of impurity incurred by sickness and the replenishment of energy by harnessing nature's energy into the sick body"[88]—Japanese conceptions that are emblemized and communicated through the three types of hospital gifts that are offered. As was discussed in Chapter 1 in connection with the sick role, illness is defined as more legitimate and desirable than in the West, and is responded to indulgently. This "indulgence over the sick" is "tacit recognition of the importance of this psychological dimension of illness, which the Japanese do not artificially separate from the physical dimension of suffering,"[89] and that they are reluctant to abstract, or to single out.

Above all, Ohnuki-Tierney's analysis affirms, Japanese biomedicine and the hospitalization process are anchored to the central meaning given to human beings and human relationships in Japanese culture: to the Japanese notion of "humans as a person among people" (*ningen*). In illness, the sick role, and hospitalization,

> the patient's self as "a human among humans" . . . comes under the limelight and reaches a new height of intensity, both positively and negatively. Every fiber of the patient's social network is tested. Many relationships are strongly reinforced, while others prove too frail and are discontinued. The patients are reassured that they are important individuals, wives, husbands, fathers, mothers, or coworkers. Their recovery rests, at least unconsciously, with their willingness to resume these roles. . . . [I]n this light, a seemingly cumbersome custom of securing "introduction to the doctor" may be seen to represent the Japanese effort to create a *human* . . . tie with the doctor, and ensure that the doctor treats the patient as a human being, rather than an ailing pathogenic object. . . .
> Paradoxical though it may sound, doctors in Japan assume total responsibility for their patients, and yet remain nonauthoritative by accommodating "human factors," instead of adhering strictly to a more narrowly defined medical judgment.[90]

In Japan, as in China, this diffuse, humanistic conception of the doctor-patient relationship, along with the cultural emphasis placed on the healing properties of harmony, peace, tranquility, and comfort, help to explain why diagnoses of cancer or fatal prognoses of any kind are generally not conveyed to the patient. Physicians believe that it is their human/professional responsibility to assume the burden of this knowledge and to protect the patient from it.

To date, Ohnuki-Tierney's detailed, interpretative, sociocultural study of hospitalization and the delivery of care in a contemporaneous, non-Western society is unique. In fact, we have no comparable study of the present-day American hospital and hospital experience, and the biomedical, social, and cultural assumptions on which they rest. It is a study that could be of great practical as well as theoretical value at this historical juncture, when hospitals in the United States are supposedly undergoing such deep and far-reaching changes that it is difficult to predict what they will look, feel, and be like by the turn of the century.

WHITHER THE CHANGING AMERICAN HOSPITAL?

Social scientists have only begun to study the implications of the converging sets of developments that have significantly altered the American hospital during the past few decades. One of these major trends is the process of "dehospitalization" that has been activated since the 1960s by the women's, consumer health, holistic medicine, and alternative therapy movements, and increasingly by government bodies.[91] This organized movement away from the hospital has been propelled by a social reaction to what is felt to be the domineering role of doctors, machines, and invasive procedures in hospital medicine, its crushing impersonality, its harmful physical and psychological side effects, its elaborate bureaucracy, and its high costs.

Nowhere is this more starkly and troublingly apparent than in the care of mental illness. What is usually termed "deinstitutionalization" has been a major movement in psychiatry since the mid-1950s.[92] It has been estimated that from 1955

number of chronically mentally ill patients in large state hospitals has
̶ percent, from approximately 560,000 to 120,000.[93] The development
̶ ̶ ̶ ̶ ̶ ̶ psychotropic drugs to treat the symptoms of mental disorders, the growing philosophical and ideological conviction about the importance of freeing as
many people as possible from the incarcerating control of "total institutions" like
mental hospitals, political advocacy to achieve this goal, and economic incentives
for extra-hospital care provided by federal programs have all contributed to the
decrease.

However beneficial it may be for certain categories of mentally ill persons to
be released from a hospital-enclosed world, deinstitutionalization has also had highly visible, disturbing consequences. While the patient populations of state hospitals
have declined, their admission rates have grown. To a significant degree, this is the
result of readmission of patients who are being hospitalized for shorter periods of
time, but who are rehospitalized more often than previously. In addition to this
"revolving door" phenomenon, many unhospitalized persons with serious chronic
mental disorders are not receiving the continuing medical and psychiatric care and
social support services necessary for them to have some semblance of a normal life
in the outside world. Very sick persons, with flagrant symptoms and signs of their
mental illness, make up a sizable number of the homeless persons who now live on
the streets of American cities.

> America's homeless crisis began in 1963 when deinstitutionalization be-
> came law through enactment of the Mental Retardation Facilities and Community
> Mental Health Center Act. Hundreds of thousands of disabled persons with
> schizophrenia, affective disorders, alcoholism, and severe personality disorders
> were released from large institutions to the streets. Once deinstitutionalized, these
> individuals created their own communities of isolation, alienation, hopelessness,
> and despair. By law, the former residents of structured institutions became the
> homeless.
> This situation occurred because a social welfare movement, based on vir-
> tually no scientifically gathered data, became public policy. . . . Once the decision
> to deinstitutionalize was in place, a sense of urgency prevailed. Patients became
> caught on colliding tectonic plates, pushed and stretched in all directions by
> psychiatrists, unions, nurses, psychologists, and social workers. The legal system,
> legislators, and the media all thought they knew . . . what was wrong with our
> mental health system. Few, however, were willing or able to provide the requisite
> care.[94]

The public distress and fear that the homeless mentally disabled evoke have
contributed to the romanticization of the advantages and accomplishments of
psychiatric hospitals that is heard in some quarters. They have also contributed to
serious talk about a policy shift in the direction of partially restoring mental hospitals to the role they formerly played in sheltering and treating mentally ill patients,
and to revisions in state laws that will make it easier to involuntarily commit mentally ill persons for outpatient and inpatient treatment.

In general hospitals as well as psychiatric facilities, the dehospitalization
movement has intersected with, and been reinforced by, the impetus for controlling
the costs of medical care that has gained momentum in American society since the
end of the financially "golden years" of the 1960s. The spiraling costs of medical

care in the United States, particularly of hospital care, which almost quadrupled from \$34.9 billion in 1972 to \$135.5 billion in 1982,[95] has "frighten[ed] thoughtful people and result[ed] in many frantic efforts on the part of policymakers and administrators to get some handle on the system or nonsystem as the case may be":

> The financial issues have become so acute that they tend to push all other matters into the background as policymakers search for mechanisms to contain costs. . . . Containing costs is only part of the problem. The challenge is to do so while providing reasonable access to medical care that is effective and humane. . . . Achieving tighter allocations, however, without significantly limiting access or high-quality and sensitive care, and doing so in a politically acceptable manner, is a baffling challenge. Although there is much puffery around one or another solution, the fact is that no one really has much confidence that we know what to do or that we could do it if we knew. In short, the problem of the costs of medical care is here to stay in one form or another.[96]

Since the early 1970s a number of regulatory mechanisms have been created in an effort to control the rise in hospital costs, without, it is hoped, compromising the quality of patient care. The Professional Standards Review Organization (PSRO) program, established under the Social Security Amendments of 1972, was designed to control the cost of health services provided by Medicare, Medicaid, and Maternal and Child Health programs by reducing days of hospitalization. Shortly after patients enter the hospital, the appropriateness of their admission and the estimated length of stay are determined by a PSRO. Any hospital stay that is longer than the established period is scrutinized in a later review. If either the admission or length of the stay is considered unjustified, reimbursement for further care is denied.

Certificate-of-need programs constitute a second set of cost-savings procedures. These were designed to control the spread of expensive new technologies by requiring regulatory approval when a hospital wishes to make a capital expenditure in excess of \$100,000 or \$150,000 a year. "Need" is determined by guidelines established by the Department of Health and Human Services and by the state in which the hospital is located.

The most recent set of cost-saving regulations are known as DRGs (Diagnosis Related Groups). Through the Tax Equity Financial Responsibility Act of 1982 and the Social Security Amendments of 1983, Medicare has been changed from a cost-based retrospective payment system to a prospective payment system based on DRGs. The DRG system classifies patients according to primary and secondary diagnoses, age, and treatment factors, sets a dollar value for each of the 467 DRGs so derived, and pays the hospital a predetermined flat rate for the type of admission, regardless of the actual services provided or the costs incurred. The average rate of reimbursement for a given DRG is based on the average costs of all hospitals in the system.

The establishment of these medical care rationing strategies has not only been driven by economics. It also stems from a value assumption that is shared by the cost-containment and the deinstitutionalization movements. Underlying both is a minimalist conviction about the nature of good medical care: namely, the belief that by and large, the fewer the days that patients spend in the hospital, and the fewer procedures they undergo, the better the quality of the care they receive is likely to be. Although this trim conception of enlightened care has evoked criticism from health professional and patient consumer groups alike, it carries a great deal of

authority in the "less-is-better" economic, political, and ethical climate that currently surrounds American medicine.

Another major set of factors transforming the hospital is what sociologist Paul
Starr has termed "the coming of the corporation"[97] to American medicine, and
physician/editor Arnold S. Relman refers to as the rise of "the new medical-industrial complex."[98] In a startlingly brief period of time, "with little initial public
notice, a vigorous and varied for-profit sector has developed in the predominantly
not-for-profit world of medical care."[99] This has happened so rapidly and unexpectedly that the precise magnitude of the for-profit sector of health service providers is
not known, though the gross revenues involved have been estimated to be as high as
$40 billion. Sociologist Bradford H. Gray indicates that:

> More than three-quarters of nursing homes are proprietary, and about 40
> percent of hemodialysis in this country is provided by profit-making units. For-
> profit organizations now provide emergency medical services, home care, mobile
> CAT screening, cardiopulmonary testing, industrial health screening, rehabilitation
> counseling, dental care, weight control clinics, alcohol and drug abuse programs,
> comprehensive prepaid HMO programs, and laboratory and related services. . . .
> Some analogous changes are also taking place in the not-for-profit health care sec-
> tor. Not-for-profit health institutions . . . have variously been forming chains, es-
> tablishing for-profit subsidiaries, selling services to other hospitals for profit, and
> taking on other attributes of the for-profit enterprises.[100]

Within this changing health care environment, Gray continues, the number of hospitals owned or managed by for-profit hospital chains "almost doubled between 1976
and 1982 (from 533 to 1,040 hospitals), a period in which the total number of hospitals in the United States decreased slightly and the number of independently-owned-
for-profit hospitals declined rapidly (many being purchased by the chains)":

> Most of the firms that own chains of hospitals (as well as those that own
> other kinds of health service facilities) were established only in the last 15 years.
> They have grown by means of purchase, construction, and contract management of
> institutions and by buying smaller chains. The growing size of the companies has
> itself attracted attention.[101]

We are only beginning to take stock of the possible implications of this
dramatic and unprecedented surge in for-profit activity in health care: for its cost,
efficiency, and quality; for the traditional service, social responsibility, and public
interest ethos of the medical profession and the hospital; for the individual and collective trust dimension of the patient/physician/health professions/medical institutions complex; and for the future development of medical education, medical
research, and care for the poor.

> The purchase of hospitals, particularly of nonprofit hospitals, by investor-
> owned hospital chains has raised questions that touch on ethics, law, research,
> medical education, costs, productivity, and more generally on how the public in-
> terest is being served. Over the past decade analysts have begun to study some of
> the effects of such hospital purchase. But little information is now available about
> how such changes in ownership may be viewed by the various affected parties,

whose attitude toward the change may in turn affect any number of factors, including both the purchase negotiations themselves and the policies under which the hospital will operate.[102]

One other occurrence is having a deeply significant impact on the practice and teaching of medicine in the American hospital: the AIDS epidemic. Particularly on the East and West coasts of the United States, in cities like New York, San Francisco, and Los Angeles, the number of AIDS-related admissions to hospitals, especially those that are teaching centers, has greatly increased and accelerated. There is a double historical irony in this tragic biomedical event. The reactions of the medical and nursing caregivers to patients with AIDS, as well as the responses of the lay public, have revealed the degree to which Americans had medically and culturally "forgotten" what it is like to deal with a serious epidemic disease, even though hardly more than forty years ago, infectious diseases were commonplace and rampant. The advent of AIDS has shattered the paradigm of expectations about illness in this era of advanced modern medicine, which Americans had come to think of as a period in which a persistent but progressively dwindling number of chronic diseases constituted the paramount threats to health. AIDS has not only drastically changed this outlook, but is filling hospital beds with very sick patients for prolonged, intensive stays, at a historical juncture when there is much concern about how the overall decrease in hospitalization is constricting clinical training opportunities for young graduate physicians.

In an impressive article written at the end of his own residency in internal medicine in a West Coast university hospital, Dr. Robert W. Wachter has given eloquent testimony to the fact that "There is a whole generation of residents at certain urban medical centers around the country whose training has been profoundly altered by AIDS."[103]

> It has yielded new insights into the complexities of the immune system and the devastating manifestations of its breakdown. It has . . . provided experience in caring for some of the most complex disorders and critically ill patients that one may see during a residency.

AIDS has also brought house officers face to face with the difficult emotional and moral challenges of the "risk and fear of transmission," "uneasiness with the patient's sexual orientation," "frustration with the limitations of technology," the ambiguity of when and whether mechanical ventilation and intensive care should be invoked, and anguish over the fact that "not in recent memory have so many relatively young, previously healthy people died so quickly, with caregivers seemingly powerless to influence the eventual outcome."[104]

If this is indeed the case, and if, as the epidemic grows, "a strong background in the care of these unfortunate patients will prove to be an indispensable attribute of a well-trained internist for the foreseeable future,"[105] then in spite of all the changes that have taken place in the American health situation, medical profession, and hospital, a life-threatening infectious disease again is becoming the same kind of comprehensive master teacher of a new generation of physicians that some of its antecedents, such as syphilis and tuberculosis, were in the not-very-distant past.

A last, historical postscript: One of the most persistent concerns about the metamorphosis of American hospitals—from predominantly benevolent, voluntary, not-for-profit institutions that have received a distinctively American mixture of private and public support[106] to a system of for-profit institutions—is the question of what will become of those who are sick and poor. The question is not as new as it seems. American physicians and hospitals have felt and implemented a long-standing ethical obligation to offer their services to the indigent. But the fact remains that throughout the entire medical history of this society, those who are poor, with long-term chronic or incurable illnesses, especially if they are also unemployed or unemployable, mentally ill or impaired, elderly, alone, or "delinquent," have constituted an unresolved problem of human suffering and of social responsibility. Persons in this predicament have received their care largely through nineteenth-century almshouses and twentieth-century public municipal hospitals.[107] Charles Rosenberg has instructively chronicled this aspect of the history and "the shaping of Philadelphia General Hospital,"[108] ending his essay with the following image:

> Class and social location still remained the primary determinant in deciding who would occupy Philadelphia's municipal hospital beds; and the problem of age, race, and chronic disease loomed if anything more prominently as the twentieth century progressed. With the retreat of the classic infectious diseases, the pace of such problems only increased. For several years after the city of Philadelphia officially closed Philadelphia General Hospital in 1977, several hundred aged chronic patients remained in its depressing wards; the city had not yet remodeled a chronic disease hospital for them. These were patients that not even the promise of third-party payment could make palatable to other city hospitals and nursing homes.[109]

This is a legacy inherited, though not created, by the "new health care for profit" hospitals. *Plus ça change, plus c'est la même chose?*

NOTES

1. Clifford Geertz, "Thick Description: Toward an Interpretive Theory of Culture," in Clifford Geertz, *The Interpretation of Cultures* (New York: Basic Books, Inc., 1973), p. 30.
2. Thomas Mann, *The Magic Mountain*, trans. H. T. Lowe-Porter (New York: Alfred A. Knopf, 1948).
3. Aleksandr I. Solzhenitsyn, *Cancer Ward*, trans. Nicholas Bethell and David Burg (New York: Farrar, Straus & Giroux, Inc., 1969).
4. Amy Clampitt, "From A Clinic Waiting Room," *What the Light Was Like*. Copyright © 1985 by Amy Clampitt. Reprinted by permission of Alfred A. Knopf, Inc. Originally appeared in *The New Yorker*, June 14, 1982, p. 42.
5. Charles E. Rosenberg, "Florence Nightingale and Contagion: The Hospital as Moral Universe," in *Healing and History*, ed. Charles Rosenberg (New York: Science History Publications, 1979), pp. 116–36.
6. Erving Goffman, *Asylums* (Garden City, N.Y.: Anchor, 1961).
7. Richard Selzer, *Taking the World in for Repairs* (New York: William Morrow and Company, Inc., 1986), pp. 238–39.
8. Rosemary Stevens, "'A Poor Sort of Memory': Voluntary Hospitals and Government before the Depression," *Milbank Memorial Fund Quarterly/Health and Society*, 60, no. 4 (1982), 552–53.
9. Charles Rosenberg, *The Care of Strangers: The Rise of America's Hospital System* (New York: Basic Books, 1987), p. 8.
10. H. H. Gerth and C. Wright Mills, trans. and eds., *Max Weber: Essays in Sociology* (New York: Oxford University Press, 1946), pp. 196–244.

11. Eliot Freidson, *Profession of Medicine: A Study of the Sociology of Applied Knowledge* (New York: Dodd, Mead & Company, 1970); see especially pp. 185–200.
12. Even in premodern times, certain attributes of nurses' roles and of the conditions under which they worked endowed them with particular kinds of authority, power, and independence in their interactions with physicians. Nurses were based more exclusively and continuously in the hospital than most doctors. As a consequence of this, and of the bedside care they gave, they often had more intimate and detailed knowledge of the physical and mental state of patients and of the daily round and workings of the hospital than physicians did. In addition, many hospitals were owned, as well as run, by congregations or orders of religious sister-nurses.
13. Gerth and Mills, *Max Weber.*
14. Zane Robinson Wolf, *Nurses' Work, the Sacred and the Profane* (Philadelphia: University of Pennsylvania Press, 1988).
15. Eviatar Zerubavel, *Patterns of Time in Hospital Life: A Sociological Perspective* (Chicago: The University of Chicago Press, 1979), p. 108.
16. Amy Clampitt, "From A Clinic Waiting Room."
17. Charles L. Bosk and Joel E. Frader, "The Impact of Place of Decision-Making on Medical Decisions," unpublished paper.
18. For two descriptive accounts of the surgical process that are especially vivid and accurate, see Mark Kramer, *Invasion Procedures: A Year in the World of Two Surgeons* (New York: Harper & Row, Publishers, 1979); and Richard Selzer, *Mortal Lessons: Notes on the Art of Surgery* (New York: Simon and Schuster, 1974).
19. Renée C. Fox, "The Autopsy: Its Place in the Attitude-Learning of Second-Year Medical Students," in Renée C. Fox, *Essays in Medical Sociology: Journeys Into the Field* (New York: John Wiley & Sons, 1979), pp. 51–77.
20. Anselm Strauss, Shizuko Fagerhaugh, Barbara Suczek, and Carolyn Wiener, *Social Organization of Medical Work* (Chicago: The University of Chicago Press, 1985), pp. 5 and 54–55.
21. The notion of "temporal order," or what Eviatar Zerubavel terms "the sociotemporal order," is the key conceptual insight on which his study *Patterns of Time in Hospital Life* is based. See especially pp. 105–30.
22. Ibid., pp. 29–30.
23. Charles L. Bosk, *Forgive and Remember: Managing Medical Failure* (Chicago: The University of Chicago Press, 1979), p. 2.
24. Zerubavel, *Patterns of Time in Hospital Life*, pp. 29–30, 35, and 107–8.
25. Ibid., p. 108.
26. Ibid.
27. Ibid., pp. 37–59.
28. Charles L. Bosk, "Occupational Rituals in Patient Management," *New England Journal of Medicine*, 303, no. 2 (July 10, 1980), 71–6.
29. Ibid.
30. Bosk, "Occupational Rituals," pp. 72–74; and Bosk, *Forgive and Remember*, pp. 103–10.
31. Bosk, *Forgive and Remember*, p. 144.
32. Renée C. Fox, *Experiment Perilous: Physicians and Patients Facing the Unknown* (Glencoe, Ill.: The Free Press, 1959), pp. 82–85. See also Renée C. Fox, "The Human Condition of Health Professionals," Distinguished Lecturer Series, School of Health Studies (Durham: University of New Hampshire, 1980), pp. 26–29.
33. Fox, "The Human Condition of Health Professionals," pp. 28–29.
34. Fox, "The Human Condition of Health Professionals," p. 30; Renée C. Fox, *Experiment Perilous*, p. 106; Renée C. Fox and Judith P. Swazey, *The Courage to Fail: A Social View of Organ Transplants and Dialysis* (Chicago: University of Chicago Press, 1974), pp. 100 and 104.
35. Wolf, *Nurses' Work.*
36. Fox, "The Human Condition of Health Professionals," p. 12.
37. Richard Selzer, *Mortal Lessons: Notes on the Art of Surgery* (New York: Simon and Schuster, 1974), pp. 92–104. Copyright © 1974, 1975, 1976 by Richard Selzer. Reprinted by permission of Simon & Schuster, Inc.
38. Fox, "The Human Condition of Health Professionals," p. 26; Renée C. Fox, "The Sociology of Modern Medical Research," in *Asian Medical Systems: A Comparative Study*, ed. Charles Leslie

178 THE HOSPITAL: A SOCIAL AND CULTURAL MICROCOSM

(Berkeley: University of California Press, 1976), pp. 106–7; Bronislaw Malinowski, *Magic, Science, and Religion and Other Essays* (Glencoe, Ill.: The Free Press, 1948), p. 70.

39. Karen A. Cise, "The Hospital Sign." This was a term paper written by Ms. Cise in February 1978 when she was a student in the course in the Sociology of Medicine (Soc. 583) that I teach at the University of Pennsylvania. The examples of hospital signs that follow are drawn both from those that she observed in two different hospital settings and from my own participant observation in many different hospital milieux.

40. William Winkenwerder, Jr., "Ethical Dilemmas for House Staff Physicians: The Care of Critically Ill and Dying Patients," *Journal of the American Medical Association*, 254, no. 24 (December 27, 1985), 3454–57.

41. Robert M. Wachter, "The Impact of the Acquired Immunodeficiency Syndrome on Medical Residency Training," *New England Journal of Medicine*, 314, no. 3 (January 16, 1986), 177–79.

42. Deborah B. Leiderman and Jean-Anne Grisso, "The Gomer Phenomenon," *Journal of Health and Social Behavior*, 26 (September 1985), 230.

43. Ibid., p. 231.

44. Patricia Benner, *From Novice to Expert: Excellence and Power in Clinical Nursing Practice* (Menlo Park, Calif.: Addison-Wesley Publishing Company, Inc., 1984), p. 1.

45. Wolf, *Nurses' Work*.

46. Benner, *From Novice to Expert*.

47. Peggy Anderson, *Nurse* (New York: St. Martin's Press, 1978).

48. Samuel Shem, *The House of God* (New York: R. Marek Publishers, 1978).

49. The following books (listed in alphabetical order) are representative of the range of ethnographic studies of hospitals or hospital units that have been made by social scientists: Ann Hill Beuf, *Biting Off the Bracelet: A Study of Children in Hospitals* (Philadelphia: University of Pennsylvania Press, 1979); William Caudill, *The Psychiatric Hospital as a Small Society* (Cambridge, Mass.: Harvard University Press, 1958); Rose Laub Coser, *Life in the Ward* (East Lansing, Mich.: Michigan State University Press, 1962); Fox, *Experiment Perilous*; Goffman, *Asylums*; Jeanne H. Guillemin and Lynda L. Holmstrom, *Mixed Blessings: Intensive Care for Newborns* (New York: Oxford University Press, 1986); Myra Bluebond-Langner, *The Private Worlds of Dying Children*. (Princeton, N.J.: Princeton University Press, 1978); Mary Elizabeth O'Brien, *The Courage to Survive: The Life Career of the Chronic Dialysis Patient* (New York: Grune & Stratton, Inc., 1983); Alfred H. Stanton and Morris S. Schwartz, *The Mental Hospital: A Study of Institutional Participation in Psychiatric Illness and Treatment* (New York: Basic Books, Inc., 1954).

50. This is William Caudill's concept (*The Psychiatric Hospital as a Small Society*).

51. Stanton and Schwartz, *The Mental Hospital*, pp. 170–90.

52. Fox, *Experiment Perilous*, pp. 141–42 and 251–52.

53. Caudill, *The Psychiatric Hospital as a Small Society*, p. 87.

54. Fox, *Experiment Perilous*. See especially pp. 237–54.

55. Stanton and Schwartz, *The Mental Hospital*, and William Caudill, *The Psychiatric Hospital as a Small Society*. Both these first-hand studies of mental hospitals were made in the 1950s, prior to the period in which psychotropic drugs were used to treat the symptoms of psychotic illness. The "mood sweeps" and "collective disturbances" they describe and analyze were far more likely to occur in the pre-psychopharmacologic era of mental hospitals than subsequently.

56. Caudill, *The Psychiatric Hospital as a Small Society*, p. 88.

57. Stanton and Schwartz, *The Mental Hospital*, pp. 342–45 and 394–95. Copyright 1954 by Basic Books, Inc. Reprinted by permission of Basic Books, Inc.

58. In their book, *Awareness of Dying* (Chicago: Aldine Publishing Company, 1965), Barney G. Glaser and Anselm L. Strauss identified "the ritual drama of mutual pretense" as one of four types of "awareness of dying contexts." "When patient and staff both know that the patient is dying but pretend otherwise—when both agree to act as if he were going to live—then a context of mutual pretense exists" (p. 64). Bluebond-Langner has organized *The Private Worlds of Dying Children* around this Glaser and Strauss concept.

59. Bluebond-Langner, *The Private Worlds of Dying Children*, pp. 198 and 231–32.

60. Emiko Ohnuki-Tierney, "Cultural Transformations of Biomedicine in Japan: Hospitalization in Contemporary Japan," *International Journal of Technology Assessment in Health Care*, 2, no. 2 (1986), 231.

61. Emiko Ohnuki-Tierney, *Illness and Culture in Contemporary Japan: An Anthropological View* (New York: Cambridge University Press, 1984), p. 7.

62. William M. Evan and R. Christopher Klemm, "Interorganizational Relations Among Hospitals: A Strategy, Structure and Performance Model," *Human Relations*, 33, no. 5 (1980), 315–37.

63. David Mechanic, "The Comparative Study of Health Care Delivery Systems," *Annual Review of Sociology*, 1 (1975), 62.

64. Anne Parsons, *Belief, Magic, and Anomie* (New York: The Free Press, 1969), pp. 151–73. Reprinted by permission from *L'Ospedale Psichiatrico* (Naples), April–June 1959.

65. Ibid.

66. Ibid.

67. Ibid.

68. Caudill, *The Psychiatric Hospital as a Small Society*, pp. 369–71.

69. For a more detailed account of Morita therapy, see William Caudill and Takeo Doi, "Interrelations of Psychiatry, Culture, and Emotion in Japan," in *Man's Image in Medicine and Anthropology*, ed. Iago Galdston (New York: International Universities Press, 1963), pp. 374–421.

70. William Caudill, "Around the Clock Patient Care in Japanese Psychiatric Hospitals: The Role of *Tsukisoi*," *American Sociological Review*, 26, no. 2 (1961), 204–14.

71. William A. Glaser, *Social Settings and Medical Organization: A Cross-National Study of the Hospital* (New York: Atherton Press, 1970).

72. Ibid., p. 191.

73. Gail E. Henderson and Myron S. Cohen, *The Chinese Hospital: A Socialist Work Unit* (New Haven, Conn.: Yale University Press, 1984); Ohnuki-Tierney, *Illness and Culture in Contemporary Japan.*

74. Ohnuki-Tierney, "Cultural Transformations of Biomedicine in Japan," p. 233.

75. Talcott Parsons and Renée C. Fox, "Illness, Therapy, and the Modern, Urban American Family," *Journal of Social Issues*, VIII, no. 4 (1952), 31–44.

76. Henderson and Cohen, *The Chinese Hospital*, pp. 110–26.

77. Ibid., pp. 151–65.

78. Renée C. Fox and Judith P. Swazey, "Medical Morality Is Not Bioethics—Medical Ethics in China and the United States," *Perspectives in Biology and Medicine*, 27, no. 3 (Spring 1984), 342.

79. Ohnuki-Tierney, *Illness and Culture in Contemporary Japan*, pp. 189–211, Ohnuki-Tierney, "Cultural Transformations of Biomedicine in Japan."

80. Ohnuki-Tierney, *Illness and Culture in Contemporary Japan*, p. 211.

81. Ibid., pp. 194–95.

82. Ohnuki-Tierney, "Cultural Transformations of Biomedicine in Japan," pp. 236–37.

83. Ibid., p. 234.

84. Ibid., pp. 236 and 238.

85. Ibid., p. 231.

86. One of the most salient, powerful, and unique characteristics of Japanese culture is this capacity to transmute whatever elements it absorbs from other societies and cultures into what is quintessentially Japanese.

87. Ohnuki-Tierney, "Cultural Transformations of Biomedicine in Japan," p. 238.

88. Ibid.

89. Ibid.

90. Ibid., pp. 238–39.

91. The discussion of "dehospitalization" and "deinstitutionalization" is drawn from Renée C. Fox, "Medicine, Science, and Technology," in *Applications of Social Science to Clinical Medicine and Health Policy*, eds. Linda Aiken and David Mechanic (New Brunswick, N.J.: Rutgers University Press, 1986), pp. 23–24.

92. The sociologist who has written the most about the "deinstitutionalization" of the mentally ill is Andrew T. Scull. See his *Decarceration: Community Treatment and the Deviant: A Radical View* (Englewood Cliffs, N.J.: Prentice-Hall, 1977), and also "Deinstitutionalization and Public Policy," *Social Science and Medicine*, 20, no. 5 (1985), 545–52.

93. Jon E. Gudeman and Miles F. Shore, "Beyond Deinstitutionalization: A New Class of Facilities for the Mentally Ill," *New England Journal of Medicine*, 311, no. 13 (September 27, 1984),

832–36. See also the brochure announcing the Program for the Chronically Mentally Ill, Co-sponsored by The Robert Wood Johnson Foundation and the U.S. Department of Housing and Urban Development, January 1986, p. 3.

94. Richard J. Wyatt, "Scienceless to Homeless," (Editorial) *Science* 234 (December 12, 1986), 1309.

95. Jonathan A. Showstack, Mary Hughes Stone, and Steven A. Schroeder, "The Role of Changing Clinical Practices in the Rising Costs of Hospital Care," *New England Journal of Medicine*, 13, no. 19 (November 7, 1985), 1201–7.

96. David Mechanic, *Future Issues in Health Care: Social Policy and the Rationing of Medical Services* (New York: The Free Press, 1979), p. xi. David Mechanic is the sociologist who has made the most notable effort to place these issues of cost containment in a larger social, cultural, and political/economic perspective. See also, David Mechanic, "Cost Containment and the Quality of Medical Care: Rationing Strategies in an Era of Constrained Resources," *Milbank Memorial Fund Quarterly/Health and Society*, 63, no. 3 (1985), 453–75.

97. Paul Starr, *The Social Transformation of American Medicine* (New York: Basic Books, Inc., 1982), especially pp. 420–49.

98. Arnold S. Relman, "The New Medical-Industrial Complex," *New England Journal of Medicine*, 303, no. 17 (October 23, 1980), 963–70.

99. Bradford H. Gray, "An Introduction to the New Health Care for Profit," in *The New Health Care for Profit: Doctors and Hospitals in a Competitive Environment*, ed. Bradford H. Gray (Washington, D.C.: National Academy Press, 1983). © 1983 by the National Academy of Sciences.

100. Gray, "An Introduction to the New Health Care for Profit," p. 3.

101. Ibid., p. 2.

102. Jessica Townsend, "When Investor-Owned Corporations Buy Hospitals: Some Issues and Concerns," in *The New Health Care for Profit*, ed. Bradford H. Gray, p. 51. Townsend's essay is based on exploratory case studies of the sale of five hospitals to investor-owned chains, the patterned issues and concerns that arose in this connection, and the ways in which they were handled.

103. Wachter, "The Impact of the Acquired Immunodeficiency Syndrome on Medical Residency Training," pp. 177–80.

104. Ibid.

105. Ibid.

106. Rosemary Stevens, "'A Poor Sort of Memory.'"

107. Emily Friedman, "Public Hospitals: Doing What Everyone Wants Done but Few Others Wish to Do," *Journal of the American Medical Association*, 25, no. 11 (March 20, 1987), 1437–44.

108. Charles E. Rosenberg, "From Almshouse to Hospital: The Shaping of Philadelphia General Hospital," *Milbank Memorial Fund Quarterly/Health and Society*, 60, no. 1 (1982), 108–54.

109. Ibid. p. 152.

CHAPTER 6

MEDICAL SCIENCE AND MEDICAL RESEARCH

This chapter concerns an intellectually fascinating and socially important sphere of inquiry in which remarkably little work has been done by social scientists. It is an area of medical sociology that does not even have an acknowledged name but might properly be called the sociology of medical science. It specifically focuses on modern biomedical science and technology and the research processes through which they are developed. Its subject matter encompasses systematic, close-up study of the influence of social and cultural factors on the form and content of medical scientific knowledge, its underlying modes of reasoning and styles of thought, its basic value premises, and the dynamics of scientific discovery. The sociology of medical science also deals with the phenomenological, everyday reality of what medical scientific work entails—including the kinds of questions that are (and are not) pursued, the methods and techniques employed, the attributes and experiences of those engaged in medical research, the social roles and settings within which it is conducted, and the circumstances and atmosphere that surround it. Analysis of the repercussions that medical scientific research and its findings have on society and culture is also an important part of the field. But its most distinctive features are associated with expert ability to identify sociocultural elements *inside* the cognitive and human framework of medical science and to analyze the consequences of their presence and shaping influence. In this respect, the sociology of medical science—a branch both of the sociology of medicine and of science—has interests in common with the history and philosophy of science and medicine, as well as the sociology of knowledge.

The development of this realm of sociology has been impeded by the positivistic tendency of many sociologists to assume that the intellectual and technical content of modern medical science—its concepts, facts, and methods—are "purely scientific," and thus fall outside the orbit of sociocultural influence. Insufficient competence in understanding relevant biomedical materials and the technical language in which they are expressed has been another deterrent. It has hampered sociologists' ability to recognize and interpret the social and cultural attitudes, values, beliefs, and symbols that are encoded in medical scientific knowledge and vocabulary. Furthermore, in sharp contrast to the substantial amount of *in situ* field research done by sociologists in a variety of medical settings, very little direct sociological observation of medical scientists at work has been conducted. For this reason, too, progress in the sociology of medical science has been slow. The statement that Robert K. Merton made in 1952 about the general condition of the sociology of science applies equally well to the present state of the sociology of medical science:

> There already exists . . . a vast literature on "scientific method" and, by inference, on the "attitudes" and "values" of scientists. But this literature is concerned with what the social scientists would call ideal patterns, that is, with ways in which scientists *ought* to think, feel, and act. It does not necessarily describe, in needed detail, the ways in which scientists actually do think, feel, and act. Of these actual patterns, there has been little systematic study. . . . It is at least possible that if social scientists were to begin observations in the laboratories and field stations of physical and biological scientists, more might be learned, in a comparatively few years, about the psychology and sociology of science than in all the years that have gone before.[1]

This chapter will do more than summarize the relatively sparse sociological writings on medical science and research that are available. It will attempt to draw them together, and at times supplement them, in a fashion that also provides a framework for more ample future work in the sociology of medical science.

We will begin by identifying the cognitive assumptions and the type of thought on which modern medical science and research are based, its underlying value orientations, and its world view. The close historical and sociological connection between Western culture and these parameters of biomedicine will be discussed, along with the variations and transformations that biomedicine may undergo in different societies. We will turn a sociological microscope on some medical scientific concepts and language and on the detailed content of the research experiences and findings of a number of investigators, in order to examine the kinds of social and cultural materials that are embedded in them. Throughout, we will be interested in what philosopher Jean Ladrière refers to as assumptions and phenomena that are not in themselves scientific, but that along with those that are, make up the "scientificness" of a science.[2]

Next to be considered are some of the implications of the fact that medical science and medical research are intrinsically relevant to the human body and mind, health and illness, and life and death, and that in certain of its forms it entails experimenting directly on human subjects. Against this background, attention will be given to the chance, uncertainty, and risk dimensions of medical research and the way these help to generate various patterns of "scientific magic."[3] The phenomenon of "the clinical moratorium" will also be dealt with here: the frequency with which it occurs in the early, highly uncertain, and risky stage of trying an experimental procedure on a patient, and "its relationship to the fundamental conceptual, technical, social, and ethical properties of clinical investigation."[4]

We will move on to some observations on the attributes of the complex social structure and organization within which modern medical scientific research is conducted. In particular, we will consider how these attributes bear on the nature of scientific teamwork, and how, in interaction with the primary values and norms of science and its reward system, they shape secondary patterns of science. Such secondary patterns include "priority disputes" over discovery,[5] also certain types of scientific deviance. The chapter will end with a reference to the "experiment perilous" and "courage to fail"[6] kinds of hospital and laboratory communities in which some type of clinical medical research is enacted and experienced.

COGNITIVE ASSUMPTIONS AND MODE OF THOUGHT

The mode of thought on which modern medical science and research are based is an emergent, eclectic product of the numerous fields of biological, physical, and behavioral science on which it draws. Biology is its cornerstone, but the phenomena with which medicine deals are both too complex and too individuated to be confined to a purely biological analysis, or to any single explanatory theory. The theoretical framework within which medical thought is hung is made up of congeries of conceptual schemes, linked by their common object of study and the style of reasoning that they share. Null hypothesis, experimental, and probability reasoning are brought to bear on what is observed, manipulated, and analyzed, within a structure of thought that also entails various forms of systematic reductionism. This type of logico-rational thought is applied to phenomena that are directly or indirectly related to human health and disease, illness and wellness. Through observation, experimental techniques, and in some instances interviewing, information is amassed and refined.

Instruments are used that enhance observation and increase control of data; in clinical research, for example, these range in power, intricacy, and size from the stethoscope, to the electron microscope, to the positron emission tomography (PET) scanner. The scientific use of concepts, chains of reasoning, facts, methods, and instruments is dependent on the existence and continual revision of a common technical language with which investigators can express and explain their observations, analyses, and interpretations to themselves and each other, as well as to nonmedical audiences.

As in all scientific fields, what Ludwik Fleck has called the "thought cycle"[7] that medical scientists learn and adopt increases their capacity to recognize particular phenomena. It also enhances the "self-fulfilling prophecy"[8] that they will "see" and discover what their training prepared them to anticipate and find. The built-in bias that results from the conceptions and preconceptions of the field and the way that scientists internalize them make it more difficult for researchers to notice and take seriously phenomena that fall outside of their habitual patterns of observation, thought, and expectation.

However systematically ordered and structured it may be, "[b]y its very nature, scientific research is a voyage into the unknown [via] routes that are in some measure unpredictable and unplannable."[9] Problems of uncertainty are inherent to it, and medical researchers are expected to be "specialists in uncertainty, who deliberately work in the realm of the uncertain and unknown, focusing on those questions that medicine still has not answered."[10] They advance knowledge "by laying bare these uncertainties, as well as by mitigating or dispelling them."[11]

Unforeseen or "chance" events are therefore inevitable in scientific research. But the occurrence of happy or lucky chance that leads to a discovery, in what

Robert K. Merton has called "the serendipity pattern,"[12] is not as aleatory as it seems. Paradoxically, as Louis Pasteur's famous dictum puts it, "Chance favors the prepared mind."

In a comparative case study of "an instance of serendipity gained and serendipity lost," Bernard Barber and Renée Fox identified and analyzed a number of the non-chance/chance factors that entered into an "accidental" discovery that was made by Dr. Lewis Thomas in 1956 and "missed" by Dr. Aaron Kellner:

> Here were two comparable medical scientists . . . both carrying out investigations in the field of experimental pathology, affiliated with distinguished medical schools, and of approximately the same level of demonstrated research ability. . . . In the course of their research, both men had occasion to inject rabbits intravenously with papain, and both had . . . accidentally encountered the same ("bizarre") phenomenon of . . . "reversible collapse of rabbit ears" . . . following the injection.[13]

Thomas went on to discover that the intravenously injected papain had caused "drastic" physical and chemical changes in the rabbits' ear cartilage and in all their other cartilaginous tissues as well; Kellner failed to note these changes. Through their focused interviews with the two scientists, Barber and Fox learned that for a long while, the explanation for the floppiness of the rabbits' ears had eluded Thomas as well as Kellner, though both men thought that they had paid sufficient attention to the rabbits' cartilage in the post-papain tissue studies they had made. In fact, both had been misled into too routinely and casually examining the cartilage because of their mutual conviction, shared by their colleagues, that it was "inert and relatively uninteresting" tissue. Thus, the preconceptions that guided and focused their research led them away from a serious consideration of what only much later seemed to Thomas to be the "obvious" explanation for the changes underlying the collapsing ears.

Thomas's capacity to break through these assumptions in a way that was conducive to discovery was the cumulative result of a number of factors. His interest in the floppy-eared phenomenon was kept alive by his scientist's belief that its "unfailing regularity" might be due to an important and powerful biological happening. He continued not only to think about it, but to describe and show it to basic science and clinical research colleagues, who were also intrigued by it. The critical event that directly resulted in his serendipitous discovery was preparing a seminar for second-year medical students to whom he wished to convey "what experimental pathology is like," especially the puzzling questions and interesting uncertainties with which it deals. Because he had reached an impasse in some of his other research, Thomas had both the time and inclination to restudy the ear-collapsing effect of papain, and he decided to "put [this] experiment on" for the students. Previously, he had only compared the histological sections made of the ears of rabbits who had received an injection of papain with his "own mental image." In order to make it an effective teaching exercise, now he made sections from the ear tissue of rabbits that did *not* receive papain, as well as from those who did, and simultaneously examined the two. This enabled him to see for the first time that the ear cartilage of the papain-injected rabbits "showed loss of a major portion of the intercellular matrix, and complete absence of basophilia from the small amount of remaining matrix."

As for Kellner, his amusement over what he called "the floppy-eared rabbits" resulted in his taking the phenomenon less seriously than Thomas. In effect, he and his colleagues closed off their interest in it by putting it to applied use as an assay test for appraising the potency and amount of papain to be injected. He was also "drawn off in other research directions by seeing other serendipitous phenomena in the same situation, and by his success in following up those leads."[14]

Despite the different experiences and outcomes associated with these particular serendipitous encounters, Lewis Thomas and Aaron Kellner had a common outlook on medical scientific uncertainty. They regarded errors and mistakes, as well as uncertainty and chance, as inherent to biology, medicine, and scientific questing. "Both investigators were as familiar with negative as with positive serendipity, preferring the latter, but were also convinced that mistakes were not inevitably unfortunate or dangerous." Quite to the contrary, in nature, in the laboratory, in scientific and in nonscientific activities, "they believed mistakes could lead to unexpectedly felicitous . . . knowledge" and understanding.[15] This was the at-once scientific and moral message that Thomas hoped to transmit to his students by organizing a whole class around a persistently baffling phenomenon that he had repeatedly tried and failed to elucidate.

Individual personality factors undoubtedly played some role in forming Thomas's and Kellner's attitudes toward uncertainty, chance, probability, and error. But their attitudes were also shaped by the culture of modern science, modern Western society, and, perhaps, to a degree, by American society in particular. The concepts of uncertainty, probability, accident, and chance do not even exist in some non-Western, nonmodern cultural traditions, and the way that they are institutionalized in modern Western scientific reasoning is incommensurable with the cognitive assumptions and modes of thought of such traditions. In the Central African culture of Zairean society, for example:

> Most happenings—illness figuring prominently among them—are interpreted either as adverse or felicitous, relatively few experiences are regarded as neutral or without meaning, and virtually none are considered to be fortuitous. They are viewed as being determinatively caused, primarily by supernatural, psychic, and inter-personal forces, within a closed system of thought and belief, whose inner logic is cogent, self-confirming, and self-fulfilling. . . . When evidence contrary to traditional interpretations presents itself, there is a tendency to develop . . . "secondary elaborations," that "excuse" or explain away the untoward occurrence and thereby protect established premises. There is no room for the concept of probability in this way of thought, nor for the formal acknowledgment of an ultimate, irreducible degree of uncertainty as an inherent property of man's attempts systematically to understand, explain, and predict physical, biological, social, cultural, and psychological phenomena.[16]

The notion of "rationality," the cornerstone concept on which modern medical science is based, is also culturally specific in several respects.[17] The way that it is defined and implemented in scientific work and the supreme importance accorded to it are not identical with the way that it is understood, expressed, and valued in other, day-to-day, nonscientific activities of modern Western societies. It deviates even more from the predominant thought patterns of a non-Western, Asian society like Japan. Japan is a society, anthropologist Emiko Ohnuki-Tierney emphasizes, that is no less modern than Western societies. Its contemporaneous science, technology, and biomedicine were largely imported from the West, but its conceptions of rationality and the rational include profoundly traditional, quintessentially Japanese symbolic dimensions.[18] In this regard and others, she goes on to say, "[the] widely held assumption that biomedicine is 'scientific' and therefore 'objective,' thus, 'culture-free,' . . . epitomizes the objectivism falsely attributed" to science and technology in general.[19] This falsely culture-free assumption, she ironically points out, is a culture-bound one, "thoroughly embedded in . . . the transformations of the culture and society of the intellectual elites in the West."[20]

In light of the cultural specificity of the cognitive concepts and the characteristic mode of thought of modern Western science, how has it been sufficiently translatable and transferable to other societies to have become the predominant world science of the twentieth century? To our knowledge, this question has not been analytically addressed by social scientists. Nor have the sorts of empirical studies been made that could ascertain whether culturally nuanced differences exist in the way that competent modern medical (and other) scientists in different societies conceptualize, reason about, and perform their scientific work. As was discussed in Chapter 5, Ohnuki-Tierney's interpretation of what she terms the "cultural transformation" of biomedicine in Japan provides a suggestive model for anthropological and sociological inquiries of this sort. For example, in the Japanese health care system, "hygienic behavior and its underlying concepts, which are perceived and expressed in terms of biomedical germ theory, in fact are directly tied to the basic Japanese symbolic structure. Contemporary concepts of dirt and cleanliness derive from symbolic notions of purity and pollution, which have been basic themes of Japanese symbolic structure throughout history."[21] In this sense, "Japanese germs" have not been displaced by Western, biomedically-defined microbes. Whether the modern, Western-derived thought structures, processes, and style of Japanese scientists have been culturally altered in a comparable fashion, with what consequences for scientific work and discovery, is a worthy topic for future social science research. Beyond this, since one of the special attributes of Japanese society is its extraordinary capacity to absorb and transmute whatever it culturally imports from other societies into something fundamentally Japanese, the general applicability of Ohnuki-Tierney's "cultural transformation" paradigm would have to be explored in the scientific milieux of other Asian and non-Asian modern societies.

Like the concepts and chains of reasoning that medical scientists utilize, their special terminology is marked by social and cultural influences. It is not as strictly technical as nonscientists might suppose, or as scientists themselves generally believe. For example, the language of immunology, a medical field that has become increasingly important both scientifically and clinically, is strikingly pervaded by two sorts of imagistic vocabulary. The first is a set of warfare terms that identify and characterize the body's "defenses" against infections, and possibly cancer. T cells and B cells are considered to be among the most crucial cells of the immune defense system against disease. They are depicted as organized sentries, guided missiles, and assassins, with the capacity to "recognize," "remember," seek out, "target," and "destroy" "invaders," such as viruses and bacteria, or "foreign" particles, cells, and tissue. Not only are there "helper" T cells that bolster the activity of B cells and "suppressor" T cells that act to shut off their activity, but also "killer" T cells that have the capacity to attack and lethally damage target cells that have acquired foreign characteristics. This whole lexicon of bellicose, sociomilitary terms (some of them inherited from germ theory, bacteriology, and an earlier "microbe hunters" era of modern Western medicine) has been projected onto the body's immune system. A second notable group of socially imprinted immunological terms refer to the body's ability to distinguish "self" from ("foreign") "not-self," using "individuality markers" to do so. It is because of the so-called natural determinants of self (known as the major histocompatibility complex) that persons receiving organ transplants are given immunosuppressive drugs in order to keep their T cells from "recognizing" the transplanted tissue as "not-self," and proceeding to "reject" it.

As David P. Willis and Renée C. Fox have commented, "It seems more than coincidental" that these "individualism, individuality, and personhood" referents have become a part of the language of immunology in a historical period when American and other Western societies are grappling with "major questions . . . about our cultural conceptions of personhood, and about what their implications are for how we relate to our individual selves, and to multiple others."[22] The warfare and the personhood languages of immunology not only converge at certain points; they also share anthropomorphic characteristics.

The special language of a field can also "technicalize" the way social and cultural sentiments, values, and beliefs are phrased, in a manner that simultaneously masks them and permits them to be expressed "scientifically." This point is demonstrated by Ilana Löwy's case study of the controversy over the value of tissue typing in cadaver kidney grafts.[23] The participants in this controversy were physicians who dealt with kidney transplantation and medical scientists who studied human tissue groups (human leukocyte antigens—HLA) and their relevance to clinical organ transplantation.

The controversy began in the 1960s, "with the HLA specialists' proposal that the newly discovered 'tissue groups' be used for the optimization of the selection of donor-recipient pairs in kidney transplants":

> The transplanters quickly agreed that the proposed innovation was helpful for the selection of the best potential living related donor among the members of a patient's family, and on the value of leukocyte antigens studies in the elimination of the presensitized recipients (i.e., recipients who already have pre-formed antibodies against the proposed kidney and who, in consequence, are at risk to reject it promptly). They disagreed however upon the value of this innovation for the selection of an adequate recipient for an available cadaver kidney. The debate on this subject was at its height in the years 1970–1973. . . . Both the transplanters and the HLA specialists who vehemently supported the efficiency of HLA typing in cadaver kidney grafts, and those who strongly opposed it, were able to produce convincing statistical data to support their respective points of view. This "battle of statistics" was ended by a partial compromise. The majority of the HLA specialists agreed at the end of the 1970s that HLA compatibility is of some, albeit limited, value in cadaver kidney grafts. The transplanters continue, however, to have differing opinions of the practical value of HLA typing in cadaver kidney grafts, and those evaluations are reflected in their clinical practice.[24]

Throughout all stages of this debate, Löwy stresses, the only arguments used were "statistical evaluations" of the effect of testing HLA compatibility on the survival of cadaver kidney grafts. But these statistically expressed differences in results and their interpretations, she contends, were significantly influenced by sociocultural factors. On a microlevel, the local history and cultural tradition of individual transplantation centers affected the use and appraisal of HLA matching. On the level of a whole country or group of countries, Löwy found that decisions concerning the importance of HLA matching for the way that cadaver kidney procurement and allocation were institutionalized was "highly dependent" on how health care services were organized in a given society and on its underlying "social philosophy" concerning equality in the distribution of those services. This, for Löwy, explains the fact that the majority of transplantation units and organ procurement agencies that firmly support HLA-antigen typing and use it as the principal criterion for what they believe is the most scientifically valid and socially equitable mode of distributing cadaver kidneys are European or Australian, whereas those that attach less importance to HLA matching in the allocation of transplantable kidneys are generally American. From her perspective (of a European immunologist and historian of science and medicine), this "testif[ies] to the fact that in the United States the importance of a classification system ensuring equality may become secondary to other economic and organizational considerations."[25]

THE VALUES AND ETHOS OF MEDICAL SCIENCE

The cognitive assumptions and mode of thought of modern medical science are interrelated with the cultural values that are embodied in its ethos.[26] As previously discussed, the value of rationality provides the *raison d'être* for all types of scientific inquiry, and a strongly-felt commitment to progress in rationally understanding the human body and mind, health and illness, and life and death is institutionalized in medical research. The pursuit of logical, orderly, generalized, but open-ended knowledge is valued for its own sake and as an expression of high intellectual faculties. In medical research, this pattern of rationality derives further support from the assumption that it is the primary means through which disease and illness will be vanquished, adventitious death overcome, and health sustained. Thus, rationality interacts with a dynamic, melioristic value complex that Talcott Parsons called "instrumental activism."[27]

The role that feeling plays in this rationality is shaped by a value conception of detached concern.[28] Medical investigators are expected to be emotionally involved in their research and to care about the knowledge and applications that it may bring forth. At the same time, they are supposed to maintain a detachment that blends objectivity with organized doubting.

This value orientation shades into universalism. Judgments of the reliability, validity, and significance of medical scientific findings, along with the opportunity to have a research career, are supposed to be as dissociated as possible from particularistic attributes or relationships. Scientific talent, competence, and performance are considered to be the most appropriate criteria of eligibility and excellence. The scientist's personal qualities and social characteristics of sex, age, race, nationality, class, religion, and political persuasion are deemed to be irrelevant.

Finally, modern medical research is poised between individualism and a collectivity orientation. Investigators are enjoined to follow the paths of knowledge that scientific inquiry open up, no matter how lonely or heterodox they may seem. But researchers are also expected to recognize that the knowledge they utilize and generate is not a personal possession. In principle, it belongs to an all-encompassing human community that extends far beyond the particular social groups and society to which the scientists belong, and beyond their own historical time. In addition, investigators are expected to be aware of the social consequences of their research, though the content and scope of these responsibilities are not clearly designated.

Rationality, instrumental activism, detached concern, universalism, and collectivism describe the ideal-typical value system of medical and other fields of science, as they have developed in modern Western societies. We have already commented on the "Western-ness" of these values. Even with societies that are both modern and Western, however, considerable variability exists in the form and degree to which these value orientations are institutionalized. For example, the social settings within which most medical research in Belgium takes place—departments, hospitals, or university institutes—are living, paradigmatic expressions of the major social and cultural variables present in all spheres of Belgian life and of the various permutations and combinations in which they appear. Each of these particularistic, relatively cloistered university worlds is a mini-expression of the ethnic-linguistic, religious and philosophical, political, economic, and social class, community, and regional variables that structure, permeate, and rend Belgian society. Thus, such factors as whether a medical researcher is Flemish, Walloon, or *Brusselaar/Brusselois*, Flemish-speaking or French-speaking, Catholic, Free Thought, or Free Mason, and which political enclave he belongs to, are determinants of his appointment to a university research position, along with his scientific ability, training and achievement. Furthermore, each university tends to recruit its teaching and research personnel from its own alumni. Thus, institutionalized particularism is a major value component and social structural feature of the way that medical research in Belgium is organized. This Belgian pattern is not totally incompatible with good quality medical research, but on a societal level, it puts restraints on the volume and originality of the work done.[29]

Recent feminist-oriented studies of the relationship between gender and science have underscored the cultural "masculinity" of the paramount ethos of modern science. Evelyn Fox Keller, a theoretical biologist and mathematician who has done some of the most distinguished work in this field, points out that the ideals and values canonized by science—reason, objectivity, impersonality, autonomy, power, control, and domination over nature—are ones that have been historically associated with masculinity.[30] This association between science and masculinity, she contends, goes back to the birth of modern science in seventeenth-century England and the "virile" Baconian vision of science, "constructed around the naming of object (nature) as female, and the parallel naming of subject (mind) as male."[31] (Francis Bacon metaphorically expressed this view of science as a "chaste and lawful marriage between Mind and Nature."[32] He wrote: "I am come in very truth leading you to Nature with all her children to bind her to your service and make her your slave."[33])

Keller does not deny that the prevailing ethos of science has been fruitful; nor does she claim that the ideals and values it upholds should be rejected. Quite to the contrary, she asserts that "the equation between knowledge and power" that Bacon's vision promised has been "realized beyond [his] wildest dreams . . . in the triumphs of modern science."[34] Furthermore, as a scientist who is herself primarily committed to "the best (maximally reliable) and fullest description of the natural world around us—in short, to the priority of the search for truth"[35]—she regards the established values of science as more than biased masculine ideology. And she does not agree with "one strand of the radical feminist critique" that demands that they be "replaced."[36]

What Keller does affirm is that the supremacy accorded to this "masculine" conception of science "normatively excludes" other values traditionally associated with femininity, which are potential wellsprings of scientific creativity and discovery: feeling and empathy, understanding, identification with nature, respect for difference and complexity, an appreciation of connectedness and relatedness, a sense of mystery, and "even love." What Keller would like to see is a science that surpasses gender, in which so-called female as well as male perspectives, concepts, and qualities are legitimated and integrated in the persons and in the research of both men and women scientists. "If we want to think about the ways in which science might [then] be different," Keller writes,"we could hardly find a more appropriate guide than Barbara McClintock."[37] Here she refers to the life and work of the scientist who, at age 81, was awarded the 1983 Nobel Prize in Medicine or Physiology for her discovery of genetic transposition (the movement of genetic elements, in an apparently uncoordinated way, from one chromosomal site to another).

THE WORLD VIEW(S) OF MEDICAL SCIENCE

The language of science, especially the metaphors and images that are coded into it, along with its value system, is closely connected to another of science's underlying dimensions—the world view on which it is predicated. This macro-view is composed of the meta-assumptions of a science—its most basic and transcendent conceptions of nature, the universe, time, matter, structure, order, life, death, organism, human, body, mind, behavior—and of science itself.

Modern scientists, those in biomedicine included, have resolutely tried to fashion and maintain a "disenchanted" outlook, in Max Weber's sense of the term. They have struggled to free their scientific thought and work from vitalistic and teleological conceptions of higher purpose and ultimate meaning in the design of nature and the universe—particularly from religious beliefs and magical notions about the influence of any supernatural forces on what is held to be the "natural" phenomena that scientists study. The predominant scientific view of nature is positivistic and reductionistic. There are a fathomable, impersonal, and essentially simple set of "laws [that] are part of the mathematical and mechanical fabric of the universe, and that . . . are also at play in biological processes."[38] And there is a dauntless belief in the knowability of these laws through science:

> Physicists, or at least some of us, believe that there is a simple set of laws of nature, of which all our complicated present physical and chemical laws are just mathematical consequences. We do not know these underlying laws, but, as an act of faith if you like, we expect that eventually we will. . . .
> We can trace the history of the present period of expansion back to its first million years, or its first three minutes, or its first ten billionth of a second, but we still do not know if time really began just a little before then, or if so, then what started the clock. It may be that we shall never know, just as we may never learn the ultimate laws of nature. But I wouldn't bet on it.[39]

For an astrophysicist like Steven Weinberg, there is no great clock maker and clock starter in the sky; and there is no deterrent in time, space, or the collective human intellect, that can limit the capacity of science to progressively explain "the rules that . . . govern the universe and everything in it."

Pushed to the extreme, such a relentless philosophical and mechanistic reductionism can become a kind of anti-metaphysical metaphysics, as sociologist Howard L. Kaye has brilliantly shown in his analysis of the writings of "the philosophical spokesmen for molecular biology," such as Francis Crick, James Watson, Jacques Monod, François Jacob, Joshua Lederberg, and Gunther Stent:

> What, then, distinguishes the philosophical spokesmen for molecular biology from their biological-humanist counterparts is their determinism and reductionism: culture is reduced to biology; biology, to the laws of physics and chemistry at the molecular level; mind, to matter; behavior, to genes; organism, to program; the origin of species, to macromolecules; life, to reproduction. . . .
>
> The reductionism . . . represents both a research strategy (one that has been spectacularly successful), and something more: a world view. . . . To speak of molecular biology's "aim" or "search" to reduce "all" of biology, all of the "behavior," characteristics, and "fundamentals" of living things to molecular mechanisms betrays a metaphysical ambition to demonstrate that organisms really *are* machines and that all of life really can be accounted for in this way.[40]

As part of his analysis, Howard Kaye points to some of the "religious language" that characterizes the field: for example, the application of the term, "the central dogma" (coined by Crick) to his and Watson's delineation of the double helical structure of DNA, and their DNA-to-RNA-to-protein account of the genetic functions of replication and instruction; and molecular biologists' reference to a genetic linkage map of all the 3 billion units of the human genome that they hope some day to produce as the "grail of human genetics."

The "aggressive, simplifying, reductionist approach and attitude" that Kaye describes may be "the dominant point of view within molecular biology,"[41] but another Nobel Laureate in the field, Albert Claude, speaks with a quite different voice:

> Looking back 25 years later, what I may say is that the facts have been far better than the dreams. In the long course of cell life on this earth it remained for our age, for our generation, to receive the full ownership of our inheritance. We have entered the cell, the mansion of our birth, and started the inventory of our acquired wealth.
>
> For over 2 billion years, through the apparent fancy of its endless differentiations and metamorphosis, the cell, in its basic physiological mechanisms, has remained one and the same. It is life itself, and our true and distant ancestor.
>
> It is hardly more than a century since we first learned of the existence of the cell: this autonomous and all-contained unit of living matter that has acquired the knowledge and the power to reproduce; the capacity to store, transform, and utilize energy; and the capacity to accomplish physical works and to manufacture practically unlimited kinds of products. We know that the cell has possessed these attributes and biological devices and has continued to use them for billions of cell generations and years.
>
> In the course of the past 30 or 40 years, we have learned to appreciate the complexity and perfection of the cellular mechanisms, miniaturized to the utmost

at the molecular level, which reveal within the cell an unparalleled knowledge of the laws of physics and chemistry. . . .

In addition, we know also that the cell has a memory of its past, certainly in the case of the egg cell, and foresight of the future, together with precise and detailed patterns for differentiations and growth, a knowledge which is materialized in the process of reproduction and the development of all beings from bacteria to plants, beasts, or men. It is this cell which plans and composes all organisms, and which transmits to them its defects and potentialities. Man, like other organisms, is so perfectly coordinated that he may easily forget, whether awake or asleep, that he is a colony of cells in action, and that it is the cells which achieve, through him, what he has the illusion of accomplishing himself. It is the cells which create and maintain us, during the span of our lives, our will to live and survive, to search and experiment, and to struggle. . . .

Of course, we know the laws of trial and error, of large numbers and probabilities. We know that these laws are part of the mathematical and mechanical fabric of the universe, and that they are also at play in biological processes. But, in the name of the experimental method and out of our poor knowledge, are we really entitled to claim that everything happens by chance to the exclusion of all other possibilities? . . .

Life, this anti-entropy, ceaselessly reloaded with energy is a climbing force, toward order among chaos, toward light among the darkness of the indefinite, toward the mystic dream of love, between the fire which devours itself, and the silence of the cold. . . .[42]

Albert Claude's profoundly emotional, almost mystical identification with the cell, and the cosmic meaning that he finds in it, are comparable to the "feeling for the organism" relationship that geneticist Barbara McClintock has with corn plants, the chief "objects of her study [that] have become subjects in their own right."[43] Like Claude, McClintock has "a deep reverence for nature," surprise and delight in the "vast complexity," "ingenuity," "flexibility," and "mystery" of living forms, a strong sense of the oneness of things, and "a capacity for union with that which is to be known."[44] As Evelyn Fox Keller comments, this view "reflect[s] a different image of science from that of a purely rational enterprise."[45]

Over and over again, [McClintock] tells us one must have the time to look, the patience to "hear what the material has to say to you," the openness to "let it come to you."

One must understand "how it grows, understand its parts, understand when something is going wrong with it. . . . You need to know those plants well enough so that if anything changes, . . . you [can] look at the plant and right away you know what this damage you see is from—something that scraped across it or something that bit it or something that the wind did."

" . . . I know every plant in the field. I know them intimately, and I find it a great pleasure to know them. . . . I have learned so much about the corn plant that when I see things, I can interpret [them] right away." . . .

"Animals can walk around, but plants have to stay still to do the same things, with ingenious mechanisms. . . . Plants are extraordinary. For instance, . . . you can't touch a plant without setting off an electric pulse. . . . There is no question that plants have [all] kinds of sensitivities. They do a lot of responding to their environment. They can do almost anything you can think of. But just because they sit there, anybody walking down the road considers them just a plastic area to look at, [as if] they're not really alive."[46]

McClintock and Claude's research carried them deeply into the universe of the cell—its structure and mechanisms, organization and functions—as it did Watson and Crick. But the conceptions of nature and the world view from which their scientific looking and listening, analyzing and interpreting emanated differed greatly in certain respects from those of the co-discoverers of the structure of the DNA and of the central dogma.

> McClintock . . . did not share in the general enthusiasm for the central dogma. The same model that seemed so immediately and overwhelmingly satisfying to so many of her colleagues did not satisfy her. Although duly impressed by its explanatory power, she remained at the same time acutely aware of what it did not explain. It neither addressed the questions that were of primary interest to her—bearing on the relation between genetics and development—nor began to take into account the complexity of genetic organization that she had always assumed, and that was now revealed to her in her work on transposition.
>
> McClintock locates the critical flaw of the central dogma in its presumption: it claimed to explain too much. Baldly put, what was true of *E. coli* (the bacterium most commonly studied) was *not* true of the elephant, as Monod (and others) would have had it. Precisely because higher organisms are multicellular, she argued, they necessarily require a different kind of economy. . . .
>
> To McClintock, transposition provided evidence that genetic organization is necessarily more complex, and in fact more globally interdependent, than such a model assumes. It showed that the DNA itself is subject to rearrangement and, by implication, to reprogramming. Although she did not make the suggestion explicit, the hidden heresy of her argument lay in the inference that such reorganization could be induced by signals external to the DNA—from the cell, the organism, even from the environment. . . .
>
> To her, such a possibility is not heresy—is not even surprising. On the contrary, it is in direct accord with her belief in the resourcefulness of natural order. Because she has no investment in the passivity of nature, the possibility of internally generated order does not, to her, threaten the foundations of science. . . . It merely confirms the existence of forms of order more complex than we have, at least thus far, been able to account for.[47]

For many years, McClintock's concept of transposition was not understood or accepted by fellow scientists. It came to seem even more out of touch with biological reality, and more peculiarly heterodox, after the central dogma gained ascendancy as the establishment view in molecular biology. Yet however much her ideas may have departed from the central dogma and its form of reductionism, in other, fundamental respects, they never strayed from the scientist's "credo" that she shared with her colleagues: "confidence in the underlying order of living forms, . . . use of the apparatus of science to gain access to that order, and . . . commitment to bringing back her insights into the shared language of science."[48] Furthermore, as the affinities between her vision of nature and science and that of Albert Claude suggest, McClintock's world view did not fall totally outside the traditions and perspectives of the scientific community either. "Had that been so," Evelyn Fox Keller points out, "she could not have had even marginal status as a scientist." For McClintock to be recognized as a scientist, "the positions that she represents, however unrepresentative, had to be, and were, identifiable as belonging somewhere in that tradition."[49] In turn, this is indicative of an important cultural as well as intellectual characteristic of science, its ethos, and its world view that is often overlooked: namely, that "in practice, the scientific tradition is far more pluralistic than any particular description of it suggests, and certainly more pluralistic than its dominant ideology."[50]

In the end, Barbara McClintock's ideas about genetic transposition were vindicated, and even accorded Nobel Prize recognition. This is a testimony to the cognitive and normative capacity of scientists to break through their established preconceptions and their self-confirming attachment to them. There is currently an outburst of discovery of mobile genetic components that belies the original absolutism and fixity of the central dogma. Still, reluctance to greatly alter the central dogma, or to make it less preeminent, and the collective ambivalence that the community of molecular biologists continue to feel about genetic transposition show up in the language that is used to describe the mobility of genes. Half-playfully, half-derisively, they are referred to as "jumping genes." They are also called "promiscuous genes," reflecting what appears to be a lingering moral indignation that scientists feel about the "unfaithful" as well as unstationary way in which genes behave.

From a sociology of science perspective, it is interesting to note that even investigators as positivistically and scientifically inclined as James Watson and Francis Crick, and as motivated by militant atheism as Crick "to try to show that areas apparently too mysterious to be explained by physics and chemistry could in fact be so explained,"[51] do not, and in fact *cannot*, ignore existential and metaphysical questions. Such questions are as inescapably involved in the kind of searching that scientific inquiry entails as they are in the quite separate but adjacent realm with which religion deals. Science and religion, each in its own way, are concerned with questions of origin and identity, order and meaning: where we come from; why we are here; where we are going; what the purpose of life is, and the reason for death. This is even more immediately and poignantly true of medical than of other forms of scientific research, because it deals so directly with the human body and mind, with human illness and its attendant pain and suffering, and with the enigma of our own ultimate mortality.

Although Watson and Crick would claim otherwise, the way that they addressed questions about the aim, purpose, and "logic of life,"[52] was no more neutral, and no less metaphysical, than McClintock and Claude's approach.

SCIENTIFIC MAGIC

By its very nature, as we have emphasized, scientific research is fraught with uncertainty, with seemingly aleatory events, and with limitations in knowledge—including those that are inherent to scientific ways of knowing. Scientific uncertainty and limitation, and the problems of meaning as well as of competence that they can raise, confront scientists of all genres. But medical researchers experience these problems in a particularly acute and often painful way. They are faced with mediate consequences for health and illness, life and death, of what they do not know or understand, and cannot control. Clinical investigators, who are also physicians, meet the stresses of uncertainty and limitation in daily, face-to-face encounters with the human subjects of their research, often very sick patients under their care, who have agreed to undergo experimental therapeutic trials.

Over the course of many years of participant observation in such medical research contexts, I have repeatedly noted certain patterned responses to those stresses that I have come to think of as "scientific magic." These forms of magic either simulate medical scientific ways of thinking and acting or lie burrowed within them. They help researchers to deal with problems of uncertainty, limitation, and meaning by "ritualizing [their] optimism," as anthropologist Bronislaw Malinowski would have put it.[53] Although scientific magic parodies some of the basic intellectual attributes and assumptions, values and beliefs, and procedures of modern medical research, it appears to be a mechanism that enables investigators to persist in their efforts to advance medical knowledge and technique according to the cognitive and moral canons of science. For this reason, and because it is recurrent, socially structured, and dissembled, I regard it as a latently institutionalized pattern in modern medical research.[54]

One of the characteristic forms of scientific magic that frequently occurs in medical research settings is what I have called "the game of chance."[55] This consists of highly ritualized, humor-accompanied, collective wagering by the members of a research group or team about the possible outcome of a particularly important or risky experiment on human subjects. The unlikelihood of its success, the occurrence of inexplicable success, the dangerous and harmful side effects it may have on its subjects, its enigmatic, unpredictable, and "bizarre" concomitants, and even whether or not the gravely ill patients who are its subject will live or die are foci of the counterphobic, often impious humor that surrounds the betting in which researchers engage.

The game of chance is a complicated phenomenon. On one level, it is a shared and regulated way of "acting out" the chance elements that are intrinsic to medical science and scientifically based medical practice. It is also a way of "acting on" them, for it involves a group of medical researchers in a game-like contest in which they pit their knowledge, experience, skill, and powers of reasoning and prediction against the unknown, adventitious, hard-to-control factors in their work. Winning the bet by guessing right represents a symbolic mastery of these chancey forces, and is a schematic victory over them. The wagering is fundamentally ironic in nature. It mimics probability-based medical scientific thinking, and it is playfully and sportingly organized around the premise that what medical investigators know and do not know, and how their knowledge and understanding affect health, illness, and patients—all have much in common with a game of chance. At the same time, the betting behavior is self-depreciatory and self-mocking, depicting the supposed expertise of medical scientists as speculative, questionable, and full of guesswork, gambles and both good and bad luck. Finally, the game of chance is a protest, a petition, and an affirmation. It is a jesting but profoundly serious, ceremonial way of declaring that what medical researchers know and are seeking to know, and how this relates to the condition of patients *should*, and indeed *does*, have more order and meaning than the throw of the dice or the turn of the roulette wheel. In this basic and ultimate sense, the game of chance ritualizes medical researchers' optimism about the import and the eventual success of their questing.[56]

A second notable pattern of scientific magic is one that is more interwoven within the process and the reporting of medical research, and to a degree camouflaged by it. This is a tendency, which seems especially characteristic of pharmacological research, to focus exuberantly on the positive features of a promising new drug during the early stages of its experiment-to-therapy trajectory, and only later in the therapeutic innovation cycle—with greater sobriety, and some chagrin—to formally acknowledge the limitations and potentially harmful side effects of that agent. There is no inherent biological reason why the discovery of the beneficial actions of a new drug should precede the identification of its disadvantages and contra-indications. Nor are there objective scientific grounds for investigators to be "surprised" and "disappointed"—as they often state that they are in the medical literature—when they encounter what they term the "vexing problem" of the undesirable secondary effects of an otherwise "remarkably effective" drug. Quite to the contrary, no all-therapeutic, side-effect-free therapy of any sort has ever been found, and there are solid scientific grounds for assuming that none ever will be.

What, then, accounts for clinical investigators' unstated but apparently persistent belief in the possibility of discovering a totally beneficent "wonder drug" or true "magic bullet," and their delayed, temporarily disappointed recognition of the drawbacks of a therapeutic agent about which they initially had such high expectations? And how does it repeatedly come to pass that this stage of dissatisfaction and restiveness about the side effects, limitations, and "non-wondrous" attributes of a drug provides impetus to search for still another new, "better" drug that, like the preceding one, is likely to be greeted with unqualified enthusiasm, which then leads to a subsequent stage of discontent with its complications and limitations—and so on, again and again?

We have closely observed and attempted to analyze this "therapeutic innovation cycle" in connection with a series of immunosuppressive drugs used to inhibit the rejection of organ transplants—concentrating especially on what was hailed as the "advent" of cyclosporine.[57] In the words of several research physicians who were engaged in the clinical trials with this agent, "It was necessary to hope for better immunosuppressive drugs. [But] this did not seem a realistic possibility until the advent of the drug cyclosporin A."[58] At the outset of its laboratory and clinical trials in the 1970s, cyclosporine was exultantly described in the medical literature as

> "novel," "unique," "interesting," and "fascinating"; a drug that is "chemically different from any other previously investigated immunosuppressive agent"; an "extremely powerful" and "most effective" drug, that is both "superior" and "important." It [was] portrayed as a "real advance"; "the most promising new pharmacological immune suppressant to emerge in recent years"; a drug that represents "the first step in a new generation of agents for clinically effective immunosuppressive therapy," and that has "opened a new chapter" in transplantation.[59]

At the present time, cyclosporine is still viewed as the immunosuppressive drug of choice. But the unqualifiedly enthusiastic accounts of cyclosporine's extraordinary properties[60] have given away to medical journal articles that now read more like this:

Cyclosporine is a unique immunosuppressive agent that inhibits activation of both B and T lymphocytes as well as certain macrophage functions. . . .

Despite the remarkable effectiveness of cyclosporine in experimental models and in the clinic, as well as the absence of potent myelosuppressive effects, cyclosporine-induced nephrotoxicity remains a vexing problem. . . .

What maneuvers might preserve the potent immunosuppressive properties of the drug while minimizing its nephrotoxicity? . . .[61]

It is to be hoped that measures will be developed that will widen the margin of safety between the dose of cyclosporine required to achieve effective immunosuppression and the dose likely to cause renal damage. Until such measures become available, however, we urge that cyclosporine be used only when its potential benefits clearly outweigh the risk of the development of irreversible renal failure.[62]

What the research physicians previously cited referred to as the "necessity to hope" is involved in the "scientifically magical" thinking that helps to set the therapeutic innovation cycle into perpetual motion. The expectant, often overly hopeful, accentuate-the-positive attitudes of medical researchers are integral to the belief in medical progress that fosters their motivation to look for improved ways of preventing, treating, and managing disease (and also the iatrogenic consequences of their medical actions), and to their ability to persevere in the face of the many uncertainties, problems, and setbacks that clinical investigation entails. The fact that their subjects are also their patients enhances their need to hope. In turn, this gives momentum to the cycle through which new drugs like cyclosporine, its antecedents, and its eventual successors, all pass.

There is a third and final pattern of scientific magic that bears mention. Like the "game of chance," it consists of highly structured and ritualized, levity-infused theatrical behavior that has been shaped by the culture of a laboratory. The laboratories in which we have observed this behavior have generally been ones in which the researchers are trying very experimental procedures or agents on animals, with all the uncertainty, potential harm to the animals, and risk to their lives that this entails. The investigators are testing these procedures in anticipation of moving from the laboratory to the clinic, when it is scientifically and ethically warranted to do so; and they ardently hope that the experimental procedures will prove to be life-saving to the very sick patients who will be the first human subjects. Other comparable laboratory circumstances in which we have observed such patterns are ones in which early clinical trials are already proceeding with patient-subjects, while the work on animals continues, as part of a tandem effort to improve the procedure, gain knowledge, and deal with the clinical complications and the high mortality rate that this phase of clinical research usually entails.

The ritualized behavior that we have seen develop under these conditions more closely resembles the magico-religious ceremonial practices classically described by cultural anthropologists than the other forms of scientific magic that we have identified. Quite commonly, too, in this type of situation, human qualities are ascribed to the animals around whom these rituals develop.

One of the most vivid examples of this scientific magic phenomenon that we have encountered were the norms and practices surrounding the naming of the calves and sheep in the laboratory and barn at the University of Utah who were recipients of experimental models of the artificial heart. It was here that the Jarvik-7 model of a permanent artificial heart that was implanted in Dr. Barney Clark, its first human recipient, was tested on animals. When I observed the animal-naming practices, it was three months after Dr. Clark's death, following the 112 days that he had survived the implant. Members of this laboratory group and the clinical team that had been involved in this pioneering trial were "still in an early phase of its post-mortem stock taking."[63] There was, as yet no second prospective human recipient:

> The principal surgeon and investigator for a given implant is the person who has the right and privilege of naming the animal-recipient. The name is usually not given to the animal until at least twenty-four hours after the implant has occurred. Dr. Donald B. Olsen, who directs the animal work, attributes this custom to the fact that in the early days of the artificial heart program, there was great uncertainty concerning whether the animal into which a heart was implanted would survive even that long. Investigators say that they try to choose a name that "fits the animal's personality" or the surrounding circumstances under which the implant is done. For example, the name Fred was given to "an extremely ugly animal, with a wonderful personality"; and a female calf who received a heart implant on Columbus Day was named Niña, after one of Columbus's ships. More often than not, the names chosen are humorous, such as Ali Baa Baa for a sheep . . . [or Ted E. Baer].
> . . . The names in which the investigators seem to take the greatest pleasure are those that make some sort of self-mockingly romantic or ironic commentary on the meaning of their experimental work, such as Alfred Lord Tennyson, Magic, or in the case of twin calves, Charles and Diana. In the last instance, the fact that "Diana gave her heart to Charles" in an experimental heart transplant added a dimension of gallows humor to the significance of their interconnected names.[64]

Many of the same elements woven into the "game of chance" are present in these naming rituals: preoccupation with uncertainty and risk, with a high mortality rate, and with the limited knowledge and dubious heroism of supposedly expert, trail-blazing researchers. In addition, this laboratory group's naming behavior expressed both affectionate and guilty attachment to their animal-subjects, and their joking acknowledgment of the animals as stand-ins for human subjects. Seen as a whole, the norms and taboos regulating the naming of the animals that the group devised, enacted, and enforced were an emblematic way of trying to achieve greater control over their experimental situation and, in so doing, to symbolically curtail untoward happenings, reduce "failure" (especially the death of the animals), and increase the probability of research and clinical "success."

THE CLINICAL MORATORIUM

However much research on animals has been done before a new therapy is moved from the laboratory to the clinic, its initial trials on human subjects inescapably involve uncertainty and risk as well as potential benefit. These inherent aspects of clinical research are most pronounced when a new treatment may offer the only hope of "saving" the life of a critically ill patient for whom all known interventions have been exhausted. In this situation, a new procedure, drug, or device may prove to be at least somewhat efficacious. But it may also cause unanticipated and sometimes calamitous injury to the already drastically sick patients whom it is considered ethical to engage in this process, contributing to a relatively short survival and painfully complicated death after undergoing the experimental procedure. The phase that transplant pioneer Francis D. Moore called the "black years" of clinical investigation[65] is a stressful and discouraging time for a research group. As the unknown and uncontrolled factors that they face mount, along with the ascending mortality rate, research physicians are subject to strong pressures to consider calling what Judith Swazey and Renée Fox have termed a "clinical moratorium."[66] We have defined a clinical moratorium as a suspension, rather than permanent cessation, of the use of an experimental procedure on patients. Depending on the particular case, it is a pause that can last for months or for years. Such moratoria are not isolated or random events. Rather, they occur frequently in the process of therapeutic innovation; they begin and end under certain identifiable circumstances; and they are generically related to the sociocultural as well as the biomedical dynamics of clinical investigation.

We have studied three sets of moratoria in detail, all associated with the evolution of cardiac surgery. The first of these is the moratorium on mitral valve surgery that lasted from 1929 to 1945.[67] This represents the simplest form that a moratorium can take. Dr. Eliot Cutler, who pioneered the cardiovalvutome procedure for operating on the mitral valve of the heart, personally decided to call a halt to further clinical trials after experiencing a mortality rate of 90 percent in ten operations. "Devastated" by his results, he unobtrusively signalled the moratorium by the subtitle of his 1929 article on "The Present Status of the Surgical Procedures in Chronic Valvular Disease of the Heart: Final Report of all Surgical Cases."[68] Mitral valve surgery was not attempted again for seventeen years, after a series of medical and surgical advances facilitated its resumption.

The second moratorium that we have followed occurred in connection with the transplantation of human hearts.[69] It began in 1969 and lasted until the early 1980s. This thirteen-year-long moratorium was more collective, cumulative, and intricate than the one on mitral valve surgery called individually by Cutler. The moratorium on cardiac transplantation was preceded by a "bandwagon" year: 105 heart transplants were performed in 1968, which the mass media hailed as "The Year of the Transplant." In 1969, the Montreal Heart Institute decided to suspend cardiac transplantation, and this precipitated widespread discussion about whether a more general moratorium should be called. A slowdown in cardiac implantation began. Gradually, a succession of cardiac surgeons ceased doing heart transplants altogether, in most cases without announcing their decision to stop. Only one carefully planned and monitored cardiac transplantation program continued to function: the NIH-supported research program at Stanford, under the direction of Dr. Norman E. Shumway, the developer of the surgical method for heart transplants.

The chief medical development that triggered what physician-journalist Lawrence K. Altman described as the "dramatic surge" in cardiac transplants (and the transplantation of other organs as well) that was visible by the end of 1982[70] was the "advent" of cyclosporine, the new immunosuppressive drug to which greatly improved survival rates of transplanted organs and patient-recipients were attributed. At this juncture, cyclosporine had ended its clinical trial period, had been approved by the Food and Drug Administration (FDA) for more general use, and had reached the zenith of the "wonder drug" phase of the therapeutic innovation cycle.

The third moratorium process we have charted is the most recent and complex of all. It concerns total artificial heart implants, especially the series of permanent implantations of the Jarvik-7 model performed by Dr. William C. DeVries.[71] In the relatively short time that has ensued since DeVries implanted the first such device in Barney Clark in December 1982, there have already been two moratorium phases in its clinical use. The first moratorium period began in August 1983, when DeVries submitted a revised protocol to the Institutional Review Board (IRB) of the University of Utah for permission to implant an artificial heart in a second patient. He had previously been authorized by the Utah IRB and the FDA to do a series of seven implants; however, the FDA had stipulated a case-by-case approval from the IRB. For reasons involving the substance of the protocol and also a web of medical and regulatory politics and policies, IRB approval for a second implant was not forthcoming until January 1984, and FDA approval was not granted until June 1984.

DeVries left the University of Utah to join the Humana Heart Institute's private group practice in Louisville, Kentucky, to continue his artificial heart work with funding from the Humana Corporation. A new round of regulatory approvals were required, and were accorded by the Audubon Hospital and the FDA in September and November 1984. On November 25, 1984, William Schroeder became the second patient on whom DeVries performed an implantation of a Jarvik-7 heart.

The next moratorium phase of the artificial heart endeavor began after DeVries's fourth implant, on Jack Burcham, in April 1985, and continues to the present (August 1987). It has two sources. First, an acceptable recipient for the fifth implant has not yet been found. The pool of candidates referred to DeVries's program has decreased markedly, due both to increased eligibility criteria for heart transplants and to the morbidity and deaths of his first four patients. Second, what might be called a "technical moratorium" was temporarily imposed on further implants by the FDA, while they reviewed a revised investigational device exemption (IDE) protocol that Symbion, the manufacturer of the Jarvik-7 heart, was required to submit after the FDA's Circulatory System Devices Panel had held a special meeting in Washington, D.C., on December 20, 1985. On that occasion, testimony for and against the use of the artificial heart was heard. The purpose of the hearings—at which medical professional society and Symbion representatives testified, as well as DeVries and his colleagues—had been to determine whether or not to recommend a moratorium on permanent implants of the total artificial heart. The technical moratorium that followed lasted from late December 1985 to late February 1986, when the advisory panel unanimously recommended, and the FDA agreed, that permanent implants could "proceed, but with caution." Thus, the decision not to call a moratorium was a qualified one, and it involved even tighter FDA regulations.

One of the most striking observations that emerges from historical comparison of these moratoria is that the social system framework within which they have occurred has become progressively more elaborate, formally institutionalized, and more public over time. In this sense, the "stories" of the mitral valve and artificial heart moratoria seem light years apart. In contrast to Eliot Cutler's simple, self-initiated and self-executed moratorium, quietly communicated to fellow physicians in a single medical journal article, the starting and stopping of the artificial heart project has involved its principal physician-investigator, his colleagues in Salt Lake

City and Louisville, several hospitals and IRBs, two corporations (Humana and Symbion), the FDA, various regulatory statutes and numerous protocols, a bevy of "new" and "old" medical experts—including bioethicists and bioengineers—and continuous, detailed media coverage. These conditions are not unique to the artificial heart or to clinical moratoria. They represent widespread changes that have taken place more generally in the social organization and value climate of American medical research and care.

It is important, however, not to overlook the fact that despite the changed sociocultural context in which a clinical moratorium now occurs, the basic factors that underlie it, and that help to induce, deter, or terminate it, have remained essentially the same throughout the period of almost sixty years that the mitral valve, cardiac transplant, and artificial heart surgery episodes span. Irrespective of the particular historical circumstances under which they take place, the starting and stopping of clinical moratoria are generated by the medical, social, and moral responsibilities, uncertainties, dilemmas, and stresses that are inherent to the process of clinical investigation. Decisions about calling, and if called, ending a moratorium involve a dynamic set of interacting, formal and informal pressures and counterpressures. These forces are set into motion by the experimental procedure itself and the state-of-the-art factors surrounding it; by the physician-investigator, with his dual, often conflicting role obligations of conducting research on patients for whom he is also obliged to care for clinically; by the investigator's research team and hospital and the larger medical collegium to which he belongs; and by the lay public—via patient-subjects, their families, the mass media, the regulatory process, and the evocation of societal values and beliefs (such as cultural conceptions of the human heart).

Moratoria classically occur in the risky and uncertainty-ridden early stages of the movement of a new drug, device, or procedure from trials on laboratory animals to trials on patient-subjects. The human morbidity and mortality that this laboratory-to-clinic phase of medical research entails put the physician-investigator under strong professional and personal pressure to call a moratorium. But clinical moratoria take place only when the pressures on the research physician to desist from certain clinical trials on patients are greater than the counterpressures galvanized by scientific and therapeutic responsibilities to continue. Here, we come finally to a core attribute of the clinical moratorium "in any season." Within the limits of what the ethics of human experimentation permit them to do, clinical investigators are *obliged* to conduct research with patients in order to advance medical knowledge and technique, and bring them to bear on diseases that cannot otherwise be adequately prevented or treated. "If for some reason an investigator wishes to interrupt or roll back this process, as is the case when a physician would call a moratorium on his own or colleagues' work, there is a sense in which the burden of proof falls on him":

> For, when he invokes a moratorium, he challenges institutionalized values that work to keep the process of clinical research ongoing. . . . A call for a clinical moratorium, then, entails the seeking of legitimation for significant others temporarily to bring a halt to an otherwise obligatory research activity, on the grounds that this suspension will ultimately serve the values of clinical investigation better than continuing the trials in question.[72]

SOCIAL STRUCTURE AND ORGANIZATION
OF MODERN MEDICAL RESEARCH

The multiple persons, groups, and institutions involved in the artificial heart moratoria, as we have stated, are indicative of the complex social structural matrix within which modern medical research now proceeds.

The historical recency of this organizational framework and the magnitude of biomedical and social change that have brought it into being are vividly suggested by a mural portrait of Jules Bordet, a distinguished medical scientist who received the Nobel Prize for Medicine or Physiology in 1919,[73] at work in his turn-of-the-century laboratory. The mural, painted by Paul Delvaux, hangs in the Institut Jules Bordet in Brussels, internationally renowned as a center for cancer research and treatment. It depicts Bordet as an elderly man,

> white-haired and white-mustached, lean, erect, dignified, and elegant; clad in a dark suit, his vest properly buttoned over a white shirt and dark tie, white handkerchief neatly arranged in his jacket pocket, a small ribbon rosette of honor affixed to his buttonhole. He stands with hands in his trouser pockets, a solitary figure in the midst of the laboratory where so much of his work was done. The laboratory is a cluttered, but orderly and austere, white-tiled room, lit from overhead by three gas lamps. The tables, shelves, cupboards of the laboratory are filled with test tubes, glass beakers, and bottles of various sizes and shapes, syringes and pipettes. On a side counter there is a Bunsen burner on which a large white casserole with a tipsy black lid has been placed. The windowsill at one end of the laboratory contains two simple microscopes under bell jars, and another assortment of pipettes and test tubes in beakers. It is late evening. The shades of the windows have been raised, so that one sees the first sliver of a new moon rising over the tiled, gabled rooftops and tidy chimneys of traditional Belgian architecture.[74]

In short, the mural is a romantic portrait of a scientist of gentlemanly origins and demeanor, a dedicated solo investigator, equipped only with his individual talent and training and very simple tools, working in his laboratory at night, in the Louis Pasteur era of medicine.

Modern medical research differs from this Bordet image in many important respects. More than the type of building that houses it, the clothing and bearing of its investigators, and the equipment it employs have changed. Modern research is characterized by a progressive division of labor and professionalization. Anatomy, pathology, and bacteriology are no longer the reigning basic medical sciences. They have been displaced by cell biology, biochemistry, immunology, genetics, molecular biology, virology, and biophysics—the disciplines considered to be at the center of the "biological revolution" that has occurred since World War II. The staggering development of new knowledge, understanding, and techniques in these fields has been so fast and so abundant that it has necessitated increased specialization and superspecialization. It has also driven a sharper wedge between basic biological and clinical research and researchers, making it both more difficult for the clinical world to keep up with modern biological advances, and more imperative that they do so in order to find ways to apply them to preventive, diagnostic, and therapeutic medicine.

The lone researcher has become an exceedingly rare phenomenon. Increased knowledge, specialization, and the intricacy and expense of biomedical technology usually require that research be conducted by teams of investigators, as a cooperative enterprise. Even in a relatively small-scale research organization, a "critical mass" of persons who have different training, competence, and experience is needed to insure that the investigative work will be carried out with "enthusiasm, momentum, and effectiveness."[75] Here, for example, is the way that Dr. Albert E. Renold, Director of the Institut de Biochimie Clinique, at the University of Geneva in Switzerland, describes his team:

> Geographically, my country is small. Institutionally, my own laboratory is a small but rather independent part of the department of medicine. . . . It deals with experimental diabetes; the secretion and action of insulin and other hormones and their regulation; and the genetics, epidemiology, and pathogenesis of diabetes, especially in animals. My institution employs at any one time some 25 people in all, no more than 10 of whom are M.D.'s or Ph.D.'s, specializing in biology, biochemistry, or biophysics.[76]

Other members of Renold's Institute include specialized technicians, secretaries, a librarian, and a number of younger medical scientists of varied backgrounds in the field of experimental diabetes, metabolism, and endocrinology. The Institute's research is enhanced by collaboration with particular members of the departments of morphology, medicine, physiology, biochemistry, and molecular biology and microbiology at the University of Geneva and by regular and programmed contacts with groups of "similar orientation at the universities of Zurich, Basle, and Lausanne."[77] In addition, one or two foreign visiting professors work at the Institute each year, on sabbatical from their own institutions (mainly in the United States, Canada, Sweden, and New Zealand). The Institute also has a very close working relationship with several university research groups in the United States—especially with an American laboratory that is conducting experiments using a "common cell line" that they share with the Institute. Dr. Renold and his research director carry on daily telephone discussions with their colleagues in other cities and countries about their research ideas, procedures, findings, and problems.[78]

As the foregoing illustrates, the communication and collaboration between medical scientists can be formal, informal, or quasiformal (e.g., "regular programmed contacts"). It is also interdisciplinary, interinstitutional, interregional, and international. What is exchanged includes information, personnel, and *matériel* such as cell lines and biological reagents. The patterns of teamwork and collaboration that have developed are in part organized responses of scientists to their recognition that cooperation is essential to the conduct of modern research—to its sheer performance, its reliability and validity, its creativity, and to the speed as well as the content of its productivity. However, more than pragmatism and expediency are involved. Commitment to teamwork and collaboration across institutional, disciplinary, and national barriers is also based on the shared moral conviction that this is the "best" and most "correct" way for scientists and science to proceed. These beliefs are integrally connected with the values of universalism and collectivism, and the importance attached to them by the scientific community:

The 1970s were a time of change; the climate of research that had favored close relationships between the European and American scientific communities was under strain as national governments turned inward on both sides of the Atlantic. Budgets for science were tightening because of inflation and demands on the resources available in the public and private sectors of national economies.

We were—and still are—concerned over the apparent slow erosion of scientific ties and cooperation between the advanced scientific communities of the world. . . .

We became convinced that it was appropriate to review some of the contributions to the area of biomedical research that grew out of the post-World War II climate of scientific collaboration at the international level. We felt that a conference devoted to international cooperation in biomedical research would emphasize its value and highlight the necessity of maintaining collaborative relationships across national boundaries through long- and short-term exchanges of research scientists. We particularly felt the importance of making younger scientists aware of the value, for their own careers, of experience in a cultural environment different from the one in which they had received their training. We therefore proposed to the Fogarty International Center a conference entitled "The Role and Significance of International Cooperation in the Biomedical Sciences."[79]

Modern medical research is carried out in status-role complexes within university, government, and business organizations or in centers or institutes that are associated with these organizations. Research is subsidized by monies that come from university, government, and business sources, and from private and public foundations. How much and what sorts of research are done in these different settings, and under these different auspices, varies from field to field, country to country, and from one historical period to another. For example, in many Continental European societies, medical research is more concentrated in university settings and is more exclusively funded by the national government than is the case in American society. Or, to take another example: In the United States, "an unprecedented growth of close ties" between molecular biologists and business enterprises has occurred in recent years.[80] This is particularly true of biotechnology, because of the range of possible applications that these techniques promise to have in "the pharmaceutical and health care industries, in agriculture, in mining, and in certain aspects of the chemical industry such as waste management."[81] The relationships that have been established between academically based molecular biologists and business corporations encompass "the vast majority of [this scientific field's] leading practitioners," to a degree that involves the "whole discipline."[82]

In effect, a great deal of modern medical research is done in relatively large and differentiated team-like groups, located within still larger formal organizations that are bureaucratic in nature. To varying degrees, these structures accommodate the changing configurations of medical science, including the rise of new disciplines and subfields, and shifts in the content and scope of basic and applied goals. In addition, medical researchers are linked to one another by informal scientific and collegial exchanges, mutually read publications, and membership in loosely organized professional societies. These ties go beyond formal affiliation with a particular university, government office, or business firm. Thus, modern medical research is not coordinated or controlled by one centralized intellectual, political, or economic body, even though the organizations within which researchers do their work, and that support it, are interconnected through the overlapping statuses and roles that scientists occupy.

Social structural conditions that favor the florescence of original and productive modern scientific research are not identically or equally present in all societies. For instance, sociologist of science Joseph Ben-David has claimed that in the 1950s and 1960s such conditions were more fully realized in the United States than in any other society in the world. Medical research, along with other scientific investigation, was regarded "as a resource to be developed according to its immanent possibilities and to be marketed as widely and imaginatively as possible."[83] An "entrepreneurial . . . system of research and higher education" prevailed, "characterized by a large number of autonomous and competing organizations, the internal structures of which were flexibly adjusted to the changing requirements of scientific collaboration and division of labor."[84] The volume and variety of support for scientific research that these organizational arrangements helped to generate and the bold idealism as well as pragmatism that underlay them attracted many talented researchers from other countries. This further enhanced the originality of the scientific work done in the United States during that period and its prolific output.

In this connection, current organized efforts by the Japanese to "redesign institutions" in order to facilitate scientific creativity should be sociologically edifying to observe:

> Things are changing. Japanese policy-makers increasingly see Japan as having reached a stage of development where it is less able to base its policies on the experiences of others. They see a growing need for Japan to base its future economic development on the creation of new technologies. Moreover, they wish to change the image of Japan to one of a nation making original contributions to science and technology. A major thrust of policy has been to overcome several of the factors seen as contributing to Japan's lack of creativity. One area of discussion is reform of the education system, which is widely felt to stifle creativity. Business firms have been rapidly building new facilities for basic research and otherwise stepping up research spending at an impressive rate. Policies have been implemented by various government agencies to improve the linkages between universities, government research laboratories, and business. . . . Whether these efforts can succeed at turning a highly successful technology fast-follower into a highly successful technology [and science] creator is an open question.[85]

SOME SECONDARY PATTERNS: SCIENTIFIC RECOGNITION, PROPERTY, COMPETITION, AND PRIORITY

Out of the interaction between the ways that modern scientific work is organized, discoveries are made, and scientists are recognized and rewarded, a number of secondary patterns of scientific behavior have developed. These exist alongside the primary normative patterns that exemplify the core values of the scientific ethos. The secondary patterns are supplements to, and variants of, the ideal norms of science, structuring the way that those norms are put into action. Under certain conditions, as we shall see, rather than implementing and reinforcing the ideal norms of science, these secondary patterns can slide into structured forms of scientific deviance.

As Robert K. Merton has lucidly analyzed and stated, the intellectual and moral *raison de'être* of science and the scientist is to extend knowledge in a particular, certified, technical form:

> On every side the scientist is reminded that it is his role to advance knowledge, and his happiest fulfillment of that role, to advance knowledge greatly. This is only to say . . . that in the institution of science originality is at a premium. For it is through originality, in greater or smaller increments, that knowledge advances. When the institution of science works efficiently . . . recognition and esteem accrue to those who have best fulfilled their roles, to those who have made genuinely original contributions to the common stock of knowledge.[86]

Because of the institutionalized norms of "disinterestedness," "humility," and what Merton calls "the communism of intellectual property" in science,[87] "once he has made his contribution, the scientist no longer has exclusive rights of access to it.":

> It becomes part of the public domain of science. Nor has he the right of regulating its use by others by withholding it unless it is acknowledged as his. In short, property rights in science become whittled down to just this one: the recognition by others of the scientist's distinctive part in having brought the result into being.[88]

The institution of science has developed a system of rewards that are conferred on those who live up to its norms. One of these forms of recognition is eponymy: "the practice of affixing the name of the scientist to all or part of what he had found."[89] This is a prominent and pervasive cultural tradition in the medical sciences:

> In the medical sciences, . . . the attention of posterity is assured to the discoverer or first describer of parts of the body. . . . In medicine, also, eponymy registers the first diagnostician of a disease; . . . the inventor of diagnostic tests; . . . and the inventor of instruments used in research or practice. . . .[90]

There is "an iconography of fame in science,"[91] which includes medals, memberships and fellowships in certain academies and societies of science, honorary degrees and titles, and what is perhaps "the preeminent token of recognized achievement in science," the Nobel Prize.[92]

Being granted a patent for a discovery or invention is still another form of recognition and reward—one that lays claim to the discovery as the personal intellectual property of the investigator to whom the patent is given. Because it runs counter to the collectivistic and "communistic" values of science, most academic scientists feel ambivalent about applying for patents on their work, to an extent that strongly disinclines them to do so. The following event in the recent history of molecular biology illustrates this. It concerns the invention of the recombinant DNA ("gene-splicing") technique in 1973 by two molecular biologists, Stanley Cohen of Stanford University and Herbert Boyer of the University of California at San Francisco. This technique made it possible for biologists to manipulate DNA molecules of living organisms with some precision. Specific segments of DNA could now be cut out of one organism's gene set and inserted into that of another. Multiple copies of a particular gene or its protein product could be made by inserting the relevant piece of DNA into bacteria and allowing the bacterial cells to grow, divide, and reproduce. Cohen and Boyer had no thought of patenting this important technique, which has become basic to what is now termed "genetic engineering":

> Cohen even resisted the suggestion of the Stanford University patent officer to do so. . . . "My initial reaction . . . was to question whether basic research of this type could or should be patented and to point out that our work had been dependent on a number of earlier discoveries by others," Cohen explain[ed]. . . . Finally persuaded that a patent would be to their universities' benefit, Cohen and Boyer agreed to let their institutions apply for one, but stipulated that they not receive the inventor's share of any royalties. Cohen assigned his share to a fund for supporting postdoctoral researchers. Boyer also assigned his share to the university. . . .[93]

The issue of patents and of molecular biologists' attitudes toward them is not only highly relevant because of the pressures of commercialization[94] to which their field's involvement with industry exposes them. It also has profound jurisprudential, philosophical, and existential implications concerning the nature of the altered forms of life that result from gene-splicing techniques, their relationship to the scientists who manipulated them into being, and their implications for the larger human community. What are these microorganisms? Are they living parts of nature, and thus belong to everyone and no one? Or is there any sense in which these living organisms are patentable property? If so, do they belong to the scientist who caused them to happen? Should he or she be recognized as a patent holder, who has special property rights with regard to these "new forms of life?"

In the case of *Diamond* v. *Chakrabarty*, in a 5 to 4 decision handed down on June 16, 1980, the United States Supreme Court ruled that such a microorganism is indeed "patentable subject matter."[95] The case involved microbiologist Ananda M. Chakrabarty, who in 1972 filed a patent application, assigned to the General Electric Company by which he was employed, in which he asserted 36 claims related to his "invention of a bacterium from the genus Pseudomonas." This bacterium, capable of simultaneously breaking down several components of crude oil, was believed to have significant value for the treatment of oil spills. The case was appealed by the Federal Government to the Supreme Court after the Court of Customs and Patent Appeals awarded a patent to Dr. Chakrabarty in 1979. The majority opinion of the Supreme Court, written by Chief Justice Warren E. Burger, justified the patentability of the new bacterium on the following grounds:

> The question before us in this case is a narrow one of statutory interpretation requiring us to construe 35 U.S.C. §101 which provides:
> "Whoever invents or discovers any new and useful process, machine, manufacture, or composition of matter, or any new and useful improvement thereof, may obtain a patent therefor, subject to the conditions and requirements of this title."
> Specifically, we must determine whether respondent's micro-organism constitutes a "manufacture" or "composition of matter" within the meaning of the statute. . . .

In choosing such expansive terms as "manufacture" and "composition of matter," modified by the comprehensive "any," Congress plainly contemplated that the patent laws would be given wide scope. The Patent Act of 1793 . . . embodied Jefferson's philosophy that "ingenuity should receive a liberal encouragement."

This is not to suggest that §101 has no limits or that it embraces every discovery. The laws of nature, physical phenomena, and abstract ideas have been held not patentable. . . . Thus, a new mineral discovered in the earth or a new plant found in the wild is not patentable subject matter. Likewise, Einstein could not patent his celebrated law that $E = mc^2$; nor could Newton have patented the law of gravity. Such discoveries are "manifestations of . . . nature, free to all men and reserved exclusively to none."

Judged in this light, respondent's micro-organism plainly qualifies as patentable subject matter. His claim is not to a hitherto unknown natural phenomenon, but to a nonnaturally occurring manufacture or composition of matter—a product of human ingenuity "having a distinctive name, character [and] use.". . .[T]he patentee has produced a new bacterium with markedly different characteristics from any found in nature and one having the potential for significant utility. His discovery is not nature's handiwork, but his own; accordingly it is patentable subject matter under §101.[96]

Even when such metaphysically laden issues as the nature and ownership of a bacterium that was "produced by the human ingenuity" of a scientist are not involved, the question of ascertaining whether a discovery is a particular investigator's "handiwork" is rarely a simple one.[97] As microbiologist Stanley Cohen stressed, the work on recombinant DNA that he and Herbert Boyer did together, like all scientific research, was "dependent on a number of earlier discoveries by others."[98] Because their work as a "team of two" identified the role that each played in the development of gene-splicing, it did not present the same order of difficulty that larger-scale research projects can pose.

The increasing extent to which present-day scientific research takes place in sizable teams of highly specialized and intricately organized workers "not only makes problematic the evaluation of contributions by [the scientific workers] *themselves.*"[99] In addition, the question of which scientists should be credited and rewarded for having made a particular discovery is compounded by what Merton terms "the strategic fact of the multiple and independent appearance of the same scientific discovery."[100] Merton goes so far as to say that "the pattern of independent multiple discoveries in science is . . . the dominant pattern" of scientific development, and that "it is the singletons—discoveries made only once in the history of science—that are the residual cases, requiring special explanation."[101] Multiple discoveries abound because they are the logical and sociological outgrowth of the process by which science develops: through "the incremental accumulation of knowledge, the sustained social interaction between [scientists], and the methodical use of [codified] procedures of inquiry. . . . Once the needed antecedent conditions obtain, discoveries are offshoots of their time, rather than turning up altogether at random."[102] This means that not only are there clustering and convergence in the phenomena and problems that scientists in a given field are investigating, but also that simultaneous independent discovery is a frequent happening. On an individual level, this seems to be especially true of the greatest, most fecund scientists, who are "involved in a multiplicity of multiples,"[103] (that is, in a considerable number of independent discoveries that are also made by others). On a collective level, the same phenomenon is characteristic of whole fields. In a so-called "hot" area of science like molecular biology, with its great density of scientists rapidly producing so many significant discoveries, the rate of multiple discoveries is likely to be particularly high.

The socioscientific conditions that foster multiple discoveries also are conducive to scientific competition. The fact that different scientists, working in differing places on similar problems, often come up with the same results, can fuel competition between them as well as provide the reliability and validity checks that are essential to the establishment of scientific knowledge. In turn, that competition can spark another closely related phenomenon: the occurrence of disputes over priority of scientific discovery. Priority disputes have taken place so frequently in the history of science that, Robert K. Merton alleges, "[t]hey have practically become an integral part of the social relations between scientists."[104] Although "[t]he bunching of similar or identical discoveries in science" is an "*occasion*" for disputes over priority, Merton goes on to say, it is "not their *cause* or their *grounds*."[105] Rather, he contends, "these conflicts are largely a consequence of the institutional forms of science itself":[106]

> The great frequency of struggles over priority . . . result[s] . . . from the institution of science, which defines originality as a supreme value and thereby makes recognition of one's originality a major concern. When this recognition of priority is either not granted or fades from view, the scientist loses his scientific property. . . . It may be that [the] concentration of the numerous rights ordinarily bound up in other forms of property into the one right of recognition by others helps produce the great concentration of affect that commonly characterizes disputes over priority. Often, the intensity [of a scientist's] affect seems disproportionate to the occasion. . . . This same concentration of property-rights into the one right of recognition may also account for the deep moral indignation expressed by scientists when one of their number has had his rights to priority denied or challenged. Even though they have no personal stake in the particular episode, they feel strongly about the single property-norm and the expression of their hostility serves the latent function of reaffirming the moral validity of this norm.[107]

The "great concentration of affect" of which Merton writes is intensified by the characteristically "deep" and often "agitated ambivalence" of scientists toward priority.[108] The ambivalence is as sociological as it is psychological.[109] It is triggered by two potentially incompatible ideal values of science: on the one hand, "the value of originality, which leads scientists to want their priority to be recognized," and on the other hand, "the value of humility, which leads them to insist on how little they have been able to accomplish."[110] The "tension between these kindred values . . . creates an inner conflict" among scientists who "have internalized both of them."[111] Such torn inner feelings can make priority disputes all the more harsh and ugly when they erupt and become public.

One of the bitterest priority disputes in recent decades was the battle over who should be given credit for discovering and identifying the virus identified as the cause of AIDS, and over who should be accorded the patent rights and royalties on the antibody blood test to detect the AIDS virus. The chief actors in this dispute were two eminent scientists—Robert C. Gallo and Luc Montagnier—and the world-famous medical institutes with which they are associated—the National Institutes of Health (NIH) in Bethesda, Maryland, and the Pasteur Institute in Paris. Gallo is the head of the laboratory of tumor and cell biology at the NIH's National Cancer Institute; Montagnier is the Pasteur Institute's chief cancer virologist.

The dispute between the United States and French teams also involved a series of legal actions between NIH's parent agency, the Department of Health and Human Services (HHS), and the Pasteur Institute over patent claims for the blood serum antibody test kit and techniques for growing the AIDS virus in permanent cell lines. After a series of patent filings, suits and counter-suits, and extensive United States-French negotiations from 1983–1987, the legal issues were settled in March 1987. The devastating import of the AIDS epidemic and the at-once nationalistic and universalistic fervor involved in efforts to deal with it were signified by the fact that the settlement was jointly announced in Washington, D.C. by the President of the United States and the Prime Minister of France on March 31:

> Under a legal agreement dated 30 March 1987, HHS and the Pasteur will share rights to the patent, and Robert Gallo . . . and his colleagues and Luc Montagnier . . . and his colleagues will be recognized as joint inventors of the AIDS antibody test-kit assay. . . .
>
> A key part of the settlement is the establishment of an AIDS foundation [whose trustees include Montagnier, Gallo, and the directors of the Pasteur Institute and NIH]. HHS and the Pasteur are to contribute to the foundation 80% of the antibody test royalties they receive from 1 January 1987 to 27 May 2002. The foundation money is to be used for research on AIDS and other retroviruses.[112]

The strong feelings surrounding this priority dispute were intensified by several factors. To begin with, the scientific characterization of the AIDS virus and the development of rapid, effective methods of screening for it bear directly on the search for ways to treat and prevent a frightening and lethal epidemic disease.

> Few diseases in modern times have raised such fears and uncertainties as the acquired immune deficiency syndromes (AIDS) and the malignancies, infections, and brain damage that can accompany it. In little more than five years AIDS has grown from a clinical oddity to a virtual epidemic, half of whose victims already have died, and the vast majority of whom will be dead within three years of their seeking medical attention. At the same time, stunning successes in the sciences of molecular biology and epidemiology have led to discovery and description in intricate detail of the virus that causes AIDS and the major pathways of its spread. But medical science has not yet been able to create a vaccine against the virus or a drug that can prevent or quell infection by it.[113]

Second, the potential royalties from the sale of blood test kits that have been developed for detecting the AIDS virus are uncommonly high, given their widespread use to routinely screen blood donations for the presence of the AIDS virus and to screen at-risk individuals or population groups. In addition, chauvinistic French and American national sentiments have been evoked by this dispute.

The still-unfolding story of this priority controversy is replete with more events and issues of relevance to the sociology of medicine and science than can be described and analyzed here.[114] There are, however, two more phenomena integral to it that deserve mention, in part because they are related to important scientific patterns discussed earlier in this chapter.

One of the features of the relations that existed between Gallo, Montagnier, and their colleagues before the controversy erupted that complicated the dispute, both scientifically and emotionally, is the fact that throughout the whole 1982 to 1985 period, when the two teams were intently working on identifying the AIDS virus and developing blood tests for detecting it, they had close and continuous working relations with each other. Their cooperation involved numerous forms of exchange. For example, Jean-Claude Chermann, a key member of Montagnier's group, who defined Gallo as "a good friend," called him in January 1983 to ask for reagents to test whether the virus that the Pasteur group had isolated was the same HTLC-I retrovirus (human T-cell leukemia virus) that Gallo had isolated and thought might be involved in AIDS:[115]

> Gallo "sent the reagents immediately." The virus did not react with monoclonal antibodies to the core protein of HTLV-I, indicating that it was a different virus. . . . The Pasteur group did some initial characterization of their virus. . . . Montagnier wrote up the results and sent a copy of the paper to Gallo in April "to ask his opinion and, if he thought it was OK, to transmit it to *Science*." Gallo called to say it was OK, but suggested some modifications, including adding a phrase stating that the new virus appears to be a member of the HTLV family. . . . Montagnier agreed to the change but the phrase has since come back to haunt him in a subsequent dispute over the naming of the virus. . . .
>
> [I]n the summer of 1983, an exchange took place between Gallo and Montagnier that would later figure prominently in the patent dispute and the rumors circulating in the scientific community. On 17 July, Montagnier attended a meeting of the National Cancer Institute ad hoc AIDS task force and he brought with him a sample of supernatant from his LAV [lymphadenopathy-associated virus] culture. Gallo says no reverse transcriptase activity could be detected in the sample, and Mikulas Popovic, a cell biologist in Gallo's lab, says he tried twice to infect fresh lymphocytes but failed. Popovic says he called Montagnier at home to tell him.
>
> Montagnier sent a second sample of supernatant on 23 September. . . . By this time [February 1984], [the] Centers for Disease Control (CDC) were cooperating closely with the French group and had confirmed many of their results. CDC researchers had also developed an antibody test using a sample of LAV sent from the Pasteur Institute in February, and in the spring of 1984 the three tests were indirectly compared. . . . [S]ome 170 serum samples were sent blind to all three labs [the Gallo, Pasteur and CDC groups]. . . .
>
> Gallo went to the Pasteur Institute to lecture on HTLV-I and HTLV-II, and in a private meeting afterwards told Montagnier and Chermann of his results. "I came back to the United States happy, confident, and feeling one of the best feelings I have had," Gallo recalls.
>
> Within a short time, however, these good feelings were soured by the mounting controversy over patents and priority.[116]

Through these and other formal and informal, personal and impersonal modes of communication and collaboration that are generic to the social structure and value system within which modern scientific research proceeds, Gallo, Montagnier, and their teams both aided and competed with each other's work. Their intermingling contributed to the priority dispute, and also made it more painful.

Part of the March 1987 legal settlement between the Pasteur Institute and the Department of Health and Human Services involved an effort to resolve the priority dispute by sorting out the contributions of Montagnier and Gallo's groups in the characterization of the virus and the development of the antibody test. This was accomplished, in part, by bringing in an eminent third party, Dr. Jonas Salk, discoverer of the Salk polio vaccine and himself no stranger to priority disputes:

> As part of the settlement, Gallo and Montagnier signed a chronology that highlights important findings in AIDS research. "The chronology is fair and substantive," said Gallo. "We didn't have any real disagreements about it." Jonas Salk . . . played a key role in constructing the chronology. "He really helped catalyze the effort," Gallo said.[117]

The second phenomenon that merits attention is the dispute that arose over naming the AIDS virus. This nomenclature controversy was a major item of contention between the Gallo and Montagnier groups. As science writer Colin Norman perceptively indicated: "Part of this contest is symbolic: whoever gets to name the virus will be broadly emphasized as its discoverer. But a legitimate scientific issue [was] at stake as well in determining how the virus should be classified."[118] The various names devised by Gallo's group centered on their contention that the AIDS virus is a variant of, or has important characteristics in common, with the human T-cell leukemia virus (HTLV), discovered in Gallo's laboratory in the late 1970s. Thus, the different viruses they isolated were successively named HTLV-I, HTLV-II, and HTLV-III. Gallo designated the AIDS retrovirus as HTLV-III and argued that this whole family should be called human T-lymphotropic viruses. The names employed by Montagnier's group were based on the premise that the virus they isolated is not related to HTLVs, but is more like viruses that belong to the so-called lentvirus family. To distinguish "their" virus from Gallo's HTLVs, they named it lymphadenopathy-associated virus, or LAV. They later settled on the term lymphadenopathy/AIDS virus, which has the same acronym (LAV) as their original choice.

A nomenclature subcommittee of thirteen scientists was convened early in 1985 by the International Committee on the Taxonomy of Viruses, and charged with the task of reconciling these differences by formulating an appropriate alternative to HTLV-III, LAV, and also to AIDS-associated retrovirus (ARV), designated by Jay A. Levy and his colleagues of the University of California at San Francisco. Gallo, Montagnier, and Jay Levy were appointed to the subcommittee. On May 1, 1986, the subcommittee published the final results of their deliberations in the correspondence section of *Nature*, in the form of a letter co-signed by eleven of its thirteen members.[119] (The same letter was printed in the Letters to the Editor section of the May 9, 1986 issue of *Science*.) The two persons who had refused to sign the letter were Robert Gallo and Max Essex of the Harvard University School of Public Health.

"We propose that the AIDS retroviruses be officially designated as the human immunodeficiency viruses," the subcommittee's letter began, "to be known in abbreviated form as HIV." From there, it went on to present the underlying reasoning on which this proposal was based:

MEDICAL SCIENCE AND MEDICAL RESEARCH   213

1. The name should conform to common nomenclature for retroviruses, beginning with the host species ("human"), ending with "virus," and containing a word that denotes a major (though not the only) pathogenetic property of the prototypic members of the group ("immunodeficiency"). . . .
2. Though the name should clearly link the viruses to the disease with which they are associated, it should not incorporate the term "AIDS," which many clinicians urged us to avoid.
3. The name should be readily distinguished from all existing names for this group of viruses and has been chosen without regard to priority of discovery.
4. The name should be sufficiently distinct from the names of other retroviruses to imply an independent virus species, a group of isolates that can presumably exchange genetic information readily with each other but not with members of other known retrovirus species. These other species include the human T-cell leukemia viruses (for example, HTLV-1 and HTLV-2), which will continue to be named according to a convention adopted by several leading investigators in September 1983. . . .
5. Retroviruses isolated from subhuman primates and found to be genetically related and biologically similar to HIV's should be designated as immunodeficiency viruses of the appropriate host species (for example, simian immunodeficiency virus [SIV] or African green monkey immunodeficiency virus [AGMIV].
6. Because HIV isolates are numerous and display considerable genetic heterogeneity, particularly in the *env* gene, it will be necessary for each laboratory to assign subspecies designations to their isolates. We recommend that each laboratory adopt a code with geographically informative letters and sequential numbers to identify their isolates (for example, the 42nd isolate at the University of Chicago could be described as HIV [CHI-42]). . . .
7. Any future isolates of human retroviruses with clear but limited relationship to isolates of HIV (for example, more than 20 percent but less than 50 percent nucleic acid sequence identity) should not be called HIV unless there are compelling biological and structural similarities to existing members of the group.

The subcommittee's letter ended with the "hope that this proposal will be adopted rapidly by the research community working with viruses." However, in a note printed just below it, the Editor of *Nature* referred to an earlier version of the letter asking that "journals publishing it should make the name HIV a condition for the publication of research articles," and went on to politely reject that suggestion. "There is much to be said for the general use of a common name," the Editor wrote, "while the present proposal seems to have much to commend it. . . . Nevertheless, *Nature* will continue its present practice of allowing its contributors to use whatever nomenclature seems to them appropriate, while reserving the right to add a clarifying note if this should seem necessary to avoid confusion." (*Science* also declined to accept the subcommittee's initial suggestion that "the editors of all journals" printing their letter "insist that published papers conform to these rules," and deleted this request from the version of the letter that it published in its May 9, 1986 issue.)

The work of the International Subcommittee on the Taxonomy of Viruses and their official proposal notwithstanding, the nomenclature dispute over the AIDS virus has not ended. It is a particularly complex and important example of how social, cultural, historical, and psychological factors influence the technical language of science, its content, acceptance, and use. And it illustrates, with considerable drama, that there is often much more in a scientific name than pure science.

MISBEHAVIOR AND DEVIANCE IN SCIENCE

Robert K. Merton concluded his famous essay on "Priorities in Scientific Discovery" by underlining how the institutional values of science that emphasize achievement, originality, and their recognition, which do so much to advance knowledge and which also impel scientists to press their claims to priority of discovery, "can generate a tendency toward sharp practices just inside the rules of the game [of science], or sharper practices far outside [of them]":[120]

> The culture of science is, in this measure, pathogenic. It can lead scientists to develop an extreme concern with recognition which is in turn the validation by peers of the worth of their work. Contentiousness, self-assertive claims, secretiveness lest one be forestalled, reporting only the data that support an hypothesis, false charges of plagiarism, even the occasional theft of ideas and, in rare cases, the fabrication of data—all these have appeared in the history of science and can be thought of as deviant behavior in response to a discrepancy between the enormous emphasis in the culture of science upon original discovery and the actual difficulty many scientists experience in making an original discovery. In this situation of stress, all manner of adaptive behaviors are called into play, some of these being beyond the mores of science.[121]

The range and sources of deviant behaviors on the part of scientists are more varied than those cited by Merton. Although he identifies such deviance with the cultural dynamics of science itself, he alleges that it occurs rarely rather than frequently. How often violations of prescribed or proscribed values and norms of science actually do take place is, of course, difficult to ascertain. Since illicit practices are involved, they are likely to be consciously or unconsciously hidden or disguised by their perpetrators in order to avoid detection. The Merton essay, written and published in the 1950s, antedates by almost twenty years the extensive reporting and discussion of various types of misconduct in science that has characterized the 1970s and 1980s. Much more visible and audible attention than in the past is now being paid to scientific wrong-doing: by the media, editors of professional journals, academic and research administrators, funding agencies, political and regulatory bodies, the general public, and scientists themselves. A small but deeply troubling series of flamboyant cases of scientific fraud, committed in prestigious institutions by well-regarded biomedical scientists, have come into public view. These cases have been powerful catalysts of the increased awareness of scientific deviance and concern about it.[122] This raised consciousness makes it even harder to determine whether deviance in science has become more prevalent. For in this connection, as in scientific research, we tend to see what we look for and to disregard what we do not seek.

A sociological case description and analysis of the spectrum of borderline to flagrantly deviant practices in which scientists have engaged is beyond the scope of this book. We will confine ourselves to some brief comments on several patterns that are notable in the newer materials on scientific deviance that are now in the public domain. To begin with, as noted, the types of misconduct are more varied than the Mertonian paradigm suggests. As sociologists Paul and Peter Meadows have commented, "so many different accounts are bringing to the surface so many variants of the pattern of . . . deception that . . . [w]e are now being confronted with the high likelihood of *companies of deviance* in the house of Science."[123]

Among the more subtle forms of deviance are those that have to do with the technical nuances in the way that scientific data are collected and processed: forms of scientific dishonesty that the "irascible genius," Charles Babbage (1792–1871)— mathematics professor at Cambridge University and prophetic visionary of the electronic computer—referred to as "trimming" and "cooking."[124] These modes of smoothing the irregularities in data or retaining only the results that fit the theory are insidious. They are not as flagrant as forging data, and can all too easily be trivialized, rationalized, or routinized. They may grow out of the relatively innocent misuse of the sophisticated equipment and methods of modern science as, for example, when researchers rely on computer results without adequately understanding the algorithms the computer is using, or when they are too trusting about the software involved. The "trimming" and "cooking" may also be artifacts of some of the unrecognized, magico-scientific practices that are quasi-institutionalized in a field, such as the "accentuate-the-positive" tendency to notice and report the favorable properties of a promising new drug before its side effects and limitations are identified.

Another, quite different area in which reported or suspected incidents of misconduct in science seem to have increased concerns the protection of human subjects and the welfare of laboratory animals who participate in biomedical research. In recent years, there has been enough disquietude over the ethicality of the conditions under which such research is conducted, and a sufficient number of cases of alleged or actual misconduct in these areas, for all federal entities involved in human or animal research (most notably the Department of Health and Human Services/Public Health Services/National Institutes of Health complex), to develop formal policies, rules, procedures, and offices to govern and monitor research, and also to investigate and handle the cases of possible wrong-doing that arise. We will return to this topic in the next chapter.

One of the most consistent patterns detected in cases of scientific deviance is the role played by the large organizational structures within which modern research is conducted in the genesis of misbehavior and its subterfuge. In a number of incidents, for example, the principal investigators or directors of research of large teams did not have the kind of direct, knowledgeable, and supervisory relationship to the work of more junior members of the group who falsified data, a relationship that could have prevented such acts from occurring in the first place, nipped them in the bud, or detected them quickly once they happened. Another recurring phenomenon is associated both with the culturally induced drive for scientific success and recognition, and the organizational framework within which scientific work and careers unfold. It emanates from the magnitude of the scientific literature, the pressure to publish, the relationship between senior and junior colleagues, and coauthorship practices:

> For many [researchers] . . . a more immediate objective is to establish credit—often defined as a long list of publications—which helps in the continual struggle to secure government grants and win academic promotion. . . . [T]he quantity of scientific papers listed on a curriculum vitae can . . . be more important than their quality.

One effect of the publishing game is an extraordinary expansion of the literature. According to the *British Medical Journal,* there are currently in the world 8000 journals devoted to biology and medicine alone. The clutter has hindered the checking mechanisms of science and lessened the deterrent for would-be cheats and plagiarists. . . .

A more subtle way of expanding one's share of credit in the publishing game is to coauthor many papers. A serious type of coauthor abuse, for example, is seen in the large laboratory where a senior scientist provides little work of inspiration, but manages nonetheless to walk away with a large measure of the credit for the efforts of his underlings. Today, it is not uncommon for the name of a prominent biomedical lab chief to appear on 500 or 600 papers produced in large measure by his juniors. A disheartening aspect of this publishing game is the impact the research mill sometimes has on the attitude of young researchers. The dislocation between work and reward makes large labs a breeding ground for cynicism—an atmosphere that encourages finagling of data or wholesale invention of results.[125]

The business milieu of which fields such as molecular biology and biotechnology have become part has also been conducive to serious deviations from collegially correct research that is properly conducted and reported. Commercial competition and secrecy have led to aberrations such as those associated with the programming of bacteria to synthesize insulin:

A team at Harvard, the young biotechnology company Genentech, and researchers at the Department of Biochemistry and Biophysics at the University of California at San Francisco (UCSF) all set out to isolate the insulin gene in rats, with the UCSF team establishing a nonprofit corporation known as the California Institute for Genetic Research. It happened that Genentech's Herbert Boyer was associated with another laboratory in the same department at UCSF. With commercial pressures added to the normal desire to publish first, the secrecy maintained by the UCSF team grew to conspicuous levels. . . . Relations were not improved when the UCSF insulin team held a press conference in May 1977 to announce their success; their departmental colleagues resented the fact that they too were hearing the news for the first time.

Colleagues' feelings were not the only casualty of the rush to success. It later emerged that the successful team had been in such a hurry that they had breached government safety rules on gene-splicing by using certain biological material before it had been certified as safe. Moreover, misleading entries were made in the laboratory logbook to conceal this fact. When the incident was reported to the departmental committee charged with overseeing recombinant DNA safety procedures, the ensuing investigation failed to bring to light any facts except those critical of the National Institutes of Health, the agency that had instituted the guidelines.[126]

What the investigative attitudes and outcome referred to above dramatically reveal is that the social controls for detecting, preventing, exposing, and penalizing scientific misconduct have been seriously deficient, inadequate, and, in their own way, ethically flawed. Nowhere is this more apparent than with regard to "whistleblowing"—a major mechanism of professional self-regulation through which colleagues draw attention to dishonest or unacceptable behavior by a scientist or group of scientists. Not only is this an interpersonally and morally difficult task from which many scientists shrink; it is also made more painful by the tendency of the research community to turn on whistle-blowers and raise questions about their motives and reputation, as if they were the wrongdoers. Both whistle-blower and accused face hostility from colleagues, attributions of disloyalty, blackballing, academic censure, dismissal, and lawsuits. It is hardly surprising that such experiences and fear of them further reduce the likelihood of whistle-blowing occurring, or of its effectiveness when it does take place.[127]

Beginning in the late 1960s, partly as a consequence of all the incidents of scientific deviance and the changed climate of professional and public opinion surrounding them, a whole new set of structural mechanisms for regulating scientific research, especially research with human subjects, have been set into place by scientific associations, journals, and academic and governmental bodies. A quite altered system of internal and external controls on the American scientific community now exists. These controls are still proliferating and being tested and monitored as they develop. Their evolution is a phenomenon of considerable importance to the sociology of science, medicine, and the professions, one that social scientists with competence in these fields should have a special interest in studying.

This chapter has concentrated on the constituent components of science, the process of scientific investigation, and the roles and experiences of researchers, with special reference to medical science and medical research. It seems fitting to close with a reminder that, in contrast to work in the physical sciences, medical research—in particular, clinical investigation—involves human subjects, many of whom are patients, their families, and teams of caretakers that include nurses and other health professionals and personnel, along with doctors. Without them, and the "experiment perilous," "courage to fail" kinds of communities that they characteristically create out of their shared situation, their hopes in science, and their willingness to give themselves to it, a great deal of the modern medical research that takes place, and the knowledge that comes from it, could not go forward.

NOTES

1. Robert K. Merton, "Foreword," in Bernard Barber, *Science and the Social Order* (Glencoe, Ill.: The Free Press, 1952), p. xxii. One of the few observation-based studies of a biological research laboratory, which combines philosophical, sociological, and literary criticism approaches, was conducted at The Salk Institute for Biological Studies in 1975–77 by a French philosopher; his work was subsequently written up in collaboration with a British sociologist; (Bruno Latour and Steve Woolgar, *Laboratory Life: The Construction of Scientific Facts*, 2nd ed. (Princeton, N.J.: Princeton University Press, 1986).

2. Jean Landrière, *La Science, Le Monde et La Foi*. (Tournai, Belgium: Casterman, 1972), passim.

3. Renée C. Fox, *Experiment Perilous* (Glencoe, Ill.: The Free Press, 1959); Renée C. Fox,"The Sociology of Modern Medical Research," in *Asian Medical Systems: A Comparative Study*, ed. Charles Leslie (Berkeley: University of California Press, 1976), pp. 106–7.

4. Judith P. Swazey and Renée C. Fox, "The Clinical Moratorium: A Case Study of Mitral Valve Surgery," in *Experimentation With Human Subjects*, ed. Paul A. Freund (New York: George Braziller, 1970), p. 315.

5. Robert K. Merton, "Priorities in Scientific Discovery: A Chapter in the Sociology of Science," in *The Sociology of Science* (Chicago: University of Chicago Press,1973), pp. 286–324. This essay was originally published in *American Sociological Review*, 22, no. 6 (December 1957), 635–59.

6. Renée C. Fox, *Experiment Perilous, op. cit.*; Renée C. Fox and Judith P. Swazey, *The Courage to Fail: A Social View of Organ Transplants and Dialysis*, (Chicago: University of Chicago Press, 1975). 2nd Ed., revised.

7. Ilana Löwy, "Ludwik Fleck on the Social Construction of Medical Knowledge," unpublished paper. Fleck was a Polish-Jewish physician-scientist, with strong philosophical and sociological interests, who wrote pioneering studies on the impact of society on the genesis of medical knowledge, in the 1920s and 1930s. His works were rediscovered by historians, philosophers, and sociologists of science after the publication of Thomas Kuhn's book, *The Structure of Scientific Revolutions* (Chicago: University of Chicago Press, 1962), in which Kuhn cited Fleck's *Genesis and Development of Scientific Fact* as among the works that had influenced his own thought.

8. Robert K. Merton, "The Self-Fulfilling Prophecy," in *Social Theory and Social Structure* (Glencoe, Ill.: The Free Press, 1949), Chap. XI.

9. Bernard Barber and Renée C. Fox, "The Case of the Floppy-Eared Rabbits: An Instance of Serendipity Gained and Serendipity Lost," *American Journal of Sociology*, 64, no. 2 (September 1958), 129.

10. Fox and Swazey, *The Courage to Fail*, p. 40.

11. Fox, "The Sociology of Modern Medical Research," p. 103.

12. Robert K. Merton, "The Bearing of Empirical Research on Sociological Theory," in *Social Theory and Social Structure*, rev. (Glencoe, Ill.: The Free Press, 1957), pp. 103–8. The term "serendipity," coined by Horace Walpole in 1754, was first used by the physiologist Walter B. Cannon to refer to the chance component of research. See his *Way of an Investigator: A Scientist's Experiences in Medical Research* (New York: W. W. Norton and Co., Inc., 1945), Chap. VI, pp. 68–78.

13. Barber and Fox, "The Case of the Floppy-Eared Rabbits," p. 313.

14. Ibid., p. 324.

15. Renée C. Fox, "The Evolution of Medical Uncertainty," *Milbank Memorial Fund Quarterly/Health and Society*, 58, no. 1 (Winter 1980), 9.

16. Renée C. Fox, "Medical Evolution," in *Explorations in General Theory in Social Science: Essays in Honor of Talcott Parsons*, Vol. 2, eds. Jan J. Loubser and others (New York: The Free Press/Macmillan, 1976), p. 780.

17. For some pertinent empirical materials and illuminating discussion of culturally different conceptions of rationality, see *Modes of Thought: Essays on Thinking in Western and Non-Western Societies*, eds. Robin Horton and Ruth Finnegan (London: Faber & Faber, 1973).

18. Emiko Ohnuki-Tierney, *Illness and Culture in Contemporary Japan: An Anthropological View* (New York: Cambridge University Press, 1984), pp. 1, 50, 224–25, and passim.

19. Emiko Ohnuki-Tierney, "Cultural Transformations of Biomedicine in Japan–Hospitalization in Contemporary Japan," *International Journal of Technology Assessment in Health Care*, Vol. 2, no. 2 (1986), 231 and 240.

20. Ibid., p. 240.

21. Ohnuki-Tierney, *Illness and Culture in Contemporary Japan*, Chap. 2.

22. Renée C. Fox and David P. Willis, "Personhood, Medicine, and American Society," *Milbank Memorial Fund Quarterly/Health and Society*, 71, no. 1 (Winter 1983), 128.

23. Ilana Löwy, "Tissue Groups and Cadaver Kidney Sharing: Socio-Cultural Aspects of a Medical Controversy," *International Journal of Technology Assessment in Health Care*, 2, no. 2 (1986), 195-218. Reprinted by permission of Cambridge University Press, Publishers.

24. Ilana Löwy, "Tissue Groups and Cadaver Kidney Sharing," pp. 197-198.

25. Ibid., p. 213.

26. The discussion of the value system of modern science that follows is indebted to: Bernard Barber, *Science and the Social Order* (Glencoe, Ill.: The Free Press, 1952), Chap. III; Robert K. Merton, *Social Theory and Social Structure* (Glencoe, Ill.: The Free Press, 1949), Chap. XVI; and Talcott Parsons, *The Social System* (Glencoe, Ill.: The Free Press, 1951), Chap. VIII. See also Fox, "The Sociology of Modern Medical Research," pp. 104–6.

27. Talcott Parsons, *Sociological Theory and Modern Society* (New York: Free Press, 1967), pp. 225–26.

28. I formulated this concept in a seminar paper that I coauthored with Miriam Massey Johnson in the 1950-1951 academic year when we were graduate students at Harvard. It was not until 1963

that I used it in a publication about one of the thematic foci of the socialization of medical students. Harold I. Lief and Renée C. Fox, "Training for 'Detached Concern' in Medical Students," in *The Psychological Basis of Medical Practice*, eds. Harold, Victor F. and Nina R. Lief (New York: Harper and Row, 1963), pp. 12–35.

29. See Renée C. Fox, "Medical Scientists in a Château," *Science*, 136, (May 11, 1962), 476–83; and Renée C. Fox, "An American Sociologist in the Land of Belgian Medical Research," in *Sociologists at Work*, ed. Phillip E. Hammond (New York: Basic Books, 1964), 345–91.

30. Evelyn Fox Keller, *Reflections on Gender and Science* (New Haven, Conn.: Yale University Press, 1985).

31. Ibid., p. 174.

32. Quoted by Keller in *Reflections on Gender and Science*, p. 36.

33. Quoted by Keller in "Contending with a Masculine Bias in the Ideals and Values of Science," *The Chronicle of Higher Education* (October 2, 1985), p. 96.

34. Ibid p. 96.

35. Ibid.

36. Keller, *Reflections on Gender and Science*, p. 177.

37. Ibid., p. 158.

38. Albert Claude, "The Coming of Age of the Cell," *Science*, 189 (August 8, 1975), 434.

39. Steven Weinberg, "Origins," *Science*, 230, (October 4, 1985), 17–18.

40. Howard L. Kaye, *The Social Meaning of Modern Biology: From Social Darwinism to Sociobiology* (New Haven: Yale University Press, 1986), pp. 55–56; see his entire Chap. 2, "From Metaphysics to Molecular Biology."

41. Kaye, *The Social Meaning of Modern Biology*, p. 55.

42. Albert Claude, "The Coming of Age of the Cell," pp. 434–35. © The Nobel Foundation 1975. This article is the lecture that Claude delivered in Stockholm, Sweden, on December 12, 1974, when he shared the Nobel Prize for Physiology or Medicine with George Palade and Christian de Duve.

43. Evelyn Fox Keller, *A Feeling for the Organism: The Life and Work of Barbara McClintock* (San Francisco: W. H. Freeman and Company, 1983), p. 200.

44. Ibid., pp. 199, 201, and 204.

45. Ibid.

46. Ibid., pp. 198–200.

47. Keller, *Reflections on Gender and Science*, pp. 170–71.

48. Keller, *A Feeling for the Organism*, p. 200.

49. Keller, *Reflections on Gender and Science*, pp. 173–74.

50. Ibid.

51. Kaye, *The Social Meaning of Modern Biology*, p. 67.

52. "The logic of life" is the English-language title of François Jacob's book on "the history of heredity," originally published in French under the title "La logique du vivant." François Jacob, *The Logic of Life: A History of Heredity* (New York: Pantheon Books, 1973); François Jacob, *La logique du vivant* (Paris: Éditions Gallimard, 1970).

53. Bronislaw Malinowski, *Magic, Science, and Religion and Other Essays* (Glencoe, Ill.: Free Press, 1948), p. 70.

54. Fox, "The Sociology of Modern Medical Research," p. 107.

55. Fox, *Experiment Perilous*, pp. 82–85 and 246–47; Renée C. Fox, "The Human Condition of Health Professionals," Distinguished Lecturer Series, School of Health Studies (Durham: University of New Hampshire, 1980), pp. 28–30. See also the discussion of the "game of chance" in Chapter 4.

56. On theoretical grounds, we would hypothesize that such a "game of chance" is not exclusive to medical researchers, but also exists in the laboratories and field stations of other types of scientists who, like their medical counterparts, are faced with perennial problems of uncertainty, limitation, risk, and chance, and who have a strong emotional as well as intellectual vested interest in effectively and meaningfully coming to terms with these problems.

57. Renée C. Fox, Judith P. Swazey, and Elizabeth M. Cameron, "Social and Ethical Problems in the Treatment of End-Stage Renal Disease Patients," in *Controversies in Nephrology and Hypertension*, ed. Robert G. Narins, (New York: Churchill Livingstone, 1984), pp. 46–53.

The only other published case study I know made by sociologists of the "belated and un-even recognition" by physicians of the side effects of a new drug, and of "resistance to recog-nizing the severity of the problem," is Philip Brown's and Steven C. Funk's interesting article, "Tardive Dyskinesia: Barriers to the Professional Recognition of an Iatrogenic Disease," *Jour-nal of Health and Social Behavior*, 27, no. 2 (June 1986), 116–32. In this essay, Brown and Funk attribute the delay of psychiatrists in recognizing, acknowledging, and acting upon the dis-covery of the pervasive central nervous system side-effects of antipsychotic drugs primarily to various "structural elements of professional dominance." They emphasize the role played by the evolution of psychiatry toward "a stricter medical model, centered on pharmacological interven-tions," and within this framework, of "the dilemma of neuroleptic compounds [that] promise some benefits to psychotic patients, yet involve serious iatrogenic suffering."

Brown and Funk cite several other articles that refer to "the 'law of the new drug,' whereby soon after a compound is developed, it is hailed as a panacea, and few side effects are noticed. Then the pendulum swings in the opposite direction, and the opinion is widely held that the drug is toxic, and has limited clinical use." Finally, there is "an accumulation of evidence of serious adverse side effects together with the demonstration of much lesser effectiveness in con-trolled studies." Dilip V. Jeste and Richard J. Wyatt, *Understanding and Treating Tardive Dys-kinesia* (New York: Guilford Press, 1982); John B. McKinlay, "From 'Promising Report' to 'Standard Procedure': Seven Stages in the Career of a Medical Innovation," *Milbank Memorial Fund Quarterly/Health and Society*, 59 (1981), 374–411; Ingrid Waldron, "Increased Prescrib-ing of Valium, Librium, and Other Drugs: An Example of the Influence of Economic and Social Factors on the Practice of Medicine," *International Journal of Health Services*, 7, no. 1 (1977), 37–62.

Neither Brown and Funk, nor the authors they cite, refer to the role of anything like "scien-tific magic" in these "stages of the career" of a new drug.

58. Thomas E. Starzl and others, "Evolution of Liver Transplantation," *Hepatology*, 2, no. 5 (1982), 614.
59. Fox, Swazey, and Cameron, "Social and Ethical Problems in the Treatment of End-Stage Renal Disease Patients," p. 49.
60. Cultural factors seem to play a role in enhancing or tempering the optimism of the medical reports. In this connection, it is interesting to note that to a greater degree in British than in American journals, the optimism surrounding cyclosporine has been accompanied by appeals to caution.
61. Terry B. Strom and Rolf Loertscher, "Cyclosporine-Induced Nephrotoxicity" (Editorial), *New England Journal of Medicine*, 311, no. 11 (September 13, 1984), 728.
62. Byran D. Myers and others, "Cyclosporine-Associated Chronic Nephropathy," *New England Journal of Medicine*, 311, no. 11 (September 13, 1984), 704.
63. Renée C. Fox, "'It's the Same, but Different': A Sociological Perspective on the Case of the Utah Artificial Heart," in *After Barney Clark: Reflections on the Artificial Heart Program*, ed. Margery W. Shaw (Austin: University of Texas Press, 1984), p. 68.
64. Ibid., pp. 89–90 (Footnote 10).
65. Francis D. Moore, "Medical Responsibility for the Prolongation of Life," *Journal of the American Medical Association*, 206 (1968), 384–86.
66. Swazey and Fox, "The Clinical Moratorium," pp. 315–57.
67. Ibid.
68. Eliot C. Cutler and Claude S. Beck, "The Present Status of the Surgical Procedures in Chronic Valvular Disease of the Heart: Final Report of all Surgical Cases," *Archives of Surgery*, 18 (January 1929), 403–16.
69. Fox and Swazey, *The Courage to Fail*, Chap. 5, "The Heart Transplant Moratorium."
70. Lawrence K. Altman, "Transplants Are Surging as Survival Rates Improve," *The New York Times* (*Science Times* section), October 5, 1982, C1–C2.
71. Judith P. Swazey, Judith C. Watkins, and Renée C. Fox, "Assessing the Artificial Heart: The Clinical Moratorium Revisited," *International Journal of Technology Assessment in Health Care* 2, no. 3 (1986), 387-410.
72. Swazey and Fox, "The Clinical Moratorium," p. 348.

73. Jules Bordet's early studies showed that anti-microbic sera include two active substances, one existing before immunization (alexine), the other a specific antibody created by vaccination. Bordet introduced the method of diagnosing microbes by sera. In 1898, he discovered hemolytic sera and showed that they act on foreign blood by a mechanism comparable to that by which an anti-microbic serum acts on microbes. He also demonstrated that the reactions of all these sera are colloidal in nature. With Gengou, he cultivated *B. pertussis*, and laid the basis for the generally accepted opinion that this organism is the cause of whooping cough.

74. Fox, "The Sociology of Modern Medical Research," pp. 107–8.

75. A. E. Renold, "Planned Integration of International Visiting Fellows and Scientists: Enhancement of Morale, Productivity, and Impact in a Laboratory Concerned with Human Diabetes and its Animal Models," *Perspectives in Biology and Medicine*, 29, no. 3, Part 2 (Spring 1986), S217. (This paper is part of a special issue devoted to the proceedings of a 1983 NIH conference on "The Role and Significance of International Cooperation in the Biomedical Sciences.")

76. Ibid., p. S214.

77. Ibid., p. S216.

78. These details are based on observations I have made at Dr. Renold's Institute in Geneva.

79. Gaetano Salvatore and Howard K. Schachman, "Introduction," *Proceedings of the International Symposium on "The Role and Significance of International Cooperation in the Biomedical Sciences," Perspectives in Biology and Medicine*, 29, no. 3, Part 2 (Spring 1986), S2.

80. *The Science Business: Report of the Twentieth Century Fund Task Force on the Commercialization of Scientific Research* (New York: Twentieth Century Fund, Inc., 1984), p. 3. © 1984 The Twentieth Century Fund, New York.

81. Nicholas Wade, "The Tree of Knowledge," in *The Science Business*, p. 24.

82. Ibid., p. 23.

83. Joseph Ben-David, *Fundamental Research and the Universities* (Paris: Organization for Economic Cooperation and Development, 1968), p. 55.

84. Ibid., pp. 45–46.

85. Leonard Lynn, "Japanese Research and Technology Policy," *Science*, 233 (July 18, 1986), 297 and 300.

86. Robert K. Merton, "Priorities in Scientific Discovery," p. 293.

87. Robert K. Merton, "The Normative Structure of Science," in *Robert K. Merton: The Sociology of Science*, pp. 267–78. (This essay was originally published in "Science and Technology in a Democratic Order," *Journal of Legal and Political Sociology*, 1 (1942), 115–26; and later published as "Science and Democratic Social Structure," in Robert K. Merton, *Social Structure and Social Theory* (Glencoee, Ill.: Free Press, 1949), pp. 307–16.)

88. Merton, "Priorities in Scientific Discovery," pp. 294–95.

89. Ibid., p. 298.

90. Ibid., p. 300.

91. Ibid., p. 301.

92. Ibid.

93. Nicholas Wade, "The Erosion of the Academic Ethos," *The Science Business*, pp. 30–31.

94. Ibid.

95. Sidney A. Diamond, Commissioner of Patents and Trademarks, Petitioner, *v.* Ananda M. Chakrabarty et al., No. 79-136, 447 U.S. 303, 65 L.Ed.2d 144. Argued March 17, 1980. Decided June 16, 1980.

96. Diamond v. Chakrabarty, 100 *Supreme Court Reporter* 2204 (1980), pp. 2207–8.

97. Howard L. Kaye astutely points out that "the reductionistic world view of contemporary biology," as exemplified by the outlook of James Watson and Francis Crick, "has, in effect, been given legal status" by this Supreme Court decision, in refusing to "distinguish between animate and inanimate matter and thereby permit[ting] the patenting of engineered forms of life." Howard L. Kaye, "The Biological Revolution and its Cultural Context," *International Journal of Technology Assessment in Health Care*, 2, no. 2 (1986), 279.

98. Nicholas Wade, "The Erosion of the Academic Ethos," *op. cit.*, pp. 30–31.

99. Robert K. Merton, "Behavior Patterns of Scientists," in *Robert K. Merton: The Sociology of Science*, ed. Norman W. Storer (Chicago: University of Chicago Press, 1973), p. 332. (This essay was originally copublished in *American Scientist*, 58 (Spring 1969), 1–23, and *The American Scholar*, 38 (Spring 1969), 197–225.)

100. Robert K. Merton, "Singletons and Multiples in Science," in *Robert K. Merton: The Sociology of Science*, p. 352.

101. Ibid., p. 356.

102. Ibid., p. 349.

103. Ibid., p. 367.

104. Merton, "Priorities in Scientific Discovery," p. 289.

105. Ibid.

106. Ibid., p. 293.

107. Ibid., pp. 294–96.

108. Ibid., p. 307.

109. The concept of "sociological ambivalence" was first coined and developed by Robert K. Merton and Elinor Barber in their essays, "Sociological Ambivalence," in *Sociological Theory, Values, and Sociocultural Change: Essays in Honor of Pitirim A. Sorokin*, ed. Edward A. Tiryakian (New York: The Free Press of Glencoe, 1963), pp. 91–120.

110. Merton, "Priorities in Scientific Discovery," p. 305.

111. Ibid.

112. Deborah M. Barnes, "AIDS Patent Dispute Settled," *Science*, 236 (April 3, 1987), 17.

113. Samuel O. Thier, "Preface," *Mobilizing Against AIDS: The Unfinished Story of a Virus* (Cambridge, Mass.: Harvard University Press, 1986), p. vii.

114. For an outstanding series of articles about research on AIDS, including an excellent account of the priority disputes involved (based on interviews with dozens of scientists in the United States and Europe), see Colin Norman, "Congress Readies AIDS Funding Transfusion," *Science*, 230 (October 25, 1985), 418–19, "AIDS Virology: A Battle on Many Fronts," *Science*, 230 (November 1, 1985), 518–21, and "Patent Dispute Divides AIDS Researchers," *Science* 230 (November 8, 1985), 640–42. Copyright © 1985 by American Association for the Advancement of Science.

115. Colin Norman, "AIDS Virology: A Battle on Many Fronts," p. 520.

116. Ibid., pp. 520–21.

117. Barnes, "AIDS Patent Dispute Settled."

118. Colin Norman, "Patent Dispute Divides AIDS Researchers," p. 641.

119. "What to call the AIDS virus?", Correspondence Section, *Nature*, 321 (May 1, 1986), 10. Reprinted by permission from *Nature*. Copyright © 1986 Macmillan Magazines, Limited.

120. Merton, "Priorities in Scientific Discovery," p. 308.

121. Ibid., p. 323.

122. Over the course of the 1980s, science writers William Broad and Nicholas Wade have done a particularly outstanding job of chronicling cases of scientific fraud: in a series of articles in *Science* magazine, and in a coauthored book, *Betrayers of the Truth* (New York: Simon & Schuster, 1982). Another interesting case study of a notorious instance of scientific fraud is Joseph Hixson's *The Patchwork Mouse* (Garden City, N.Y.: Anchor Press, 1976). Hixson, a science writer, tells the detailed story (alluded to in Chapter 1 of this book) of the "painted mouse" fraud by William T. Summerlin, a young surgeon/dermatologist/investigator at the Sloan-Kettering Institute for Cancer Research in New York City, in 1973–1974. See also science writer Barbara J. Culliton's two excellent articles on this case: "The Sloan-Kettering Affair: A Story Without a Hero," *Science*, 184 (May 10, 1974), 644–50, and "The Sloan-Kettering Affair (II): An Uneasy Resolution," *Science*, 184 (June 14, 1974), 1154–57.

The subject of deviant research has attracted strong journalistic interest, and the publications of science writers like the ones cited have had a significant amount of professional and public impact. Curiously and regrettably, it does not seem to have inspired serious social science research to any meaningful degree.

123. Paul Meadows and Peter Meadows, "Anomaly Revisited: Rules and Roles in Research," in *The Dark Side of Science*, eds. Brock K. Kilbourne and Mana T. Kilbourne, Proceedings of the 63rd Annual Meeting of the Pacific Division, American Association for the Advancement of Science, San Francisco, 1, part 2 (August 30, 1983), 66.

124. Charles Babbage, *Reflections on the Decline of Science in England* (Farnborough, England: Gregg, 1969). This is a facsimile report of the 1st edition, London, Fellowes, 1830.
125. William J. Broad, "Frauds from 1960 to the Present: Bad Apples or a Bad Barrel?" in *The Dark Side of Science*, pp. 29–30.
126. Nicholas Wade, *The Science Business, op. cit.*, pp. 31–32.
127. Judith P. Swazey and Stephen R. Scher, eds., *Whistleblowing in Biomedical Research* (Washington, D.C.: U.S. Government Printing Office, 1982).

CHAPTER 7

THE SOCIOLOGY OF BIOETHICS

Bioethics is a social and cultural as well as an intellectual happening. The term came into use toward the end of the 1960s, in connection with an area of inquiry and action that was just beginning to develop in the United States.[1] What has since become the flourishing field of bioethics is structured around problems associated with modern biomedicine, particularly some of its frontier scientific and technological advances. But bioethics is not just the name of a new discipline. It also refers to a wider, more organized, professional and public concern about so-called "ethical matters" that has taken on the characteristics of a social movement.

Bioethics, in both these senses, surfaced in American society in the late 1960s, a period of acute social and cultural ferment. From its outset, the value and belief questions with which it has been preoccupied have run parallel to those with which the society has been grappling more broadly. Its name, empirical focus, and technical vocabulary notwithstanding, the matters it treats are not exclusively medical and ethical. They have more general moral, social, and religious connotations. "Bioethics is not just bioethics, . . . and [it] is more than medical," Fox and Swazey have written. "Using biology and medicine as a metaphorical language and a symbolic medium, bioethics deals . . . with nothing less than beliefs, values, and norms that are basic to our society, its cultural tradition, and its collective conscience."[2]

As the field has evolved over a period of almost two decades, it has attracted greater public notice and participation, more media attention, and increasing government interest and involvement. Although its overall configuration and focus have remained relatively constant, bioethics has undergone several shifts that are congruent with those taking place on the larger American scene. For example, a certain "economization" of bioethics seems to have occurred: a tendency to highlight some of the same allocation of scarce resources and cost containment themes that current political administrations stress.

By the mid-1970s, under the same name and significantly influenced by the intellectual content of bioethics in the United States, the orbit of bioethics had extended to a number of Western European countries. European bioethics is gradually differentiating itself from its American counterpart in its emphases, framework of analysis, institutional structure, and ethos.[3] We mention the European variations in passing, partly because of their historical and sociology of knowledge interest, but mainly to underscore the culturally specific features of American bioethics with which the present chapter will be largely concerned.

It is because American bioethics is embedded in the country's value and belief system and is an emanation of important sociocultural as well as biomedical developments that it is an apt subject with which to conclude this book. An analysis of the key sociological characteristics of American bioethics will provide an overview of fundamental interrelationships between the society, its culture, and modern Western biomedicine. Along with a review and discussion of the relatively sparse sociological literature on bioethics,[4] the chapter will include some analysis of the restricted role that social scientists have played in this field and the medical and social implications of their limited participation.

BIOMEDICAL FOCI

Bioethics has concentrated its attention on a particular group of advances in biology and medicine. With strikingly little acknowledgement of the improvement in identifying, controlling, and treating disease that these advances represent, bioethics has focused on actual and impending problems that medical scientific progress has brought in its wake:

> ... [D]evelopments in genetic engineering and counseling, life support systems, birth technology, population control, the implantation of human, animal, and artificial organs ... [and] the modification and control of human thought and behavior are principal foci of [bioethical] concern. Within this framework, special attention is concentrated on the implications of amniocentesis . . . *in vitro* fertilization, the prospect of cloning, . . . organ transplantation, the use of the artificial kidney machine, the development of an artificial heart, the modalities of the intensive care unit, the practice of psychosurgery, and the introduction of psychotropic drugs.[5]

Cross-cutting its interest in these areas of biomedical development is the strong involvement in issues of human experimentation that the field of bioethics has shown from its inception. In fact, it was growing professional and public concern about moral aspects of experimentation with human subjects, particularly in the sphere of medical research, that played the major triggering role in the genesis of bioethics. During the field's early years (from the late 1960s to the mid-1970s), the greatest interest and energy were invested in this area. Bioethical analysis and recommendations were centered on the general importance and difficulty of obtaining the informed, voluntary consent of human research subjects for the procedures they underwent. Special attention was paid to the worrisome situations of potential subjects who were especially vulnerable, disadvantaged, or unable to speak for themselves: for example, infants and children, the mentally disabled, the dying, institutionalized persons, such as prisoners and the mentally infirm, uneducated and very poor individuals, and members of minority groups that have been the object of much societal prejudice and discrimination.

Human experimentation remains a central preoccupation of bioethics. However, in the mid-1970s, concern about life and death and personhood issues at the beginning and end of the life cycle began to take up more medical, philosophical, and legal space in bioethical discussion. In this second phase, bioethics became increasingly involved in definitions of life and death and personhood, with the humane treatment of emerging life, and with the care of the dying, particularly with the justifiability of foregoing life-sustaining forms of medical treatment.

The mid-1980s constitute a third phase in the evolution of bioethics—its progressive "economization." The following excerpt from a 1986 meeting announcement by the Society for Health and Human Values identifies some of the components in this focus on "ethics and the new economics of health care":[6]

> We are soliciting papers which deal with either the conceptual or the practical aspects of the economic frameworks in which health care is being delivered in the United States, now and in the future. Topics such as the effects of a prospective payment system (e.g., DRG's), for-profit hospitals, arguments on the right to health care in a free market economy, the moral responsibilities of physicians in various organizational structures, rationing of health care and expensive technology, etc., are especially welcome. . . .

Along with the thematic shifts through which bioethics has passed, there have been fluctuations in the prominence accorded to particular medical scientific advances and types of medical treatment. For example, in the mid-1970s, when discussion of the case of Karen Ann Quinlan was at its height,[7] and again in the 1980s, at the peak of concern about so-called Baby Doe cases,[8] adult and neonatal intensive care units and various life support modalities received a great deal of bioethical notice. Or, to take another example, a resurgence of interest in cardiac transplantation occurred in the mid-1980s, in synchrony with the increase in transplants that the immunosuppressive drug cyclosporine helped to effect, the temporary bridge-to-transplantation use of artificial hearts, and the creation of a National Task Force on Organ Transplantation in 1985.[9]

Such shifts and fluctuations in the salience of different bioethical themes and topics result from a complex process of interaction between concrete medical scientific and clinical events, the settings and the circumstances in which they occur, professional and public reactions to them (including those of the media and the polity), and the work agendas of the interdisciplinary community of bioethicists. The subject matter with which bioethicists are involved at any given time is partly self-determined, partly responsive to current biomedical happenings, and partly set by the phenomena and questions that they are invited or commissioned to analyze by a wide range of groups. These groups include professional organizations, medical institutions, academic milieux, private foundations, government agencies and commissions, legislative bodies, the courts, and the media.

SOCIAL ORGANIZATION AND INSTITUTIONALIZATION OF BIOETHICS

As the foregoing suggests, bioethics now functions within a complex, multi-institutional framework that encompasses private, public, local, and national sectors of the society. Its initial organization toward the end of the 1960s was much simpler, more inconspicuous, and largely confined to the activities of the pioneering centers and programs that established the field. Preeminent among these were the Institute of Society, Ethics, and the Life Sciences in Hastings-on-Hudson, New York (The Hastings Center); the Center for Bioethics of the Kennedy Institute of Ethics, Georgetown University, Washington, D.C.; and the Society of Health and Human Values, then located in Philadelphia and now based in McLean, Virginia. These three groups have continued to play an important leadership role in the intellectual development of bioethics and its involvement in social action. But in the course of the last fifteen years, they have been joined by scores of other independent, academic, professional, and public interest associations, institutes, departments, and programs that have a major commitment to reflection, research, teaching, publishing, and action in matters pertaining to bioethics. These burgeoning organizations have received sponsorship and support from a wide array of private foundations, scholarly bodies, and government agencies.[10]

The expansion and increasing institutionalization of bioethics have also contributed to "a veritable explosion of literature on bioethical issues."[11] This literature is so vast and appears in such diverse and widely scattered sources that a number of bibliographies have been published to facilitate its use. The best known of these is the *Bibliography of Bioethics*, edited by LeRoy Walters, Director of the Georgetown University/Kennedy Center for Bioethics, which has been published annually since 1974 and seeks to be as comprehensive as possible for all English-language bioethical materials.[12] The fact that it examines 68 reference tools for pertinent citations, searches four databases, and directly monitors 102 journals and newspapers for articles and citations is an indicator of the impressive scope and volume of the literature on bioethical topics. There is also an *Encyclopedia of Bioethics*, published in 1978 under the editorship of Warren T. Reich, another scholar associated with the Georgetown/Kennedy Center for Bioethics.[13] As Reich commented in his Introduction "[I]t is unusual, perhaps unprecedented, for a special encyclopedia to be produced almost simultaneously with the emergence of its field." He also recognized and justified the encyclopedia's role in shaping and furthering the institutionalization of bioethics, and its function in "systematizing" the "plethora of contemporary [bioethical] literature."[14]

One of the most remarkable features of the way in which bioethics has developed is the extent to which it has pervaded the public domain. American courts and legislatures, at every level of the system, are involved with bioethical questions—deliberating on them, rendering decisions about them, and formulating guidelines, regulations, and laws that bear upon them. Issues concerning research with human subjects and the availability and foregoing of life-saving and life-sustaining medical treatment have been particularly important aspects of this legislative and judicial action.

There have also been two consecutive national commissions established to study and report on a number of bioethical problems in medicine and research. The first of these was the National Commission for the Protection of Human Subjects of Biomedical and Behavioral Research, created in 1974 by Title III of the National Research Act (Public Law 93-348), with members appointed by the Secretary of Health, Education and Welfare. This Commission was charged to conduct "a comprehensive examination and study to identify the basic ethical principles which should underlie the conduct of biomedical and behavioral research involving human subjects," and to develop "guidelines which should be followed in such research to assure that it is conducted in accordance with such principles."[15] From 1975 through 1978, the Commission published a series of reports on various aspects of experimentation with special populations of human subjects from whom it is problematic to obtain informed consent: human fetuses and pregnant women, children, prisoners, the institutionalized mentally ill or retarded, and possible candidates for psychosurgery. The recommendations presented in these reports provided the bases for the regulations governing human experimentation adopted by the Department of Health, Education, and Welfare, and by its successor, the Department of Health and Human Services.

The second commission, the President's Commission for the Study of Ethical Problems in Medicine and Biomedical and Behavioral Research, was authorized by Congress is November 1978 in Title III of Public Law 95-662, and its original members were named by President Carter. Its mandate was broader than that of the National Commission; it was not confined to ethical issues in research with human subjects, and it was accorded the flexibility to modify the list of topics it was asked to study, either as it or the President saw fit. The Commission began its work in January 1980, and was officially terminated at the end of March 1983.[16] Over the course of those three years, it published reports on making health care decisions, securing access to health care, defining death, deciding to forego life-sustaining treatment, screening and counseling for genetic conditions, genetic engineering, compensation for injured research subjects, and whistle-blowing in biomedical research. It also issued two biennial reports, required by its Congressional mandate, on protecting human subjects and implementing human research regulations. Another effort, in collaboration with the NIH's Office for Protection from Research Risks and the Food and Drug Administration was a guidebook for Institutional Review Boards.[17] A number of these reports have had considerable influence on public opinion and public policy, medical and hospital practice, legislative action, and legal decision-making. The Commission's volumes on *Defining Death* (July 1981) and on *Deciding to Forego Life-Sustaining Treatment* (March 1983) have probably had the most impact.

The "going public" of bioethics has been amplified by the continuous, extensive, and prominent coverage that the issues it deals with have received from the print media and television. Media interest in bioethically relevant events and questions has escalated over the years, reaching especially high points when there are identified human cases that dramatically personify the medical questions and the societal values and beliefs that are involved. For example, through media attention, pioneer artificial heart recipients Barney B. Clark and William J. Schroeder were not only made American culture heroes; they were also seen as very human embodiments of the painfully complicated ethical questions and uncertainties that surround the process of human experimentation and therapeutic innovation. As in a morality play, their cases became symbolic foci of collective conscience issues that radiate far beyond medicine and medical research.[18]

There is, however, a certain inflation in the public and professional notice being given to bioethical questions. In part, this is due to the expansive way in which the term "ethical" is used in this connection. A kind of "everything is ethics" syndrome has developed. It consists of a generalized tendency to attach the label "bioethical" to a diverse array of medical science and technology-associated problems that are moral, social, and religious in nature, as well as strictly ethical. Accompanying this trend is the propensity to call all intellectuals and professionals lecturing and writing about value issues relevant to medicine, "ethicists"—whether they are philosophers, religionists, biologists, physicians, lawyers, or social scientists. In turn, these patterns are part of the "bioethics bandwagon" that now exists on the American scene.

Despite its expansionary characteristics, certain kinds of concerns and ways of thinking about them, although germane to the area of bioethics, are defined as outside its orbit or as peripheral to the field. This is all the more striking because of how comprehensive—even engulfing—the scope of bioethics appears to be.

What is included or excluded in bioethics, and emphasized or deemphasized by it, can be better understood through an analysis of its ethos.

THE ETHOS OF BIOETHICS[19]

The chief intellectual and professional participants in American bioethics and shapers of its ethos have been philosophers (particularly philosophical and religious ethicists), theologians (predominantly Christian), jurists, physicians, and biologists. Certain public officials who have played a prominent role in the involvement of local and national government in bioethical matters have also influenced the outlook and emphases of the field.[20] In addition, the thought and presence of economists have been more strongly felt in bioethics during the 1980s, as allocation of scarce resources and cost-containment problems have become more salient. In comparison, the participation of anthropologists, political scientists, and sociologists has been quite limited. This is a complex phenomenon, resulting as much from the prevailing *Weltanschauung* of present-day American social science as from the framework of bioethics.[21] We will return to the relationship between bioethics, social thought, and sociology in later sections of this chapter.

The values and beliefs highlighted by American bioethics represent a particular cross section of the society's cultural tradition. From the outset, the conceptual framework of bioethics has accorded paramount status to the value complex of individualism, underscoring the principles of individual rights, autonomy, self-determination, and their legal expression in the jurisprudential notion of privacy. By and large, what bioethics terms "paternalism" is negatively defined, because however well-meaning and concerned with the good and the welfare of another person it may be, it interferes with and limits an individual's freedom and liberty of action.

The notion of contract has played a major role in the way that relations between autonomous individuals are conceived in bioethics. Self-conscious, rational, functionally specific agreements between independent individuals are presented as ethical models. The archetype of such contractual relations is the kind of informed, voluntary consent agreement between research subjects and investigators that the field of bioethics helped to formulate and translate into public policy.

Truth-telling is another value precept stressed by bioethics. In keeping with the overall orientation of the field, bioethics attaches special importance to the rights of patients or research subjects to "know the truth" about the discomforts, hazards, uncertainties, and "bad news" that may be associated with medical diagnosis, prognosis, treatment, and experimentation.

As already indicated, concern about the just and fair distribution of scarce, expensive resources for advanced medical care, research, and development is another major value preoccupation of bioethics, one that has increasingly come to the forefront in the 1980s. The view of distributive justice underlying it is structured upon an individual rights-oriented conception of the general or common good, in which greater importance is assigned to equity than to equality.

"Cost containment," an essential value component of this outlook on rightful distribution, has evolved from the status of an ethical response to an empirical situation of economic scarcity, to something approaching a categorical moral imperative of bioethics.

Finally, what is usually referred to as "the principle of beneficence" or "benevolence" is also a key value of bioethics. The enjoinder to "do good" and "avoid harm" that this entails is structured and limited by the supremacy of individualism. The benefiting of others advocated in bioethical thought is circumscribed by respectful deference to individual rights, interests, and autonomy; and minimizing the harm done to individuals is more greatly accentuated than the maximation of either personal or collective good.

The weight that bioethics has placed on individualism has relegated more socially-oriented values and ethical questions to a secondary status. The concept and the language of "rights" prevails over those of "responsibility," "obligation," and "duty" in bioethical discourse. The skein of relationships of which the individual is a part, the sociomoral importance of the interdependence of persons, and of reciprocity, solidarity, and community between them, have been overshadowed by the insistence on the autonomy of self as the highest moral good. Social and cultural factors have been primarily seen as external constraints that limit individuals. They are rarely viewed as forces that exist *inside* as well as outside of individuals, shaping their personhood and enriching their humanity.

The restricted definitions of "persons as individuals" and of "persons in relations" that dominate bioethics have downplayed "values like decency, kindness, empathy, caring, devotion, service, generosity, altruism, sacrifice, and love."[22] All of these involve "emphasis on . . . feeling, on connection and relatedness,"[23] and on responding to known and unknown others in a self-transcending way.

The basic values of bioethics and its cognitive characteristics and style of thought are closely allied. The capacity to think rationally and logically about ethical questions, with as much rigor, clarity, consistency, parsimony, and objectivity as possible, is accorded high intellectual and moral standing. Bioethics proceeds in a largely deductive manner, formalistically applying its mode of reasoning to the phenomenological reality it addresses. An array of cognitive techniques are used to distance and abstract bioethical analysis from the human settings in which the questions under consideration occur, to reduce their complexity and ambiguity, and to control the strong feelings that many of the medical situations on which bioethics centers can evoke in those who contemplate them, as well as those who live them out.

Much of the bioethical literature is based on the assumption that the value questions that have arisen in the field of biomedicine have been "caused" or "created" by medical scientific and technological advances. Partly because of its biomedical and technological determinism, bioethical analysis does not usually take note of the fact that some of the same cultural questions that have crystallized around biological and medical developments have also been central to many non-medical issues that have surfaced in American society during the past fifteen to twenty years. Thus, the examination of bioethical matters is enclosed within a framework that does not easily open onto a consideration of larger, more encompassing concerns about the general state of ideas, values, and beliefs in American society at this historical juncture. In fact, there is a sense in which bioethics has taken its American societal and cultural attributes for granted, ignoring them in ways that imply that its conception of ethics, its value system, and its mode of reasoning transcend social and cultural particularities. In its inattention to its "American-ness" and its assumption that its thought and moral view are *trans*cultural, American bioethics has been more intellectually provincial and chauvinistic than it has recognized.

This inclination, along with the dominance that bioethics assigns to individualistic ethical questions, bend it away from involvement in social problems. Nowhere is this more apparent than in the context of neonatal intensive care units (NICU). Bioethical attention has been riveted on the justifiability of nontreatment decisions. Relatively little attention has been paid to the fact that a disproportionately high number of the extremely premature, very low birth weight infants, many with severe congenital abnormalities, cared for in NICUs are babies born to poor, disadvantaged mothers, many of whom are single nonwhite teenagers. Bioethics has been disinclined to regard the deprived conditions out of which such infants and mothers come as falling within its purview. These are defined as *social* rather than ethical problems—a dichotomous distinction that permeates bioethical thinking. In effect (to use a term coined by a philosopher-founder of bioethics, Daniel Callahan), these kinds of social problems are "de-listed" as ethical problems in a manner that removes them from the sphere of moral scrutiny and concern.

Bioethics deals with religious variables in a comparable fashion. When questions of a religious nature arise in bioethics, there is a tendency to screen them out or "reduce" them, and fit them into the field's circumscribed definition of ethics and ethical. This is particularly notable with regard to issues concerning what sort of life-sustaining medical treatment, if any, should be used to preserve the lives of severely mentally or physically defective or terminally ill persons. The "strictly ethical" manner in which bioethics generally defines and approaches such an ultimate question contrasts with the way in which it has been understood and dealt with in American courts. Judges have repeatedly acknowledged that these medical and moral problems are also "spiritual," "theological," and "metaphysical," as they have put it. For this reason, mindful of the American doctrine of separation of church and state, they have tried to identify the religious facets of the questions before them, and have consistently advised that any government intervention into these "difficult and sensitive" decisions "should . . . reflect caution and sensitivity."[24] In the words of one judge, "Courts temporal are not ideally suited to resolve problems that originate in the spiritual realm."[25]

These cognitive and value traits of bioethics are an emergent product of a number of converging factors. American philosophy and philosophers have had the greatest molding influence on the field. It is principally American analytic philosophy—with its emphasis on theory, methodology, and technique, and its utilitarian, neo-Kantian, and "contracterian" outlooks—in which the majority of the philosophers most active in bioethics were trained. Their philosophical positivism is reinforced by the principles and rules of "being scientific" that physicians and biologists have been educated and socialized to apply to their own professional work, and that they have brought to bioethics. In turn, the rationalism of American law, its emphasis on individual rights, and the ways in which it has been shaped by Western-American traditions of natural law, positivism, and utilitarianism overlap with and enhance key attributes of the philosophical and scientific thought in bioethics.

As has been indicated, the law has shown less of a tendency than analytic philosophy to collapse medical, moral, social, and religious issues into an undifferentiated amalgam called ethics. Nevertheless, in order for the courts and legislatures to make concrete decisions about the swelling numbers of bioethical cases and problems that have been coming before them, they, too, must logically "reduce" the questions involved, and "technicalize" them; otherwise, they would have to declare these matters to be nonjusticiable, or beyond the application of legal principles. Thus, for example, issues concerning the "definition of death" are transformed into statutory, medico-legal criteria for pronouncing death, either on the basis of irreversible cessation of circulatory and respiratory functions or irreversible cessation of all functions of the entire brain.[26] As another example, rather than speculate on the answer to "the difficult question of when life begins" raised by abortion, the courts turn to the biological concept of "fetal life after viability," and to the legal concept of "right of personal privacy."[27] Comparably, "failure to follow procedural requirements in [their] promulgation becomes the primary basis on which Baby Doe rules are declared invalid by the Court, despite its broader commentary on life-sustaining medical treatment for newborn infants who are gravely ill or have serious congenital defects."[28]

In the philosophical, medical, and legal spheres of bioethics, applied pragmatism also plays an important role in how bioethical problems are conceptualized and analyzed. Physicians, nurses, other medical professionals, hospital administrators, patients, families, biologists, lawyers, judges, legislators, politicians, business executives, and their associates are called upon to decide what to do and what not to do in real-life settings, and then act on the basis of their determinations. In addition, intellectuals and academicians who are considered to be bioethicist experts, most frequently those with philosophical training, are often asked to help professional practitioners and policymakers arrive at reasonably specific and clear ways of resolving particular bioethical problems that they face. The practical necessity of systematically managing the complexity and uncertainty that such decision-making and applied action entail augments the cognitive predisposition of bioethics toward utilitarianism, positivism, and reductionism.

Despite the significant contributions of highly esteemed religious ethicists and theologians to bioethics, the field is studiously secular in its perspective. This secularism is partly a consequence of the professional socialization that philosophers, biologists, physicians, and jurists undergo in their respective fields. It is also an instrumental, political, and moral response to a basic societal question that the whole phenomenon of American bioethics poses: The United States is an advanced modern, highly individualistic, pluralistic, and religiously resonant society, founded on the precept of governance "under law" rather than "under men," and the sacredly secular principles of separation of church and state and freedom of belief. How can or should such a society try to achieve collective and binding consensus about the kinds of bioethical issues that are now in the public domain? The society is experiencing great difficulty in resolving, on behalf of its entire citizenry, these more-than-medical ethical matters that lie at the heart of its moral, religious, and cultural tradition. The problem is complicated and made more acute by the degree to which such questions have entered the polity. Siphoning off their religious content and framing them in as secular a way as possible provides an institutionally supported, reductionistic way of defining them, which is compatible with the ethos of bioethics and makes them more amenable to logical analysis and technical solution. The problem is that, in the end, this masks their essential nature, and because this is true, does not conclusively dispel them.

Bioethical thought and discourse have two other distinctive characteristics. As is to be expected, the major intellectual shapers and spokespersons in this field have been professionals, scholars, and academics. The extent to which the literature and commentary it has generated are "locked into . . . upper middle class professional and guild enclaves"[29] was brought home to the members of the Medicine and Society Advisory Board of the Duke Endowment and the North Carolina Humanities Committee when they went to various groups and communities in their state to discuss bioethical and other "humanistic" questions associated with health, illness, and medicine. What they found was that "'grassroots' audiences, or 'the people,' or the 'out-of-school-adult-public' (especially North Carolina's nonprofessional public) know 'the issues,' but know them in their own language, i.e., what they mean to them, how they feel and think and tell about their experiences of illness and medicine and health."[30]

Finally, in a number of respects, the ideological orientation of bioethics could be characterized as conservative—even though the field has separated its ethics from theological principles and historical religious tradition, and despite the fact that philosopher William Bennett, U.S. Secretary of Education and former Chairman of the National Endowment for the Humanities, has chastised bioethics for what he regards as its skew toward "ethical relativism" and away from "traditional . . . American cultural ideals."[31] But the way that bioethics has defined and focused on the value complex of individualism, the degree to which it has played down a social perspective on personal and communal moral life, its parsimonious acceptance of a cost-containing framework of health care analysis, and the extent to which its rationality and methodology have distanced it from the phenomenological reality of medical ethical situations have converged to form a gestalt that is congruent with other fundamentals of a conservative outlook. Daniel Callahan alleges that conservatism is inherent to "ethical analysis and prescription," in the sense that "only rarely can [they] . . . lead the way in social and cultural change. . . . This is not to say [he continues] that ethics cannot or should not have a radical or reforming role":

> [I]t can oppose current practices, point out a subversion of important principles, and espouse higher ideals. But that is a relatively rare situation. Its more normal role is to try to interpret and structure the flux of behavior, experience, and intuition, and from there to develop general moral visions and goals together with specific principles and rules to exemplify them.[32]

INCIPIENT CHANGES IN THE ETHOS OF BIOETHICS

A certain amount of intellectual and moral stock-taking has been occurring in the bioethical community since 1980, as a consequence of the experience and greater maturity of insight it feels it has gained over its relatively brief history. Self-criticisms, as well as critical commentaries by observers of bioethics, have started to appear in print. Prominent spokespersons for the field, like Daniel Callahan, have taken the lead in declaring that bioethics (or "biomedical ethics," as he prefers to call it), "must now move into a new phase, one that will force a rethinking of its role, its methodology, and its relation to other disciplines and institutions."[33]

One of the major foci of the auto-critique in which bioethicists have begun to engage is what they now call the field's "excessive emphasis" on the "language of 'rights'" of American individualism and of American courts,[34] and its elevation of the principle of "autonomy" to a position of such overriding importance that it was "given a kind of moral clout sufficient to trump every other value."[35]

The stock-taking that has been occurring in bioethics includes not only an appraisal of its central philosophical precepts, but questions about how relevant those precepts, and their applications, have been for clinical medicine. From their perspective as faculty in a program in psychiatric ethics, for example, philosopher Colleen Clements and physician Roger Snider charged that medical ethics has represented an "assault upon medical values":

> Physicians are decidedly ambivalent about these ethical contributions [in clinical settings]; on the one hand, they are eagerly searching for assistance in resolving the increasingly complex ethical dilemmas now so common in medical practice. On the other hand, they are wary and disappointed because, until now, the ethicists' contributions have been of dubious value. In this article we will argue that the currently dominant school in medical ethics, that of a patient autonomy-rights model based in rationalist philosophy and liberal political theory, has been used to subvert values intrinsic to medicine, that it has done so without adequately establishing the merits of its case, and that the unfortunate result has been the attempted replacement of the historic medical value system by an ill-fitting alternative.[36]

Most philosopher-bioethicists still contend that "autonomy's temporary triumph"[37] (and even its triumphalism) were "indispensable" for general moral and specifically medical-ethical reasons:

> Among . . . the benefits of giving moral priority to autonomy . . . are a recognition of the rights of individuals and of their personal dignity; the erection of a powerful bulwark against moral and political despotism; a becoming humility about the sources or certainty of moral claims and demands; and a foundation for the protection of unpopular people and causes against majoritarian domination. . . .[38]

> The issues and themes of the medical ethics that emerged in the 70s were largely shaped by the problems bequeathed to us by clinicians and patients of the day . . . that led us . . . to see medical ethics as a conflict between the old Hippocratic paternalism (having the physician do what he or she thought was best for the patient) and a principle of autonomy. . . .[39]

The drive for autonomy that was the major moral mark of the 1960s and 1970s in medical ethics was indispensable. It brought patients into a full partnership with physicians in their medical care. There can be no return to those good old days that understood doctors to be good old boys who could work out moral problems among themselves in the locker room.[40]

The issue that is being raised by bioethicists in the 1980s is "not whether and how to get rid of autonomy." Rather, it is how to keep it from becoming such "a moral obsession" that it "pushes other values aside,"[41] particularly those that pertain to *social* ethical questions, "a search for morality in the company of others, community as an ideal, and interdependence as a perceived reality":

> But is a society based upon an individualistic search for autonomy, and a cherishing of moral independence, a good community? There is little to suggest that it is. By flying in the face of those goods that have constituted valid communities, we have left nothing with which to build bonds between and among people. Community requires constraints, limits, and taboos, just as it requires shared ideals, common dreams, and a vision of self that is part of a wider collectivity. By bringing into the medical relationship the most sterile and straitened notions of an autonomous self, ethics has borrowed not from the richest portion of our tradition but from the thinnest. . . .[42]

These admonitions about an "ethic based on maximizing individual autonomy at the expense of personal obligation to the human community—past, present and future,"[43] constituted the major motif at the June 1984 symposium on "Autonomy, Paternalism, and Community," organized by the Hastings Center to celebrate its fifteenth anniversary. Repeated affirmations were voiced about the necessity to progress beyond what its Director, Daniel Callahan, had termed a "minimalist ethic" in a 1981 publication—an individualistic ethic based on the proposition that "one may morally act in any way one chooses so far as one does not do harm to others."[44] Central to all the symposium discussions was a preoccupation with "the just allocation of scarce resources," which was cited as "perhaps the dominant theme of bioethics today,"[45] and with the fact that because of its strong individualistic focus, ethics had contributed relatively little to such large-scale, societal, health care delivery and policy issues. The statements made on this important rites-of-passage occasion seemed to presage greater future involvement of bioethics in "large, structural, moral and political decisions." "The idea of an 'applied ethics' is growing, and that idea must encompass not only the individual decision maker but the policymaking process as well," Callahan stated.[46]

In connection with the "future agenda"[47] of bioethics, several other items are increasingly mentioned. One is the need to make a greater effort to overcome "the current problems with medical ethics thinking and its application in medicine," which philosopher Colleen D. Clements calls "bioethical essentialism."[48] The first step in this direction that she advocates is "the acceptance of the uniqueness and diversity of cases, which implies situation-relative definitions of action guides. It is most unethical to routinely apply policies and procedures equally to cases," she declares.[49] Callahan makes the same point in more colloquial language:

Those in ethics have learned, mainly by hard experience, that they will make little sense to practicing physicians if they are not fully aware of the experience and details of clinical practice. It is simply not enough for those in ethics to roll up to the bedside the ghost of Immanuel Kant, John Stuart Mill, or G. E. Moore and provide instant moral diagnoses. It is hardly better to do the same with the writings of John Rawls. If the ultimate strength of ethics lies in its capacity to develop coherent modes of ethical analysis and comprehensive moral systems, it needs at the moment greater skill in penetrating the often confused dynamic of the clinical setting. Only after a detailed analysis of the actual experience of the clinician (or a patient trying to work out a moral choice) can it be in any position either to invoke traditional theories or develop new ones.[50]

Clements's enjoinder to reject ethical essentialism includes another component that she herself says is likely to be criticized by the current philosophical schools that predominate in bioethics. This "second step" entails recognizing that "only probable generalizations can be made about the relationship 'good.' Nevertheless, they can be made, and ethics can have naturalistic content."[51] "To travel that path," she continues, "we need to give up the 'quest' for certainty, universality, and necessity, as Dewey put it," and the deductive philosophical tradition that insists that "one cannot derive value from fact, *ought* from *is*, without making a major error."[52] Rather than holding that "ethical ways of knowing be only deductive," Clements proposes a research program that takes what she calls "the more optimistic Humean choice": the application of scientific induction to ethics, and bioethics specifically, so that its ideas will be "grounded in and justified by biological thought."[53]

Of special interest to sociologists are recent statements by bioethicists about the importance of learning to work closely with those in the social sciences, as well as in medicine and the law, as the field becomes more involved with social, cultural, and cross-cultural dimensions of moral life, the actual experience of patients, families, and caretakers of different backgrounds, and with policy issues that are national and international in scope.[54]

The Kennedy Institute of Ethics, for example, is collaborating with the Georgetown Center for Population Research and the Hebrew Home of Greater Washington, in an action-research project concerned with "frail elderly" persons in long-term care, which includes four social workers on its staff. In terms of international dimensions, the Institute has established an Asian Bioethics Program (directed by a Japanese Doctor of Law), which describes itself as "a resource and reference center in the United States on the issues relating to ethics and values caused by the impact of scientific, technological, and biomedical development in Asian countries." The program also serves as a bioethics "think tank" for the Institute of Medical Humanities, School of Medicine, Kitasato University where it cosponsored the First and Second "Japan-U.S. Symposium for Bioethics," in 1985 and 1986. The *Bibliography of Bioethics*, published by the Kennedy Center, is making plans to progressively include French-Canadian, French, Dutch, German, and Japanese materials in its citations.

The other major bioethics center in the United States, the Hastings Center, also has decided that bioethics in other countries and societies now merits serious attention, and that the time has come to begin examining issues in an international and cross-cultural context. In 1985–86, Hastings took "two initial steps" toward "international bioethics": organizing international summer workshops, and establishing a new category of "International Fellows" of the Center.[55] In summer 1987, the Center held a conference on "Biomedical Ethics: An Anglo-American Dialogue," which its convenors hoped "will make an important contribution to the growing interest in comparative biomedical ethics."[56] The paucity of social scientists invited to participate in this "dialogue," however, indicates that the bioethics community is still doubtful or unaware of their possible contributions to the field, even in a cross-cultural realm.

RELATIONS BETWEEN BIOETHICS AND SOCIAL SCIENCE

Such discernible shifts in a more social and cultural direction notwithstanding, then, the incorporation of social science and scientists into bioethics has not proceeded very far. The August 1986 issue of the *Hastings Center Report* also illustrates this point. It features four articles on "Caring for Newborns," written by an Israeli, Indian, Japanese, and American author respectively.[57] These articles emphasize and describe how the social structure, cultural values, religious traditions, and world-views of the eight different societies that they cover, their respective stages of socioeconomic development, and their polities affect their "strategies" of caring for "imperiled or impaired" newborns. Another major article in the same issue summarizes and discusses a 1984 – 1985 study of the ethical dilemmas confronting physicians practicing in a rural American setting, and how they are like and unlike those of their urban counterparts.[58] The article highlights the ways that distance from other professional facilities, the interrelationship of private and professional roles in a small community, and their non-specialized practice influence what rural physicians consider to be ethically justifiable courses of professional action.

Despite the social and cultural subject matter and perspective of these five articles, none is written by or cites a social scientist. Two of the authors are physicians; one is a medical student; two are jurists; and one is a scholar in the field of medical jurisprudence and humanities.

As the foregoing suggests, the relations between bioethics and social science continue to be tentative, distant, and susceptible to strain. On the bioethics side, the ethos of the field has still not evolved far enough from its individualism and autonomy starting point to accord the kind of recognition to the principles of relatedness, reciprocal obligations, and community, or to what sociologist Emile Durkheim termed the "non-contractual," fiduciary framework of social life,[59] to be firmly convinced that social scientific competence can be useful in the analysis of medical ethical phenomena. (Here, it is relevant to note that, although the Kennedy Institute of Ethic's project on the "frail elderly" entails collaboration with demographers, and *in situ* interventionist research involving nursing home patients, family members, and social workers, its chief goal is to "facilitate the expression of autonomy" by older persons in "long-term care decision-making.")

One of the inadvertent consequences of the continuing professional dominance of philosophy and philosophers in the field is the tendency on the part of influential members of the "invisible college" of bioethicists to regard the social sciences as disciplines whose subject matter and value concerns are alien to those of the humanities, and to view most social scientists as insufficiently humanistic in their education and their perceptions. The overall trend is to equate social science with the "amassing" of quantitative data and information, relevant to "policy formulation and implementation," which only uses large-scale surveys and "the techniques of linear programming and of cost-benefit, risk-benefit, and systems analysis."[60] At the same time, social science is seen as less rigorously scientific than biomedicine. Social scientists who work in a more ethnographic, *en plein air*,[61] qualitative fashion are often defined by philosophically-oriented bioethicists as "closet humanists," who are "not really" social scientists. Although this is usually considered to be a compliment by those who make the allegation, it often carries with it the implication that such social scientific humanism-in-disguise is more prone to "relativism" and "subjectivism" and to "moral laxity and logical confusion"[62] than is the discipline of philosophical ethics.

This tension in bioethics goes beyond the "science vs. humanities" or "two cultures" divide that C. P. Snow delineated.[63] Something like a "three cultures split" is involved, with "the 'Third Culture' Snow forgot" being the social sciences that fall in a rather negatively evaluated "intermediary sort of . . . sub-area."[64] Numerous physicians, biologists, and jurists, as well as moral and religious philosophers active in bioethics share this perspective, which is institutionalized across the primary disciplines that have fashioned the matrix of bioethics. In this connection, it is significant that the great expansion in the teaching of bioethics to medical students and house staff that has occurred in recent years, has progressively displaced the behavioral science teaching about psychological, social, and cultural dimensions of health, illness, and medicine that was prominent in the 1950s and 1960s.[65] In most instances, the fact that medical ethics or "human values" has been substituted for social science in the curriculum has neither been deliberately planned by medical educators, nor recognized by them as such.

The limited involvement of social scientists in bioethics, however, is not solely attributable to the unwelcoming ambivalence with which they are viewed by the shapers and gatekeepers of the field. The ethos of the social sciences also contributes to the minor role that they have played in bioethics. For example, some of the cognitive and value characteristics of contemporary sociology that we have identified at various points in the course of this book are of relevance here. Most sociologists have not chosen to concentrate on the kinds of problems with which bioethics is concerned; and many are unaware either that bioethics exists, or of its potential sociocultural import. This is related to sociologists' greater propensity to work in a social structural or social organizational frame of analysis than to focus on systems of values and beliefs—the very cultural variables that are core to bioethics—and to their positivistic preference for quantitative rather than qualitative methods of research. In turn, these intellectual inclinations and disinclinations are reinforced by an ideological conviction that is held by a substantial number of sociologists, especially those who espouse a critical, reformist, or radical approach to the field: namely, that dealing with culture and cultural tradition, which are slow and difficult to change, is inherently more conservative than being interested in what are assumed to be more malleable and rapidly modifiable social structures. The lack of pertinent interdisciplinary competence in the sociological profession has been another deterrent. Some ability to handle relationships between social and cultural variables, on the one hand, and biomedical, philosophical, and/or legal considerations, on the other, is requisite for work in bioethics. There is a dearth of sociologists who have this trained competence, or who seem willing to acquire it.

The branch of sociology that one would expect to have the most affinity for an analysis of social and ethical implications of biomedical advance and technology is the sociology of medicine. And indeed, as will be seen, among the relatively few sociologists who have contributed to the bioethics literature, most are known for their work on medicine. But in this subspecialty, too, sociologists have been less interested in areas that bear directly on the concerns of bioethics, such as the sociology of medical science, medical research, and therapeutic innovation, and the nexus between the sociology of medicine and of law, and more involved in such matters as the "sick role," and "illness behavior" of patients, the "professional dominance" and "organized autonomy" of physicians, the process of medical socialization, and the social system of the hospital. The field's stronger commitment to "basic" academic than to "applied" work also acts as a deterrent to sociologists' participation in bioethics. Still, the fact remains that the kinds of studies and analyses that sociologists have made of illness, medical care, the hospital, and the medical professions are germane in many respects to the situations and value questions that are central to bioethics. It is the ethos of the two fields, and the way that they converge to produce reciprocal blindspots, that seem to prevent both sociology and bioethics from recognizing this.

RELEVANT SOCIOLOGICAL LITERATURE: PRE-BIOETHICS WORKS

The chief substantive bioethical topics about which sociologists have written are experimentation with human subjects, particularly the phenomena and issues surrounding informed consent; death and dying, and extending or foregoing life-sustaining treatment; genetic screening and counseling; artificial and transplanted organs; resource allocation and cost containment; and for-profit enterprise in health care. In contrast to many of the bioethical articles and books written by non-social scientists, most of the sociological publications are based on empirical research. They present and analyze systematically gathered data, a substantial proportion of which were collected through first-hand studies conducted by the authors themselves, using survey, historical, or field methods of research. The relatively slender corpus of sociological/bioethical works that have been produced is quite evenly distributed between qualitative and quantitative approaches, and a number of studies have utilized both.

There are two sets of pioneering sociological studies that antedate bioethics, and that have considerable *ex post facto* pertinence to the current interests of the field. The first is a small group of empirical studies of the social context of terminal illness and death in the modern American hospital, the primary setting where death takes place in our society. The investigations are first-hand inquiries into how the social organization of the hospital affects and is affected by the care of terminal illness and the "dying trajectory" that occurs within its confines, and of how patients and their families, doctors and nurses, and hospital personnel continuously involved in "death work" (for example, morgue attendants), experience and cope with these end-of-life events. Such sociological monographs on "death and dying" in the hospital include Diana Crane's *The Sanctity of Social Life* and Renée C. Fox's *Experiment Perilous* (discussed at some length in Chapters 4 and 5); Barney G. Glaser and Anselm L. Strauss's trilogy of ethnographies, *Awareness of Dying, Time for Dying*, and *Anguish;* and David Sudnow's field study, *Passing On.*[66] With the exception of Crane's study, the research on which these books are based was conducted in the late 1950s and the 1960s, before bioethics had crystallized as an intellectual and social phenomenon.

The books were also written in a period when there was as yet relatively little public or even medical discussion of death and dying, although a sizable literature on death and dying had developed, particularly professional articles written by psychiatrists and psychologists.[67] It was a time just prior to what historian Michel Vovelle has termed the societal "rediscovery of death" that surfaced at the end of the 1960s.[68] When the cluster of sociological works on death in the hospital appeared, it was commonly believed (to use historian Philippe Ariès's language) that death had become a hidden, solitary, "unnameable . . . taboo," and that this "modern attitude toward death, . . . born in the United States at the beginning of the twentieth century," had deep roots in American society and culture.[69] Congruent with this "forbidden death" thesis was the often-heard, more psychiatrically-phrased contention that the "denial of death" was basic to modern American national character.

None of the sociologist authors cited approached their research with facile sociocultural assumptions of this sort. However, they all observed a number of social conditions surrounding death in the hospital that created the impression of denial: the routinization and ritualization of the practices and procedures of hospital personnel; their outward display of impersonal efficiency, equanimity, and vigorous "do something" care; and what Glaser and Strauss termed the mutual "pretext of unawareness" that was often enacted by patient, family, and medical and nursing staff in the face of the uncertainties and anxieties of the dying process. These sociological works were sensitive to the fact that nurses and physicians who care for dying patients need special mechanisms and sources of support to help them navigate in situations that arouse the deepest kind of anxiety and questioning about human suffering, moral worth, meaning, and their relationship to our mortality.

Several authors gave accounts of critical symbolic cases: for example, a dying child, a patient with intractable pain who dies a lingering death, the unexpected death of a mother giving birth to a baby, the death of a suicidal, alcoholic, or "criminal" patient. These types of cases brought such questions so acutely to the surface that the "normal sentimental order" was shattered, and the hospital staff's institutionalized ways of dealing with death temporarily broke down. However, all the authors reached the conclusion that, on balance, the professional training and socialization processes of nurses and physicians, and the social organization of the hospital and its daily round, were more conducive to emotionally distant, technically proficient care of dying patients than to close, deep, humanly skilled engagement with them. More often than not, the hospital death bed was surrounded by socially patterned silence, to which patients, families, nurses, and doctors tacitly contributed.

At least two of the authors, Glaser and Strauss, were moved to formulate recommendations about how the social and psychological aspects of hospital care of the dying could be improved to make it both more compassionate and efficacious.[70] On the basis of their research findings, they suggested a series of interconnected reforms in the training of nurses and physicians, in their professional subcultures, and in the social system and organization of the hospital. These proposals went beyond mere institutional "tinkering," or "humanizing the [professional] curriculum a little more," and related the hospital to "the world outside." In this latter connection, they recommended that "medical and nursing personnel should encourage discussion of issues that transcend professional responsibilities for terminal care," especially the question of the circumstances under which procedures for prolonging life should be initiated, maintained, or discontinued. "While the physician and nurse can decide for particular patients," Glaser and Strauss wrote, "they cannot decide the wider issue. That must be debated by the more general public. With some certainty, one can predict that this issue will increasingly be discussed openly as medical technology becomes increasingly efficient."[71]

Though virtually never acknowledged in the bioethical literature, this corpus of sociological monographs contain what are now historically valuable *in situ* observations on the attitudes and behaviors surrounding terminal illness and death in the American hospital. These works also anticipate (and in the case of Glaser and Strauss advocate) a number of changes relevant to death and dying that have in fact occurred in American society in the last 15 years—changes with which the field of bioethics has been actively involved. These include the rupturing of personal, professional, and social silence around terminal illness, dying, and death; attention to the stages of dying in the care of the terminally ill, as epitomized by the trail-blazing clinical work, writing, and impact of psychiatrist Elisabeth Kübler-Ross;[72] the growth of hospice programs inspired by and adapted from the system of medical, psychological, social, and spiritual comfort-giving care created by British nurse-physician Dame Cicely Saunders at St. Christopher's Hospice in London;[73] and the continuing, very public wrestling with issues concerning the definition of death, quality of life, terminally ill patients' "right to know" and "right to die," and the foregoing of life-sustaining treatment.

The second group of bioethically-relevant sociological studies from the pre-bioethics period dealt with medical research and the use of human subjects, particularly with the complex social dynamics and problems involved in obtaining and implementing the informed voluntary consent of subjects in different types of medical research settings. Three books belong to this category of sociological works: Renée Fox's *Experiment Perilous* (1959), *Research on Human Subjects: Problems of Social Control in Medical Experimentation* by Bernard Barber, John J. Lally, Julia Loughlin Makarushka, and Daniel Sullivan (1973), and *Human Subjects in Medical Experimentation: A Sociological Study of the Conduct and Regulation of Clinical Research*, by Bradford H. Gray (1975).[74] The social research on which Fox's study was based predates bioethics by some fifteen years; Barber and Gray's studies were conducted at the end of the 1960s and start of the 1970s, on the threshold of the emergence of bioethics.

Experiment Perilous by Renée Fox was the first, and is still the only, sociological study of a clinical research unit. As indicated in Chapter 5, it is a participant observation-based, descriptive analysis of a metabolic research ward—Ward F-Second—located in a renowned northeastern university hospital. The book centers on the entwined problems of the patients and physicians of F-Second, their reciprocal stresses, and the socially patterned ways that they evolved for coming to terms with these problems and stresses. Out of their common predicament of chronic and terminal illness, high medical uncertainty and risk, severe therapeutic limitation, and constant closeness to death, and in response to their dual, often conflicting roles of physician-investigators and patient-subjects, the men of F-Second created a tragicomic hospital community in which doctor and patient were collegially committed to medical research.

As Fox has written, there are a number of respects in which this work is "more contemporaneous now than it was at the time of its initial publication."[75] The experiences, dilemmas, and questions associated with human experimentation, biomedical advance, and inexorable and fatal illness around which *Experiment Perilous* and Ward F-Second itself were structured are now bioethical and public issues of paramount importance in American medicine and society. In the early 1950s, when Fox was a participant observer on Ward F-Second, this was not yet the case. The book has also grown in medical-empirical relevance. The use of the artificial kidney machine to effect hemodialysis, the transplantation of human organs, the trials of immunosuppresive therapy, and the conduct of certain forms of cardiac surgery, all of which were pioneered on Ward F-Second in the 1950s, are among the medical developments that are most often invoked today when bioethical issues are discussed.

In *Research on Human Subjects*, Bernard Barber and colleagues hold that in the universe of American institutional settings in which medical research with human subjects is carried out, the attributes of Ward F-Second are relatively rare. Their conclusion was drawn from the two bodies of data on which their book was based: a nationally representative questionnaire survey of 239 biomedical research institutions, and a more intensive comparative study (via 331 personal interviews) conducted in a university hospital and research center, and a community teaching hospital.

Barber and his coauthors found that in research situations where the procedures being tried are dramatically innovative, dangerous, or painful, where there is a continuing relationship between researchers and their subjects, and where the physician-investigators are responsible for caring for their patient-subjects, a Ward F-Second-type situation was likely to prevail. Under such circumstances, medical researchers do tend to be keenly aware of the risks and suffering to which they are exposing their subjects, humanly concerned about them, and acutely troubled by the research-therapy conflicts involved. It is in this kind of situation, too, Barber et al. claim, that research physicians are most likely to live up to the highest ethical standards of human experimentation. They treat their subjects as collaborators and coadventurers, explain the risks and benefits of the experimental procedures in scrupulous detail, make it clear to subjects that they can withdraw from the experiment at any time, and thereby obtain the most fully informed voluntary consent possible.[76] In contradistinction to the F-Second model, the Barber team found that:

> In most research projects . . . the investigator is not faced with a decision about serious, life-threatening procedures for his patient-subjects. [T]here is . . . evidence . . . that there are mechanisms which protect investigators from emotional involvement in research by limiting their contact with their subjects. . . . Much research is brief, involving simple measurements on large numbers of subjects. Much research could be, and some is, conducted without the knowledge and cooperation of the subjects. The patients' involvement is not necessarily conscious, long-term, or painful. . . . [Thus] only a minority of research projects have the characteristics of risk and patient contact which seem to make researchers aware of research ethics. . . .[77]

In the almost fifteen years that have elapsed since this was written, partly as a consequence of the reductionistic paradigm of medical research that now prevails, the sort of holistic clinical research discussed by Fox and by Barber et al., carried out with a relatively small number of patients on a special F-2-like unit, has become even more uncommon than it was at the beginning of the 1970s. Using the Barber and Fox studies as baselines, it would be interesting to inquire into the implications for "research ethics" of the progressive decline in what physician-scientist E. H. Ahrens, Jr. terms "patient-oriented research."[78]

Barber and coauthors schematically described the diverse types of medical research with human subjects that were being conducted nationally, and the variation that they found in the "expressed standards and self-reported behavior" of biomedical researchers concerning the "key issues of informed consent and the risk-benefit ratio. [Their] data . . . show two types of patterns," they go on to say:

> They show, first, that a majority of biomedical researchers using human subjects are very much aware of the importance of informed voluntary consent, that a majority express unwillingness to take undue risk when confronted with hypothetical research proposals, and that a majority do not themselves actually do studies in which the risk-benefit ratio is unfavorable for the patient-subjects. These patterns we call "strict." But the data also show that there is a significant minority that manifests a different type of pattern, what we call "more permissive," in each of these three respects: unawareness of the importance of, or concern with, consent; willingness to take undue risk; and actually doing studies that involve unfavorable risk-benefit ratios.[79]

In the opinion of Barber et al., "the fact that the more permissive pattern exists suggests that there is indeed a problem in this area, that the increased concern . . . by both the biomedical research community itself and the lay community over ethical standards of researchers whose studies use humans subjects is not without some objective basis."[80] As sociologists, they were especially interested in the dual value-commitment of research physicians to "science and therapy," the dynamic equilibrium between these value and role obligations that they are ideally expected to maintain, and the ways in which social structural factors present in the "science community" can exert pressure on research physicians to "put science ahead of humane therapy," and to adopt more "permissive" or "deviant," rather than more "strict," "conformist" patterns of ethical behavior.[81]

Barber and colleagues identified "the structure of competition" among scientists "for recognition and reward" as a major source of such pressure. They found that "those biomedical researchers who [were] failures in the social structure of . . . competition" for recognition and reward in the scientific community at large, "but who [were] still striving to achieve success in that competition [were] more likely than others to be those who have the permissive standards and behavior with regard to the use of human subjects in research."[82] In local research settings, the Barber data revealed that "those who [had] been less rewarded by . . . rank than . . . colleagues who . . . performed no more satisfactorily . . . on any one of a number of criteria" used to accord rank at a given research institution, were "more likely to be led to take advantage of human subjects in order to increase their chances of promotion by publishing significant scientific work."[83]

Within this framework of the "dilemma of science and therapy," "structure of scientific competition," and relative "success/failure/deprivation," the Barber group examined the impact of social control structures and processes on medical researchers' ethical standards and behavior regarding informed, voluntary consent, the balance between benefit and risk, and humane therapeutic concern about their subjects. The three major types of social control that they considered were the professional socialization relevant to ethical research that medical students and doctors undergo; the patterns of informal interaction that characterize the collaborative groups and teams within which physicians generally carry out their research; and the peer group review of research with human subjects that has been made mandatory by governmental and many nongovernmental funding agencies. In all three of these spheres, the Barber study found inadequacies that they considered problematic and in need of reform:

> Our data show that the first type of social control, socialization, which is supposed to instill in researchers the knowledge, values, and norms necessary for satisfactory ethical performance with regard to the use of human subjects, is given scant attention in the formal medical school curriculum. . . . [S]ocialization into scientific values does occur in medical school but socialization into humane treatment of human subjects has yet to be brought into proper place in medical education.

> The collaboration groups and other informal interaction networks in which our sample of biomedical researchers operate provide a second environment of social control for them in regard to standards and behavior in the treatment of human subjects. Our data show that like tends to select like for collaboration groups, that both the strict and the more permissive are more likely to work with their own kind, and that this collaboration of similars may contribute to deviance in groups where the more permissive predominate.

> Finally, as is mandated by the National Institutes of Health for all the human research it subsidizes and as our data show in the case for all research in 85% of the institutions in our nationally representative sample, peer review committees exercise social control over biomedical research using human subjects. Our data show . . . that the committees are fairly effective. . . . However, there is serious need for improvement in the use of the peer review committee as a control device. In our Intensive Two-Institution Study, for instance, 8% of our respondents *volunteered* the information that one or more of their investigations using human subjects had not come before the peer review committee, which, in each of the two institutions . . . is supposed to review all research on humans.[84]

As sociologist Charles Bosk has pointed out, Barber et al.'s claim that "physicians receive almost no ethical training through their socialization" is heavily premised on "[the] absence of formal courses, seminars," and the like that existed at the time of their study. Bosk suggested that "their survey research methodology [might have been] too distant from the rhythms of everyday [clinical] life" aspects of medical training to have captured "the moral and ethical dimensions" that are more latently built and coded into it.[85] In contrast to the late 1960s-early 1970s period that the Barber study describes, the courses in medical ethics that now abound in medical school and residency training curricula include much didactic material on human experimentation. However, what kind of socialization and social control influence they have on medical students and house staff, if any, is not at all clear.

There is one other set of findings to which Barber and colleagues attached considerable moral weight. They reported that in the two medical institutions where they conducted interviews with medical researchers, "the studies with the poorest Risks-Benefits Ratio for Subjects more frequently involve[d] ward and clinic patients than more favorable studies" did.[86] Conversely, "studies involving great therapeutic benefit for the subjects [were] more likely than those of lesser benefit to be done using subjects the majority of whom [were] private patients."[87] The Barber group firmly stated that this "problem of the ethics of the differential treatment of ward and clinic patients as against private patients has not been adequately faced by the biomedical research profession."[88](However, in a study published in 1978 by sociologist Bradford H. Gray, et al., these findings were not confirmed on a national level.)[89]

Barber and his associates were candid about the limitations of their work. They recognized that "the proper treatment of human subjects in experimentation" they had studied was "only one" of a number of ethical problems that arise in clinical research. And they "explicitly . . . disclaim[ed] having made any total explanation of the variations in the ethical standards and practices of biomedical researchers using human subjects."[90]But theirs was one of the first systematic, empirical studies of ethical practices as well as standards in medical research designed to contribute to sociological theory and understanding, and to generate "specific and useful suggestions for policy change and reform."[91] It did, in fact, help to raise public and political consciousness about the existence of ethically problematic research with human subjects, notably through Barber's presentation of their major findings at 1973 U.S. Senate hearings on "quality of health care: human experimentation."[92] Out of these hearings, Congress subsequently created the National Commission for the Protection of Human Subjects of Biomedical and Behavioral Research.

As its subtitle states, Bradford Gray's *Human Subjects in Medical Experimentation* also is "a sociological study of the conduct and regulation of clinical research." Gray's inquiry, however, is more exclusively focused on the complex process of obtaining informed consent from subjects, as "a key element in distinguishing the ethical from the unethical in research."[93] Summarizing the overall intent and import of his work, Gray has described it as a study that "emphasized the difference between informed consent and a signature on a consent form by describing a situation in which the informed consent transaction was little more than a bureaucratic detail, in which key information was not understood by many subjects, and in which many subjects understood the request to participate to be advice to participate."[94]The medical research context that Gray examined in the greatest detail was a double-blind study of several drugs for inducing labor, conducted at "Eastern University" Medical Center. "Women were referred into the research project by resident physicians in the hospital clinic or by private physicians. Consent forms were presented to the women by the nurses who prepared them for labor and who initiated the infusion of the drug."[95] Out of the 51 patients involved as subjects, as many as 20 patients were unaware that they were participating in research at the time that they began receiving a labor-inducing drug. In this project, and in others that he explored in the same medical center, Gray found that in many instances the subjects' signatures on consent forms were obtained in a routinized way. Only "cursory, euphemistic, verbal" explanations were given to the subjects.[96]A considerable number of the women who served as subjects did not understand the procedures they had ostensibly agreed to undergo, or the possible risks that they entailed. Nor did they realize that they had the option to refuse to sign the consent form. Some subjects were not only persuaded, but pressured to take part in the project by residents acting on behalf of the senior research physicians whom they were eager to please. The relationship of the patient-subjects to the obstetrician-researchers was limited to occasional contact during labor and delivery. Gray found that the women who participated in the study had a variety of reasons for doing so. Only a few expressed altruistic motives, such as the desire to help other patients or to advance medical knowledge. Among the better-educated women with private physicians, the research was used as "a tool for manipulating the system: space in the hospital was tight and these women . . . wanted to control the timing of their delivery and saw in the research a way to do so."[97] At the other end of the spectrum, motivationally and socially, were the many women who were "unaware subjects."[98] These were mostly women with low levels of education and no private physician, "who did not even realize that they had been entered into a research project," or that the drug they were asked to take might be for study purposes rather than for their own medical conditions, despite the "explanations about the experiment" that they had received and the consent form they had signed.[99]

These socially structured deficiencies and inequities in the informed consent process for specific research projects parallel the findings of Barber and associates. Gray's study, like theirs, disclosed and documented "real-life" problems in the effectiveness of professional social control mechanisms that were supposed to protect human subjects and insure the ethicality of the medical research in which they participated. Along with Barber and colleagues, Gray expressed an interest in helping to further policy change in this area, as well as in advancing sociological knowledge and understanding.[100] His book ended, as did Barber's, with an exhortation to the medical profession to work as hard on ethical problems as they had on medical scientific ones, and with the hope that sociology could contribute to this "continuing quest"[101] through information provided by direct social research and social analysis.

STUDIES OF INSTITUTIONAL REVIEW BOARDS AND OF INFORMED CONSENT

Over the course of the fifteen-year history of bioethics, the professional recognition that social science has received has come mainly in the pragmatic form of enlisting sociologists to conduct empirical research on matters pertaining to human experimentation, in connection with the work of the National Commission for the Protection of Human Subjects of Biomedical and Behavioral Research, and the President's Commission for the Study of Ethical Problems in Medicine and Biomedical and Behavioral Research.

Because of his prior work, Bradford Gray was recruited by the National Commission as a staff member. Under his aegis as project director, a major study of institutional review boards (IRBs) was carried out for the Commission by Robert A. Cooke and Arnold S. Tannenbaum, with the facilities of the Survey Research Center of the University of Michigan's Institute for Social Research.[102] The IRB is a committee responsible for systematically reviewing and evaluating the ethicality of all but the most risk-free studies involving human subjects that take place in its institution. It is an organized, now federally mandated social control mechanism, an "ethical filter,"[103] whose primary purpose is to safeguard the rights and welfare of human subjects. It is a relatively new social invention that has evolved over the past three decades in the United States, and has progressively developed since the mid-1960s into the codified and regulated form in which it currently exists.[104] The IRB's size, composition, and procedures must meet certain regulatory requirements established by government agencies concerned with research, notably the Department of Health and Human Services and the Food and Drug Administration. For example, it must be composed of not fewer than five persons; it cannot consist of a single professional or lay group; and its membership must include persons who are not employees of the institution and who represent the lay-community. The concrete task of the IRB is to judge the research that comes before it with regard to informed consent, confidentiality, the risk-benefit ratio, the equitable selection of subjects, adequate research design, and so forth.[105] As of 1986, IRBs were reviewing "research . . . carried out in more than seven hundred universities, medical schools, hospitals, psychiatric institutions, research centers, and other institutions around the country."[106]

The data presented by Cooke, et al. in their report to the National Commission encompassed 61 institutions during the period of July 1, 1974 to June 30, 1975. Close to 3,900 persons were interviewed (chiefly via a survey questionnaire) about their experiences with this research and with the review process. Slightly more than 2,000 of these persons were research investigators; over 800 were members of review boards or persons especially knowledgeable about them; and close to 1,000 were research subjects or their proxies.

In its overall results, the Commission survey found that most researchers and IRB members held favorable opinions of the IRB system and supported it, despite certain imperfections that they saw in it. It appeared that, in general, the IRBs were relatively effective in dealing with the risk/benefit dimensions of the research submitted to them, although the survey did discover some tendency for IRBs to put too much time and energy into evaluating projects that entailed little or no risk.[107] IRBs did not seem to be as successful in improving the readability or comprehensiveness of the consent forms used by about 80 percent of the research projects surveyed. Despite the fact that boards did request modifications in these forms, important information was missing from a considerable number of the ones that IRBs approved, many of which also remained unduly complex in sentence structure and word length.

The survey deliberately investigated the generalizability of one of the serious ethical shortcomings that Bernard Barber and colleagues discovered in their study: does risk fall disproportionately on special groups or classes of persons? Unlike the Barber team, Cooke and colleagues did *not* find that children, women, minority, or low income persons were more likely than others to participate in projects that were above average in risk, or that they were less likely to participate in projects intended to benefit the subjects. The single most prevalent reason reported for participating in research was the expectation of medical, psychological, or educational benefits. Almost all of the subjects who were respondents in the survey felt that their participation was voluntary; most reported positively on the experience; and the majority felt that they had benefited directly from it and would be willing to take part in a similar study again.

One of the most important general accomplishments of the survey was its documentation of a disquietingly large amount of variation in the composition of IRBs, the institutional and administrative support that they received, their procedures, and in all the dimensions of their performance. In short, although IRBs were intentionally accorded flexibility and latitude in the way that they fulfilled Federal regulations for protecting human subjects, the evidence pointed to a great difference among institutions in the degree to which they had developed strong, expert, and effective local review boards. And yet, the survey indicated that it was very difficult, if not impossible, to tell how well a particular IRB was carrying out its work, simply by examining a list of its members, an inventory of its work load, and a description of its review procedures. This was demonstrated by the fact that, on the aggregate level, virtually no statistical relationship was found between the composition, procedures, performance, and decisions of the IRBs. It was on the basis of these results that the National Committee decided that a full assessment of an IRB should be based on its performance in its own institutional context, and recommended in 1978 that Federal compliance activities should include routine site visits and audits of IRBs. While this recommendation has not been implemented, it was pursued by the President's Commission. This Commission asked Bradford Gray, as a special consultant, to organize an exploratory study of the possible value that IRB site visits might have, and of how they ought to be conducted. On the basis of visits to 12 IRBs at 10 institutions between October 1981 and June 1982, the conclusion was reached that this was, indeed, a viable, useful, and edifying device for evaluating IRBs: "relatively brief site visits conducted by knowledgeable, experienced persons *can* identify problems in the operations of IRBs that are correctable by an institution once it has become aware that the problem exists."[108]

The second major piece of sociological research of bioethical import that was carried out under Commission auspices was the study of informed consent in the patient-practitioner relationship undertaken by Charles W. Lidz and Alan Meisel.[109] Conceptually, methodologically, and empirically, this investigation had a number of characteristics that distinguished it from most bioethical inquiries, and that differentiated it even more sharply from the kinds of studies that government bodies and other policy-making organizations ordinarily sponsor or conduct. The study, titled *Informed Consent and the Structure of Medical Care*, was qualitative rather than quantitative in nature. It was based primarily on first-hand field research, employing participant observation and semi-structured interviews as its principal methods. It was situated in the routine, everyday treatment settings of two inpatient wards (a medical cardiology service and a surgical service) and a surgical outpatient clinic in a university teaching hospital. It was designed to explore the complex social reality of how informed consent actually operates in various clinical settings, within the larger framework of the process of medical and surgical decision making. The study's thickly descriptive "reams of data on about 200 patients, 35 doctors, 20 nurses, and countless family members, in a handful of different clinical settings"[110] were the antithesis of the taut, impersonal, and statistically-expressed data of conventional bureau and agency reports. These kinds of materials were deliberately sought in order to examine the reality-situation fit between the rational, linear, autonomy-driven, uniform model of informed consent envisioned by the law and by the prevailing theory of biomedical ethics, and the way that it actually occurs in practice.

At the time that they began this study, Lidz and Meisel were completing a four-year, group research project on informed consent and decision making in psychiatry. That study documented a "substantial divergence" between the law-and-ethics conception of informed consent and its operation in clinical practice.[111] They brought this research-borne perspective to the President's Commission study, along with a classical sociological interest in "finding out which characteristics of the structure of providing medical care are likely to affect the processes of making disclosure and obtaining consent."[112] They started with the four-fold hypothesis that these processes would be influenced and shaped by the setting in which medical care is provided, the nature of the patient's disorder, the professional identity and status of the care providers, and the routine or non-routine nature of the medical care involved. Rather than treating informed consent as a unitary phenomenon, they broke it down into three distinct components: "disclosure"—including both what patients are told about particular diagnostic, therapeutic, and experimental procedures, and what they ask about; what and how much patients understand of the information made available to them; and the dynamics of medical decision-making, especially the roles of health providers, patients, and family members in the process.

The major conclusion that Lidz, Meisel, and colleagues reached was a startling one. "In its pristine form," they declared, "law's vision of how medical decisions should be made [as] embodied in the informed consent doctrine . . . does not exist in reality."[113] According to the researchers, the legal model of informed consent requires the following elements:

> Information is "disclosed" to patients by their physician or other health care personnel designated to do so. Physicians make reasonable efforts to ascertain whether patients understand the treatment decision at hand and provide the information necessary for them to do so. Patients make a decision either to undergo or forego the procedure in question. Patients make their decisions voluntarily. No coercion, duress, or undue influence is imposed by health care personnel. When patients are incapable of understanding the issues in the treatment decision—that is, when they are "incompetent"—health care personnel should invoke some sort of proxy decision-making process. All of these factors are supposed to lead to patients actively and autonomously participating in a decision-making process with the physician. The final decision is supposed to be made by the patient.[114]

Informed consent, in this paradigmatic sense, is so "largely absent from the clinic," Lidz et al. found, that "[e]ven the vocabulary of the informed consent doctrine is inappropriate to a description of the medical decision-making process as it actually operates; an entirely different vocabulary must be employed if reality is to be more accurately portrayed":

1. "Disclosure" does not typically occur. Rather, patients learn various bits of information, some relevant to decision making, some not, from doctors' and nurses' efforts to obtain compliance and from "situational etiquette."
2. "Decisions" are not made by patients. "Recommendations" are made by doctors to patients.
3. "Consent" does not exist. Instead what we find is "acquiescence," the absence of "objection," or occasionally a "veto."[115]

Furthermore, they pointed out, the law's conception of medical decision-making is implicitly based on an assumption that is "invalid in a substantial number of situations. This is an assumption that medical practice is discrete—that is, broken into distinct parts, or decision units—and that there can be consent by the patient to each of these individual parts."[116] However, they go on to say, the intricacy, uncertainty, and the logic of medical practice belie this:

Much of medical practice is so complex, uncertain, and unknowable in advance (except in the most general terms) that there really can be nothing like *informed* consent. Because of the complexity of practice and the structure of medical logic, there rarely exists a set of alternatives from which the patient could choose. Moreover, the explanation of the consequences of an "alternative" is complicated by the fact that the results of any procedure may reveal that yet another procedure might need to be performed.[117]

As Lidz and Meisel had anticipated, "[t]here was a great variety in what doctors told patients, what patients learned from other sources, what patients understood, and how decisions were made":

The ways in which decisions were made varied from rather close conformity with the legal model in a few situations, to a type of decision-making that bore almost no resemblance to the legal model. There were a variety of intermediate patterns, some involving a lesser degree of "disclosure" than legally required and some involving a different temporal order of events than contemplated by the legal model. . . . In general the physician was clearly the dominant actor in terms of making decisions about what treatments, if any, a patient was to have. Both doctors and patients saw the process this way.[118]

The structure of the medical care setting and the nature of the patient's medical problem and condition seemed to play a significant role in the systematic differences that Lidz and Meisel observed. For example, surgery outpatients were found to be more active participants in the decision-making process than inpatients. They asked more questions; they often had a better idea of what they wanted; they tended to negotiate more for treatment; and doctors seemed to take seriously their ability to "walk away" if they were not satisfied with these negotiations. The most striking differences in decision-making patterns that Lidz and Meisel saw were between patients with acute illness and those with chronic, long-standing disorders. Patients suffering from acute illness, who did not also have a chronic problem, were "given enough information so that they could agree to the therapeutic recommendations made by medical personnel, and . . . would not be too surprised and unable to deal with untoward results. This, for example, was the main purpose of preoperative teaching by surgical nurses."[119] But it was patients with long-term, chronic, incurable disorders, receiving medical treatment that could best be managed with their active cooperation,[120] who "came closest to playing the role envisioned by the informed consent doctrine":

They were given more information by medical personnel, they understood it better, and both they and medical personnel viewed them as having a greater say in what treatment they received. These patients were sometimes so well educated that they spoke about their illness in the same jargon as the medical personnel. Their understanding of information relevant to their illness and treatment grew over time.[121]

In effect, these expert, collegially oriented patients, like those studied by Fox, were exemplars of the participatory rights of patients in their own medical care and in relationship to medical professionals that the ideal principles of the law and of bioethics advocate.

The results of the Lidz and Meisel study strongly suggested that the reasons why decisions about care were not usually made according to legal and ethical precepts of informed consent are far more complex than "noncooperation on the part of physicians or patient ignorance."[122] The deterrents to the model of informed consent appeared to be deeply sociological. They were intricately interrelated to the social organization of the hospital; the social system characteristics of its many different services and units; the social attributes, context, and dynamics of medical diagnostic and therapeutic reasoning; the professional training and socialization of doctors and nurses; and the institutionalized roles of different types of patients as well as of health care professionals.

The findings on the systematic variation that existed between informed consent, and acute and chronic patient roles, are especially interesting from a basic sociological and a social action point of view. The patients with acute illnesses whom the Lidz-Meisel team observed and interviewed tended to "take on a set of behaviors and attitudes" compatible with a temporary and relatively passive conception of the sick role: one in which they entrusted themselves to the doctor's care, believing that "decisions about their treatment should be primarily or completely up to their physicians because of their technical expertise and commitment to the best interests of the patients."[123] Patients with acute illness conditions desired information about their treatment "to facilitate compliance with treatment decisions," and as a "courtesy" and "a sign of respect for them as persons." They rarely wanted information in order to exercise "decisional authority," and even less often to "veto" a decision that a physician was contemplating or had already made.[124] Lidz and Meisel were "struck by the fact that overwhelmingly, . . . when [such] patients [were] given information about their treatment, . . . [they] were not very interested in much of what was told to them." "Even when they were interested in the information, they still often acted as if the final decision ought to be left to the doctor."[125] In contrast, as indicated, it was persons with long-standing chronic illnesses, and a self-conception of their patient status and role as relatively permanent ones, who had the most chance over time to learn about their medical conditions and actively participate in their management, and were the most highly motivated to do so. Furthermore, the data indicated that under these circumstances physicians and nurses were inclined to "modify their behavior in the interest of patient learning and participation in their treatment. They seemed to accept that the patient would have to know new things and behave differently as a result of having an incurable chronic disease."[126] These particular sociomedical conditions apparently helped physicians to reconcile and simultaneously fulfill what they otherwise often experienced as conflicting professional responsibilities: doing what they considered to be medically best for the patients, while providing them with as much autonomy, equality, and participatory influence in their medical care as possible.

From these quintessentially sociological findings, Lidz, Meisel and colleagues concluded that the legal and ethical doctrine of informed consent had virtually no empirical impact on medical decision making and the structure and dynamics of doctor/nurse/patient relationships in the settings they studied. Even in those special situations of chronic illness, where the informed consent model was more closely approximated, it was not informed consent principles and policies per se that made the difference, Lidz and Meisel alleged. Rather, it was the convergence of medical, social, and cultural factors indwelling in the tradition and context of medical care, and in the attitudes, values, and role-sets of patients and medical professionals. For this reason, Lidz and Meisel admitted, despite all the data that they had systematically collected for the President's Commission study and their prior study of decision making in psychiatry, in the end, they were unable to answer most of the questions they had posed for themselves concerning the empirical "benefits" and "costs" of informed consent to patients and the medical and nursing staff.

Nevertheless, "on deontological grounds," they affirmed that "informed consent must not be abandoned," because it represents "values fundamental to our society," particularly "rationality," and "the autonomy of the individual."[127] They recommended that serious and thoughtful efforts be made to encourage and implement informed consent through means that were less strictly legal and focused on consent forms, and more responsive to the social reality within which medical care takes place. Their concrete suggestions included involving patient groups, nurses, and family members more actively and extensively in the communication of medical information and in decision-making; fine-tuning the ways in which physicians and nurses inform and teach patients and engage them in decisions, taking into account such things as whether the patient is acutely or chronically ill, hospitalized, or an outpatient; and enriching medical education efforts to encourage physicians to talk with patients about their diagnosis, therapy, and prognosis—"not simply because the law requires it." "Informed consent should be the result of the natural interaction between medical care personnel and patients, rather than of attempts to 'obtain informed voluntary consent' in a reifying manner," Lidz and Meisel declared.[128] At the end of their President's Commission report, and even more vehemently in the closing pages of their book on informed consent and psychiatry, they invoke the larger process of social change that they believe fuller realization of informed consent necessarily entails. And they caution that as a consequence, no matter how earnest and imaginative the steps taken to foster it, "the path to achieving the goal of involving patients in a decision-making partnership will be, at best, a long, slow, gradual, difficult and winding one."[129]

Some legal scholars who are professionally concerned with bioethical issues have taken special note of the kinds of insights into the dynamics of informed consent that this phenomenological approach and sociological perspective have produced. Lidz and Meisel's work is liberally cited by psychologist and health policy expert Ruth R. Faden and philosopher Tom L. Beauchamp in their book on *A History and Theory of Informed Consent*. And Charles Lidz reports that numerous physicians who are both actively involved in bioethics and in clinical medicine have expressed appreciation for what they feel to be the accuracy and usefulness of the first-hand observations that he and his colleagues have reported and analyzed.[130]

By and large, however, bioethical reflection on informed consent is conceptually unaffected by these sociological studies, and the empirical knowledge and insights they have produced. The theory by which bioethical discussion of informed consent continues to be structured is dominated by the principles and language of analytically-oriented moral philosophy and of legal doctrine; and the chief practical considerations on which it still focuses are matters relating to consent forms—their composition, mode of administration, functions, and limitations.

STUDIES OF ORGAN TRANSPLANTATION AND DIALYSIS

Two sets of sociologists, Roberta Simmons and Susan Klein Marine, and Renée Fox and Judith Swazey, have been engaged for many years in the study of dialysis and organ transplantation—the cluster of surgical, medical, and technological means for treating certain end-stage diseases that have occupied a central and consistently dramatic place in the field of bioethics since its inception. They have each published a well-known coauthored book on this subject (and also many articles): *Gift of Life: The Social and Psychological Impact of Organ Transplantation*, and *The Courage to Fail: A Social View of Organ Transplants and Dialysis*.[131] Particular biographical and situational factors contributed to their initial interest in these heroic, innovative therapies. In Roberta Simmons's case, for example, her faculty position at the University of Minnesota, where there is an internationally renowned transplant center, and her marriage to Dr. Richard Simmons, a distinguished surgeon-transplanter, who is a director of that center, were influential. (More recently Richard Simmons became chairman of the Surgery department at the University of Pittsburgh, and Roberta Simmons became a professor of sociology in the departments of Psychiatry and Sociology at that university.) Renée Fox's interest was initially generated by her participant-observer experiences in 1951–1954, when she witnessed the early clinical trials with the artificial kidney machine, and the pioneering attempts to do human kidney transplants, that took place on the metabolic ward where she did the research for *Experiment Perilous*. It was their shared conviction that the importance of transplantation and dialysis lay in their psychosocial and cultural significance as well as their medical and surgical importance, and their mutual recognition of the significant value and belief issues that are associated with the history and meaning of these innovations, which involved Simmons, Klein and Simmons, and Fox and Swazey in their long-term study of these biomedical developments.

Gift of Life is more intently focused on the microdynamic impact that kidney transplantation has on recipients, donors, and families than *The Courage to Fail*. It is based on an ensemble of quantitative and qualitative studies of all kidney transplant recipients, donors, and families at the University of Minnesota Hospital during a three-year period. The scope of *The Courage to Fail* is broader in several respects. It deals with cardiac as well as renal transplantation, includes some consideration of liver and bone marrow transplants, and details the first clinical implantation of an artificial heart and the evolution of the artificial kidney. The book is developed within the framework of a larger sociology of science interest in medical research and the process of therapeutic innovation. It is based on data gathered over a period of four years through field research in a number of dialysis and transplant centers, in various regions of the country, among which two centers receive special attention. These materials are presented in the form of cases of various "sizes," ranging from the experiences of individual patients, physicians, nurses and family members to the "story" of particular events (for example, a clinical moratorium on heart transplants, and the passage of the federal law providing insurance coverage for dialysis and kidney transplants), to narrative accounts of the way that special medical centers have dealt with the cardinal issues that surround dialysis and transplantation. The differences in the form and focus of their books notwithstanding, both groups of authors single out "the gift of life," allocation of scarce material and non-material resources, and quality of life aspects of transplantation and dialysis as the phenomena that endow them with their deepest social, cultural, ethical and existential significance.

It is the "gift-exchange" dimensions of organ transplantation, these authors agree, that constitute its most distinctive features, and that make it one of "the most sociologically intricate and highly charged events in modern medicine."[132] A vital organ is donated by one individual in order to give life to another person who is terminally ill. If a kidney transplant is called for, a family member may come forward and offer a "living related" donation;[133] all other organ transplants are cadaveric ones, donated by a newly dead person and his/her family.[134] From the inception of clinical organ transplantation in the United States, this procedure and the exchange process that it entails have been defined and experienced as a supreme gift of life and self by the physicians, nurses, donors, recipients, and family members who have participated in it. This conception of organ transplantation has been conveyed to the American public through the media, and codified in the Uniform Anatomical Gift Act that makes it legally possible to will all or parts of one's body after death. American society relies on a system of voluntary and free organ donation. The buying and selling of organs is ethically and legally proscribed in this society;[135] and the routine "harvesting" of organs from those who have died is neither allowed nor favorably regarded.

Among the most impressive of the findings reported by Simmons, Klein, and Simmons in *Gift of Life* was the unambivalent and unhesitant willingness to make a live kidney donation to a close relative that most of the family members in their study manifested. "In the majority of cases the decision to donate was an immediate, instantaneous one, made with no deliberation and usually with no regret." However "spontaneous" this decision and act appeared to be, Simmons and her colleagues, like Swazey and Fox, realized that organ donation is implicitly structured by a powerful set of norms that shape the feelings and behavior of both donors and recipients. As Fox and Swazey have indicated,[136] these are the same norms identified and analyzed by Marcel Mauss in his classic monograph, *The Gift*: the obligations to give, to receive, and to repay.[137] In his exploration of "obligation and spontaneity in the gift,"[138] Mauss not only emphasized the importance of the "symmetrical and reciprocal" properties of these three "obligations" but also of recognizing that what is exchanged in the form of gifts has "emotional" and symbolic as well as "material" value and meaning. In this sense, the gift and the obligations attached to it are "not inert." "The spirit of the thing given" and received is "alive and often personified." It "pertains to a person," and because it does, it creates or reinforces "a bond" between donor and recipient.[139]

In the case of organ transplantation, where the scarce, life-saving "things" that are given and received are literally as well as emblematically parts of persons, Simmons et al., and Fox and Swazey found a dramatic exemplification of Mauss's paradigm, and of his Durkheimian conviction that "the theme of the gift," with its associated phenomena, meanings, and dilemmas, is fundamental to individual and collective "morality," and to interpersonal and societal "solidarity."[140] For example, underlying the "instantaneous" and seemingly conflict-free decision to offer a kidney to a family member described by the majority of live related donors in the Simmons study was the kind of "obligation and spontaneity in the gift" that Mauss identified. Family members who volunteered to be donors were impelled by "an intense desire to save the life of a person who [held] high value for [them]," by "feelings of family obligation" (especially strong in the case of parents who "almost always [felt] that their role require[d] them to make this sacrifice"), and also by "subtle . . . family pressures."[141] The "intensely forged ties of closeness," "long-term exhilaration and life-appreciation," and enhanced sense of esteem, worth and meaning with which many live donors and recipients emerged from this experience were related to the emotional and symbolic significance of what had been exchanged between them, and its bonding and transfiguring force.[142]

On the other hand, the same "obligation to give," together with the symbolic attribute of live organ donation, also contributed to the cases of "black sheep donors" that Simmons and colleagues, Fox and Swazey, and a number of transplant teams have documented.[143] Here, persons with a strong sense of having committed serious wrongs in the past that have hurt and offended members of their family, offer themselves as live donors, or in effect are offered up by their relatives. Guilt, punishment and self-punishment, expiration and redemption all enter into this literally and figuratively sacrificial act.

In keeping with Mauss's "obligation to receive," the terminally ill patient to whom a family member has tendered the gift of a live kidney is under "reciprocal" pressure to accept it. To refuse to do so is not only life-denying in the biomedical sense, but also implies a rejection of the person who is the gift-of-life donor, and of the kinship that links him or her to the prospective recipient. If the gift is accepted, and the live transplant does take place, strains that arise from the Maussian "obligation to repay" can and do occur. The donor has made a priceless gift; the recipient has received and accepted an inherently unreciprocal gift from the donor.

> As a consequence, donor and recipient may find themselves psychologically and sociologically locked in a creditor-debtor vise that binds them to one another in a mutually fettering way. Because a part of him(her)self is inside the recipient, the donor may feel impelled to watch over the transplanted kidney and the life of the individual who now carries it. The recipient, in turn, may feel that his (her) debt to the donor is so enormous and unrepayable that the donor has the right to ask anything of him (her) and to participate illimitably in his (her) life.[144]

Fox and Swazey called this dimension of transplantation "the tyranny of the gift." They attached more importance to it than Simmons et al., and to the psychological and social suffering that it could entail for donors, recipients, and their families. Fox and Swazey saw it as a phenomenon that occurred frequently, in heart and liver as well as kidney transplants, regardless of whether the organ donated was a live or cadaveric one. In the latter case, they observed, it is the family of the deceased donor, the recipient, and his or her relatives who can become welded together in a comparably "tyrannical" way.

The fact that donating a vital organ is what philosopher Hans Jonas terms a "supererogatory gift, beyond duty and claim," surpassing reciprocation, adds layers of painful meaning to its being biologically rejected by the recipient's body. Fox and Swazey have pointed out that the "rejection reaction" language of immunology virtually invites the live related donor and recipient to experience this occurrence as the "repudiation," "wasting," or "discarding" of the gift of life. Among the responses that they observed under these circumstances were feelings on the part of live donors that they had been rejected as persons—that their qualities, sacrifice, and motivation for giving of themselves in this way had not been accepted by the recipients, or that their gift "had not been good enough." In turn, recipients often experienced chagrin and guilt over the possibility that the rejection had somehow resulted from their failure to have the "right attitude" toward the donors and (quasi-animistically), toward the organ itself.

Simmons and colleagues and Fox and Swazey agree that the same gift-exchange phenomena that accompany live related organ donations are also associated with cadaveric transplants. However, the circumstances under which they occur alter the way in which these gift-of-life concomitants are played out. Most cadaver organs are obtained from young, healthy, single persons, who have been fatally injured in a vehicular accident, or who have committed suicide. These deaths are not only sudden and unexpected; they are also especially tragic and fraught with problems of meaning. Simmons, Fox and Swazey found that grief-stricken families may be powerfully pushed in the direction of donating the organs of a son, daughter, or sibling who has died in this way, by their intense need to make redeeming sense out of what they may otherwise experience as an existentially absurd event. Simmons and coauthors described what they called the "altruism and humanitarianism," and the "feelings about immortality," that played a major role in family members' decision to donate. Relatives of cadaver donors whom they interviewed said that "in the decision process they empathized with the recipient's family and thought about what is would be like if their own child were 'lying there waiting for an organ.'"[145] A considerable number of the families viewed the transplant as "a continuation" or "extension of life": in the organ-specific sense that "part of the cadaver-patient would still be alive . . . as long as his kidneys still functioned," or in the words of one mother, in the larger sense of "a psychological and a spiritual transplant" of her daughter's "joy and . . . what her life was."[146]

Some respondents in the Simmons study "reported that they had to envision a potential recipient in making their decision. The fantasized recipient was generally a child of the same sex as the cadaver-patient."[147] Whether or not donor families engaged in this kind of projection, most of them had a strong desire for information about the recipients, and "even a year after the transplant, many cadaver-donor families [felt] a need to know whether the donation was successful or, in other words, whether the death had any meaning."[148] Simmons et al. interpreted this quest for information as a way of seeking "reciprocation" for the enormity of what the family had given. Fox and Swazey were also impressed with the anthropomorphic connotations of the interest that the donor family displayed in the recipient. They observed that especially in the case of cardiac transplants, where the special symbolic and religious meaning of the human heart in Western Judeo-Christian tradition seems to have had a subliminal influence, the sense that part of the donor's self had been transferred to the recipient where the part, and hence the person, lived on, was often present. Both donor families and recipients of cadaver transplants expressed the belief that some of the human and social as well as the biological qualities of the person whose organ they received were transplanted into them with the organ. Thus, they were interested in knowing about the cadaver donor and his or her family—"for example, about the donor's sex, age, race, height and weight, marital status, education, occupation, religion, personal qualities, and life history."[149] In a tropism-like way, the donor family, the recipient, and the recipient's family are drawn together by their reciprocal need to know about each other; by what Mauss referred to as the "personified spirit" of the gift; by the wish of the donor family to "have something back" for their gift in the form of continuing knowledge about the health and the life of the individual who received their deceased relative's organ; and by the desire of the recipient and his or her kin to express their gratitude to the donating family, and also to find some meaningful, non-material mode of repaying them.

Because these gift-exchange attributes of organ transplantation can lead to complicated and painful entanglements between recipients and their families, and donor families, medical teams have generally adopted a policy of anonymity about cadaver transplants. With some exceptions, the prevailing norm in transplant units is not to reveal the identity of the donor to the recipient and family, or to tell the donor's family who the recipient is.[150] Simmons, Klein, and Simmons described a local variant of this policy in their account of how the University Transplant Services that they studied handled these matters:

> The current policy . . . is to send a letter to the family of the cadaver-patient shortly after the surgery thanking them for their donation and telling them something about the operation(s). Although the recipients are not named, the letter generally mentions which organs were used, the sex and age, and some other basic information about the persons who received them, and some statement about the success of the transplants. The University does not give the name of the recipient so as to protect the recipient from the well-meaning but possibly guilt-provoking concern of the cadaver-patient's family. While many recipients have stated that they would like to thank the donating family, the University staff feels that the stress of being a transplant patient is significant enough without exposing the patient to the grief of the donor's family.[151]

The ever-present possibility that the transplanted organ will eventually be rejected by the recipient's body, and the disturbing effect that knowing this has happened is likely to have on a donor family, also underlies the policy of anonymity that most transplant centers try to maintain. In the course of their research on heart transplants, Fox and Swazey learned of numerous instances where a donor family who had found a way to make personal contact with a recipient and became involved in his life, underwent a "double grief reaction" when he rejected the transplanted heart and died. They mourned both for the "final demise" of their relative, and for the passing of the person in whom a living part of that relative had resided.[152] The majority of the kidney donor families who were interviewed by Roberta Simmons and her colleagues indicated that although they were eager to know that the organ gift was "a successful and valuable one, . . . they did not wish to know if the transplant had been unsuccessful."[153] In addition, Fox and Swazey have come to feel that "another less consciously intended role that this patterned anonymity plays is that it insulates the members of the transplant team from the discomfort they may feel in having to deal with manifest expressions of the magical and religious symbolic significance of giving and receiving organs for donors, recipients, and their families."[154]

Fox and Swazey have analyzed hemodialysis as well as transplantation in a gift-exchange framework. Whether dialysis is conducted in a medical center or at home, they explain, it entails "the continuous exchange of life for death" through the donation of time, energy, skill, and concern by persons who help to run the dialysis machine and attend the dialysis patient:

In the case of home dialysis, this exchange is all the more remarkable because it requires and permits a lay person (usually the patient's spouse) to assume an unprecedented amount of responsibility for operating a complex life-support system. As a consequence, home dialysis in particular confronts patients with the problem of receiving and reciprocating a recurrent gift of life.[155]

In *Gift of Life* and *The Courage to Fail*, and in other of their publications, Simmons et al., and Fox and Swazey have examined some of the ways in which the gift-exchange aspects of transplantation and dialysis open onto and interact with questions concerning the allocation of scarce resources, quality of life, and the foregoing of life-sustaining treatment. In their common sociological view, the unfolding story of dialysis and transplantation is a paradigmatic case history of the individual, institutional, and societal forms in which these questions that surround modern medicine are occurring, of the organized attempts that have been made to resolve them, and of how painfully unsimple it is to do so.

In a case study of "The Democratization of Dialysis,"[156] Fox and Swazey examine the intended and unintended consequences of the passage of the Chronic Kidney Disease Amendment to the Social Security Act by the U.S. Congress in 1972 (Public Law 92-603), through which Medicare insurance coverage was extended to virtually all patients with end-stage renal disease. Through this legislation, these patients became the first, and thus far the only, victims of catastrophic illness in the United States to receive special coverage of their treatment costs by the federal government. In principle, this legislation should have eliminated most financially-based problems of equity of access to dialysis and renal transplantation on the American scene. But, in fact, this has not proven to be the case. The passage of the law immediately raised several macro-level questions of allocation that were at once economic, political, and moral: Why should renal disease have been singled out for special coverage? And what are the implications of this decision for the federal financing of other catastrophic illnesses, and for the provision of a more broadly based form of national health insurance? These questions have not been dispelled over time. Quite the contrary, as "cost containment" became a more dominant economic and ethical preoccupation in American society during the 1970s and 1980s, the fact that the costs of this kidney disease program have been almost double the original estimates, and continue to mount, has reactivated debate over these questions.

In effect, to a degree that is unique among societies of the world, the United States has opted to try to provide dialysis and/or kidney transplants for all patients in end-stage failure who wish to avail themselves of it, regardless of their financial status, social background, age, or medical condition. Roberta Simmons and Susan Klein Marine contrast this American policy with the end-stage renal program of the United Kingdom:

> The current approach [to end-stage renal disease in Great Britain] is characterized by limited access (particularly to older patients) and an emphasis on low-cost, non-hospital-based therapies (home dialysis and transplantation). Patients who may be rejected for treatment include not only the elderly, but also diabetics and those with physical handicaps or mental illness. In addition, patients must have facilities appropriate for home dialysis, which creates a bias against accepting many lower-class patients.[157]

Donor organs are one of the principal resources involved in the treatment of end-stage renal, cardiac, liver, and lung diseases: very scarce, infinitely precious, tangible gifts of life of great nonmaterial meaning. Simmons, Marine, Fox, and Swazey have all been continuous participant observers in the process by which American society has struggled since the late 1950s to find an efficient, fair, and humane way to increase the supply of scarce organs, and to allocate them. As they have noted, the system of organ donation and procurement that has been institutionalized in the United States is based on the profoundly American values of individualism, freedom of choice, personal responsibility, voluntarism, generosity, and the Judeo-Christian-derived universalistic belief that we should be our stranger's as well as our brother's and our sister's keepers.

The procuring of organs is premised on informed, voluntary, and free donation. The buying and selling of organs or their routine "harvesting" from those who have died, is ethically and legally proscribed. The whole system is a decentralized one, made up of about 90 local Organ Procurement Agencies, linked by a computerized United Network of Organ Sharing, whose use is voluntary, and with no universally shared criteria for determining how organs should be distributed between them.[158]

Despite all the imperfections and limitations of this system, more organs are donated in the United States than in any society in the world. And yet there is a continuing, even escalating shortage of transplantable organs. As the success of transplantation has improved, the demand for organs has grown. But, as Swazey has pointed out, there are many other, more "complicated reasons for the imbalance between the need for and supply of donor organs":

> Although surveys indicate that most Americans favor organ donation, only some 15 percent has taken the step of signing donor cards. . . . Consent must be obtained from the next-of-kin, even if the newly dead prospective donor had signed an Anatomical Gift form. . . .[O]f those who die each year, relatively few are medically acceptable organ donors. Age, general medical condition, and the reasons for and manner of death rule out many prospects. . . . And even if a gift of life is given, it is not always used. Some organs prove to be unsuitable for transplantation. Sometimes a suitable recipient, in terms of tissue-typing compatibility, cannot be located within the time-span in which a donor organ can be preserved. And sometimes, because the sharing between organ procurement groups is not always ideal, an organ is discarded, unused because there is not a recipient in the procuring group's area.[159]

The evolution of dialysis and renal transplantation has not only revealed that the funding of such treatments for end-stage disease and open access to them do not necessarily dispel allocation of scarce resource problems. Such a policy also may augment questions about quality of life, and about decisions to stop treatment that are entwined with problems of allocation. Since the passage of Public Law 92-603, for example, the percentage of older, sicker patients of lower socioeconomic status on dialysis has significantly increased. Studies of the clinical outcomes of chronic dialysis with this changed population suggest that a larger proportion of dialysis patients than previously suspected are severely debilitated. In the face of these new sociomedical conditions surrounding long-term dialysis, a very old and stark set of questions have been raised afresh, and on a larger scale: "Who shall live when not all can live?" "Should all those who can be kept alive live?"[160] When "the main effects" of a long-term, life-supporting and life-maintaining treatment such as dialysis become only those of "discomfort and pain," should "patients, physicians, and families . . . be willing to consider discontinuing treatment?"[161]

One case study in *The Courage To Fail* concerns the saga of Ernie Crowfeather, a 29-year-old, "bright, charming, part American Indian" man with end-stage renal disease who, for his medical caretakers, and also for Fox and Swazey, became "the personification" and the tragicomic "epitome" of all these allocation of scarce resources, quality of life, and stopping treatment problems.[162] After thirty months of treatment for his disease, which included peritoneal dialysis and hemodialysis prior to a kidney transplant, rejection of the organ, followed again by peritoneal dialysis, in-center hemodialysis, home dialysis, and in-center dialysis once more, punctuated by a community campaign to raise money for the continuation of his treatment, several arrests and imprisonments for theft, numerous bouts of heavy drinking, drug dependency, and both marital and employment problems, Ernie Crowfeather terminated his treatment. He used the check that he had received for dialysis at the VA hospital to go on a last binge, and to repay some debts to family members and friends. He was found in a motel room, rushed to the emergency service of a local hospital, and died there that night, leaving all who had been involved with him, his predicament, and his medical care still grappling with "the life and death issues, the sense of obligation to actively intervene, the problems of meaning, the uncertainties, and the feelings of guilt and failure that terminal kidney disease, [long-term] dialysis, and transplantation can trigger."[163]

Physicians, nurses, social workers, and other medical professionals engaged in the fields of dialysis and transplantation have been responsive to the continuing sociological studies that Roberta Simmons and colleagues, Judith Swazey, and Renée Fox have conducted in this area. They have reviewed their books and extensively cited their articles in the medical literature, invited these sociological authors to give many lectures and make rounds in numerous institutional settings, and formally and informally expressed appreciation for both the clinical usefulness of their microdynamic analyses and the larger perspective that the macro-framework of societal and cultural analysis undergirding their empirical research provides.

The reactions of medical professionals contrast sharply with those of bioethicists. In the major publications of the bioethical community, the writings of Simmons et al., Swazey and Fox are rarely mentioned when dialysis and transplantation are discussed. Rather, there is an overall tendency to refer primarily to the works of certain in-group, nonsociologist bioethicists, who are defined as authoritative experts on the medical ethical and policy questions associated with these modes of treatment for end-stage disease.[164]

There is at least one notable exception to this pattern which, as we have indicated, extends beyond dialysis, transplantation, and social scientists who have studied them. The work that sociologist Robert W. Evans has done in this field is widely recognized and used by physicians, health policy analysts and policymakers, who also actively seek his consultant advice. His data and analyses are respected as source materials by bioethicists as well, although they do not rely on Evans's findings to the degree that physicians and health policy persons do.

Evans has specialized competence in technology assessment and resource allocation in health care. He has applied this expertise and his methodological command of large-scale survey research to the area of dialysis and organ transplantation since the late 1970s. He is best known for the National Kidney Dialysis and Transplantation Study that he conducted from 1981 to 1984 for the Health Care Financing Administration (HCFA). [HCFA is the agency of the federal government responsible for administering Medicare and Medicaid, and the End Stage Renal Disease (ESRD) Program that has been funded since 1973 with Medicare monies.] The major objective of this study was to "collect and analyze data necessary to better understand the current status of chronic renal disease patients," with the "hope" that the results forthcoming from it would be used "to formulate future health policies which adequately reflect the needs of the chronic renal disease patients, to insure the highest standards of practice within the medical community, and to promote the efficient use of public resources":

> Nearly 1,000 patients from eleven dialysis and/or transplant centers across the country were personally interviewed. . . . Respondents represented four different treatment modalities: home hemodialysis, in-center hemodialysis, continuous ambulatory peritoneal dialysis/continuous cycling peritoneal dialysis, and kidney transplantation. Following the interview, with the patient's written consent, medical data were abstracted from his or her medical record. In addition, the patient's primary nephrologist, social worker, or renal nurse familiar with the patient's functional status listed the patient's physical impairments and assessed his or her ability to work. Finally, the eleven participating dialysis and/or transplant centers were surveyed to determine various characteristics of the facility relating to treatment. . . .
>
> [T]he five major areas on which the study focused [were]: 1) quality of life, 2) rehabilitation, 3) disability, 4) quality of care, and 5) cost of treatment.[165]

During the same period that he was responsible for the kidney dialysis and transplantation study, Evans was also Principal Investigator for the National Heart Transplantation Study (1981–1985), once again sponsored by HCFA. The data collected for this study were very similar to those gathered in the dialysis and renal transplant investigations:

> 152 living donor heart transplant recipients were interviewed, and the medical records of these and 289 additional patients were abstracted with consent. All patients were associated with six major heart transplant centers in the United States. From the living donor heart transplant recipients, data were collected on their quality of life, the impact of their heart transplant on their family, their ability to cover expenses associated with their heart transplant, and their feelings about the experience they had been through.[166]

This study was commissioned primarily because the federal government was facing the question of whether or not to assume the costs of heart transplantation for Medicare recipients, drawing on the precedent set for end-stage renal disease. The federal funding issue was raised by the end of a decade-long moratorium on heart transplants, marked improvement in the survival rate of heart transplant recipients due to progress in pre- and post-operative care as well as in the surgery itself, and consequently, the increasing claim by transplanters that the procedure is no longer experimental. Evans points out that "the economic consequences" of the End-Stage Renal Disease Program have been "staggering," In 1985, for example, "more than 80,000 patients with chronic kidney failure accounted for Medicare expenditures in excess of $2 billion." He goes on to say that "it is debatable whether we will be able to afford a similar outcome for another disease again," a sentiment that is strongly felt in the present climate of "economic uncertainty" and "effort[s] to contain costs."[167]

The heart transplantation study was also launched in a policy framework influenced by the impact of bioethics on the thinking of federal agencies like the Department of Health and Human Services (HHS). "In June 1980, the late Patricia Roberts Harris, then Secretary of [the Department], announced that HHS would require new technologies to pass muster on the basis of their 'social consequences' before financing their wide distribution." For both medical and political reasons, heart transplantation became the first modality to undergo this kind of assessment—one that would entail an examination of "the patient selection process; the long-term social, economic, and ethical consequences of the procedure; and the potential for wide distribution of the heart transplantation procedure."[168] These broadly defined evaluation goals provided a grid for the national study that Evans designed and conducted.

"The debate on Medicare reimbursement—and on heart transplantation in general," Evans has written, "ostensibly rests on whether the benefits of this procedure are worth its huge perceived costs." From the data that he amassed and analyzed on patient survival, quality of life, and the comparative economic costs of the procedure, Evans concluded that "the argument in favor of Medicare funding for heart transplantation is at least as compelling as that for kidney dialysis, as well as that for the treatment of patients with acquired immune deficiency syndrome (AIDS) or cancer."[169] The macro-allocation issue underlying the "heart transplant dilemma" and the "debate" over it, he points out, is a moral as well as an economic one: "how much [are] we as a society . . . willing to spend on the care of dying patients or patients facing life-threatening diseases?"[170] He also argues that on the grounds of "fairness to patients," efficiency, and progress, "if it can be shown that a new technology or patient management strategy is equally cost-effective as other treatment approaches, we must . . . choose to cover the new treatment approaches or reconsider, and perhaps rescind, the coverage of previously accepted technologies."[171]

Since 1984, Evans has been directing two new research projects, sponsored by HFCA and the Department of the Navy, concerned with the donation, procurement, and allocation of scarce transplantable organs and tissues. The articles based on these studies that he has published so far deal principally with the role that the attitudes and behavior of the medical community and the general public play in this connection, and with the politically and ethically complicated question of what kind of involvement, if any, the government should have in promoting organ donation.[172]

Roger Evans has published some fifty articles, chiefly in medical journals. He is defined more as a medical professional than as a social scientist. Many physicians are not aware of the fact that he is a social scientist, or that his respected competence in research and analysis are grounded in sociological training. He is far less well known among sociologists than among medical and health policy professionals. In large part, this is related to what Samuel W. Bloom has described as the way in which "the tension between academic and applied orientations endemic in sociology," and its "struggling with 'insider-outsider' ambiguity," have been institutionalized in the subfield of medical sociology.[173] Medical sociology views itself as a primarily academic discipline. It is ambivalent about and resistant to applied work, and its so-called "technocratic" propensities. And it is wary about how functioning "inside medicine," rather than "outside" it can "subvert the role of [an] independent scholar."[174] Evans's career as a sociologist of medicine has been based in a non-academic institution (the Battelle Human Affairs Research Centers in Seattle, Washington); he is a medical "insider"; and most of his research has been sponsored and funded by federal agencies that have needed the data and analyses his studies provide to help them with their policy decisions and administrative responsibilities. From a "sociology of sociology" point of view, these characteristics of his professional history have made Evans more marginal to social science than to the medical and bioethical communities. In turn, the same "institutional trends in medical sociology" that push a Roger Evans to the periphery of his profession, also contribute to the "three-cultures split" that rends bioethics.

COST CONTAINMENT, RATIONING, AND FOR-PROFIT ENTERPRISE IN HEALTH CARE

At this juncture in the 1980s, the content and outlook of American bioethics have been influenced by the facts that "cost containment strategies are sweeping through the health care system like fire through parched underbrush,"[175] and that the social organization of health care is swiftly undergoing major alterations, especially in the area of for-profit services. Sociologists have been contributing several kinds of work to the concerned debate about the phenomena and issues that these changes entail.

First, they have been supplying relevant bodies of information in the form of systematically collected and analyzed socio-medical data, of which Roger Evans's studies are a prime example.

Second, they have designed and conducted a number of original empirical studies that examine some of the questions surrounding these recent trends in American medicine. One important study of this sort is the Institute of Medicine (IOM) project on the provision of health care by investor-owned organizations, directed by sociologist Bradford H. Gray, with the collaboration of a 22-member IOM-appointed Committee on Implications of For-Profit Enterprise in Health Care.[176] The inquiry not only investigated "factual matters about organizational behavior but also the value conflicts raised by changes taking place in the organization of health care in America . . . [conflicts that] color people's interpretations of data and persist after all empirical studies have been reviewed":

> Thus, some observers believe that the rise of for-profit health care threatens the values and ideals that should guide the activities of health professionals and health care organizations and that, if realized, distinguished professional work from commerce. Concern has also been expressed that the growth of for-profit health care may exacerbate current problems in the health care system. Problems frequently mentioned include inadequate availability of services for people who lack the means to pay, duplicative high-cost technologies and facilities for health care delivery, deficiencies in the availability of good primary care and services for patients with chronic disease, and highly variable rates of elective surgery.
>
> It is feared that something essential will be lost if a service ethos—expressed in terms such as caring, community responsiveness, fiduciary responsibility—is abandoned or replaced with a principle based on economic goals.[177]

The overall findings of the IOM study-report are equivocal:

> The differences between for-profit and not-for-profit organizations in their values, tax status, and sources of capital have prompted both theory and assumptions about their behavior regarding hospital costs, pricing, quality, service to patients who are unable to pay, involvement in research and education, access to capital, and relationships with medical staffs. . . . [T]he committee's examination of the evidence shows that many of these assumptions are false and that others are only partly true. . . .
>
> The committee concludes that available evidence on differences between for-profit and not-for-profit health care organizations is not sufficient to justify a recommendation that investor ownership of health care organizations be either opposed or supported by public policy.[178]

More specifically, the report shows that on a per-day basis, charges are higher in for-profit than in not-for-profit institutions, and that on average, for-profit institutions have been slightly less efficient. According to available indicators of quality of care, however, there are no appreciable differences between for-profit and not-for-profit hospitals. The data also showed that for-profit hospitals have rendered less uncompensated care to uninsured patients than their not-for-profit counterparts, and that their capability of greater access to capital in some places has allowed them to build or renovate needed facilities.

Most of the IOM study committee agreed that although "our current path toward an increasingly competitive environment, with more investor-ownership, more for-profit activities by not-for-profit institutions, and larger multi-institutional networks, raises enough issues to warrant careful monitoring,"[179] it is hard to find grounds for being critical of for-profit institutions at the present time, particularly when business needs are driving not-for-profit institutions as well. However, there were seven members of the committee who took exception to this conclusion, and wrote a "supplementary statement" to the report. They declared that in their opinion, its "major finding . . . is that the investor-owned hospital chains have so far demonstrated no advantages for the public interest over their not-for-profit competitors,"[180] and that "we would have little to gain, and possibly much to lose, if for-profit corporations came to dominate our health care system."[181] This dissenting minority included sociologist Eliot Freidson, and two prominent bioethicists, jurist Alexander Morgan Capron, former Executive Director of the President's Commission for the Study of Ethical Problems in Medicine and Biomedical and Behavioral Research, and philosopher Daniel Wikler, a former Commission staff member.

Sociologists like David Mechanic and Paul Starr have made a third sort of contribution to the current debate. They have set forth a larger societal and historical framework within which to analyze, interpret, and evaluate the sorts of resource allocation, rationing, cost control, and for-profit issues in health care that have become matters of great medical, economic, political, social, and ethical concern during the 1980s.

A substantial part of Mechanic's work that is addressed to these matters appears in his book, *Future Issues in Health Care: Social Policy and the Rationing of Medical Services*, and in *From Advocacy to Allocation: The Evolving American Health Care System*, a collection of some of his essays.[182] In his introductions to these volumes, Mechanic voices his convictions about what he regards as the non-disjunctive" relationship between basic and applied medical sociology, and about the valuable role he believes a social science perspective and analytic framework can and should play in fashioning, implementing, and evaluating policy:

> The American health care system is in the throes of a scientific, philosophical, and economic revolution. It is a time of ferment and uncertainty. . . . In the past several years I have had the opportunity to participate in a variety of health policy efforts and to write on health matters in different public forums in addition to pursuing empirical research on health and illness behavior and health care organization. The purpose of this volume is to bring together that part of my work in recent years that is directed more to policy and clinical issues than to substantive research themes in medical sociology. While I see no disjunction between my interests in policy and clinical issues and more basic issues I research, the choice to select only a part of my work has a number of rationales. . . . [Most] importantly, the essays that appear here have all been published in journals and books that my social science colleagues do not typically know although they are important references for physicians, policy analysts, and policymakers in health.[183] . . .
>
> In this book I examine cost-containment problems, but in the context of impending problems of health need and medical care. If there is a single thread that ties these discussions, it is the importance of understanding behavior in designing and implementing social policy, for it is the perceptions and responses of those affected that will ultimately determine the fate of public policy. . . . Controlling cost—like increasing access, improving the capacity of the care system, and providing sensitive and high-quality care—will come not by one major thrust but by long-term efforts to understand how to affect the behavior of patients and physicians and how to design incentives that will not be diverted or perverted.[184]

But it is Paul Starr's book, *The Social Transformation of American Medicine*,[185] particularly its analysis of "the growth of corporate medicine," that has received the greatest amount of attention and had the most powerful impact on a variety of medical, social science, and policymaking circles. Published in 1982, the book had an explosively illuminating effect on its vast, largely admiring readership.[186] This is partly because it authoritatively identified what he called "the coming of the corporation" to the American medical scene, situated it historically and sociologically, and raised cogent questions about its value implications, as well as its medical, economic, and political consequences, at a time when concerned awareness about this "transformation" was beginning to surface but had not yet fully crystallized. In his Preface, Starr explains that for him, too, the significance of the rise of the corporation in American medicine emerged gradually:

> I have divided this history into two books to emphasize two long movements in the development of American medicine: first, the rise of professional sovereignty; and second, the transformation of medicine into an industry, and the growing, though still unsettled, role of corporations and the state. . . .
>
> This last question became more salient while this book was in progress. When I began work in 1974, it was widely thought that medical schools, planners, and administrators were emerging as the chief counter-weight to private physicians. Government seemed to be assuming a major, perhaps dominant role in the

organization of medical care. Decisions that had formerly been private and professional were becoming public and political. Eight years later this is no longer clearly the direction of change, but neither is the status quo ante being restored. Private corporations are gaining a more powerful position in American medicine; if leading members of the Reagan administration have their way, the future may well belong to corporate medicine. However, the origins of this development precede the current administration; the forces behind it are more powerful than the changing fashions in Washington. Precisely because of what is now taking place, it has become more necessary to understand medicine as a business as well as a cultural phenomenon—and perhaps most important, to understand the relation between the two.[187]

It would seem that the sociological works that have the most influence in the bioethics subculture are ones, like those of Paul Starr and David Mechanic, that are written by academics with considerable prestige and that deal with ethical questions related to the political economy of medicine. And yet, even though Starr's *Social Transformation of American Medicine* turned out to be what amounts to a scholarly best-seller, it has figured far less prominently in the bioethics than in the medical, policy analysis, and social science literature. In the end, it has had little effect on the conceptual framework, the knowledge base, and the ethos of bioethics.

It seems appropriate to end this chapter with an invitation to sociologists to be more present and active in bioethics, not only as conceptual, empirical, and policy contributors to it, but also as analysts of the social and cultural phenomenon that it represents. For if it is true, as we alleged at the outset, that "bioethics is not just bioethics," that it is "more than medical," and that it deals with "nothing less than beliefs, values, and norms that are basic to our society, its cultural tradition, and its collective conscience,"[188] then it is vital that the best, most insightful, and morally sensitive sociological thinking be integral to it.

NOTES

1. It is unclear who coined the term bioethics. Biologist and cancer researcher Van Rensselaer Potter was one of the first to use it in print, in his book *Bioethics: Bridge to the Future* (Englewood Cliffs, N.J.: Prentice-Hall, 1971). For Potter, bioethics referred to the new ethical values and practices which he felt were necessary to save Western civilization, and humankind more generally, from impending social disaster. Potter saw bioethics as based on a "science of survival," and "built on the science of biology . . . enlarged beyond the traditional boundaries to include the most essential elements of the social sciences, and the humanities, with emphasis on philosophy." (see Howard L.Kaye's interpretive analysis of how and why such apocalyptically survivalist themes are salient motifs in the writings of many prominent contemporary biologists: H. L. Kaye, *The Social Meaning of Modern Biology: From Social Darwinism to Sociobiology* (New Haven: Yale University Press, 1986), and "The Biological Revolution and Its Cultural Context," *International Journal of Technology Assessment in Health Care*, 2, no. 2 (1986). As our discussion of bioethics will indicate, the way Potter used the term bioethics is not what it has commonly come to mean.
2. Renée C. Fox and Judith P. Swazey, "Medical Morality Is Not Bioethics—Medical Ethics in China and the United States," *Perspectives in Biology and Medicine*, 27, no. 3 (Spring 1984), 336 and 360.
3. See, for example, sociologist François-Andre Isambert's comparative analysis of French and American bioethics in his essay, "Révolution Biologique, ou Reveil Éthique," *Éthique et*

Biologie (Cahiers Science–Technologie–Société), Paris: Éditions du Centre National de la Recherche Scientifique, 1986, 9–41, especially pp. 27–38. According to Isambert, French bioethics did not really "take off" and begin to develop intellectually and institutionally until the 1980s, some "ten to fifteen years later" than in the United States. Its scope has not been as wide and diverse as American bioethics. Thus far, it has been especially centered on issues associated with infertility and reproductive technologies, and with the theme of procreation more generally. The secularization of French society notwithstanding, its culture is still deeply influenced by Catholicism. This may contribute to the French bioethical preoccupation with procreation. The same pattern is notable in the bioethics of Belgium, which is also a Catholic country in the same sense. French bioethics has been more secondarily involved in matters concerning human experimentation, death, dying, and "euthanasia," genetic screening and counseling, and genetic engineering. Isambert regards the creation of the Comité Consultatif National d'Éthique pour les Sciences de la Vie et de la Santé [National Advisory Ethics Committee for the Life Sciences and Health], installed in December 1983, as the most significant development to date in the progressive institutionalization of bioethics in France.

4. At the risk of immodesty, since I am one of the only sociologists who has written about bioethics as a social and cultural phenomenon, I will have to draw heavily on my own work in some sections of this chapter. The chief publications in which I have essayed this kind of sociological analysis of bioethics are: Renée C. Fox, "Ethical and Existential Developments in Contemporaneous American Medicine: Their Implications for Culture and Society," *Milbank Memorial Fund Quarterly/Health and Society* (Fall 1974), 445–83; "Advanced Medical Technology—Social and Ethical Implications," *Annual Review of Sociology*, 2 (1976), 231–68; (with Judith P. Swazey) "Medical Morality Is Not Bioethics"; "Medicine, Science, and Technology," in *Applications of Social Science to Clinical Medicine and Health Policy*, eds. Linda H. Aiken and David Mechanic (New Brunswick, N.J.: Rutgers University Press, 1986), 13–30. An essay by Bradford H. Gray and Marian Osterweis, "Ethical Issues in a Social Context," in the same volume (Aiken and Mechanic), provides an informative and useful topical survey of works by sociologists that are relevant to medical ethical issues and dilemmas treated by bioethics.

5. Fox, "Ethical and Existential Developments in Contemporaneous American Medicine," pp. 446–47.

6. This meeting on "Ethics and the New Economics of Health Care," sponsored by the Southern Regional Branch of the Society for Health and Human Values, was held at the Medical College of Virginia in March 1986.

7. In 1976, the New Jersey Supreme Court granted Joseph Quinlan's request to be appointed guardian of his daughter, Karen Ann Quinlan, who had been in a "persistent vegetative state" for more than a year. The court empowered him to discontinue the life-supporting respirator on which she was being maintained, if attending physicians and the hospital ethics committee agreed that there was "no reasonable possibility" that she would return to a "cognitive, sapient state." This court decision overruled the position taken by Karen Ann Quinlan's physicians, and overturned the Superior Court of New Jersey's ruling on the case in 1975. Karen Ann Quinlan was taken off the respirator, but lived for almost ten more years in a nursing home, breathing on her own, without returning to consciousness. [See *In re Quinlan* 70 N.J. 10 355 A.2d 647, *cert. denied* 429 U.S. 922 (1976).]

8. The term "Baby Doe cases" has grown up around instances in which, out of a process of consultation between medical professionals in a neonatal intensive care unit (NICU) and parents, the decision has been made to withhold some medical or surgical treatment vital to maintaining the life of an infant. The Baby Doe-type cases that have received the most bioethical and public attention have involved infants afflicted either with Down's syndrome or spina bifida, who have both correctable life-threatening defects and also serious, irreparable, permanent handicaps. Around such Baby Does, highly publicized court cases have occurred, precipitated in part by the direct intervention of the federal government. At the specific request of the White House in 1962, the Department of Health and Human Services (HHS) established so-called "Baby Doe rules," and at one point a "Baby Doe hotline," to govern the NICU situation, and to report persons to the HHS who were suspected of withholding medical or surgical treatment or nutrition from an infant in the NICU. For several sociologists' perspectives on these developments, on the numerous revisions in the Baby Doe rules since 1962 and on the continuing controversy surrounding this situation, see Gray and Osterweis, "Ethical Issues in a Social Context," pp. 553–55, and Renée C. Fox, "Medicine, Science, and Technology," *op. cit.*, pp. 17–21. Several books published in 1986–87 examine the ethical issues involved in NICU treatment of handicapped

newborns and in government intervention in this area of medicine. See Joanne B. Ciulla, "The Legacy of Baby Doe," *Psychology Today*, 21, no. 1 (January 1987), 70–75.

9. The Congress held oversight meetings in 1983 and 1984 into the shortage of donor organs in the United States. As a consequence of those hearings, it passed the National Organ Transplant Act (P.L. 98-507), which brought the Task Force on Organ Transplantation into being. The Task Force was established by the Secretary of Health and Human Services in January 1985. It consisted of two work groups, on immunosuppressive therapies and on reimbursement. It delivered its report on immunosuppressive therapies to the Secretary and the Congress in October 1985, and its second, more general report on the procurement and allocation of scarce organs and on the funding of organ transplants, in July 1986.

10. For a list of some of these bioethics organizations and the agencies that have been sponsoring and funding their work, see, Renée C. Fox, "Advanced Medical Technology—Social and Ethical Implications," p. 415.

11. LeRoy Walters, "Introduction," *Bibliography of Bioethics*, 9 (New York: The Free Press/Macmillan, 1983), p. 3.

12. The *Bibliography of Bioethics* is one of the ongoing research projects of the Kennedy Institute of Ethics. It has received financial support for its publication from the Joseph P. Kennedy, Jr., Foundation, the National Library of Medicine, and the National Institutes of Health.

13. The *Encyclopedia of Bioethics* project was made possible by a matching grant from the National Endowment for the Humanities. It is a four-volume work, published by The Free Press and edited by Warren T. Reich. A new edition is presently being considered.

14. Warren T. Reich, "Introduction," *Encyclopedia of Bioethics* (1978), xvi.

15. Section 202(a) (1) (A) of the National Research Act of 1974.

16. Due to delays in appointing and funding this Commission, it did not hold its first meeting until January 14, 1980, when its original members were sworn in at the White House by Judge David L. Bazelon. Its "sunset" date was originally December 31, 1982, but because of its late start, this was extended to March 31, 1983 by Public Law 97-377 (December 20, 1982). Partly as a consequence, as the terms of the Commissioners with one-, two-, and three-year appointments expired, President Reagan was able to replace them with others of his own choosing. By August 1982, he had named eight new Commissioners (out of a Commission of eleven members). I served as a member of this Commission from July 1979 until February 1982.

17. In each case, the Commission's report was in a single volume; for some subjects, supporting materials and documents were published in the form of one or more appendix volumes. The entire set of volumes, published *in seriatim* by the U.S. Government Printing Office in Washington, D.C., were ordered in great numbers by a wide range of professionals, public officials, academics, science and medical writers, etc. The reports and their contents are listed and summarized in the Commission's final report, *Summing Up: The Ethical and Legal Problems in Medicine and Biomedical and Behavioral Research* (Washington, D.C.: U.S. Government Printing Office), March 1983.

18. For a sociological analysis of the cultural content and meaning of the case of Dr. Barney C. Clark, see Renée C. Fox, "'It's the Same, but Different': A Sociological Perspective on the Case of the Utah Artificial Heart," in *After Barney Clark: Reflections on the Utah Artificial Heart Program*, ed. Margery W. Shaw (Austin: University of Texas Press, 1984), pp. 68–90. Other comparably symbolic figures that come to mind include Karen Ann Quinlan, Jamie Fiske, and "Baby Fae."

19. Parts of the discussion of the ethos of bioethics in this chapter are heavily dependent on Fox and Swazey, "Medical Morality Is Not Bioethics," especially pp. 352–58.

20. Two such prominent public figures, for example, are Senator Albert Gore, Jr., who has been a Congressional leader on issues concerning organ transplantation, and Colorado Governor Richard D. Lamm, who has been actively involved in questions of death, dying, and life-prolonging treatments.

21. Fox, "Advanced Medical Technology."

22. Fox and Swazey, "Medical Morality Is Not Bioethics," p. 355.

23. This phrase is taken from Evelyn Fox Keller's depiction of Barbara McClintock's "vision of science." Evelyn Fox Keller, *Reflections on Gender and Science* (New Haven, Conn.: Yale University Press, 1985), p. 173. It is interesting and more than coincidental that these concepts and values, which coincide with our most familiar stereotypes of women, are de-emphasized both in the dominant ethos of science and of bioethics. For a more extensive discussion of

Keller's work on gender and science and of her biography of Barbara McClintock, see Chapter 6.

24. In the United States District Court for the District of Columbia, American Academy of Pediatrics, National Association of Children's Hospitals and Related Institutions, Children's Hospital National Medical Center, Plaintiffs, v. Margaret M. Heckler, Secretary, Department of Health and Human Services, Defendant, Civil Action No. 83-0774, filed 14 April1 1983, U.S. District Judge Gerhard H. Gesell presiding.

25. Judge Irving R. Kaufman, "Life-and-Death Decisions," Op. Ed. page of *The New York Times*, October 6, 1985.

26. See the Uniform Determination of Death Act, drafted by the President's Commission for the Study of Ethical Problems in Medicine and Biomedical and Behavioral Research in collaboration with the American Bar Association, the American Medical Association, and the National Conference of Commissioners of Uniform State Laws, in President's Commission for the Study of Ethical Problems in Medicine and Biomedical and Behavioral Research, *Defining Death*, (July 1981), pp. 119–20, and the review and analysis of state legislation on the "determination of death," and judicial developments in the "definition" of death, pp. 109–46.

27. Supreme Court of the United States, Roe et al. v. Wade, District Attorney of Dallas County, Appeal from the United States District Court for the Northern District of Texas, No. 70-18. Argued December 13, 1971; reargued October 11, 1972; decided January 22, 1973.

28. American Academy of Pediatrics, National Association of Children's Hospitals and Related Institutions, Children's Hospital National Medical Center v. Margaret M. Heckler, cited above in Footnote 26.

29. Personal letter (July 17, 1986), from Ruel Tyson, Professor in the Department of Religious Studies of The University of North Carolina at Chapel Hill.

30. Memorandum to North Carolina Humanities Committee, from Medicine and Society Advisory Board Members, June 20, 1986, p. 3. The memo goes on to refer to one of the major paradoxes that the Committee has faced in their attempt to broaden and enrich the perspective and discussion on these issues with the public. Particularly "rural audiences . . . tend to underestimate what they can do, . . . do not take seriously their own capabilities and resources, . . . and commonly do not think that they know anything unless it is ordained by the expert."

31. William J. Bennett, "Getting Ethics," *Commentary*, 70, no. 6 (December 1980), 63–5. See philosopher Samuel Gorovitz's spirited rejoinder to what he refers to as Bennett's indicting attack on bioethics: Samuel Gorovitz, "Baiting Bioethics" (Survey Article), *Ethics*, 96 (January 1986), 358 and 368–72. In this same article, Gorovitz also characterizes the article comparing American bioethics and Chinese "medical morality" that I coauthored with Judith Swazey ("Medical Morality Is Not Bioethics"), as "another biting attack" on bioethics, and debates it at some length. (See pp. 358 and 363–69.)

32. Daniel Callahan, "Contemporary Biomedical Ethics" (Shattuck Lecture) *New England Journal of Medicine*, 302, no. 22 (May 29, 1980), 1228.

33. Ibid.

34. Ibid., p. 1230.

35. Daniel Callahan, "Autonomy: A Moral Good, Not a Moral Obsession," *Hastings Center Report*, 14, no. 5 (October 1984) 42.

36. Colleen D. Clements and Roger O. Snider, "Medical Ethics' Assault Upon Medical Values," *Journal of the American Medical Association*, 250, no. 15 (October 21, 1983), 2011.

37. Robert M. Veatch, "Autonomy's Temporary Triumph," *Hastings Center Report*, 14, no. 5 (October 1984), 38–40.

38. Daniel Callahan, "Autonomy: A Moral Good, Not a Moral Obsession," p. 40.

39. Veatch, "Autonomy's Temporary Triumph," p. 38.

40. Daniel Callahan, "Autonomy: A Moral Good, Not a Moral Obsession," p. 42.

41. Ibid.

42. Ibid.

43. Robert S. Morison, "The Biological Limits on Autonomy," *Hastings Center Report*, 14, no. 5 (October 1984), 43 and 48.

44. Daniel Callahan, "Minimalist Ethics," *Hastings Center Report*, 11, no. 5 (October 1981), 19–25.

45. Willard Gaylin, "Autonomy, Paternalism, and Community," *Hastings Center Report*, 14, no. 5 (October 1984), 5.

ontemporary Biomedical Ethics," p. 1233.

Clements, "Bioethical Essentialism and Scientific Population Thinking," *Perspec-logy and Medicine*, 28, no. 2 (Winter 1985), 188.

49. Ibid., p. 4.

50. Callahan, "Contemporary Biomedical Ethics," p. 1233.

51. Clements, "Bioethical Essentialism and Scientific Population Thinking," p. 204.

52. Ibid., p. 205.

53. Ibid., p. 206. For a luminous sociological analysis of some of the problems of "biologizing ethics," see Howard L. Kaye, *The Social Meaning of Modern Biology* (New Haven: Yale University Press, 1986), and our discussion in Chapter 6.

54. Callahan, "Contemporary Biomedical Ethics," p. 1233. Callahan makes a stronger statement about the help that the social sciences could derive from the field of ethics than about the potential benefits of social science to ethical analysis, research, and methodology.

55. Daniel Callahan, "At The Center," *Hastings Center Report*, 16 (August 1986).

56. Letter from Daniel Callahan to Renée C. Fox, November 7, 1986.

57. "Caring for Newborns: Three World Views," (Arthur I. Eidelman, "In Israel, Families Look to Two Messengers of God"; K. N. Siva Subramanian, "In India, Nepal, and Sri Lanka, Quality of Life Weighs Heavily"; Rihito Kimura," In Japan, Parents Participate but Doctors Decide"; Nancy K. Rhoden, "Treating Baby Doe: The Ethics of Uncertainty") *Hastings Center Report*, 16, no. 4 (August 1986), 18–42.

58. Ruth Purtilo and James Sorrell, "The Ethical Dilemmas of a Rural Physician," *Hastings Center Report*, 16, no. 4 (August 1986), 24–28.

59. This is a reference to Durkheim's conceptual insight about the "non-contractual aspects of contract," developed in his *Division of Labor*. Certain of the more existentially and theologically oriented philosophical contributors to bioethical thought also highlight the "faith," "trust," and "commitment" parameters of a moral social life. For example, James F. Gustafson emphasizes "fidelity," and William F. May, "covenant."

60. Callahan, "Contemporary Biomedical Ethics," p. 1233.

61. This is a phrase used by anthropologist Clifford Geertz in his 1981 Bicentennial Address to the American Academy of Arts and Sciences, entitled, "The Way We Think Now: Toward an Ethnography of Modern Thought," *Bulletin of The Academy of Arts and Sciences*, XXXV, no. 5 (February 1982), 18.

62. Ibid., p. 22.

63. C. P. Snow, *The Two Cultures and the Scientific Revolution* [The Rede Lecture, 1959] (New York: Cambridge University Press, 1959).

64. Geertz, "The Way We Think Now," p. 27.

65. By 1985, the teaching of medical ethics in American medical schools had advanced to the point where the *New England Journal of Medicine* published a "Special Report," authored by a group of medical and non-medical bioethicists who had reached the conclusion that "the field is now sufficiently developed and the need for application of ethical knowledge and skills in medicine sufficiently compelling to justify a recommendation that all medical schools require basic instruction in the subject." Charles M. Culver, and others "Basic Curricular Goals in Medical Ethics," *New England Journal of Medicine*, 312, no. 4 (January 24, 1985), 253–56. See also Janet Bickel "Human Values Teaching Programs in the Clinical Education of Medical Students," *Journal of Medical Education*, 62 (May 1987), 369–78.

66. Diana Crane, *The Sanctity of Social Life: Physicians' Treatment of Critically Ill Patients* (New York: Russell Sage Foundation, 1975); Renée C. Fox, *Experiment Perilous* (Glencoe, Ill.: The Free Press, 1959); Barney G. Glaser and Anselm L. Strauss, *Awareness of Dying* (Chicago: Aldine Publishing Company, 1965); Barney G. Glaser and Anselm L. Strauss, *Time for Dying* (Chicago: Aldine Publishing Company, 1968); Anselm L. Strauss and Barney G. Glaser, *Anguish: A Case History of A Dying Trajectory* (Mill Valley, California: Sociology Press, 1970); David Sudnow, *Passing On: The Social Organization of Dying* (Englewood Cliffs, N.J.: Prentice-Hall, Inc., 1967).

67. See Robert A. Kalish, "Death and Dying: A Briefly Annotated Bibliography," in *The Dying Patient*, eds. Orville G. Brim and others (New York: Russell Sage Foundation, 1970), pp. 327–80.

68. Michel Vovelle, "Rediscovery of Death Since 1960," in *The Social Meaning of Death*, Special Issue of *Annals of the American Academy of Political and Social Science*, ed., Renée C. Fox, 447 (January 1980), 89–99.

69. Philippe Ariès, *Western Attitudes Toward Death: From the Middle Ages to the Present*, Patricia M. Ranum, trans. (Baltimore: The Johns Hopkins University Press,1974), pp. 85–107.

70. Glaser and Strauss, *Time For Dying*, pp. 251–59.

71. Ibid.

72. The famous book in which Elisabeth Kübler-Ross identified and clinically described the five stages through which dying persons supposedly pass (denial and isolation, anger and resentment, bargaining and an attempt to postpone, depression and a sense of loss, and acceptance) is: *On Death and Dying* (New York: Macmillan Co., 1969). This book, in which she presented a number of firsthand cases drawn from her intensive experience with over 200 incurably ill and progressively dying patients, became an overnight best-seller. By 1981, it had sold several hundred thousand copies. See Renée C. Fox's analysis of "Elisabeth Kübler-Ross and the 'On Death and Dying' Movement," in "The Sting of Death in American Society," *Social Service Review*, 55, no. 1 (March 1981), 49–51. See also Carol P. Germain, "Nursing the Dying: Implications of Kübler-Ross' Staging Theory," in *The Social Meaning of Death*, 46–58.

73. See Dame Cicely Saunders, Dorothy H. Summer, and Neville Teller, eds., *Hospice: The Living Idea* (London: Edward Arnold, 1981); and Dame Cicely Saunders and Mary Baines, *Living with Dying: The Management of Terminal Disease* (Oxford: Oxford University Press, 1983). See also Constance Holden, "The Hospice Movement and Its Implications," in *The Social Meaning of Death*, 59–63, and Fox, "The Sting of Death in American Society," pp. 51–53.

74. Renée C. Fox, *Experiment Perilous* (Glencoe, Ill.: The Free Press, 1959); Bernard Barber, John J. Lally, Julia Loughlin Makarushka, and Daniel Sullivan, *Research on Human Subjects: Problems of Social Control in Medical Experimentation* (New York: Russell Sage Foundation, 1973); Bradford H. Gray, *Human Subjects in Medical Experimentation: A Sociological Study of the Conduct and Regulation of Clinical Research* (New York: John Wiley & Sons, 1975).

75. Renée C. Fox, "Introduction to the Paperback Edition," *Experiment Perilous* (Philadelphia: University of Pennsylvania Press, 1974), p. 11.

76. John J. Lally and Bernard Barber develop these ideas in greater detail in their article, "'The Compassionate Physician': Frequency and Social Determinants of Physician-Investigator Concern for Human Subjects," *Social Forces*, 53, no. 2 (1974), 289–96.

77. Barber, Lally, Makarushka, and Sullivan, *Research on Human Subjects*, p. 113.

78. Personal communication.

79. Barber, and others, *Research on Human Subjects*, pp. 6–7.

80. Ibid., p. 29.

81. Ibid., p. 92.

82. Ibid., pp. 80–1.

83. Ibid., pp. 8 and 91.

84. Ibid., pp. 8–9.

85. Charles L. Bosk, *Forgive and Remember: Managing Medical Failure* (Chicago: University of Chicago Press, 1979), p. 190.

86. Barber, and others, *Research on Human Subjects*, p. 57.

87. Ibid., p. 55.

88. Ibid., p. 57.

89. Bradford H. Gray, Robert A. Cooke, and Arnold S. Tannenbaum, "Research Involving Human Subjects," *Science*, 201 (September 22, 1978), 1094–1101.

90. Barber, and others, *Research on Human Subjects*, pp. 9–10.

91. Ibid., p. 185.

92. Bernard Barber, Testimony before Subcommittee on Health, Committee on Labor and Public Welfare, U. S. Senate, March 8, 1973, in *Quality of Health Care—Human Experimentation*, 3, (Washington, D.C.: Government Printing Office, 1973), 1043–49.

93. Bradford H. Gray and Marian Osterweis, "Ethical Issues in a Social Context," in *Applications of Social Science to Clinical Medicine and Health Policy*, eds. Linda G. Aiken and David Mechanic (New Brunswick, N.J.: Rutgers University Press, 1986), p. 547.

94. Ibid.

95. Ibid.

96. Gray, *Human Subjects in Medical Experimentation*, p. 221.

97. Gray and Osterweis, "Ethical Issues in a Social Context," p. 547.

98. Gray, *Human Subjects in Medical Experimentation*, pp. 128–39.

99. Gray and Osterweis, "Ethical Issues in a Social Context," p. 547.

100. These parallels between the works of Gray and of Barber et al. are not "purely accidental." While planning his research, Gray spent time with Barber's Research Group on Human Experimentation at Columbia University. In this setting, Barber, et al., were gathering their data, and gave Gray the benefit of their experience to that point. Subsequently, Barber urged Gray to prepare his study for publication as a book, and wrote the foreword to it. Gray's work was also influenced by Diana Crane's. As he stated in the preface to his book, his "original interest in this area was stimulated by Diana Crane in her seminar in sociology of science at Yale." It was there that he generated the idea for his study, which became his doctoral dissertation, and subsequently his book, *Human Subjects in Medical Experimentation*.

101. Barber, and others, *Research on Human Subjects*, p. 198.

102. Robert A. Cooke, Arnold S. Tannenbaum, and Bradford H. Gray, "A Survey of Institutional Review Boards and Research Involving Human Subjects," in *Report and Recommendations Institutional Review Boards*, Appendix, The National Commission for the Protection of Human Subjects of Biomedical and Behavioral Research (Washington, D.C.: Government Printing Office, 1977).

103. Gray and Osterweis, "Ethical Issues in a Social Context," p. 548.

104. For more details concerning the history of the IRB see William J. Curran, "Governmental Regulation of the Use of Human Subjects in Medical Research: The Approach of Two Federal Agencies," in *Experimentation with Human Subjects*, ed. Paul A. Freund (New York: George Braziller, 1970); Robert M. Veatch, "Human Experimentation Committees: Professional or Representative?" *Hastings Center Report*, 5, no. 5 (October 1975), 31–40; Robert J. Levine, *Ethics and Regulations of Clinical Research* (Baltimore: Urban & Schwarzenberg, 1981), pp. 207–43; and Ruth R. Faden and Tom L. Beauchamp, *A History and Theory of Informed Consent* (New York: Oxford University Press, 1986), especially Chap. 6, pp. 200–34.

105. According to Robert J. Levine (*Ethics and Regulations of Clinical Research*, p. 211), "most of the IRB's time is devoted to considerations of risks and hoped-for benefits and to informed consent. . . . Except when reviewing protocols designed to involve the 'special' or other obviously vulnerable populations, the IRB spends relatively little time considering whether subjects are to be selected equitably. The responsibility for rigorous review for scientific design and investigators' competence is in the majority of cases delegated to the funding agencies."

106. Gray and Osterweis, "Ethical Issues in a Social Context," p. 548.

107. Based on this finding, the National Commission recommended that some types of very-low-risk research be exempted from IRB review, and that "expedited" procedures be allowed for other types. Included among what was defined as low-risk research were certain sorts of social science inquiries. These recommendations were accepted and were incorporated into the regulatory guidelines for IRBs.

108. President's Commission for the Study of Ethical Problems in Medicine and Biomedical and Behavioral Research, *Implementing Human Research Regulations: The Adequacy and Uniformity of Federal Rules and of Their Implementation*, Second Biennial Report, March 1983 (Washington, D.C.: Government Printing Office, 1983), p. 97. See Chapter 4 for a fuller description of the study.

109. Charles W. Lidz and Alan Meisel, with the assistance of Janice L. Holden, John H. Marx, and Mark R. Munetz, *Informed Consent and the Structure of Medical Care*, Section C in President's Commission for the Study of Ethical Problems in Medicine and Biomedical and Behavioral Research, *Making Health Care Decisions: The Ethical and Legal Implications of Informed Consent in the Patient-Practitioner Relationship*, Volume Two: Appendices, Empirical Studies of Informed Consent (Washington, D.C.: Government Printing Office, October 1982), 317–407. Lidz is a sociologist, Meisel a jurist, Holden a nurse, Marx a sociologist, and Munetz a psychiatrist, and they were all colleagues at the University of Pittsburgh at the time that this study was made.

110. Ibid., p. 320.

111. Ibid., p. 319. See also Charles W. Lidz, and others, *Informed Consent: A Study of Decisionmaking in Psychiatry* (New York: The Guilford Press, 1984).

112. Ibid., p. 319.

113. Ibid., p. 399.

114. Charles W. Lidz, and others, "Barriers to Informed Consent," *Annals of Internal Medicine* 99, no. 4 (1983), p. 539.

115. Lidz, and others, *Informed Consent and the Structure of Medical Care*, pp. 400–401.

116. Ibid., p. 401.

117. Ibid.

118. Ibid., p. 391.

119. Ibid., p. 395.

120. Patients in this category who showed these characteristics included those with arteriosclerosis, diabetes, cardiomyopathy, chronic bowel obstruction, and end-stage renal disease.

121. Lidz, and others, *Informed Consent and the Structure of Medical Care*, p. 395.

122. Lidz, and others, "Barriers to Informed Consent," p. 543.

123. Ibid., p. 540.

124. Ibid., pp. 540–41.

125. Lidz, and others, *Informed Consent and the Structure of Medical Care*, p. 403.

126. Charles W. Lidz, Alan Meisel, and Mark Munetz, "Chronic Disease: The Sick Role and Informed Consent," *Culture, Medicine, and Psychiatry*, 9, no. 1 (1985), 1–7.

127. Lidz, and others, *Informed Consent and the Structure of Medical Care*, p. 404; and Lidz, and others, *Informed Consent: A Study of Decisionmaking in Psychiatry*, p. 328.

128. Lidz, and others, *Informed Consent: A Study of Decisionmaking in Psychiatry*, p. 333.

129. Ibid., p. 334.

130. Personal communication.

131. Roberta G. Simmons, Susan D. Klein, and Richard L. Simmons, *Gift of Life: The Social and Psychological Impact of Organ Transplantation* (New York: John Wiley and Sons, 1977), (reissued by Transaction Books in 1987); Renée C. Fox and Judith P. Swazey, *The Courage to Fail: A Social View of Organ Transplants and Dialysis* (Chicago: University of Chicago Press, 1974 and rev. 1978).

132. Judith P. Swazey, "Transplants . . . The Gift of Life," Guest Editorial, *Wellesley* (Alumnae Magazine), 70, no. 4 (Summer 1986), 15.

133. Because the kidneys are paired vital organs, the loss of a single kidney is not life-threatening. It is for this reason that the American medical profession permits live as well as cadaveric kidney transplants to take place. However, it has largely confined live transplants to kidneys from living related donors. It is only in the United States that live kidney transplants of any type have been done with any frequency and regularity.

  It should not be taken for granted sociologically that the live transplantation of a vital organ other than a kidney is forbidden since its removal would cause the death of the donor. The fact that the desire to donate a singular vital organ, like a heart or a liver, is defined as unacceptably self-destructive, suicidal, and/or pathological, rather than as a noble, sacrificial act of laying down one's life for another is worthy of sociological reflection.

  Even more interesting is the reluctance that the medical profession has shown to encourage or permit kidney transplantation from unrelated living donors. A very small percent of U.S. transplantation centers use such donors. A somewhat larger percent of these centers say that they would allow spouses to donate kidneys to one another, although not all that respond this way have yet done so. The rationale for a live kidney transplant is that if there is a good tissue match between donor and recipient, a severe and rapid rejection reaction is less likely to occur than with a cadaver transplant. If donor and recipient are biologically related, there is a higher probability that such a good tissue match may exist. However, the fact that more transplanters are willing to consider spouses as live donors than other biologically "non-related" candidates suggests that the reasons underlying the reluctance of the physicians to do such kidney transplants are not purely biological.

  In the words of one physician who finds it "objectionable and unacceptable" to permit a "living stranger donor" to give a kidney, because it is "unclear" what such a "prospective donor's motivation would be, if not financial," a donation by "someone closely related to the patient through marriage" is likely to be "an act of self-sacrifice and love." Gabriel Danovitch, M.D., (letter to the editor), *New England Journal of Medicine*, 315, no. 11 (September 11, 1986), 713–14.

    For a speculative discussion of some of the non-biomedical factors that may contribute to the "disturbance" many physicians feel about transplants from unrelated living donors, see Renée C. Fox, Judith P. Swazey, and Elizabeth M. Cameron, "Social and Ethical Problems in the Treatment of End-Stage Renal Disease Patients," in *Controversies in Nephrology and Hypertension*, ed. Robert G. Narins (New York: Churchill Livingstone, 1984), p. 54.

134. Even if a person legally certifies willingness to make an organ donation after death by signing an Anatomical Gift form, consent to donation is always obtained from the deceased person's next-of-kin.

135. The 1984 National Organ Transplantation Act, passed by the U.S. Congress, explicitly prohibits the sale of organs for transplantation. However, a black market does exist, particularly for kidneys from live donors.

136. See Fox and Swazey, *The Courage to Fail* (second, revised edition), especially Chapters 1 and 12; Fox, Swazey, and Cameron, "Social and Ethical Problems in the Treatment of End-Stage Renal Disease," pp. 53–58; Renée C. Fox, "Organ Transplantation: Sociocultural Aspects," in *Encyclopedia of Bioethics* (1978), 3, 1166–69.

137. Marcel Mauss, *The Gift: Forms and Functions of Exchange in Archaic Societies*, Ian Cunnison, tr. (Glencoe, Ill.: The Free Press, 1954), pp. 10–12 and 37–41.

138. Ibid., p. 63.

139. Ibid., pp. 8–10.

140. Ibid., pp. 66–67.

141. Simmons, Klein, and Simmons, *Gift of Life*, p. 197.

142. Ibid., pp. 196–97.

143. Ibid., pp. 161–64, 191–92, 210, and 433; Fox and Swazey, *The Courage to Fail*, pp. 24–25.

144. Fox, Swazey, and Cameron, "Social and Ethical Problems in the Treatment of End-Stage Renal Disease Patients," p. 56.

145. Simmons, Klein, and Simmons, *Gift of Life*, p. 351.

146. Ibid., p. 352.

147. Ibid.

148. Ibid., p. 371.

149. Fox, Swazey, and Cameron, "Social and Ethical Problems in the Treatment of End-Stage Renal Disease Patients," p. 57.

150. The mass media attention that certain transplant stories receive may break this norm of anonymity. Public awareness of the need for transplantable organs has been increased by the personal appeals made by families, or sympathetic celebrities, via TV, radio, and newspapers, to secure an organ for a dying child or, less frequently, an adult. But one of the consequences of what Judith Swazey has called "such dramatic identified-life requests" is that the identity of the donor and donor family, as well as that of the recipient and recipient family, may be publicly revealed.

151. Simmons, Klein, and Simmons, *Gift of Life*, p. 369.

152. Fox and Swazey, *The Courage to Fail*, pp. 29–30.

153. Simmons, Klein, and Simmons, *Gift of Life*, pp. 370 and 375.

154. Fox, Swazey, and Cameron, "Social and Ethical Problems in the Treatment of End-Stage Renal Disease," p. 58.

155. Renée C. Fox, "Advanced Medical Technology—Social and Ethical Implications," p. 441.

156. Fox and Swazey, *The Courage To Fail*, 345–75.

157. Susan Klein Marine and Roberta G. Simmons, "Policies Regarding Treatment of End-Stage Renal Disease in the United States and the United Kingdom," *International Journal of Technology Assessment in Health Care*, 2, no. 2 (August 1986), pp. 259–60. Reprinted by permission of Cambridge University Press.

158. In early 1986 the Task Force on Organ Transplantation, created by the National Organ Transplantation Act passed by the Congress in 1984, called for a national computer network to keep track of all available organs and all people needing them, ranking the requests in terms of the urgency of need. Such a National Organ Procurement and Transplantation Network has long been seen as essential to "a unified national system of organ sharing," and had been a central

provision of the National Organ Transplantation Act. However, its implementation was delayed by the reluctance of the Reagan administration to fund it.

159. Swazey, "Transplants . . . The Gift of Life," pp. 14–15.

160. Fox, Swazey, and Cameron, "Social and Ethical Problems in the Treatment of End-Stage Renal Disease," p. 63.

161. Steven Neu and Carl M. Kjellstrand, "Stopping Long-Term Dialysis: An Empirical Study of Withdrawing Life-Supporting Treatment," *New England Journal of Medicine*, 314, no. 1 (January 2, 1986), 19.

162. Fox and Swazey, *The Courage to Fail*, pp. 266–301.

163. Ibid.

164. In the *Hastings Center Report*, for example, published by the Institute of Society, Ethics, and the Life Sciences of Hastings-on-the-Hudson, New York, Arthur Caplan is the primary author, source person, and referent in this area.

165. Marilyn M. Hoe, Roger W. Evans, and Julie T. Elsworth, *National Kidney Dialysis and Kidney Transplantation Study: A Summary of Results* (Seattle, Wash.: Battelle Human Affairs Research Centers, 1985), p. 5. For a fuller account of the results of this study, see, Roger W. Evans, and others, *Selected Findings From the National Kidney Dialysis and Kidney Transplantation Study* (Seattle, Wash.: Battelle Human Affairs Research Centers, 1985).

166. Roger W. Evans, Diane L. Manninen, Anthony M. Maier, Louis P. Garrison, Jr., and L. Gary Hart, "The Quality of Life of Kidney and Heart Transplant Recipients," *Transplantation Proceedings*, XVII, no. 1 (February 1985), 1579. A Final Report on this study was published by the Battelle Human Affairs Research Centers in Seattle, Washington, in 1985.

167. Roger W. Evans, "The Heart Transplant Dilemma," *Issues in Science and Technology*, II, no. 3 (Spring 1986), 92 and 100.

168. Ibid., p. 92.

169. Ibid.

170. Ibid.

171. Ibid., p. 100. Roger W. Evans, "The Heart Transplant Dilemma," *op. cit.*, p. 100. After this chapter was completed, HCFA did approve Medicare coverage for heart transplants. The final regulations issued in April 1987 seek both to ensure successful transplant outcomes, and contain the government's expenditures for them. Coverage will be approved "only in certain facilities with a record of successful transplants and with careful selection criteria that limit transplants for patients older than the mid-50s . . . Medicare is anticipated to pay for only about 100 of the nearly 2,000 transplants that will be done [in 1988] . . . The program's costs could range from about $12.5 million to $70 million during the next five years." Sharon McIlrath, "Rules Limit Medicare Pay for Heart Transplantation," *American Medical News*, 30, no. 15 (April 17, 1987), 2, 34.

172. See, for example, Thomas D. Overcast, Roger W. Evans, and others, "Problems in the Identification of Potential Organ Donors," *Journal of the American Medical Association*, 251, no. 12 (March 24/30, 1984), 1559–62; Diane L. Manninen and Roger W. Evans, "Public Attitudes and Behavior Regarding Organ Donation," *Journal of the American Medical Association*, 253, no. 21 (June 7, 1985), 3111–15; Roger W. Evans, and others, "Donor Availability as the Primary Determinant of the Future of Heart Transplantation," *Journal of the American Medical Association*, 255, no. 14 (April 11, 1986), 1892–98.

173. Samuel W. Bloom, "Institutional Trends in Medical Sociology," *Journal of Health and Social Behavior*, 27, no. 3 (September 1986), 265–76.

174. Ibid.

175. Victor R. Fuchs, "Has Cost Containment Gone Too Far?" *The Milbank Quarterly*, 64, no. 3 (1986), 479.

176. Bradford H. Gray, ed., *For-Profit Enterprise in Health Care*, Committee on Implications of For-Profit Enterprise in Health Care, Institute of Medicine (Washington, D.C.: National Academy Press, 1986).

177. Ibid., p. 182.

178 Ibid., pp. 185, 191.

179 Ibid., p. 201.

180 Ibid., p. 205.

181 Ibid.

182 David Mechanic, *Future Issues in Health Care: Social Policy and the Rationing of Medical Services* (New York: The Free Press, 1979); David Mechanic, *From Advocacy to Allocation: The Evolving American Health Care System* (New York: The Free Press, 1986).

183. Mechanic, *From Advocacy to Allocation*, p. ix.

184. Mechanic, *Future Issues in Health Care*, p. xii.

185. Paul Starr, *The Social Transformation of American Medicine* (New York: Basic Books, Inc., 1982).

186. The book was selected by *The New York Times Book Review* as one of the six best nonfiction books of 1983, and won the American Sociological Association's C. Wright Mills Award, the Bancroft Prize in American history, and a Pulitzer Prize.

187. Paul Starr, *The Social Transformation of American Medicine*, pp. ix–x.

188. Renée C. Fox and Judith P. Swazey, "Medical Morality Is Not Bioethics," pp. 336 and 360.

AN UNFINAL CONCLUSION

This book encompasses a broad gamut of medical sociological works. However, as I indicated at the outset, it constitutes neither an exhaustive nor a completely objective survey of the field. The way in which I have done research and taught over the years as a medical sociologist—the methodological style of my work, its conceptual, empirical, and thematic foci, and the angle of vision that underlies it and results from it—has influenced the choices that I made in reviewing the literature.

As this book goes to press, new medical sociological works of merit continue to appear. I have resisted citing and discussing them, because at some point in the writing of a book like this, one must simply stop, however arbitrary that cutting-off point will inevitably seem.

Its gaps, points of fixity, and limitations notwithstanding, medical sociology is a dynamically ongoing field—one that I hope will continue to develop creatively, and to move beyond the participant observer view of it that I have presented here. In that spirit, I end this book, with a conclusion that is not a finale.

INDEX